Intangible Heritage

The development and ratification of the UNESCO *Convention on the Safeguarding of the Intangible Cultural Heritage* (2003) has seen a significant increase in international debate about not only the nature and value of intangible heritage, but also the meaning and character of heritage more generally. Greeted with enthusiasm by many countries, the convention was also met with wariness and apprehension in much of the West, and the idea of 'intangible heritage' is a relatively unexplored concept in many Western countries.

Intangible Heritage fills a significant gap in the available heritage literature and represents an important cross-section of ideas and practices associated with intangible cultural heritage. The volume brings together authors from the USA, Europe (UK, Germany, Iceland), Africa (Morocco, Zimbabwe), Japan, Tehran and Australia to document and analyse the development of the 2003 convention and its consequences. The opening chapters identify the principles, philosophies and assumptions underlying the convention and discuss the implications these will have, not only for the development of management and conservation/preservation practices, but also for the re-examination of the dominant ideas about the role and meaning of heritage in contemporary societies.

The convention is also reviewed against community and Indigenous cultural concerns and aspirations. Case studies documenting material and cultural politics of intangible heritage are also presented, while other chapters explore the theoretical implications for existing definitions of heritage. The collection brings together a range of areas of expertise, including anthropology, law, heritage studies, archaeology, museum studies, folklore, Indigenous studies and ethnomusicology, and both academics and heritage professionals discuss the theoretical and practical implications of intangible cultural heritage, and the very idea that we can talk about 'heritage' and 'intangible heritage' is challenged.

Laurajane Smith is a Reader in Cultural Heritage Studies and Archaeology at the University of York, UK. She is author of *Uses of Heritage* (2006) and *Archaeological Theory and the Politics of Cultural Heritage* (2004), and editor of *Cultural Heritage: Critical Concepts in Media Studies* (2007).

Natsuko Akagawa is at the Cultural Heritage Centre for Asia and the Pacific, Deakin University Melbourne, Australia. Her research interests are intangible cultural heritage, cultural landscape and tourism/management issues related to heritage.

Key Issues in Cultural Heritage

Series editors: William Logan and Laurajane Smith

Also in the series:

Places of Pain and Shame, Dealing with "Difficult Heritage"
William Logan and Keir Reeves

Intangible Heritage

Edited by
Laurajane Smith and Natsuko Akagawa

Routledge
Taylor & Francis Group

LONDON AND NEW YORK

First published 2009
by Routledge
2 Park Square, Milton Park, Abingdon, Oxon OX14 4RN

Simultaneously published in the USA and Canada
by Routledge
270 Madison Avenue, New York, NY 10016

Routledge is an imprint of the Taylor & Francis Group, an informa business

Typeset in Garamond by
Taylor & Francis Books
Printed and bound in Great Britain by
CPI Antony Rowe, Chippenham, Wiltshire

British Library Cataloguing in Publication Data
A catalogue record for this book is available from the British Library

Library of Congress Cataloging in Publication Data
Intangible heritage / edited by Laurajane Smith and Natsuko Akagawa.
    p. cm.
"Simultaneously published in the USA and Canada"–T.p. verso.
Includes bibliographical references.
    1. Convention for the Safeguarding of the Intangible Cultural Heritage
(2003) 2. Cultural property–Protection. 3. Intangible property. 4. Cultural
property–Protection–International cooperation. 5. Cultural property–
Protection (International law) 6. Nature conservation. 7. Nature
conservation–International cooperation. I. Smith, Laurajane. II. Akagawa,
Natsuko.
    CC135.I56 2008
    930.1–dc22
                    2008026697

ISBN 13: 978-0-415-47396-5 (pbk)
ISBN 13: 978-0-415-47397-2 (hbk)
ISBN 13: 978-0-203-88497-3 (ebk)

Contents

Illustrations

Contributors

Noriko Aikawa-Faure, former Director of the Intangible Cultural Heritage Unit of UNESCO. She is currently an Adviser to the Assistant Director-General for Culture of UNESCO and a Visiting Professor at the National Graduate Institute for Policy Studies in Japan.

Natsuko Akagawa, Cultural Heritage Centre for Asia and the Pacific, Faculty of Arts and Education, Deakin University Melbourne, Australia.

Regina Bendix, Professor of Cultural Anthropology and European Ethnology at the University of Göttingen, Germany.

Janet Blake, Specialist in International Cultural Heritage Law and Senior Lecturer in Law, Environmental Sciences Research Institute at the University of Shahid Beheshti, Tehran.

Denis Byrne, leads the research programme in culture and heritage at the Department of Environment and Climate Change (New South Wales), Sydney. He is also an Adjunct Professor at the Transforming Cultures Centre, University of Technology Sydney, Australia.

Valdimar Tryggvi Hafstein, Assistant Professor of Folklore/Ethnology at the University of Iceland, Reykjavík. He is currently a Visiting Professor, teaching in the departments of Anthropology and Scandinavian at the University of California, USA.

Frank Hassard, was schooled in the Ruskin-Morris philosophy and practice of buildings preservation, and is currently a Research Associate of Buckinghamshire New University. He is an independent writer and adviser on key issues in heritage, UK.

Amanda Kearney, Centre for Australian Indigenous Studies, Monash University, Melbourne, Australia.

Mary Kenny, Associate Professor of Anthropology at Eastern Connecticut State University, USA.

Christina Kreps, Associate Professor of Anthropology and Director of Museum Studies and the Museum of Anthropology at the University of Denver, USA.

Henrietta Marrie, born and raised in the Aboriginal community of Yarrabah southeast of Cairns, Australia. Program Officer for the Christensen Fund for Northern Australia, she has worked at the United Nations Environment Programme Secretariat of the Convention on Biological Diversity.

Dawson Munjeri, the Deputy Permanent Delegate of Zimbabwe to UNESCO and was, until 2002, Executive Director of National Museums and Monuments of Zimbabwe. A member of the Intergovernmental Experts Draft Group on the *Convention for the Safeguarding of the Intangible Cultural Heritage.*

Anthony Seeger, Professor, Ethnomusicology and Director, Ethnomusicology Archive, Department of Ethnomusicology, University of California Los Angeles, USA. He was Secretary General of the International Council for Traditional Music from 2001 to 2005.

Ahmed Skounti, Anthropologist, Assistant Professor at the Institut national des sciences de l'archéologie et du patrimoine, Rabat and Marrakech, Morocco. A UNESCO expert in intangible cultural heritage and participated in the preparation of the *Convention for the Safeguarding of the Intangible Cultural Heritage.*

Laurajane Smith, Reader in Cultural Heritage Studies and Archaeology at the University of York, UK.

Emma Waterton, Research Council UK (RCUK) Academic Fellowship in Heritage and Public History at the Research Institute for the Humanities, Keele University, UK.

Abbreviations

ACCU	Asia Pacific Cultural Centre for UNESCO
AHD	Authorized Heritage Discourse
ANZAC	Australian and New Zealand Army Corps
CBD	*Convention on Biological Diversity*
COP	Conference of the Parties
DCMS	Department for Culture Media and Sport, UK
DRIP	United Nations *Declaration on the Rights of Indigenous Peoples*
ECCO	European Confederation of Conservator-Restorers' Organisations
FAO	United Nations Food and Agriculture Organization
ICCPR	United Nations International Covenant on Civil and Political Rights
ICCROM	International Centre for the Study of the Preservation and Restoration of Cultural Property, Rome
ICH	Intangible Cultural Heritage
ICHC	*Convention for the Safeguarding of the Intangible Cultural Heritage* (Intangible Cultural Heritage Convention)
ICOM	International Council of Museums
ICOMOS	International Council on Monuments and Sites
ICP	Intangible Cultural Property
ICTM	International Council for Traditional Music
IFMC	International Folk Music Council
IFPC	Intangible Folk Cultural Property
IGO	Intergovernmental organizations
IGCSICH	Intergovernmental Committee for the Safeguarding of the Intangible Cultural Heritage
ILO	International Labour Organization
IPHAN	Instituto do Patrimônio Histórico e Artístico Nacional (Institute of National Historic and Artistic Heritage), Brazil
IPR	Intellectual Property Rights
ITK	Traditional Knowledge and Folklore

ITPGRFA	*International Treaty on Plant Genetic Resources for Food and Agriculture*
NGO	Non-Governmental Organisation
NMAI	National Museum of the American Indian, USA
NMMZ	National Museums and Monuments of Zimbabwe
RLICHH	Representative List of the Intangible Cultural Heritage of Humanity
SPAB	Society for the Protection of Ancient Buildings, UK
SPHAN	*Serviço do Patrimônio Histórico e Artístico Nacional, Brazil*
TEK	Traditional Ecological Knowledge
UIHS	UNESCO Intangible Heritage Section
UN	United Nations
UNCCD	United Nations *Convention to Combat Desertification in those Countries Experiencing Drought and/or Desertification, Particularly in Africa*
UNCTAD	United Nations Conference on Trade and Development
UNEP	United Nations Environment Programme
UNESCO	United Nations Educational, Scientific and Cultural Organisation
UNPFII	United Nations Permanent Forum on Indigenous Issues
WH	World Heritage
WHC	*Convention Concerning the Protection of the World Cultural, Natural Heritage* (World Heritage Convention)
WHO	World Heritage Organization
WIPO	World Intellectual Property Organisation
WTO	World Trade Organization
WWW	World Wide Web

Series General Co-Editors' Foreword

The interdisciplinary field of Heritage Studies is now well established in many parts of the world. It differs from earlier scholarly and professional activities that focused narrowly on the architectural or archaeological preservation of monuments and sites. Such activities remain important, especially as modernisation and globalisation lead to new developments that threaten natural environments, archaeological sites, traditional buildings and arts and crafts. But they are subsumed within the new field that sees 'heritage' as a social and political construct encompassing all those places, artefacts and cultural expressions inherited from the past which, because they are seen to reflect and validate our identity as nations, communities, families and even individuals, are worthy of some form of respect and protection.

Heritage results from a selection process, often government-initiated and supported by official regulation; it is not the same as history, although this, too, has its own elements of selectivity. Heritage can be used in positive ways to give a sense of community to disparate groups and individuals or to create jobs on the basis of cultural tourism. It can be actively used by governments and communities to foster respect for cultural and social diversity, and to challenge prejudice and misrecognition. But it can also be used by governments in less benign ways, to reshape public attitudes in line with undemocratic political agendas or even to rally people against their neighbours in civil and international wars, ethnic cleansing and genocide. In this way there is a real connection between heritage and human rights.

This is the time for a new and unique series of books canvassing the key issues dealt with in the new Heritage Studies. The series seeks to address the deficiency facing the field identified by the Smithsonian in 2005 – that it is 'vastly under-theorized'. It is time to look again at the contestation that inevitably surrounds the identification and evaluation of heritage and to find new ways to elucidate the many layers of meaning that heritage places and intangible cultural expressions have acquired. Heritage conservation and safeguarding in such circumstances can only be understood as a form of cultural politics and this needs to be reflected in heritage practice, be that in educational institutions or in the field.

It is time, too, to recognise more fully that heritage protection does not depend alone on top-down interventions by governments or the expert actions of heritage industry professionals, but must involve local communities and communities of interest. It is imperative that the values and practices of communities, together with traditional management systems, are fully understood, respected, encouraged and accommodated in management plans and policy documents if heritage resources are to be sustained in the future. Communities need to have a sense of 'ownership' of their heritage; this reaffirms their worth as a community, their ways of going about things, their 'culture'.

This series of books aims then to identify interdisciplinary debates within Heritage Studies and to explore how they impact on the practices not only of heritage management and conservation, but also the processes of production, consumption and engagement with heritage in its many and varied forms.

William S. Logan
Laurajane Smith

Chapter 1

Introduction

Laurajane Smith and Natsuko Akagawa

In 1972, the *Convention Concerning the Protection of the World Cultural, Natural Heritage* (World Heritage Convention) (WHC) embodied a particular under-standing and conceptualisation of the nature of both cultural and natural heritage. It has since had an extensive and defining impact on the development of national and international cultural heritage polices and practices, and it continues to frame international debate about the nature, consequences and value of cultural and natural heritage. In particular, the WHC has stressed the concept of 'the shared heritage' of humanity through its central focus on the concept of the 'universal value' of heritage. However, the WHC has been criticised for legitimising a particular Western – if not Western European – perception of heritage in terms of both policy and practice (Byrne 1991; Pocock 1997; Cleere 2001; Sullivan 2004, among others). The World Heritage List has been shown to be not only Eurocentric in composition, but also dominated by monumentally grand and aesthetic sites and places (Arizpe 2000: 36; Cleere 2001; Yoshida 2004: 109). The 2003 *Convention for the Safeguarding of the Intangible Cultural Heritage* (Intangible Cultural Heritage Convention; ICHC) has been characterised by some as a counterpoint to the WHC, an attempt to acknowledge and privilege non-Western manifestations and practices of heritage. Certainly, debates about the utility of the Convention have continually reinforced its relevance to Asian, African and South American countries and Indigenous heritage practices. Whatever the innovations and/or limitations of the ICHC it marks a significant interven-tion into international debate about the nature and value of cultural heritage.

This volume examines that intervention, drawing on the unique insights of several authors intimately involved with the negotiations over the Convention. The first part of the book traces the history of the Convention and identifies the debates and concepts that influenced its development and drafting. The second part of the volume reviews the utility of the ICHC against a range of issues, concerns and practices, while exploring the diver-sity of the ways intangible heritage may be understood and expressed. Those directly involved in the negotiations and drafting of the ICHC, and/or those who have policy and practical experiences in assessing and managing intangible heritage, have contributed several chapters to the first two sections of the book. Part 1 provides a detailed and up-to-date account of the historical policy processes, and provides a useful historical and contemporary guide to understanding the aims and philosophies underpinning the ICHC. The third section takes the philosophical debate beyond the boundaries set by the ICHC and explores the concept of 'intangible heritage' more broadly. Chapters in this section consider the implications the debate on intangible heritage has for a broader more critically engaged definition of 'heritage'.

The ICHC was adopted by UNESCO's General Conference in October 2003 and entered into force on 20th April 2006. The guidelines for its implementation are under negotiation at the time of writing. Certainly, the consequences of this Convention are yet to be fully realised or determined. Thus, Part 1 of this volume offers a number of chapters that document the history of the Convention and outline some of the key concepts and philosophies underlying it and against which its future implementation can be assessed and reviewed. Aikawa-Faure's contribution provides an overview of the lengthy process of negotiation and insight into the complexity of the negotiations and renegotiations that took place. In doing so, she reveals the degree of conceptual tensions that arose between State Parties in its drafting. Both Skounti and Hafstein also identify and explore some of these tensions. Skounti discusses the tensions that exist between local and global conceptualisations of heritage, and between the idea of heritage as 'fixed', immutable and focused on 'the past', with that of a mutable heritage centred very much on the present. Hafstein explores the tensions and debates that arose over the idea of a heritage 'list' – revealing the range of philosophies underpinning varying conceptualisations of heritage, and the differing aspirations for the new Convention. Blake identifies and discusses the attempt of the new Convention to engage with cultural communities, and outlines the implications this has for both the politics of cultural rights of communities and the development and nature of the ICHC. Collectively, what these chapters draw attention to, is the extent of the conceptual shift over the idea of 'heritage' that is prompted by the existence of the new Convention. The jury, we believe, is still out on the degree to which this shift has actually occurred within international debates and practices, but the Convention certainly seems to signal that how heritage is defined and understood not only as a category, but as a concept and set of practices, needs to be not only broadened but redefined.

The Convention has most frequently met with guarded enthusiasm within the literature and professional practice, with many supporting the need for such a Convention, but wary about its logistical, political and cultural consequences. The logistical issues have included concerns over human rights abuses (Kurin 2004; Brown 2005; Logan 2007), the need for new language and terminology (van Zanten 2004), how to measure and define the value of intangible heritage (Blake 2001; Brown 2005), and how to safeguard and manage a heritage that is mutable and part of 'living culture' without fossilising, freezing or trivializing it (Nas 2002; Amselle 2004; Arizpe 2004; van Zanten 2004: 41), among other issues. These practical and logistical concerns stem from the dominant perception of 'heritage' that underpins many of UNESCO's practices and previous Conventions. As one of us (LS) has previously argued, this idea of heritage draws heavily from the history of Western European architectural and archaeological conservation and preservation debates. A Western Authorized Heritage Discourse (AHD) that defines heritage as material (tangible), monumental, grand, 'good', aesthetic and of universal value dominates, if not underwrites, much of UNESCO's heritage policy (Smith 2006). The AHD not only defines what heritage 'is', but also how it needs to be assessed and managed. The dominance of the West, and in particular Western Europe, within UNESCO policy is well documented (Byrne 1991; Cleere 2001; Matsuura 2001; Yoshida 2004) and the ICHC has been defined as part of the response to address that imbalance (Aikawa 2004; Bedjaoui 2004; Schmitt 2008). The ICHC challenges the AHD – the underpinning foundations of UNESCO's concept of heritage – at both a practical and philosophical level. Some of these practical issues are highlighted in Seeger's chapter in Part 1 of this volume. Seeger examines his own experiences as Secretary General of an NGO involved in the evaluation process of intangible heritage under the Proclamation of Masterpieces of the Oral and Intangible Heritage of Humanity, 1998, the programme that preceded and helped lead to the development of the ICHC (see Aikawa-Faure, Blake and Skounti, this volume). The practical, policy and conceptual issues Seeger highlights illustrates the depth of challenge the ICHC offers to the Western AHD.

That there is a challenge is revealed in the discomfort some Western countries have with the new Convention. As Aikawa-Faure notes in her contribution, there were tensions between some Western countries who did not see the relevance or necessity of the Convention (see also Smith and Waterton this volume), while concerns were also expressed by those countries with Indigenous populations. As Kurin (2004: 66) points out, while there were no votes against the Convention, a number of countries, notably Australia, Canada, the UK, Switzerland and the USA, abstained from voting.

In the face of the dominance of the AHD, it is necessary to consider whether the Convention will really change anything. Kirshenblatt-Gimblett (2004: 57) makes the point that in creating yet another list separate from the World Heritage List the new Convention will potentially create an equally exclusive and excluding list (see also Brown 2005). The ICHC will develop two new lists: 'the List of Intangible Cultural Heritage in Need of Urgent Safeguarding' and 'the Representative List of the Intangible Cultural Heritage of Humanity'. The existing list of 90 examples of intangible heritage that were proclaimed under the Masterpieces programme will be incorporated into these lists. As both Kirshenblatt-Gimblett (2004) and Hafstein (this volume) point out, the very act of creating a list is not only an act of exclusion, it is also a performance of meaning making. In this process 'heritage' is 'identified' and 'assessed' against predefined 'criteria'. This process inevitably recreates or over-writes new meanings and values onto the heritage in question. Whether we are dealing with tangible or intangible heritage, the primary values and meaning of that heritage become framed and understood through its position on a list and its status against a set of criteria. As Kirshenblatt-Gimblett states:

> World Heritage is first and foremost a list. Everything on the list, whatever its previous context, is now placed in a relationship with other masterpieces. The list is a context for everything on it.
>
> (2004: 57)

If the listing and the assessment and management practices that are employed in the service of the ICHC simply recreate yet another self-referential list, what will be achieved? UNESCO is a project of cultural legitimisation – it recognises, authorises and validates certain cultural expressions as 'heritage' (Smith 2006: 111). How that is done and by whom, and under what framing criteria and philosophies, will be important in determining how far UNESCO's definition of 'intangible heritage' really breaks from current dominant Western perceptions. It needs to be stressed that lobbying for the ICHC has come from a range of non-Western countries, and Japan in particular has used its international standing in a variety of ways to intervene and influence the development of the Convention (Aikawa-Faure, this volume). However, critics of the Masterpieces programme maintain that the resulting list tends to privilege colourful and exotic examples of intangible heritage, that represent nationally valued cultural events or performances, and which coincide with romanticised Western perceptions, while Indigenous works remain under-represented (Kurin 2002, 2004; Kirshenblatt-Gimblett 2004).

The issues raised in debates over the drafting and implementation of both the Masterpieces programme and the ICHC are revealing about the tensions that exist between the differing philosophical and conceptual constructs that underpin dominant and authorised definitions of 'heritage', which we might now label 'tangible heritage' and 'intangible heritage'. These issues have included questioning the legitimacy of the idea of 'universal' value used in the WHC to refer to intangible heritage (Blake 2001), and, as noted above, concern about human rights, the cultural politics of identity and the mutability of intangible expressions as 'living cultures', to use a phrase often found in these debates. What we find interesting in these debates is the degree to which they are 'seen' or framed as issues of *particular* relevance to intangible heritage. In essence, the mutability and contemporary nature of intangible heritage appear to give a sense of urgency or deeper concern about these issues. Perhaps it is the physical and bounded nature and the sense of 'pastness' of the cultural heritage items and places on the World Heritage List that make the cultural politics surrounding these sites and their listing much more 'manageable' and 'containable'? Because, of course, no heritage is unconnected with controversy, dissonance and cultural/identity politics. The vast ethnographic literature in heritage studies documents the extent to which all heritage – even the grand and monumental – is dissonant and contested (see Tunbridge and Ashworth 1996; Graham *et al.* 2000; Littler and Naidoo 2005; Smith 2006). The contested nature of heritage (either 'tangible' or 'intangible') means of course that the idea of 'universal' heritage values cannot be sustained (Lowenthal 1998: 227). In Part 2 of the volume, authors critically review the nature of intangible heritage and discuss the political and cultural tensions surrounding its expression, and ask is the ICHC capable of addressing the cultural complexity of heritage? Munjeri's chapter, drawing on a wide range of examples from around the world, frames this section of the volume by asking if the weaknesses and limitations of preceding Conventions 'may yet be replicated with respect to the intangible cultural heritage'. Kenny's chapter also, although less explicitly focused on the ICHC, draws our attention to the complexity of the cultural politics and identity issues that can surround intangible heritage. What both chapters demonstrate is that the contemporary practices of 'intangible' heritage make the immediacy of the consequences of heritage practices for local communities' political and cultural aspirations more obvious and apparent. However, this is simply a shift in focus, as the cultural politics that both chapters document are integral aspects of *all* heritage, which is simply made more apparent by forcing our attention onto the contemporary practices of heritage. If nothing else, the *idea* of intangible heritage forces a recognition of the inherent dissonant nature of heritage because of the immediacy of its production and consumption.

Marrie and Kearney both review the ICHC against some of the stated cultural and political aspirations of Indigenous peoples. Marrie assesses the ICHC against an array of international policy documents, Conventions and treaties and considers its ability to engage with Indigenous concerns. Kearney likewise assesses the utility of the ICHC and calls into question some of its underlying concepts and assumptions. In particular, she considers its ability to support the local aspirations of Indigenous communities, drawing on examples from Australia. Like Munjeri, Kearney examines the ways in which international definitions and assumptions about the nature and value of intangible heritage may constrain the diversity of local expressions. These definitions not only constrain what may be recognised as heritage, but also the development of meaningful and useful practices of management and curation. Kreps takes these points further and examines the curatorial practices employed in Indonesia and various Indigenous communities. Practices of 'management' and 'curation' become integral to the performance of intangible heritage and Kreps critically examines the implications of this for museum practices. As Munjeri, Kearny and Kreps point out, and echoing observations made in Skounti and Hafstein's chapters, a re-theorisation of 'heritage' is required to meet the challenges offered by the recognition of intangible heritage.

Indeed, we would question the practical and theoretical utility of polarising debate between 'tangible' and 'intangible' heritage. Heritage only becomes 'heritage' when it becomes recognisable within a particular set of cultural or social values, which are themselves 'intangible'. Any item or place of tangible heritage can only be recognised and understood as heritage through the values people and organisations like UNESCO give it – it possesses no inherent value that 'makes' it heritage. As Munjeri states, 'cultural heritage should speak through the values that people give it and not the other way round [...] the tangible can only be understood and interpreted through the intangible' (2004: 13, see also Arizpe 2004: 131). All heritage is intangible, not only because of the values we give to heritage, but because of the cultural work that heritage does in any society (Smith 2006). This 'work' is glimpsed in the chapters of Part 2, but is explicitly examined in Part 3 of the volume.

The re-theorisation of heritage as a cultural practice, rather than simply a site, place or intangible performance or event, has been developing within the broader heritage literature. Harvey (2001) has argued that heritage is best identified as a 'verb' rather than a 'noun', and a number of authors have examined heritage as a body of knowledge and as a political and cultural process of remembering/forgetting and communication (Urry 1996; Dicks 2000; Graham 2002; Peckham 2003; Smith 2006). This project of re-theorisation is taken further by Byrne and Bendix in Part 3. Byrne's chapter offers a wide-ranging examination of the experience of heritage and its engagement with emotions, memories and forgetting. Questioning the tendency of traditional management definitions and practices to essentialise heritage and strip it of its social context, Byrne explores the emotional qualities of heritage and the consequences of this for heritage practice. Bendix observes that 'cultural heritage does not exist, it is made' and reviews the ways in which cultural anthropology has understood the nature and consequences of 'heritagitisation'. Debates about re-theorisations of heritage as offered by Byrne and Bendix, and by the literature cited above, and as requested by those like Deacon et al. (2004: 11) arguing for a more inclusive sense of heritage, are however, impeded by the dominant discursive constructions of heritage. As noted above, not all countries and commentators have been comfortable with the conceptual and philosophical challenges offered by the international efforts to recognise intangible heritage. The last two chapters in the volume deal with these issues as they relate to the UK. Hassard's chapter is predicated on the fact that the UK has yet to ratify the ICHC, and that its own national emphasis on material and monumental heritage impedes that government's ability to see the relevance of the Convention. Hassard, through an examination of the history of conservation debates in England, argues that the idea of intangible heritage is not necessarily contrary to Western conservation philosophy. Indeed, survey work by Smith (2006) within England, which asked visitors to heritage sites and museums to define 'heritage', showed that the idea of heritage as memory, workplace skills, family histories, oral histories, 'traditions' and so forth, was prevalent in many people's definitions of heritage. These definitions, however, were more likely to be expressed by those from the working communities surveyed by Smith and whose sense of heritage and identity was marginalised by the English AHD. This AHD not only defines heritage as material, monumental and nationally significant but also privileges the heritage of elite classes. The chapter by Smith and Waterton develops the idea of the English AHD, demonstrates the way it is expressed within English heritage policy, and the conceptual barriers this puts in place to limit debate about the nature, meaning and consequences of heritage. This is perhaps not a positive note upon which to conclude the volume, but the challenges offered by a widening and more inclusive debate about the nature, value and consequences of heritage are fraught, and thus will be resisted. They are fraught not only because they are complicated and complex, but because the debate may destabilise some community's and nation's sense of place.

Heritage is intimately linked with identity – exactly how it is linked and its inter-relationship are yet to be fully understood – however, a key consequence of heritage is that it creates and recreates a sense of inclusion and exclusion. At global, national and local levels, heritage, however defined, is used to define a sense of place. Current and dominant definitions about 'tangible' and 'world heritage' establish an international hierarchy of cultural relevance, status and sense of place. Ultimately, whatever the ICHC does or does not achieve, the development of international debate about intangible heritage – and thus the nature of heritage more generally – has the potential to rework not only definitions of heritage but global and local senses of place.

Acknowledgements

We would like to thank Lalle Pursglove for her patience, and Gary Campbell and Emma Waterton for their support in preparing this volume.

Bibliography

Aikawa, N. (2004) 'An historical overview of the preparation of the UNESCO International Convention for the Safeguarding of the Intangible Heritage', *Museum International*, 56 (1–2): 137–49.

Amselle, J.L. (2004) 'Intangible heritage and contemporary African Art', *Museum International*, 56 (1–2): 84–9.

Arizpe, L. (2000) 'Cultural heritage and globalisation', in E. Avrant, R. Mason and M. de La Torre (eds), *Values and Heritage Conservation*, Los Angeles: The Getty Conservation Institute.

—— (2004) 'Intangible cultural heritage, diversity and coherence', *Museum International*, 56 (1–2): 130–5.

Bedjaoui, M. (2004) 'The Convention for the Safeguarding of the Intangible Cultural Heritage: the legal framework and universally recognized principles', *Museum International*, 56 (1–2): 150–5.

Blake, J. (2001) *Developing a New Standard-Setting Instrument for the Safeguarding of Intangible Cultural Heritage: Elements for Consideration*, Paris: UNESCO.

Brown, M.F. (2005) 'Heritage trouble: recent work on the protection of intangible cultural property', *International Journal of Cultural Property*, 12: 40–61.

Byrne, D. (1991) 'Western hegemony in archaeological heritage management', *History and Anthropology*, 5: 269–76.

Cleere, H. (2001) 'The uneasy bedfellows: universality and cultural heritage', in R. Layton, P. G. Stone and J. Thomas (eds), *Destruction and Conservation of Cultural Property*, London: Routledge.

Deacon, H., Dondolo, L., Mrubata, M. and Prosalendis, S. (2004) *The Subtle Power of Intangible Heritage*, South Africa: HSRC Press.

Dicks, B. (2000) *Heritage, Place and Community*, Cardiff: University of Wales Press.

Graham, B. (2002) 'Heritage as knowledge: capital or culture?' *Urban Studies*, 39 (5–6): 1003–17.

Graham, B., Ashworth, G. and Tunbridge, J. (2000) *A Geography of Heritage: Power, Culture and Economy*, London: Arnold.

Harvey, D.C. (2001) 'Heritage pasts and heritage presents: temporality, meaning and the scope of heritage studies', *International Journal of Heritage Studies*, 7 (4): 319–38.

Kirshenblatt-Gimblett, B. (2004) 'Intangible heritage as metacultural production', *Museum International*, 56 (1–2): 52–64.

Kurin, R. (2002) 'Comments', *Current Anthropology*, 43 (1): 144–5.

—— (2004) 'Safeguarding intangible cultural heritage in the 2003 UNESCO Convention: a critical appraisal', *Museum International*, 56 (1–2): 66–76.

Littler, J. and Naidoo, R. (eds) (2005) *The Politics of Heritage: The Legacies of 'Race'*, London: Routledge.

Logan, W.S. (2007) 'Closing Pandora's Box: human rights conundrums in cultural heritage protection', in H. Silverman and D.F. Ruggles (eds), *Cultural Heritage and Human Rights*, New York: Springer.

Lowenthal, D. (1998) *The Heritage Crusade and the Spoils of History*. 2nd edn. Cambridge: Cambridge University Press.

Matsuura, K. (2001) 'Preface', *First Proclamation of Masterpieces of the Oral and Intangible Heritage of Humanity*, Paris: UNESCO.

Munjeri, D. (2004) 'Tangible and intangible heritage: from difference to convergence', *Museum International*, 56 (1–2): 12–20.

Nas, P. (2002) 'Masterpieces of Oral and Intangible Culture: reflections on the UNESCO World Heritage list', *Current Anthropology*, 43 (1): 139–48.

Peckham, R.S. (ed.) (2003) *Rethinking Heritage. Cultures and Politics in Europe*, London: I. B. Tauris.

Pocock, D. (1997) 'Some reflections on World Heritage', *Area*, 29 (3): 260–8.

Schmitt, T.M. (2008) 'The UNESCO concept of safeguarding intangible cultural heritage: its background and *Marrakchi* roots', *International Journal of Heritage Studies*, 14 (2): 95–111.

Smith, L. (2006) *Uses of Heritage*, London: Routledge.

Sullivan, S. (2004) 'Local involvement and traditional practices in the World Heritage System', in E. de Merode, R. Smeets and C. Westrik (eds), *Linking Universal and Local Values: Managing a Sustainable Future for World Heritage*, Paris: World Heritage Centre.

Tunbridge, J. and Ashworth, G. (1996) *Dissonant Heritage: The Management of the Past as a Resource in Conflict*, Chichester: J. Wiley.

Urry, J. (1996) 'How societies remember the past', in S. Macdonald and G. Fyfe (eds), *Theorising Museums*, Oxford: Blackwells.

van Zanten, W. (2004) 'Constructing new terminology for intangible cultural heritage', *Museum International*, 56 (1 and 2): 36–44.

Yoshida, K. (2004) 'The museum and the intangible cultural heritage', *Museum International*, 56 (1–2): 108–12.

Convention for the Safeguarding of the Intangible Cultural Heritage

Reflections on history and concepts

From the Proclamation of Masterpieces to the *Convention for the Safeguarding of Intangible Cultural Heritage*

Noriko Aikawa-Faure

Introduction

The UNESCO *Convention for the Safeguarding of the Intangible Cultural Heritage* (ICHC) was adopted without dissenting vote by the General Conference at its 32nd session in October 2003 and entered into force on 20th April 2006. By September 2008, more than 100 states were parties to it. The early adoption of this Convention, and its swift entry into force, was without precedent. Since November 2006, the Intergovernmental Committee had been preparing operational directives for the implementation of the Convention that were approved by the General Assembly of the States Parties in June 2008. The first inscriptions on the two lists created by the ICHC, the 'List of the Intangible Cultural Heritage in need of urgent safeguarding' (henceforth Urgent List) and the 'Representative List of the ICH of Humanity' (henceforth Representative List), will take place towards the end of 2009.

Prior to this Convention, UNESCO had carried out a number of activities to promote the safeguarding of Intangible Cultural Heritage (ICH) world-wide. Among them, the landmark undertakings were the *Recommendation on the Safeguarding of Traditional Culture and Folklore* 1989 (henceforth 1989 Recommendation), the dissemination of the *Living Human Treasure* system launched in 1993, and the *Proclamation of Masterpieces of the Oral and Intangible Heritage of Humanity* established in 1998. Throughout these activities, the concept of ICH developed in response to political, economic, social and cultural environments. This chapter traces the development of the concept of ICH during the preparation of the ICHC. Since 1993, I was responsible for the programme of ICH in UNESCO Headquarters, and was directly involved in the assessment regarding the application of the 1989 Recommendation by the member states and the development of the Proclamation of the Masterpieces of the Oral and Intangible Heritage of Humanity (henceforth, Proclamation of Masterpieces) and the ICHC. First, the chapter examines how, and in what context, the Proclamation of the Masterpieces programme was launched. It identifies the speed with which the 'cultural debates' of the Marrakech meeting (1997) were transformed into political debates within UNESCO. Second, it describes how criticisms of the 1989 Recommendation triggered the creation of the ICHC. Third, it details the progressive development of the conceptual framework for the ICHC through a review of the debates held during three expert meetings: Turin (2001), Elche (2001) and Rio (2002). Each of these marked a significant stage for the elaboration of the definition and scope of the ICHC. I also describe how consensus emerged among different views and approaches, notably within the Turin meeting, which established the underpinning concepts of the Convention. The progressive and delicate transformation process from academic to political debates during these meetings, as well as subsequent meetings held in UNESCO, is also described. Moreover, I attempt to demonstrate how the Proclamation of Masterpieces programme and the process of the preparation of ICHC were interwoven in the course of their parallel development, notably through the Elche and Rio meetings, as well as UNESCO Executive Board sessions. This demonstrates how the Proclamation of the Masterpieces programme served as a lever for the creation of the ICHC. The concluding section reviews the difficult discussions that took place between 2006 and 2008 by the Intergovernmental Committee of the ICHC over the development of the operational directives. The key issue was how to identify appropriate mechanisms to ensure the participation of practitioner communities, an issue championed as one of the most significant principles throughout the conferences and meetings examined in this chapter.

Proclamation of Masterpieces of the Oral and Intangible Heritage of Humanity – Marrakech Meeting

The underpinning concept of the Masterpieces programme was elaborated during the 'International consultation on the preservation of popular cultural spaces – Declaration of the oral heritage of mankind [sic]'.[1] This small-scale meeting, held in Marrakech in June 1997, was attended by 11 international experts and five Moroccan experts. Most of the participants were experts on oral traditions from disciplines such as anthropology, ethnology, literature, oral history and sociology. Actors, writers, poets, Ministers of Culture of Vanuatu, and Côte d'Ivoire also participated. While examining the oral expressions performed at the Jamaa'el-Fna Square in Marrakech, the meeting aimed to explore possible mechanisms through which UNESCO could effectively alert the international community to the urgent need for safeguarding oral heritage worldwide.

There were several factors driving UNESCO to take this initiative. During the first half of the 1990s, demands coming from its member states, mostly developing countries, prompted serious consideration of the protection of ICH. As Federico Mayor (1992), the then Director-General of UNESCO, stated: 'UNESCO could no longer remain a stranger to the interest [in ICH] expressed by the international community'. First, increasing frustrations were directed to the World Heritage Committee by countries from the southern hemisphere who protested that the World Heritage List hardly reflected a geographical balance as its selection criteria were not necessarily suitable for the cultural features of southern countries. Their rich cultures, it was argued, are expressed more in their living form than in their monuments and sites. UNESCO was therefore urged to take corrective measures to right this 'imbalance' by encompassing intangible components in the selection criteria. The World Heritage Committee, in response to this claim, expanded the criteria by adding a new category entitled 'cultural landscape' in 1992, which attempted to encompass intangible components. However, the pin-pointed 'imbalance' was hardly rectified. Second, following the Rio Earth Summit (1992), the significance of Indigenous peoples knowledge had been increasingly recognised by international communities, as had its vulnerability to economic exploitation by multi-national industries. Third, the report *Our Creative Diversity*, pointed out that intangible heritage had been, and was still, neglected (Pérez de Cuéllar 1995). Thus, it was argued that the concept of cultural heritage should be revisited in order to ensure that both tangible and intangible aspects were encompassed.[2] This argument was reiterated during the Intergovernmental Conference on Cultural Policies for Development in Stockholm, April 1998 (UNESCO 1998: Objective 3, para. 3).

Following the growing recognition of ICH, WIPO and UNESCO jointly organised a World Forum on the protection of folklore in Phuket, April 1997. This aimed to launch an international legal instrument to protect intellectual property rights of folklore. This initiative encountered a strong opposition from the countries that had been benefiting from the free use of traditional expressions. It appeared obvious, then, that a considerable obstacle would be placed in the path of negotiations. After their fact-finding missions of 1998, WIPO decided to increase the scope of the future treaty by adding the IPR protection of traditional knowledge and genetic resources to the expression of folklore. Given that this scope was much larger than UNESCO's mandate, WIPO pursued, as of 1999, the negotiation without UNESCO. UNESCO therefore needed to pursue its own action for the safeguarding of ICH in response to its member states' demands. Albert Sasson, former Assistant Director-General for the Bureau of Programme Planning at UNESCO, was sent to the Marrakech meeting to represent Federico Mayor, who took a particular interest in this meeting. As he stated in his opening speech:

UNESCO could begin preparing an international Convention specifically for ICH to promote its protection (with a global approach) but such a procedure would take a long time especially when it refers to a domain, which is difficult to define because it is intangible and evolving permanently. Therefore before launching a procedure for a new international normative instrument, UNESCO tries to raise awareness of its Member States that the majority of their ICH are threatened with disappearing if they do not take urgent measures for the safeguarding these treasures which constitute their source of identity.

(Sasson 1997: 5)

However, the immediate issue that pushed UNESCO to organise the Marrakech meeting was the appeal made to Federico Mayor in 1996 by the Spanish writer, Juan Goytisolo, to save Jamaa'el-Fna Square. This 'cultural space', where popular 'artists' had been performing since the Middle Ages, was threatened with being 'cleaned up' by the municipal authorities in favour of a modern urbanisation of the city. Goytisolo suggested that UNESCO could save this 'cultural space' by honouring it with an international recognition. Mayor, receptive to this appeal, supported Goytisolo's suggestion (Fuentes 1997). I was instructed to follow Goytisolo's suggestion and to develop a programme with an international dimension, taking the Marrakech case as a pilot study. UNESCO entrusted Marc Denhez, a Canadian heritage lawyer who had just finished his legal assessment of the 1989 Recommendation, to explore the different possibilities for UNESCO to grant international recognition to 'cultural spaces' worldwide that were under threat. The purpose of establishing such mechanisms was to encourage member states to become conscious of the significance of their ICH.

Denhez examined different frameworks whereby UNESCO could honour and distinguish certain actions, performances, persons and projects. Being a heritage lawyer, he immediately looked into the mechanism of the World Heritage List. He also examined the mechanisms and efficacy of different UNESCO prizes such as: the Sultan Qaboos Prize for Environmental Preservation; the UNESCO Prize for Peace Education; the Félix Houphouët-Boigny Peace Prize; and the Aga Khan Award for Architecture. It is worth mentioning here that an important prize for the ICH programme was then under negotiation with the United Arab Emirates. Denhez considered that drafting a new Convention modelled on the *World Heritage Convention* (WHC), or rearranging the WHC to include ICH, should be the logical solution. However, it was considered that it could take too many years to meet the urgent demands of member states. In addition, the model of the WHC is not necessarily applicable to ICH (Denhez 1997: 4). Denhez, therefore, proposed a mechanism combining the World Heritage List and the UNESCO Prize system as a framework for the new programme then entitled 'Proclamation of the Oral Heritage of Humanity'. He argued that the 'award system has a major impact on World consciousness and furthermore from the procedural standpoint the award system has the virtue of speed as well as of being more aptly tailored to the subject-matter' (Denhez 1997: 5). Regarding the programme title, he argued that the programme bears a prestigious title, as 'it is important to reassure the prospective donors that "prestige" will be attached to any support they provide' (Denhez 1997: 6). Denhez (1997) suggested the following three objectives of the programme:

i)   To grant an official recognition to a selection of 'cultural spaces' where there is an outstanding concentration of ICH and oral traditions.
ii) To encourage their safeguarding and to promote participation of individuals, groups, institutions or governments in the management of the safeguarding actions.
iii) To raise awareness of all stakeholders to the importance of ICH.

He proposed to apply the same definition given to the 'traditional cultures and folklore' in the Recommendation of 1989 to 'oral history' in this programme. Denhez (1997) also suggested the selection criteria should be defined as: i) cultural and ii) organisational. He thought the cultural criteria should be inspired by the general terms used for UNESCO Prizes (see, for instance, the Sultan Qaboos Prize). He also took the example of criteria used by the 'living human treasures' systems practised in different countries, and those of the World Heritage Operational Guidelines. For the organisational criteria, he was inspired by criteria used by the Getty Foundation. He finally proposed cultural criteria in a simplified form: 'its authenticity, its cultural and social role to the community concerned today, its creative value, its testimony to a cultural tradition and history of the community concerned, its skill, its distinctive characteristics and the danger of its disappearing' (Denhez 1997b: 7). With respect to the organisational criteria, to which he attached more weight, he proposed more detailed criteria that privileged the transmission and emphasised the primary roles of practitioner communities. The nomination files, Denhez (1997a) suggested, should be accompanied by:

i)   an action plan;
ii) indication of the linkage between the action plan and the measures foreseen in the Recommendation of 1989;
iii) measures to empower the community concerned to preserve and promote its own oral heritage, name of responsible parties who will enter into a binding contract with UNESCO;
iv) name of the recipient of the award and the credentials of the proposed recipient and the way in which the recipient will apply the proceeds of the award in support of the action plan.

In assessing the action plan, the jury should consider:

i)   the mandate of public authorities and of NGOs in assuring the protection and transmission of the relevant cultural values;

ii) the arrangement to raise awareness of the value of this heritage and the importance of its preservation among peoples belonging to the community concerned;

iii) the role assigned to the bearers of the heritage;

iv) the arrangement with the local communities to preserve and promote this heritage;

v) the arrangement to record this heritage;

vi) the arrangements with the bearers of these traditions, to advance the relevant skills, techniques or cultural expressions;

vii) arrangements with the bearers of these traditions, to pass on the relevant skills, techniques or cultural expressions to trainees and youth generally;

viii) recipients of an award should preferably be local NGOs.

(Denhez 1997b: 8)

Denhez finally suggested creating a jury to make selections as well as establishing a fund/prize for the new programme.

He presented his proposed *System to Honour Cultural Space with Remarkable Intangible Heritage* to the 1997 Marrakech meeting. The meeting, after examining the Jamaa'el-Fna case, scrutinised Denhez's proposal. Experts agreed that UNESCO would confer on the idea of a list modelled on the World Heritage List. The term 'Cultural Space' was defined as: 'locations where cultural activities occur, having the characteristic of shifting over time and whose existence depends on the presence of these forms of cultural expression' (UNESCO 1997a: 9). According to experts, the principal goal of the project should be to encourage governments, municipalities, NGOs and local communities to undertake activities to identify, preserve, and promote their oral heritage. There should be two principal selection criteria: i) exceptional universal value as a general cultural criterion; and ii) organisational criteria. Experts stressed that 'a continual or permanent existence of cultural expression within the cultural space' and 'respect for tolerance, multiculturalism and the role of women' should be included within the cultural criteria (UNESCO 1997a: 9). In connection with organisational criteria, emphasis was placed on the integral participation of the communities concerned in the undertaking of protective measures. A caveat was formulated that before launching national protective measures, traditional apprenticeships and processes for the transmission of skills associated with oral heritage should be studied with a view to respect the traditional social structures within which the apprenticeships and transmission occur (UNESCO 1997a: 8). Participants underscored the importance of the creation of a financial mechanism, such as a fund/prize, to be connected to the new programme to ensure its efficient implementation. As there were a number of points which needed further discussion, the representative of the Director-General announced that what mattered most was to confer on UNESCO the immediate mandate of putting this system into operation, even if the contents and procedures of this initiative required ongoing consideration over the long term (UNESCO 1997a: 10).

As outlined above, the proclamation programme started as a small-scale prize project applying the mechanism of the World Heritage List in a simplified manner. Its principal purpose was to honour or distinguish certain oral heritage in order to prevent outside forces undermining their existence. Therefore, a 'distinctive notion' expressed in the term 'masterpiece' was indispensable to this programme. In addition, it was unconceivable to launch a new programme of this kind without having substantial financial support from outside UNESCO, as any increase in the ICH budget was unlikely. Therefore, exploring a prize or extra-budgetary funding was integral to the successful running of the programme. This was another reason why the notion of 'prestige' needed to be attached to the project to attract sponsors, as was suggested by Denhez. It deserves mentioning that the amount of the budget for an ICH programme for the biennium (1996–97), was $1,310,800 of which merely $853,500 (USD) was available to be implemented by the Headquarters of UNESCO. In addition, more than 50% of this amount was cut to finance so-called urgent activities. Although the Marrakech meeting was modest, it precipitated an important process. In October 1997, immediately after the meeting, Morocco and Guinea (supported by Saudi Arabia, Cape Verde, UAE, Spain, Lebanon, Mali, Uzbekistan, Portugal, Dominican Republic and Venezuela) submitted a draft resolution to the 29th UNESCO General Conference proposing that UNESCO set up a new project entitled 'Proclamation of Masterpieces of Oral Heritage of Humanity' (UNESCO 1997b).[3] During the debates of the General Conference, many countries championed the ICH programme, and recommended that it should be prioritised (Aikawa 2007: 59). After the adoption of the draft resolution by the General Conference, this new project came under the scrutiny of the subsequent sessions of UNESCO's Executive Board.

A draft Regulation of the Proclamation of Masterpieces of the Oral Heritage of Humanity, in which the criterion regarding authenticity was removed, was submitted to the Executive Board session in May 1998 (Document 154EX13+CORR). The Board members were supportive of this project in principle, but rejected the proposed Regulations as a whole. Most of the opponents were highly contributing countries, such as Western European countries, who did not seem to find much merit in such a programme, and tended to consider it as merely consuming the budget. Other countries having Indigenous peoples on their soils seemed to find it rather disturbing. The Board decided to enlarge the scope of the project by adding 'intangible cultural heritage' to the title and thus the scope of the project was modified. The Board requested that the Director-General 'conduct a thorough consultation with all of the Member States and to resubmit the proposal ... to the following session of the Board in October 1998' (154X/ 52 Decision 3.5.1). Between May and September 1998, the Secretariat undertook a series of consultations with different groups of the member states and produced a revised version of the Regulations. The project of the Proclamation of Masterpieces gave rise to many intense debates between member states on a range of issues. These included the notion of 'masterpiece', the notion of 'universal value' and the 'method of the implication of the practitioners communities'. Debates on the issue of ICH were pursued on a governmental level, and the member states did not allow the Secretariat to further develop the conceptual framework by organising expert meetings. The Proclamation project thus 'cleared the political ground' for the preparation of the ICHC. In September 1998, the Regulations of the project were finally adopted by the 155th session of the Executive Board after numerous modifications including the suppression of organisational criteria. Even if it was decided that the candidature files should be accompanied by safeguarding action plans, the elimination of the organizational criteria, conceived as the principal criteria, caused a certain degree of damage to the whole framework of the programme. The Board then requested – and received – a progress report for the 157th session in October 1999 (155EX/Decision+Appendix). Following the decision of the Executive Board (155EX/decisions: 3.5.5 para. 4), the implementation guidelines were drafted and nine members of the jury were nominated. The submitted report (157EX/8) encompassed the results of the International Conference entitled 'A Global Assessment of the 1989 Recommendation on the Safeguarding of Traditional Culture and Folklore: Local Empowerment and International Cooperation', co-organised with the Smithsonian Institution in Washington DC in June 1999. The Conference concluded that the underpinning concept of the 1989 Recommendation was obsolete in the contemporary world political, social and cultural context and therefore a new international normative instrument needed to be created.

While examining the progress report of the Proclamation of Masterpieces programme, the Board, however, expressed its doubt about the decisions already taken. Some members, mostly from developed countries, vigorously debated issues such as the notion of the term 'masterpiece', the selection method of jury members and the roles of NGOs. At this point, the Board members were reminded by the Representative of the Director-General that the presented report was an implementation report of decisions already taken by the previous session of the Board. She then suggested that the Board might review the regulations after at least one round of the proclamation had been experienced. Thus, the project, which was almost jeopardised, was nevertheless launched as an 'experimental' programme (Aikawa 2007: 63). One of the reasons why some developed countries were particularly opposed to the Proclamation of the Masterpieces project at this time (October 1999), may have been because they realised that this Proclamation programme was meant to pave the way for an initiative to create a new Convention for the protection of ICH as was recommended by the Washington Conference.

From the 1989 Recommendation to a new normative instrument – Washington Conference

The review of the 1989 Recommendation revealed that it had had little impact among the member states. In reply to the appeal by UNESCO to all member states to report on the action they had taken to give effect to this Recommendation, a mere six countries sent reports to UNESCO. These reports were too limited in number to be submitted to the General Conference in 1991 (Aikawa 2001: 13). Admittedly, this lack of interest shown by member states stemmed from the fact that the Recommendation was 'soft law', without binding force. It could also be because the instrument gave neither a specific mandate to UNESCO, nor any explanation of how it should be implemented. Alternatively, it could be due to its shortcomings, deriving from the dilemma posed by the opposition between two approaches: the global cultural approach and the intellectual property approach (Aikawa 2004: 140). Between 1995 and 1999, upon the initiative of the Czech Republic, a worldwide appraisal of the safeguarding of traditional and folk heritage was carried out, taking the 1989 Recommendation as a reference point. A series of surveys were then undertaken through a detailed questionnaire, and seminars were organised in eight regions of the world (Czech Republic, Mexico, Japan, Finland, Uzbekistan, Ghana, New Caledonia and Lebanon) to address an assessment for each geographical region (Aikawa 2001: 16). At the culminating International Conference held in Washington DC in 1999, which summarised the eight regional stocktaking meetings, experts considered that the 1989 Recommendation was no longer adequate for the world geo-political, social and cultural situation. The principal criticisms addressed the definition of 'folklore and traditional culture'[4] and its scope, as well as its fundamental approaches to the safeguarding actions. The Conference concluded that the scope of the term 'folklore', as defined in Article A of the Recommendation, was too limited and its use was inadequate. Moreover, the definition given to the term 'folklore' was much too product oriented, while related symbols, values and processes were neglected. In the approaches applied, too much weight was placed on research and the researchers, while the practitioners and communities who had a primary stake in creating, performing, enacting, preserving, and disseminating their traditional cultures were neglected. The Conference, having considered the concepts underpinning the 1989 Recommendation to be obsolete, recommended that the UNESCO member states[5] be invited to submit to the forthcoming 30th General Conference (1999) a draft resolution requesting that UNESCO undertake a feasibility study for the adoption of a new standard-setting instrument for the protection of traditional culture and folklore (Aikawa 2007: 64).

The process for the preparation of the new international Convention (adopted in 2003) was thus set in motion in 1999. The 30th session of the General Conference (October 1999) adopted the draft resolution submitted by the

Czech Republic, Lithuania and Bolivia and supported by Bulgaria, Côte d'Ivoire, Slovakia and Ukraine (30C/DR.84). Janet Blake[6] was entrusted in 2000 to conduct a preliminary study on the question of developing a new standard-setting instrument for the protection of traditional culture and folk-lore (Blake 2001a). What those member states endowed with rich ICH expec-ted for such an instrument was nothing but an international Convention. Hence, while pursuing the process of developing a Convention, the new project for the Proclamation of Masterpieces was launched in the year 2000.

The strongest impetus given to the development of the Intangible Cultural Heritage programme was the arrival in November 1999 of Koiichiro Matsuura as Director-General of UNESCO. The new Director-General chose ICH as one of the eight priority programmes of the organisa-tion. A few days before the Executive Board (159th session), he organised an information meeting (on 5 May 2000) to explain to the representatives of the member states that the Proclamation project would be launched in parallel with the preparation of the new normative instrument. The Director-General announced that 'this feasibility study might lead to the creation, in the medium-term, of a Convention accompanied by an intergovernmental com-mittee and a fund after the manner of the World Heritage Convention' (Matsuura 2000). Another impetus was the donation of $3,200,000 by the Japanese government in 2000 for both the Masterpieces programme and the development of the new instrument.

Definition and scope of ICH for a normative instrument

Turin meeting

Following the authorisation given by the General Conference to proceed with the preparation of the new instrument, UNESCO, at the invitation of the Italian government, organised an International Roundtable entitled 'Intangible Cultural Heritage – working definitions' at Turin in March 2001. It was the first expert meeting convened to reflect upon the conceptual framework of the future international instrument. The purpose of the meet-ing was to clarify the definition, scope and relevant terminology of ICH. Participants of the meeting were carefully selected to ensure an equitable balance in terms of geography and expertise. There were four anthro-pologists,[7] two folklorists,[8] three specialists in international law studies,[9] one linguist,[10] one ethnomusicologist,[11] two members of the Executive Board of UNESCO,[12] one diplomat,[13] one official of a cultural administration[14] and one specialist in biotechnology.[15]

At the beginning of the meeting, UNESCO indicated some requirements to be observed while developing the definition of ICH and identifying the scope of the domains to be regarded in the new instrument. These were to respect the specific mandate[16] of UNESCO in order to avoid overlap with other UN Agencies such as WIPO, ILO, WHO, CBD, UNCTAD, and to take full account of UNESCO's current priority policy in the field of culture, which was the promotion of cultural diversity and cultural identity. Therefore, priority should be given to the social, intellectual and cultural processes of the communities that generate such identity (UNESCO 2001a). Prior to the meeting, UNESCO undertook an extensive worldwide survey of the definitions used by member states, IGOs, NGOs and other institutions for the term 'intangible cultural heritage' or other equivalent terms, such as 'folklore', 'traditional culture', 'oral heritage', 'traditional knowledge' and 'Indigenous heritage'. The results of the survey provided by 36 entities were presented to the participants of the meeting for their consideration.

Working definitions currently in use by various member states as well as by intergovernmental organisations

Two anthropologists assessed the results of the survey and made suggestions regarding the purposes, scope and definition of the future instrument for the safeguarding of ICH.

Manuela da Cunha[17] presented her analysis of the survey results (2002), pointing out that:

i)   A shift in focus from products to the process of production had occur-red, such that traditional knowledge was no longer considered an anti-quity, but was valued for the way it was acquired and used. This was a particular issue for the Organization of African Unity. Therefore, the protection of cultural heritage necessarily entails the protection of the social and environmental context in which it exists. In the same vein, it is necessary to support producers of cultural heritage as participant agents in its protection and conservation.

ii)   A duality was noticeable between the definitions of 'internal' and 'external' assertions of cultural identity.

iii) Major changes had taken place in many countries where there was the shift of notion from denial of the legitimacy of local identity as inimical elements to national identity to acknowledgement of pluri-ethnicity and pluri-identity.

As a result of her analysis, da Cunha (2002) recommended that a primary objective of the new instrument should be to maintain living processes rather than exclusively historic processes. Therefore, more recent definitions needed to be developed, taking into consideration the current situation concerning ICH worldwide, which may be summarised as:

i)   A growing acknowledgement of the general importance of local culture.
ii)   Increasing recognition of Indigenous and traditional knowledge.

iii) Acknowledgement of inter-relatedness of ecological knowledge, genetic resources and the way of life of local and Indigenous people, and the growing understanding of the concerns of Indigenous and local communities.
iv) Recognition of the importance of equity in sharing benefits and control by producers of cultural goods as well as the principle that the prior informed consent (control) is the prerequisite for registering any of their knowledge.

Manuela da Cunha (2002) concluded that UNESCO should take a more 'holistic view of protection' in relation to economic issues, while also privileging cultural producers as beneficiaries and agents. Finally, she suggested the adoption of a wide-ranging definition of ICH as provided by Elika Daes[18]: i) folklore and crafts, ii) bio-diversity, iii) Indigenous knowledge.

Loudes Arizpe[19] presented her proposals regarding the definition of the scope, working definition and elements that should be protected through an international legal instrument. She emphasised that 'enactment is an essential and defining aspect of ICH in a sense that this heritage exists and is sustained through the acts of people' (2001). Arizpe noted that as UNESCO is an IGO, its role and activities should be acceptable to the majority of member states, and as such, a balance is necessary between member states' political consensus and scientific rigour. She then gave the following list of justifications for establishing an international legal instrument for the safeguarding of ICH (2001):

i)   To conserve human creations that may disappear forever, taking into consideration the importance of valuing human creations and enhancing the diversity of human creation.
ii) To give world recognition to a certain kind of ICH.
iii) To strengthen identity in compliance with UNESCO's mandate to promote peace.
iv) To enable social co-operation in the era of individualism.
v)   To provide historical continuity in addressing the apparent psychological need for people to feel that they belong to some historical tradition.
vi) To foster enjoyment.

She stressed that the emphasis needed to be placed on viewing ICH holistically and understanding it as:

a process of creation, comprising skills, enabling factors (enabling creation and conservation, access to knowledge, objects and practices of past cultures; museums and research, dialogue with other cultures and copyright for the protection of creations), products (to conserve knowledge or product, practices or performances, the meaning given to physical heritage), meanings (meanings concern identity, aesthetic enjoyment, emotive sentiments, expressive culture and historical reasons), impacts (the fact that ICH has an impact on people's perception of belonging to a certain group could create some difficulty in preparing an international legal instrument) and economic value (to be left with other organizations such as WIPO and WTO).

(Arizpe 2001)

Arizpe also suggested that UNESCO should identify within its new international instrument those domains which have not yet been dealt with by other organisations and which had a comparative advantage to UNESCO. She then listed principal elements of ICH as follows:

life (birth, rites of ages and betrothal, wedding and death), social (kinship, community, settlements, border and nation), biodiversity (botany, zoology, pharmacopoeia, agriculture), land (nature beliefs, names, landscape and property), symbolic (signs, representations, rituals and flags), spiritual (cosmo vision animistic beliefs, sacred books, liturgies), literary (oral literature such as legends and epic stories and printed literature), performing arts (high arts and local arts), and festive (season's calendar, games, religious festivals, school festivals).

(Arizpe 2001)

In eliminating elements that had already been dealt with by other IGOs, governments or organised religious institutions, Arizpe identified the domains that UNESCO should focus on in developing a new instrument. These were: 'i) the area between nature and culture; ii) areas concerning Indigenous people's culture; iii) social co-operation and social cohesion; iv) oral tradition; and v) local arts and crafts' (2001).

The presentation of two different views on the scope for the future instrument generated an animated debate among experts. Arizpe favoured a limited scope of domains in order not to overlap with the domains already covered by other organisations and bodies, while da Cunha proposed a larger scope, focusing on the traditional knowledge related to biodiversity of Indigenous peoples. Views of participants were also divided between anthropological concerns with local practitioner communities and political concerns with the states' roles, and between those considering ICH as product and those as process. The issue on the cultural rights of Indigenous peoples and economic aspects of ICH protection gave rise to controversial discussions. In the end, the final report of the meeting (UNESCO 2001c: 7) notes the following consensus emerged:

i)   The definition should reflect 'participatory democracy' rather than 'representative democracy'. Therefore, a greater recognition should be given to the agency of traditional custodians of ICH as creators with expertise and conscious intention to transmit their traditions.

ii) In conformity with the Washington Conference conclusion, a greater recognition should be given to the agency of traditional custodians of ICH as creators with expertise and conscious intention to transmit their traditions. Therefore, the term 'community' should be the keyword for the future instrument. However, as the term 'community' bears multiple meanings, the definition needs to be carefully examined. In addition, a question of how to treat ICH expressed by a cross-border community and the possibilities to address the protection of 'communal property right' within the legal framework were raised.

iii) A question of concrete steps to be taken to implement active participation of actors/creators of culture in the protection of cultural heritage was discussed, i.e. the question of whether actors/creators of culture should be considered or not as experts. Against some reservation expressed, it was stressed that an international legal instrument should work with people and not on people.

iv) With respect to creation and innovation, ICH should be regarded as being continually shaped according to the circumstances and social environment in which it occurs. In the same vein, the notion of intercultural exchange and the sharing of diversity need to be reflected in the working definition.

v) Referring to 'traditional knowledge', in spite of the general tendency to associate it exclusively with Indigenous peoples, it was suggested that UNESCO should consider 'traditional knowledge' in a broader sense as encompassing all communities of a given country including Indigenous people's communities.

vi) The issues of protecting people's rights to practice ICH is a human rights issue. The knowledge of Indigenous people cannot be protected unless their rights to access the resources relating to this knowledge are protected. Therefore, protecting ICH is also a means of protecting the rights to live and to be secure.

vi) However, the future international normative instrument should not only protect the rights of custodians as individuals but also encourage a system whereby *the State recognises the importance of a particular cultural expression in a broader sense.*

vii) With reference to the consistency of customary law and normative law, a growing recognition of the role of customary law should be taken into account.

viii) While accepting the shift in anthropological concepts about product, production and process, the *product* must also be recognised as an element of ICH.

ix) A *distinction* should be made between the use of heritage for *commercial purposes* and *internal activities of communities.*

Terminology in the field of ICH and related areas

Peter Seitel[20] also proposed definitions of the terms 'cultural process', 'traditional cultural process', 'traditional culture', 'traditional knowledge' and 'safeguarding of traditional cultures'. He was opposed to the establishment of an international directorate of ICH after the manner of the 1972 World Heritage Convention, and he argued that, 'such selective programs have no effect on the vast majority of traditional practitioners. Such gestures seem to benefit more the interests of cultural professionals than those of the vast majority of cultural bearers' (Seitel 2001: 9). Instead, he proposed the following two programmes be dealt with by the future international agreement: i) a code of ethics[21] that would govern legal and economic relationships between traditional practitioners as members of traditional cultures and the institutions of national societies, which include commercial, cultural, administrative, and educational and media institutions; ii) the creation of cultural registers of ICH on the web in order to ensure that all traditional cultures have access to establishing collegial relationships with other traditional cultures and with relevant NGOs and organisations. According to Seitel, 'Creation of such cultural registers would be useful for the legal defence of IPR in support for WIPO's efforts in this area' (2001: 10).

Without referring to the proposed two programmes, discussions continued and the following points emerged as indispensable elements of the scope and limits in a normative instrument: i) the importance of practitioners and their agency; ii) the significance of creative process as well as product; iii) the transmission of skills and know-how; and iv) the context of creation and transmission.

Several key terms offered for inclusion in the title of the instrument were also examined carefully. These included 'traditional culture', which was characterised as opposed to modernity, and 'intangible heritage', which was understood as oppositional to tangible heritage, which in turn has a long history in UNESCO's programmes. 'Folklore' was seen as a problematic term, and 'treasures' was seen as having a paternalistic connotation, while 'oral heritage' was considered too limited in scope, but none of them appeared to be entirely satisfactory for the instrument.

Preliminary study on the advisability of regulating internationally, through a new standard-setting instrument, the protection of traditional culture and folklore

Two legal experts presented their papers concerning the scope and definition of an instrument to be developed. Janet Blake (2001a) introduced her preliminary conclusions to be presented to the UNESCO Executive Board at its 161st session in May 2001. Blake argued that the definitions of ICH should not imply that ICH is a 'common or universal heritage of humanity', but the protection of this heritage should be considered as a matter of 'universal interest'. This argument was generally accepted. Experts considered that the system of the WHC, which refers to 'world heritage of mankind' (1972: Preamble, paragraph 7), and which is based on the fundamental idea of 'outstanding and universal value', was an inadequate model, since such a criterion could not be applied to ICH due to its intangible nature.

Blake (2001a) enumerated the following realms of actions to be covered by the instrument:

- Recording and inventorying of ICH in danger of which safeguarding activities need to be supported by the instrument.
- Revitalisation of the continuing creative process of traditional culture through measures that member states would be invited to put in place.
- Strengthening measures enabling the communities to continue to create and maintain and transmit their culture in traditional contexts.
- Prevention of the unauthorised use of ICH and its distortion.
- Restitution of items of cultural property, associated with ICH (to complement the 1970 *Convention on the Means of Prohibiting and Preventing the Illicit Import, Export and Transfer of Ownership of Cultural Property*).
- Raising awareness of the value of ICH.

Blake (2001a: 6) underscored three major elements to be encompassed in the new legal framework:

i)   Inclusion of protocols to reinforce international cooperation and assistance to enable states to carry out the necessary safeguarding measures, following the example of the WH Fund of the 1972 Convention.
ii) Respect for customary rules regarding cultural secrecy.
iii) Practitioners and communities to be involved in the preservation, maintenance management, and so forth of their ICH.

A controversial debate again took place when Blake brought up the issue of practitioner communities' participation in implementing the instrument. Views were divided again between those giving voices to encourage communities' initiative versus those prioritising the state's control. While many participants supported the view that the instrument should, through states, enable communities to develop their own ways of preserving their heritage, others argued that such an instrument should, to a certain extent, be prescriptive at the international level and interactions between states and communities should be encouraged. A compromise was finally accepted that the active involvement of local communities and civil society should be given priority on condition that the states and agencies connected with UNESCO were consulted. A consensus was, however, reached on the importance of the official recognition of exemplary ICH, as it has positive effects on the tradition-holder communities in that it encourages their efforts to preserve and transmit their skill and knowledge.

Blake finally recommended two types of instrument: an instrument similar to the 1972 WHC or an instrument of general cultural heritage protection, which would need a sui-generis legal system to be enacted. She then concluded that the domains included in the definition of ICH for the instrument would influence the type of instrument chosen (2001a: 15–16).

Finally, Francesco Francioni,[22] the Chair of the Roundtable, presented his proposal on the possible working definition for the UNESCO instrument. He first tackled the question of how international law may address the problem of intangible heritage. As an instrument, it should provide regulations concerning the authorisation, procedure on the enjoyment, licensing, time limits and the public policy exceptions, and so forth. Francioni noted that the IPR paradigm can perform a useful function for the protection of ICH. However, he argued, one should take into account the fact that UNESCO's mission goes beyond the IPR approach and that the IPR aims to safeguard the economic utilisation of the end product of a cultural process. Francioni then gave the following reasons why the IPR approach is not adequate for the protection of ICH. First,:

> [the] IPR approach focuses on the end product of a specific artistic or cultural tradition, rather than on the societal structures and processes from which the cultural product is derived ... In the field of ICH, the end product is only the tip of the iceberg represented by the complexity and richness of the intellectual, political and cultural processes in which the heritage is rooted.
>
> (Francioni 2001: 1)

Furthermore, he argued that many expressions of ICH are not traceable to a specific act of invention, and are collective expressions of social necessities that were transmitted from generation to generation, while the IPR approach requires an act of invention or discovery:

> The collective character of most forms of ICH, may represent a further obstacle to the use of IPR as an instrument for international protection ... With ICH it is difficult to identify the title holder as custodian by whom IPR are to be exercised or a legal process is preceded to licence the commercial use of the relevant heritage.
>
> (Francioni 2001: 2)

This analysis was met with general agreement. He then went on to examine the definitions given in three UNESCO Conventions related to cultural heritage, namely the *Convention for the Protection of Cultural Property in the Event of Armed Conflict*, 1954, the 1970 Convention (see above) and the 1972 WHC in order to identify criteria upon which the domains to be protected are delineated. From this analysis of these Conventions, he underscored the need to identify the criteria by which certain expressions of ICH will become subject to the protection of the instrument. Francioni (2001) then proposed several components be included in the definition of the instrument to be developed; these, in summary, were:

i)   the concept of 'important' or 'significant' ICH;
ii)   a reference to the universal value of certain types of intangible cultural heritage to the extent that loss or destruction of such heritage amounts to loss and impoverishment of the 'common cultural heritage of humanity' (a criterion taken from the preamble to the 1954 Hague Convention);
iii) a general, synthetic and inclusive clause encompassing all forms of ICH followed by an indication of some essential typologies in line with Article 1 of the WHC;
iv)   the general definition should be inter-faced with references to operational criteria used in determining the eligibility of intangible cultural heritage proposed for inclusion within the scope of international protection;
v)   as a caveat to the method of definition, the definition should reflect the intrinsic value of the heritage as conceived and perceived by the people, group or community to which such heritage belongs.

The proposals made by Francioni caused some controversy in debates, notably the reference made to 'outstanding universal value'. However, the following framework of the instrument, as well as its definition, were accepted: i) the use of a general definition of ICH to be safeguarded; ii) that a Convention would be developed; iii) the term 'safeguarding' would be used instead of 'protection'; iv) the aim of the instrument would be to enhance the custodians' role, transmission, learning processes, processes of creation and cooperation surrounding ICH; and v) codes of ethics should be integrated into the instrument. The Roundtable finally adopted the following action plan encompassing a 'summary of the conclusions' drawn from the debate, 'objectives', a 'definition' and 'scope of the domains' for an international normative instrument to be prepared for the safeguarding of the ICH (UNESCO 2001b: para. 12). This action plan laid the cornerstone of the ICHC.

Action plan for the safeguarding of the ICH as approved by the international experts on the occasion of the international round table on 'Intangible Cultural Heritage – Working Definitions'

The summary conclusions of the Turin meeting for the Action Plan (UNESCO 2001b) were:

(i)   International efforts to safeguard intangible cultural heritage must be founded on universally accepted human rights, equity and sustainability and on respect for all cultures that also have respect for other cultures.

(ii)   Intangible cultural heritage is fundamentally safeguarded through creativity and enactment by the agents of the communities that produce and maintain it.

(iii)   Any instrument dealing with intangible cultural heritage should facilitate, encourage and protect the right and capacity of communities to continue to enact their intangible cultural heritage through developing their own approaches to manage and sustain it.

(iv)   Sharing one's culture and having a cultural dialogue fosters greater overall creativity as long as recognition and equitable exchanges are ensured.

(v)   The loss of intangible cultural heritage can only be prevented by ensuring that the meanings, enabling conditions and skills involved in their creation, enactment and transmission can be reproduced.

(vi)   Any hierarchical approaches should be avoided in dealing with ICH.

(vii)   The term 'intangible cultural heritage' is acceptable on condition that the question of the interface between tangible and intangible heritage is carefully studied taking into account that in many cultures no distinction is made between two aspects of cultural heritage.

(viii) Among different domains, languages and oral traditions, which are major supporting components for the transmission of ICH, should be given priority.

The Action Plan proposed that the objectives for an international legal instrument should be:

(i)   to conserve human creations that may disappear forever;
(ii)   to give world recognition;
(iii) to strengthen identity;
(iv)   to enable social cooperation within and between groups;
(v)   to provide historical continuity;
(vi)   to enhance the creative diversity of humanity;
(vii) to foster enjoyment.

(UNESCO 2001b)

The definition of the term 'intangible cultural heritage', which was the term retained, was proposed as:

peoples' learned processes along with the knowledge, skills and creativity that inform and are developed by them, the products they create, and the resources, spaces and other aspects of social and natural context necessary to their sustainability; these processes provide living communities with a sense of continuity with previous generations and are important to cultural identity, as well as to the safeguarding of cultural diversity and creativity of humanity.

(UNESCO 2001b)

The suggested scope of the domains to be covered by this instrument included 'oral cultural heritage; languages; performing arts and festive events; social rituals and practices; cosmologies and knowledge systems; beliefs and practices about Nature' (UNESCO 2001b). The elements of these domains should be specified by a group of experts in the course of the elaboration of the instrument.

The Action Plan was presented to the 161st session of the Executive Board in May 2001, together with the Preliminary Feasibility Study drafted by Janet Blake. The Executive Board, after lengthy debate, finally endorsed two documents and decided to authorise the Director-General to continue pursuing the preparation of a new international legal instrument (161EX/Decisions, 3.4.4: 14). The 161st session of the Executive Board was indeed crucial for the preparation of the Convention because it decided to allow the Director-General to continue the process of preparation for the new instrument.

Elche Jury meeting

The Proclamation of the Masterpieces of the Oral and Intangible Heritage of Humanity was also under scrutiny at the same session of the Board (161EX/14) in May 2001. The board examined two items concerning ICH: one related to the preparation of an international legal instrument (161EX/15) and the other related to the Proclamation of the Masterpieces programme (161EX/14). During the debate, the members of the Board highlighted the complementary nature of the two programmes underscoring that the experiences acquired from the latter should contribute to a deepening of the conceptual deliberation of the former. In fact, the first round of the Proclamation programme, took place a few days before the Board session, and declared 19 Masterpieces out of 32 candidates. The Board members, notably those whose candidatures were not proclaimed, found that the selection criteria, in particular the notion of 'outstanding value', were not precise enough and therefore it was necessary to set up further detailed selection criteria.

The board expressed its wishes to further reflect upon the conceptual aspects of ICH and harmonise its definition with the Proclamation programme and the future normative instrument.[23] In response to this request, UNESCO convened an extraordinary jury meeting in September 2001 in Elche, Spain. The principal outcomes of the meeting were:

i)   The endorsement of the Turin definition of ICH.
ii) The clarification of the criterion 'outstanding value' as follows:
     a. the outstanding value to the community concerned and for the maintenance of cultural diversity;
     b. long-lived practice of the custodian communities;
     c. specific creation linked to a particular cultural space.

iii) The setting up of the following definition of the term 'Masterpieces': 'Based on the fact that any culture may hold masterpieces and without restriction by any specific historical and cultural reference, a masterpiece (in the field concerned) is understood as a cultural manifestation of exceptional value, defying any formal rules and not measurable by any external yardstick, which conveys the freedom of expression and creative genius of a people' (2001d: 23b).

iv) Harmonising priority domains with the Turin Action Plan: 'in the vast domain covered by the oral and intangible heritage of humanity, as defined [Turin definition cited], the selection of masterpieces may include, but not be limited to, areas such as cultural events closely linked to languages, oral tradition, the performing arts and craft skills' (UNESCO 2001d: para. 6).

v) Clarification regarding the treatment of 'languages'. Languages, as such, are not eligible, but cultural expressions closely linked to languages are eligible. In this case the 'orality' of the expression needs to be demonstrated as a defining feature.

vi) Respecting consistency with the ideals of UNESCO (in particular with the Universal Declaration of Human Rights).

vii) Clarification regarding priority order among domains determined that no priority should be set up among domains, but that the jury should be allowed to set some specific domains in each submission period. *The Guide for the Presentation of Candidature Files* for the Proclamation programme was modified accordingly for the subsequent appeal of candidatures.

31st General Conference and Rio meeting

The 31st UNESCO General Conference decided in October 2001 that the most appropriate legal instrument for achieving the goal of affording urgent and adequate protection of important ICH would be an international Convention and its preliminary draft would be examined at its 32nd session in October 2003 (UNESCO, EX164/19, 2002). The great majority of member states at the General Conference expressed the view that the new Convention should follow the example of the widely supported WHC, while also recognising the importance of the full participation of the bearers and transmitters of this heritage. However, some delegates stressed the need to further clarify the concept of ICH, in particular those countries that were not in favour of the development of a Convention for ICH. Other delegates underscored the need to avoid overlap with other international organisations such as WIPO (UNESCO 2001e: item 8.6). At the moment of the adoption of the cultural commission's report, 18 member states expressed, in writing, their reservations about deciding the nature of the instrument as an 'international convention' giving as a reason that it was 'premature as the issue is delicate and complex one requiring a cautious approach'. These countries were Argentina, Barbados, Denmark, Finland, France, Germany, Granada, Greece, Mexico, Norway, the Netherlands, Portugal, Sweden, Spain, St. Lucia, St. Vincent Grenadine and the UK (UNESCO 2001e). The General Conference, however, decided finally that 'this instrument should be an international convention, [taking into account] that UNESCO is the only organization whose mandate refers expressly to the safeguarding of this aspect of the cultural heritage' (31st General conference, Resolution 30).

In the light of the debates at the General Conference, and the decision to adopt an international Convention, the Director-General convened an expert meeting[24] in Rio de Janeiro on 22–24 January 2002, in order to identify the proprietary domains that the future 'convention' should encompass within the vast domain of ICH as defined in Turin. Some 20 experts who were not only anthropologists, ethnologists, historians and lawyers, but also five members of UNESCO Executive Board (Algeria, Morocco, Egypt, Lithuania and Benin) including its Chairperson, Madame Bennani (Morocco), and the President of the French National Commission for UNESCO, attended the meeting. UNESCO, at this point, needed a political understanding and the support of its Executive Board to further the process of the development of the Convention. Koichiro Matuura, stated in his opening speech that the presence of certain members of the Executive Board, notably its Chairperson Madame Bennani, who were also experts in this domain, would help to develop a text conducive for obtaining a consensus of all of the member states, including those opposed to the creation of a Convention in this field (DG/2002/03). The meeting was chaired for the first time by Mohammed Bedjaoui (Algeria, former Judge and President at the International Court of Justice), who chaired six subsequent intergovernmental and non-governmental meetings until the last intergovernmental meeting of June 2003.

Brazilian experts explained their National Registry system and the mechanism they had established in 2000 to facilitate the participation of practitioner communities. The meeting compared the role of UNESCO in the field of ICH with other IGOs. Experts reaffirmed that UNESCO should not duplicate the activities of other organisations, particularly in the field of economic rights for which specialised agencies such as WIPO and WTO have specific expertise. UNESCO should focus upon the cultural dimension of ICH covering the domains not yet covered by other organisations. The meeting then examined the impact of the first Masterpieces Proclamation. Madame Bennani and Madame Karvelis (Lithuania, one of the vice-chairs of the Executive Board) who were also members of the international jury of the Proclamation programme, reported on the discussions of the recent extraordinary jury meeting of Elche, and the impact of the first Proclamation. The impact survey of the 19 Proclaimed Masterpieces was undertaken seven months after the Proclamation. The most outstanding impact was that the Proclamation process raised community awareness of the significant value of their ICH and the need for its urgent safeguarding. It encouraged the people concerned to take pride in their heritage and could thus help them affirm their cultural identity. At a national level, four countries (Dominican Republic, Uzbekistan, Morocco and Guinea) had already started a procedure for establishing legal protection measures. The Philippines and Dominican Republic had already established their national committee for the safeguarding of ICH. Many states had engaged in consultation with local communities, associations, universities and NGOs in order to define the modalities for their participation in the implementation of the safeguarding action plans.

In respect to the priority domains for a future Convention, experts examined the results of the Turin meeting and the discussions from the Elche meeting. They, yet again, endorsed the relevance of the Turin conceptual framework in general, and its definition in particular. Experts stressed that a flexible concept of 'safeguarding' should be adopted which respects both the internal dynamics of a particular cultural expression, and the diversity of ICH. They therefore considered that the new Convention should be developed within the framework of the UNESCO Universal Declaration of Cultural Diversity, adopted unanimously in October 2001, linking the preservation of ICH with cultural diversity, seen as a source of creative inspiration and sustainable development. It was in the Rio meeting that a political link between ICH and cultural diversity was established for the first time. This link was further strengthened at the Third Round Table of Ministers of Culture: 'Intangible Cultural Heritage – Mirror of Cultural Diversity'[25] held in Istanbul, September 2002. The setting up of this link was pivotal for the successful and early adoption of the ICH Convention. By linking ICH to Cultural Diversity, states supporting the latter, mostly French-speaking countries, tacitly and progressively joined those defending the former, which were mostly Asian and Eastern-Central European countries and other developing countries. The meeting also reaffirmed the significant link between ICH and the tangible cultural and natural heritage, between cultural diversity and the maintenance of biodiversity, with special reference to Indigenous peoples, as specified in Article 8(j) of the Convention on Biological Diversity.

With regard to the priority domain of protection, experts underscored that, at the national level, each member state should determine or revise freely, in consultation with the communities concerned, in accordance with the criteria that they consider appropriate. In doing so, the scope suggested in Turin should be taken into account. With regard to international safeguarding, the Convention should include a mechanism to promote public awareness of the various aspects of intangible cultural heritage, identifying these aspects on the basis of internal criteria (i.e., the importance of intangible heritage in forming and maintaining a social group's identity) and external criteria (e.g., respect for human rights and the capacity to foster intercultural dialogue). The meeting concluded that the Convention should draw on, for this purpose, experiences gained in connection with the Proclamation of Masterpieces, particularly concerning the detailed selection criteria worked out in Elche.

Conclusion and Recent Developments

All the debates, which took place through the meetings in Marrakech, Washington, Turin, Elche and Rio from 1997 to 2002, attest to the progressive building up of the definition and scope of ICH for the ICHC. Experiences of the Proclamation of Masterpieces had been extremely useful from political, conceptual and operational aspects. The programme served notably as a gauge to measure the political 'temperature' of each member state vis-à-vis the issue of ICH. It also contributed to refining the definition and scope of ICH for the Convention. Although this small-scale programme was prepared rather hastily, without much conceptual elaboration, its impact among member states was much stronger than expected. The primary goal of the programme, 'raising awareness of the significance of the Intangible Cultural Heritage', had been achieved rapidly at the state's level. The proclaimed Masterpieces, of which there are now 90, will be integrated into the Representative List of Intangible Cultural Heritage of Humanity within the framework of the ICHC.

The principles recurrently championed throughout these meetings, and the subsequent intergovernmental expert meetings were that ICH should refer to a process and not to a product. Therefore, ICH is not static but is permanently developing, and that its safeguarding should take a practitioner-/community-centred approach in order to ensure its viability and continuity. More concretely, tradition bearers and practitioner communities should play significant roles at every step of the safeguarding actions, from policy-making to evaluation of safeguarding actions. Moreover, respect for Human Rights and respect for cultural identity, cultural diversity, creativity, and mutual appreciation were considered integral to the safeguarding process. These principles are fully embodied in different parts of the Convention, notably in the Preamble, Article 1 (Purposes), Article 2 (Definitions) and Article 15 (Participation of communities, groups and individuals). One of the most significant and 'characterising' principles of the ICHC is that concerned with the participation of practitioner communities, which is expressed in several parts of the Convention (Articles 1, 2–1,11, 14-(a)(ii), 15, 21(b) and reflected in Articles 12 and 13(d)(ii)). The difficulties seem to remain, nevertheless, in developing the practical methods of the implementation of this principle. The issue of the mechanism of the participation of communities or their representatives, practitioners, and Indigenous peoples has been one of the most difficult themes throughout the current negotiation of the drafting of the operational directives in the Intergovernmental Committee as reviewed hereunder.

At the first session of this Committee (Alger, November 2006), this issue emerged in the discussion of the 'accreditation of NGOs to act as an advisory capacity to the committee' (Article 9 ICHC). This advisory capacity could involve the evaluation of nomination files, monitoring and granting international assistance. The Secretariat proposed to establish 'an umbrella advisory body, composed of representatives of accredited NGOs (which gather experts and research institutions) and of a limited number of private persons with widely recognized competence in the field of ICH' (ITH/06/1.COM/ CONF.204/6). For the purpose of consulting communities, the Secretariat proposed two options: either to create a separate body, composed of practitioners and tradition bearers, which would play a subordinate role to the umbrella advisory body, or to include a number of rotating representatives of communities in the proposed body (ITH/06/1.COM/CONF.204/6, para. 7). The Committee did not accept the Secretariat's proposal of an 'umbrella advisory body' as the Committee members, in general, preferred not to follow the system practised by the WHC where only two NGOs (of which the members are mostly from the North) monopolise the advisory function of the Committee. They underscored the need to maintain the plurality of the advisory bodies and their flexible relationship with the Committee. The countries of Latin America, such as Bolivia, Peru, Mexico and Brazil, favoured an advisory mechanism that would give voice to Indigenous populations and communities, while India noted the importance of using NGOs representing all areas of the world. Algeria and Senegal drew attention to the fact that in developing countries there are many competent centres of expertise and research institutions that are not organised as NGOs. They therefore wished, in addition to the NGOs, practitioners and communities, that experts and centres of expertise with known skills should be consulted (UNESCO 2006: 15–16). As the Committee could not reach an agreement, it decided to invite the state parties to submit (written) proposals regarding the accreditation and the representativeness criteria of practitioners of ICH. The Committee further requested that the Director-General submit a proposal on the criteria that would determine the accreditation of practitioners of ICH, NGOs, experts and centres of expertise with recognised competence in the field of ICH, at its second session in Tokyo, September 2007 (Decision 1.COM6 – Advisory Assistance to the Committee, para. 5 and 6). The written comments received from state parties showed diverse views (ITH/07/1.EXT.COM/CONF.207/INF.2Rev, para. 21).[26] At the following extraordinary session of the Committee (Chengdu) May 2006,[27] the Secretariat, rather than complying with the request made by the Committee in Alger, presented a proposal that reflected a strict legal interpretation of the text of the Convention which referred exclusively to NGOs (Article 9 Accreditation of advisory organisations). Many members then regretted that the presented document did not refer to practitioners, experts or centres of expertise other than NGOs. During the debate, a confusing discussion took place mixing Article 8, concerning possibilities to invite any public or private bodies, private persons to the committee's meetings, and Article 9, concerning the accreditation of NGOs as advisory organisations to the Committee.[28] Finally, the Committee adopted the criteria and modality for the accreditation of NGOs (DECISION 1.EXT.COM 10). After a lengthy discussion, consensus was not reached, thus, the Secretariat was requested to submit a document referring specifically to the 'participation of communities or their representatives, practitioners, experts, centres of expertise and research institutes' to the session in Tokyo, September 2007 (Decision 1. EXT.COM 10).

At the session in Tokyo, the Secretariat presented its proposal drawn up on the basis of the state parties' written comments sent since the Chengdu meeting. However, the Committee considered that the proposal 'did not take sufficient note of the importance the Committee accorded to this issue and did not permit an in-depth discussion on the other aspects of the participation of communities and their representatives, practitioners, experts, centres of expertise and research institutes in the implementation of the Convention' (UNESCO 2007a: para. 214). Some members noted the difference in nature and function of the two categories of groups: on one hand 'communities, practitioners and Indigenous groups' and 'experts, centres and research institutes' on the other. In fact, Latin American countries and Estonia emphasised the role of the former, and African countries and Romania stressed the importance of the indispensable participation of the latter. In this context Peru, Romania and Japan pointed out that 'communities and practitioners' and 'centres of expertise and research institutions' should be dealt with separately. The Committee, however, concurred in not separating them, stressing the necessity to involve all of these groups as closely as possible in implementation of the Convention (UNESCO 2007b: 4).

The Committee, considering that the document presented by the Secretariat, again, did not comply with the request made by the Algiers and Chengdu meetings, decided to pursue further reflection on this difficult issue. A working group was established, and the Committee Chair designated Japan to lead the working group. The group concluded that a questionnaire would have to be sent to state parties, a subsidiary body was established and a meeting organised before the next session of the Committee (UNESCO 2002: para. 278). France offered to organise an expert meeting that could reflect further. The committee requested that the Secretariat consult state parties on the possible modalities for the participation of 'communities or their representatives, practitioners, experts, centres of expertise and research institutes' in the implementation of the Convention. Further, they decided to create a subsidiary body of the Committee to prepare, on the basis of comments provided by the state parties, a document on this issue for the next session (UNESCO 2007a: Decision 2. COM 8 para. 3–6). The Committee elected Belgium (Group I),[29] Romania (Group II), Peru

(Group III), Japan (Group IV), Senegal (Group V(a)) and Algeria (Group V (b)) to constitute the body.

The Secretariat collected comments from state parties and meetings of the subsidiary body that took place in Paris and Bucharest in December 2007, and in Vitré (France) in January 2008. At the third meeting of the subsidiary body in Vitré the role of the experts and research institutions was strongly emphasised to the detriment of that of communities and practitioners. The results of these three meetings were presented at the second extraordinary session of the Committee in Sofia in February 2008. In Sofia, the Committee slightly increased the role of communities and practitioners, and drafted a text concerning the participation of communities and other elements for an independent chapter to be included in the 'operational directives'. It is to note that in addition to this chapter, other chapters, as for example, those concerning the inscriptions on the Urgent List,[30] the Guidelines for the use of the resources of the ICH Fund,[31] and International assistance,[32] also set the parameters for participation of entities other than NGOs. In June 2008, the General Assembly authorised entities such as public or private bodies, private persons, practitioners, and experts to be 'involved' in advisory services (Resolution 2GA6). However, an imbalance emerged as while NGOs will need accreditation to offer advice, in conformity with Article 9 of the convention, other 'entities' will not.

As was shown in the negotiations of the Committee, the principle of community participation is extremely difficult to implement because of its wide-ranging political implications. In fact, among all the meetings that UNESCO convened to prepare the Convention (more than 10 governmental and non-governmental meetings), the Washington meeting and the jury meetings of the Proclamation were the only ones that benefited from the 'active participation' of 'representatives of communities and practitioners'. In the Washington meeting (1999), seven representatives of communities and practitioners out of 36 invited participants attended the meeting. In conformity with the Regulations[33] of the Proclamation programme, three out of 18 members of the international jury were practitioners (three singers of traditional music from Uzbekistan, Bolivia and Georgia). During the three sessions of the Intergovernmental Committee held so far, where the significant roles of the communities and practitioners have been so strongly emphasised, none of the sessions, however, witnessed the presence of representatives from communities, practitioners or grass root NGOs as observers. This shows how difficult it is for an intergovernmental organisation to mobilize grass roots populations.

The first extraordinary Committee meeting in Chengdu reconfirmed that the Urgent List take priority over the Representative List. The elements of ICH proclaimed as Masterpieces were selected upon the criterion of 'outstanding value', whereas the Representative List,[34] to which the elements of the Masterpieces will be incorporated, will not bear the distinctive notion, even though this list had been entitled 'Treasures/Masterpieces' during the negotiations of the Convention, until the last day of the last session in June 2003 of the intergovernmental expert meeting (Aikawa 2008: 24). Even though no definition has yet been officially given to the term 'representative', it is obvious that 'representative' in this case means 'representative of each community' to ensure that there will be no hierarchy between the items inscribed and those not inscribed in this list. Moreover, this list is far from being selective as there will be neither prestigious selection criteria nor limits in the number of items to be presented to, or be inscribed on, the lists. In addition, with regard to the evaluation of candidates a Subsidiary Body of the Committee will undertake the task without outside expertise.

The ICH inscribed on the Urgent List, after an elaborate evaluation will not be selected for its 'outstanding universal value' but for the 'fear of losing diversity'. The ICHC, of which the first inscription will take place in 2009, might not be developed in the same manner as WHC. Perhaps, it might take a similar path to the Convention of Biological Diversity, both of which are 'the common concern'[35] of humanity.

Notes

1 Organised by UNESCO, Marrakech, Morocco, 26–28 June 1997.
2 The report also stated that 'it is time for a broader anthropological approach to gain currency' and concluded that it 'shares the view of those who consider that the heritage in all its aspects is still not being used as broadly and effectively as it might be, nor as sensitively managed as it should be' (Pérez de Cuéllar 1995: 176–7).
3 UNESCO 29th General Conference, DR 64.
4 1989 Recommendation, Article A. Definition: 'Folklore (or traditional and popular culture) is the totality of tradition-based creations of a cultural community, expressed by a group or individuals and recognized as reflecting the expectations of a community in so far as they reflect its cultural and social identity; its standards and values are transmitted orally, by imitation or by other means. Its forms are, among others, language, literature, music, dance, games, mythology, rituals, customs, handicrafts, architecture and other arts'. This definition, given in the sole existing international legal instrument concerning intangible cultural heritage, had been in use in UNESCO since 1989 including the programme for the promotion of 'Living Human Treasure system' launched in 1993 and the programme of the Proclamation of the Oral and Intangible heritage of humanity launched in 1998.
5 USA was not a member state of UNESCO as it had withdrawn from UNESCO in 1984 and rejoined in 2003.
6 Then Honorary Visiting Research Fellow, University of Glasgow, Law Studies specialising in Cultural Heritage Law, who assumed the role of rapporteur at the Washington Conference in 1999.
7 Lourdes Arizpe (Mexico, former Assistant Director-General for Culture of UNESCO 1994–98), Manuela Carneiro da Cunha (Brazil), Georges Condominas (France, Jury member of the Proclamation of Masterpieces), Ralph Regenvanu (Vanuatu, jury member of the Proclamation of Masterpieces).
8 James Early (USA) and Peter Seitel (USA).
9 Francesco Francioni (Italy), Janet Blake (UK), Leila Takla (Egypt).

10 Herbert Chimhundu (Zimbabwe).

11 Kwabena C. Nketia (Ghana).

12 Olabiyi Yai (Benin, specialist in African languages and oral literature, member of UNESCO Executive Board), Ugné Karvelis (Lithuania, writer, jury member of the Proclamation of Masterpieces, member of UNESCO Executive Board).

13 Ali Suleman Sahli (Libya).

14 Hajime Endo (Japan).

15 Albert Sasson (Morocco, Former Assistant Director-General of UNESCO).

16 UNESCO constitution Article 1, paragraph 1: 'The purpose of the Organization is to contribute to peace and security by promoting collaboration among the nations through education, science and culture in order to further universal respect for justice, for the rule of law and for the human rights and fundamental freedoms which are affirmed for the peoples of the world, without distinction of race, sex, language or religion, by the Charter of the United Nations'. And paragraph 2-c: 2, to realise this purpose, the organisation will: '(c) Maintain, increase and diffuse knowledge: By assuring the conservation and protection of the world's inheritance of books, works of art and monuments of history and science, and recommending to the nations concerned the necessary international Conventions. In its preamble, it is also mentioned: 'that ignorance of each other's ways and lives has been a common cause, throughout the history of mankind [sic], of that suspicion and mistrust between the peoples of the world through which their differences have all too often broken into war'.

17 Professor, Department of Anthropology, University of Chicago.

18 Rapporteur of UN High Commissioner for Human Rights.

19 Professora Investigadora, Centro Regional de Investigaciones Multidisciplinariaz (CRIM), Universidad Nacional Autonoma de Mexico (UNAM), Former Assistant Director-General for Culture of UNESCO (1994–98).

20 Folklorist, Smithsonian Center for Folklife and Cultural Heritage, Smithsonian institution.

21 Establishment of a code of ethics was also argued for by Estonia at the second session of the Intergovernmental Committee for the safeguarding of the ICH, Tokyo, September 2007.

22 Vice-Rector, University of Sienna.

23 161EX/SR.12,para.6.14. Oral report of the Chairperson of the Programme and External Relations.

24 The meeting was organised thanks to the Brazilian government's and Japanese government's financial contribution.

25 Istanbul Declaration: The first round table of Ministers of Culture: 'Culture and creativity in a Globalized World' held in Paris, November 1999. The second round table of Ministers of Culture: 'Cultural Diversity: Challenges of the Marketplace' held in Paris, December 2000.

26 Several states proposed that the advisory body, or bodies, include representatives of communities that bear or create ICH elements (Algeria), representatives of Indigenous peoples and communities (Peru), creators, bearers and practitioners (Mexico), representatives of groups and communities of practitioners and bearers (Slovakia), representatives from the communities whose ICH is proposed for inscription (Croatia), representatives from communities and groups in general (Spain), international organisations that embody and represent Indigenous peoples (Estonia), communities already part of a national network of organisations (Belgium), and resource people (France). Senegal was not in favour of accrediting practitioners, but suggested that experts and NGOs always be obliged to consult them (ITH/07/1.EXT.COM/CONF.207/INF.2Rev, paragraph 21).

27 At the first extraordinary session (Chengdu, May 2007), this point arose again (item 10: Advisory assistance to the Committee).

28 'an earnest attempt to accommodate all the various positions ... (the decision) was offered as a compromise among the various positions, by separating matters relating to the NGOs' functions from those referring to Articles 8.3 (Refers to the possibilities to establish the committee's ad-hoc consultative bodies) and 8.4 (refers to the possibilities to invite any public or private bodies), private persons to the committee's meetings)' (rapporteur's oral report p. 6).

29 Group I (Western Europe and North America), Group 2 (Central and Eastern Europe), Group III (Latin America and the Caribbean), Group IV (Asia and Pacific), Group V-a (Sub-Sahara Africa), Group V-b (Arab states).

30 'nominations shall be examined by preferably more than one advisory organization accredited in conformity with Article 9.1 of the Convention and/or private persons with recognized competence in the field of ICH in conformity with Article 8.4 of the Convention' (Operational Directive 5).

31 'The resources may further be used for the costs of advisory services to be provided, at the request of the Committee, by non-governmental and non-profit-making organizations, public or private bodies and private persons' (Operational Directives 60d) and 'for the cost of public or private bodies, as well as private persons, notably members of communities and groups, that have been invited by the Committee to its meetings to consult them on specific matters' (Operational Directives 60e).

32 The 'secretariat shall seek examination for complete requests over USD 25,000' (Operational Directives 72).

33 Regulations relating to the proclamation, 4 a 'a jury of eighteen members ... ensuring a balance between creative workers and experts ... '.

34 Criteria for the Representative List, subject to approval by the General Assembly in June 2008:
R.1. The element constitutes intangible cultural heritage as defined in Article 2 of the Convention for the Safeguarding of the Intangible Cultural Heritage.
R.2. Inscription of the element will contribute to ensuring visibility, awareness of the significance of the intangible cultural heritage and dialogue, thus reflecting cultural diversity worldwide and testifying to human creativity.
R.3. Safeguarding measures are elaborated that may protect and promote the element.
R.4. The element has been nominated following the widest possible participation of the community, group or, if applicable, individuals concerned and with their free, prior and informed consent.
R.5. The element is included in an inventory of the intangible cultural heritage present in the territory(ies) of the submitting state(s) party(ies). (Decision 1EXT COM 6).

35 ICHC, 'the universal will and the common concern to safeguard the ICH of humanity', Preamble 6th paragraph; CBD, 'Conservation of biological diversity is a common concern of humanity', Preamble 3rd paragraph.

Bibliography

Aikawa, N. (2001) 'The UNESCO Recommendation on the safeguarding of Traditional culture and Folklore (1989): Actions Undertaken by UNESCO for Its Implementation', in P. Seitel (ed.), *Safeguarding Traditional Cultures: A Global Assessment*, Washington D.C.: UNESCO-Smithsonian Center for Folklife and Cultural Heritage.

—— (2004) 'An historical overview of the preparation of the UNESCO International Convention for the Safeguarding of the Intangible Cultural Heritage', *Museum International*, 56(1–2): 137–49.

—— (2007) 'The conceptual development of UNESCO's programme on intangible cultural heritage', J. Blake (ed.), *Safeguarding Intangible Cultural Heritage – Challenges and Approaches*, Builth Wells: Institute of Art and Law.

—— (2008) 'UNESCO Convention for the Safeguarding of the Intangible Cultural Heritage – from its adoption to the first meeting of the Intergovernmental Committee', *Proceedings of the 30th International Symposium on the Conservation and Restoration of cultural Property*, Tokyo: National Research Institute for Cultural Properties.

Arizpe, L. (2001) 'Intangible cultural heritage – perception and enactments', unpublished Power Point presentation, International Round Table on Intangible Cultural Heritage – Working Definitions, 14–17 March, Turin.

Blake, J. (2001a) *Developing a New Standard – Setting Instrument for the Safeguarding of Intangible Cultural Heritage: Elements for Consideration*, Paris: UNESCO.

—— (2001b) *Report on the Preliminary Study on the Advisability of Regulating Internationally, Through a New Standard-setting Instrument, the Protection of Traditional Culture and Folklore,'* 16 May, Paris: UNESCO.

da Cunha, M. (2002) 'Notions of intangible heritage, towards working definitions', unpublished oral presentation to the International Round Table on Intangible Cultural Heritage – Working Definitions, 14–17 March, Turin.

Denhez, M. (1997a) *Background Memorandum on a Proposed System to Honour Cultural Spaces with Remarkable Intangible Heritage*, Paris: UNESCO.

—— (1997b) *Working Paper on a Proposed System to Honor 'Cultural Space' with Remarkable Intangible Heritage, Annex (Draft) Statutes for the Proclamations of the Oral Heritage of Humanity and for the Fund/Prize for Intangible Heritage, Paragraph 6.(i) Cultural Criteria*, Paris: UNESCO

Francioni, F. (2001) *Intangible Cultural Heritage – Working Definitions*, unpublished meeting paper, Turin: UNESCO.

Fuentes, Carlos (1997) *Patrimonio Oral*, El Pais, 24 September.

Matsuura, K. (2000) Director-General's speech, May 5 2000, given at the information meeting.

Mayor, Federico (1992) *Spiritual Heritage*, Speech given at the occasion of his induction as a member of the Royal Academy of Fine Arts of San Fernando, Madrid, 2nd March.

Pérez de Cuéllar, Javier (1995) *Our Creative Diversity*, Paris: World Commission on Culture and Development, UNESCO.

Sasson A. (1997) *Intervention of the Representative of the Director-General of UNESCO,* Marrakech, June.

Seitel, P. (2001) 'Proposed terminology for intangible cultural heritage: toward anthropological and folkloristic common sense in a global era,' unpublished conference document, UNESCO.

UNESCO (1989) *Recommendation on Safeguarding Traditional Culture and Folklore.*

—— (1997a) *Final Report, International Consultation on the Preservation of Popular Cultural Spaces – Declaration of the Oral Heritage of Mankind, Marrakech, Morocco, 26–28 June.*

—— (1997b) *29th General Conference*, Draft Resolution 64.

—— (1998) *Intergovernmental Conference on Cultural Policies for Development, Stockholm, 30 March – 2 April 1998*, Paris, UNESCO.

—— (2001a) 'Annotated Agenda, International Round Table on Intangible Cultural Heritage – Working Definitions, Turin, 14–17 March', unpublished document.

—— (2001b) *Action Plan for the safeguarding of the ICH as approved by the international experts on the occasion of the International Round Table on 'Intangible Cultural Heritage – Working Definitions'*, organized by UNESCO in Turin, March 2001.

—— (2001c) *Final Report*, International Round Table on Intangible Cultural Heritage – Working Definitions, 14–17 March, Turin, Paris: UNESCO.

—— (2001d) *Proclamation of Masterpieces of the Oral and Intangible Heritage of Humanity, Guide for the Presentation of Candidature Files*, Paris: UNESCO.

—— (2001e) *31st General Conference*, Oral report of the Chairperson of Commission IV (31C/INF.24), Paris, UNESCO.

—— (2006) *Summary record of the first session of the Intergovernmental Committee*, Alger, November.

—— (2007a) *Summary Record, Intergovernmental Committee for the Safeguarding of the Intangible Cultural Heritage, Second Session, Tokyo, Japan 3 to 7 September 2007*, Paris: UNESCO.

—— (2007b) *Rapporteur's Oral Report, Intergovernmental Committee for the Safeguarding of the Intangible Cultural Heritage, Second Session, Tokyo, Japan 3 to 7 September 2007*, Paris: UNESCO.

United Nations (1992) *Convention on Biological Diversity*.

Chapter 3

UNESCO's 2003 *Convention on Intangible Cultural Heritage*

The implications of community involvement in 'safeguarding'

Janet Blake

Introduction

The 2003 *Convention on the Safeguarding of the Intangible Cultural Heritage* (ICHC), secured a high number of ratifications in a short space of time.[1] This reflects the concern of the international community to respond urgently to threats to this vulnerable heritage. The willingness of so many states to commit themselves to this Convention is noteworthy, particularly in view of the fact that this represents an important departure in terms of the cultural heritage regulation, and is a unique instrument in the cultural heritage field. This departure is mainly as a result of the character of its subject matter – one that is primarily without material form and whose expressions and physical manifestations are, in fact, secondary. In this sense, it is the mirror image of the previous cultural heritage Conventions where the material heritage (movable cultural property, monuments and sites) was the central subject of protection and any intangible values contingent on these. For example, in the 1972 World Heritage Convention, under the 2002 revision of the Operational Guidelines, the 'associated intangible values' of cultural properties were recognised as an element in the value for which such properties might be inscribed on the World Heritage List (Luxen 2000; Deacon and Beazley 2007), while the spiritual significance of movable items of cultural property is also recognised in the 1970 Convention.[2] UNESCO's 1989 *Recommendation on Safeguarding Traditional Culture and Folklore* opened the path for the development of this Convention, but was much more limited in its ambitions and did not impose on member states any binding obligations.

One of the most significant aspects of this Convention, and a focus of this chapter, is the central role it gives to the cultural communities (and groups and, in some cases, individuals) associated with ICH that is unprecedented in this area of international law. This is a response to the very specific character of ICH that exists only in its enactment by practitioners and, therefore, whose continued practice depends wholly on the ability and willingness of the cultural group and/or community concerned. This introduces a clear cultural rights dimension to the safeguarding of ICH that, although present in other areas of cultural heritage protection, is much more explicitly drawn in relation to intangible cultural heritage and is another noteworthy characteristic of this Convention.

With the introduction of intangible cultural heritage into the picture, cultural heritage preservation has become a much more complex and political question than it was when preservation institutions restricted their interest to monuments and artefacts. Since ICH is embedded in the social and cultural lives of the cultural communities, safeguarding when exercised as a public policy will interfere directly in processes taking place in the present and developed by real, human collectives (Arantes 2007). Moreover, inclusion of the idea of ICH within the broader rubric of cultural heritage provides opportunities to democratise the process by which we give value to heritage, giving a larger role to local people especially in the developing world. Indeed, the question of assigning value or significance to ICH raises a further one – is it necessary for ICH expressions or practices to be highly valued outside the immediate cultural community in order to be defined officially as heritage? (Deacon *et al*. 2004: 11). The implications of these and other questions run deep and must be addressed.

The purpose of this chapter, then, is to explore the implications of this new approach in cultural heritage treaty-making and, in particular, what it means for the implementation of the Convention itself and national cultural policy-making. In order to do this, I attempt to place the 2003 ICHC in the wider context of the evolution in thinking about 'culture' in international policy-making over the last quarter century – moving from a high art to a more anthropological conception – and how this has informed both the development of cultural heritage law and human rights thinking. I also situate the references to the community (group and individual) of the 2003 ICHC within international law, in particular human rights and environmental law in which these notions are much more often applied.

However, before taking this discussion further, it is useful to present a brief outline of the main elements of the Convention itself, with a focus on the references in the text to the role of the cultural community (see also Aikawa-Faure this volume).

The Convention and the cultural community

The purposes of the Convention are given in Article 1 and are:

(i)   To safeguard ICH.
(ii) To ensure respect for ICH.
(iii) To raise awareness at local, national and international levels of the importance of ICH and thus to ensure a mutual appreciation of it.
(iv) To provide for international cooperation and assistance.[3]

These four purposes already show us that the Convention is operating on three main levels – 'local, national and international' – and that it represents an interplay between the three. Of course, since it is states that make international law, the national (i.e. state) level will always be a primary one for the implementation of any treaty. However, in this Convention it is the way in which these three levels relate to each other that is of importance. The international safeguarding actions (international cooperation and assistance and the international lists) are seen as raising awareness of the ICH within the communities as well as at the level of the state and encouraging and facilitating national implementation of safeguarding measures. Equally, as we shall see, the relationship between the state and local levels in implementation is crucial and it is here that this Convention breaks new ground and raises many important questions as to how this is to be done. Last, there is also a relationship between the local and international levels whereby the 'global' culture may be one of the threats to this heritage and so a global response (in the form of an international treaty) is needed. This last point is picked up later in the essay, showing how the 2003 ICHC can be seen also as a response to cultural as well as economic globalisation and the place of the local community in this picture.

'Intangible cultural heritage' is defined in Article 2(1) and, here again, the centrality of the community (group or individual) to ICH as much as its importance for their sense of identity is clearly drawn out.[4] First, the identification of any 'ICH' as such is dependent on the recognition by 'communities, groups and individuals' who are continuously recreating it and to whom it provides a sense of community. Paragraph 2 sets out the domains of the ICH while paragraph 3 defines 'safeguarding' for the purposes of the Convention. This last is important since the notion of safeguarding – placed at (i) in the Convention's purposes – runs throughout the whole of the Convention text from national safeguarding measures to international safeguarding activities, policies and programmes.

Following the model of the 1972 Convention,[5] the ICHC establishes two international lists of ICH – the Representative List of the Intangible Cultural Heritage of Humanity and the List of Intangible Cultural Heritage in Need of Urgent Safeguarding – on which ICH will be inscribed according to criteria to be developed by the ICH Committee. The first is designed to raise awareness of the ICH both internationally and locally, the second to respond with greater urgency in cases where ICH is in immediate danger. Beyond achieving greater 'visibility' for ICH at all levels, the purpose of the listing mechanism is to encourage better national safeguarding of all ICH (not only that listed) and this is shored up by the requirement on parties to draw up national inventories of ICH on their territory (Article 12). A set of national measures for safeguarding is set out in Articles 11–15 and it is in this section that the most important references to the cultural community's role in safeguarding and management of ICH are to be found.

In recognition of the fact that the safeguarding of ICH is not just a matter of national measures but also requires a clear commitment from the international community, a framework for international cooperation and assistance is provided for. This is supported by the establishment of an Intangible Heritage Fund to support parties in their safeguarding activities as well as assist in the implementation of the Convention's other provisions. In terms of institutional mechanisms, two main organs are also established – the General Assembly of the States Parties as its sovereign body (Article 4) and an Intergovernmental Committee for the Safeguarding of the Intangible Cultural Heritage (henceforth 'ICH Committee') (Article 6) whose task is to ensure implementation of the Convention, especially those provisions relating to the listing of ICH and the provision of international assistance.[6] A system for parties to report on their activities under the Convention is also provided for.

Culture and development – the wider context

The adoption of the ICHC is in many ways the culmination of a revision of our way of thinking about the relationship between culture and development over the preceding two decades (Arizpe 2004, 2007). During the 1960s and 1970s, development had been conceived very much as a purely economic phenomenon whereby growth in a country's gross domestic product was the main, if not sole, indicator of success. Within this picture of development, culture was often viewed as a break on development, particularly the 'traditional cultures' of the poorer countries, and theories of development generally supported 'acculturation' policies. By the 1970s, in reaction to this in Africa and Latin America, there was an intellectual shift towards the notion of 'endogenous development' in which local and ethnic cultures (and languages) were given value (Arizpe 2007).

The World Conference on Cultural Policies (1982)[7] presented a view of culture which may be typified as an 'anthropological' one that sees culture as the way of life and form of social organisation of a group, along with their traditions and other cultural manifestations. In such a view, of course, the intangible elements of cultural heritage are given a more important role and the notion of cultural heritage is expanded beyond the monuments and sites themselves to their socio-cultural and economic contexts (Garcia-Canclini 1998; Aikawa 2004; Klamer 2004). The UN World Decade for Cultural Development (1987–97) reinforced this view of cultural heritage as a source of cultural identity for groups, communities and whole nations and as playing a key role in development. It was at this time that UNESCO officially noted the need to highlight the function of the cultural heritage for the community as a living culture of the people, and that its safeguarding 'should be regarded as one of the major assets of a multidimensional type of development' (UNESCO 1990: para. 209, cited in Aikawa 2007).

In 1995, the World Commission on Culture and Development in its report stressed the creative and constitutive role played by culture in development and, in particular, intangible cultural heritage, and made clear the centrality of the cultural group or community to this (UNESCO 1996: 24).[8] This was further linked with the achievement of sustainable development and the importance to this of local know-how and traditional knowledge and practices that ensure sustainable use of natural resources (Warren *et al.* 1995; Leach 1998). Such a conception of culture and development would imply the application of bottom-up approaches that are community-driven and exploit this invaluable local know-how and other aspects of intangible cultural heritage. From this, then, it is easy to understand how safeguarding ICH has a direct connection not only with local development but also with community empowerment within that process. If we accept here Sen's (2004: 4) view of well-being (i.e. human development) as a set of capabilities that people have, with culture as one of these capabilities, we reach that of 'intangible development' (Zakayeva 2003) as the set of capabilities that allow groups, communities and even nations to define their own futures in a manner of their own choosing.

It is important, however, when presenting this picture of the potential role of ICH in development not to ignore the fact that traditional cultural attitudes may also act as a break on participatory local development where, for example, community leaders may resist threats to established power relationships or capture resources intended for the whole community for themselves (Abraham and Platteau 2004; Douglas 2004). This is, of course, an issue of direct significance when considering the participatory approach towards identification, safeguarding and inventorying required by the ICHC.

References to 'communities', 'groups' and 'individuals' in the ICHC

As noted above, the centrality of cultural communities (groups and individuals) to the identification of ICH and its continued viability, as well as the essential role it plays in constructing the identity of such entities, is explicitly stated in the definition of ICH. Hence, we can expect that this Convention will take an approach towards identifying and safeguarding ICH that places the community at its centre and that requires of state parties a participatory approach to this endeavour.

It is not without significance that Part III dealing with national safeguarding should open with a provision (Article 11) covering the 'role of States Parties'. This signals that the ICHC is not following a standard approach in cultural heritage instruments here and that it needs some explanation; at (b) we see what this is, in its requirement that parties identify and define the elements of ICH on their territory 'with the participation of communities, groups and relevant nongovernmental organizations'. This provision then applies to Article 12 which requires parties to draw up one or more inventories of ICH 'to ensure identification [of ICH] with a view to safeguarding'. The importance of this should not be understated since the identification of ICH is not only fundamental to its safeguarding but it also addresses a deeply political issue as to what and whose ICH is to be given value by the process.

The most explicit and far-reaching reference to the role that the Convention envisages for communities and others is to be found in Article 15 that reads:

> Within the framework of its safeguarding activities of the intangible cultural heritage, each State Party shall endeavour to ensure the widest possible participation of communities, groups and, where appropriate, individuals that create, maintain and transmit such heritage, and to involve them actively in its management.

This requires parties to take a participatory approach – and one that is effective – in relation to the range of activities described as 'safeguarding' in Article 2(3), namely: 'measures aimed at ensuring the viability of the intangible cultural heritage, including ... [its] identification, documentation, research, preservation, protection, promotion, enhancement, transmission ... revitalization'. It is thus a wide range of activities to which this applies and, furthermore, parties are also required here 'to involve them actively in its management'. This latter does not allow parties simply to pay lip-service to the notion of participation but requires them to ensure a much deeper involvement from the community. This last part echoes more recent developments with the operation of the 1972 Convention where local and indigenous communities have become increasingly involved in the management of properties inscribed on the World Heritage List, especially the 'mixed' cultural and natural sites such as Uluru-Kata Tjuta National Park (formally Ayers Rock – Mount Olga) in Australia.

Reference to 'communities', 'groups' and 'participation' in international law

The ICHC is not unique as far as international treaties are concerned in making reference to the 'communities', 'groups' or 'participation'; rather it is its use in the context of a cultural heritage instrument that is new. These are notions that already have a currency in the fields of human rights and environmental law, and it is worth examining their use in these areas in order to elucidate their use in the ICHC. Equally, what this brief review of international law will also show is that the ICHC may break new ground in seeking to provide a clear understanding[9] of what is meant by 'community' or 'group' and thus potentially contribute to their broader understanding in international law. However, since their definition in relation to the ICHC is specific to that Convention's subject matter, it may not be easy to extrapolate from this to a wider meaning.

During the preparation of the experts' draft of the ICHC, a *Glossary* of relevant terms was produced by an expert meeting held at UNESCO which defines a 'community' as: 'People who share a self-ascribed sense of connectedness. This may be manifested, for example, in a feeling of identity or common behaviour, as well as in activities and territory. Individuals can belong to more than one community'. Further definitions are also given for 'cultural community' and 'local community'. It was on the basis of these understandings that the term is employed in the Convention text.

'Communities', 'groups' and 'individuals' in international law

In considering the question as to how these terms are and have been understood in the human rights context, we should bear in mind that there is a difference between the meaning of a term such as 'community' to an anthropologist, for example, and its legal definition(s). However, I wish to start by considering the significance of another term used in the ICHC that is of relevance to this discussion.

A notable aspect of the ICHC is that it concerns not the 'protection' – the standard term used hitherto in the cultural heritage field[10] – but the 'safeguarding' of ICH. Although this term is employed by UNESCO's 1989 Recommendation on the Safeguarding of Traditional Knowledge and Folklore, the ICHC gives it both a specific definition (in Article 2(3)) and a centrality to the whole Convention text that is new. Its use in relation to ICH implies a far broader approach, not only protecting ICH from direct threats to it but also requiring of parties positive actions that contribute to its continuing viability. These actions go beyond such measures as identifying and inventorying ICH and include fostering the conditions within which it can continue to be created, maintained and transmitted.

Since the community is the essential context for this, it must imply the continued capability of the cultural communities themselves to practise and transmit their ICH. Hence, the community is placed at the centre of this Convention rather than the heritage itself and the safeguarding of ICH must take into account the wider human, social and cultural contexts in which the enactment of ICH occurs. Moreover, the measures to be taken by parties to achieve this include guaranteeing the economic, social and cultural rights of the communities (groups and individuals) that ensure the continuing viability of the community. It is wholly appropriate, therefore, to begin an examination of the use of the terms 'community', 'group' and 'individual' in international law with the human rights field.

From a brief survey of the use of the terms 'people', 'group', 'minority' and 'community' in international human rights law, it becomes clear that they are to some degree interchangeable and that there is no absolute and agreed meaning for any of them. Even the term 'people' with its associated legal baggage of the right to self-determination[11] has no clearly agreed meaning even though it is clear under international law what the requirements are for a people to be capable of claiming self-determination (Cassese 1995).[12] Hence, the way in which we understand and use these terms is, to a large degree, context-dependent. What is important, then, is to determine the parameters in which we are working in order to understand their meaning for the purposes of the 2003 ICHC. To reach this, there are some indications from legal doctrine that can help us.

When asked to provide an elucidation of the term 'community', the Permanent Court of International Justice[13] noted that '[t]he existence of communities is a question of fact; it is not a question of law'. This suggests that we should follow 'ordinary meaning' when considering such terms, while always remaining aware of the wider legal context and the potential pitfalls of apparently ascribing rights not recognised in international law. If we look at a more standard human rights terminology, the accepted under- standing of 'minorities' in relation to Article 27 of the United Nations International Covenant on Civil and Political Rights (1966) (ICCPR)[14] relies on both objective criteria (such as ethnicity, language etc.) and the subjective one of self-identification or 'solidarity' (Capotorti 1976; Thornberry 1991). This raises an interesting question – can a group that has no consciousness of itself as a group or a community be said to 'exist' legally, despite the exis- tence of objective criteria that sets it apart from other elements in a state's population? In other words, is it primarily their sense of distinct cultural identity and their desire to preserve it that gives minorities this cultural right? This would seem closely related to the way in which the relationship between the community and its ICH is presented in Article 2(1) of the ICHC. The 1989 ILO *Convention on Tribal and Indigenous Peoples*[15] also places high importance on 'self-identification' as a criterion for determining the groups to which the Convention applies.[16]

Article 27 (ICCPR) is also noteworthy in not referring directly to min- orities *qua* minorities as the right holders but rather to individual *members of minorities* who exercise the rights 'in community with' other members. Hence, the right attaches to individuals but can only be exercised within the community context. This reflects a strong prejudice in the human rights canon against ascribing rights on a collective basis, although the International Law Commission Commentary on this article suggests that the phrase 'in community with' does actually imply some communal or collec- tive character since, logically, such rights can only be exercised within the context of an existing, viable minority community. The recently adopted UN Declaration on the Rights of Indigenous Peoples[17] is unusual in making explicit the collective nature of the rights in question. Although this is not a binding text, it suggests the possibility of further development in this direction in future in relation to indigenous rights.

The 1966 UNESCO Declaration on the Principles of International Cultural Co-operation[18] refers to the right of 'every people' to develop its culture; the African Charter (OAS 1981)[19] talks of the right of 'all peoples' to their economic, social and cultural development. The African Charter also contains a very interesting provision in Article 29 that adds a new dimension to the relationship between the individual and the community by placing the duty on the individual 'to preserve and strengthen positive African cultural values in his relations with other members of the society ... and, in general, to contribute to the promotion of the moral well-being of society'. The UNESCO Declaration on Racial Prejudice (1978)[20] uses the unusual formulation 'all peoples and all human groups' (Preamble) and refers to the 'right of all groups to their own cultural identity'. This is, of course, extremely germane to the subject matter of the ICHC and it is intriguing that here the term 'groups' is favoured over that of 'communities'.

In view of its close association with the right to self-determination, the terms 'communities' or 'groups' are generally less potentially controversial than that of 'peoples' (Brownlie 1988), although, with the exception of provisions that deal specifically with self-determination, these terms are used fairly interchangeably. It is possible, however, to identify certain different nuances in meaning between 'communities', 'groups' and 'minorities'. Much, then, is dependent on the context of the instrument in which they are used. The 1992 CBD, for example, talks in Article 8(j) of preserving and maintaining the 'knowledge, innovations and practices of indigenous and local communities embodying traditional lifestyles', and the 2001 United Nations Food and Agriculture Organization (FAO) treaty[21] refers to the contribution of 'indigenous and local communities and farmers' to conserving plant genetic resources. Neither treaty defines exactly who these 'communities' are and we are left to interpret this in terms of each particular instrument as well as in the wider context of international law. Despite this, it is possible to understand that these are communities primarily defined by their specific knowledge/know-how and their way of life and so that they are 'cultural' communities in the sense that the communities of the ICHC also are.

These terms and the related rights create theoretical dilemmas for human rights law that should be noted here since they may also be of relevance in implementing those provisions of the ICHC that directly affect communities and groups. First, can collective rights exist? The classic theoretical position is that some 'individual' rights (such as the enjoyment of culture) presuppose the existence of a community of individuals and the underlying assumption here is that the rights of groups are taken care of automatically by protecting individuals' rights. Moreover, individuals do not exist *in abstracto* but, in reality, are defined by their membership of certain (cultural, ethnic, linguistic, etc.) groups. The African Union, for example, has undertaken work that seeks to challenge the 'Western' system of individual rights by developing a notion of 'community' or 'peoples' rights held directly by the collective.[22]

Second, even if we do accept some collective rights as held by groups, there is always the potential for conflict between the needs of the group and those of the individuals within it. For example, an individual's right to choose not to be part of a certain cultural identity set against the right of that group to exist. In such circumstances, we must always recognise the primacy of individual over collective rights (Niec 1998). The corollary to this is that the 'community' or 'group' should be defined in terms of the individual members that make it up. To some degree the ICHC avoids this dilemma by defining the community or group in relation to its ICH, although awareness that certain individuals may not wish to be associated with the ICH in question has always to be taken into account (Sunder 2001). Moreover, certain elements deeply embedded in many cultures clash directly with widely recognised human rights norms, which then sets up a clash between those norms and the right to cultural identity. We should also remember that an individual can claim multiple identities – the choice is the individual's not the community's (Stavenhagen 1998).

Third, can we define 'cultural identity' and 'community' independently of each other since the former requires reference to some group or community to which it attaches while the latter cannot easily be defined without reference to cultural criteria? (Prott 1988). Thus, there is some circularity to be addressed here in identifying a 'cultural community'. Lastly, once we have identified a 'community' there remains the issue as to who, in practice, can exercise the rights ascribed to it or represent it in other ways. Many cultural communities are heterogeneous in character; it is difficult to find a 'representative' who speaks for the group (and all individuals within it), and principles of democratic participation must come into play in dealing with this issue. This question is taken up again later in relation to the implementation of the ICHC.

Community involvement in development and participation in international law

A similar participatory approach to that of the ICHC may be found in Conventions dealing with sustainable environmental protection, for example,[23] and it is therefore useful to consider in brief how these notions have developed and operate in contemporary international law. This linkage with the ICHC is made even stronger by recognition of the important role played by ICH in 'achieving truly sustainable development' (UNESCO 2002: paragraphs 3 and7)[24] connecting it directly to the requirement of a participatory approach to development in order to achieve sustainable development (UNCED 1992: Principle 10). By examining the nature of this requirement and its expression in various international treaties and other texts, I seek to throw some light on the nature of community participation or involvement in safeguarding ICH.

Sustainable development as expressed in the Rio Declaration[25] comprises both substantive and procedural elements, and the latter contain an international obligation on governments to operate in certain ways. Principle 10 places the requirement on states to take a participatory approach to development issues. Principle 22 specifically refers to the vital role of 'indigenous people and their communities, and other local communities' in environmental management and development and a concomitant requirement on states to 'recognise and duly support their identity, culture and interests and enable their effective participation in the achievement of sustainable development'. These two principles together have inspired the various international treaties that make reference to participation by indigenous and local communities.[26]

The 1992 UN *Convention on Biological Diversity*,[27] for example, makes one of the most explicit references in Article 8(j) to the role of local and indigenous communities' knowledge and practices for preserving biodiversity.[28] In relation to this article, parties undertake *inter alia* to establish mechanisms to ensure effective participation by indigenous and local communities in decision-making and policy planning. The specific content of such mechanisms is examined below. According to the 1994 *Convention to Combat Desertification*,[29] parties should be guided by the need to ensure that decisions on the design and implementation of programmes 'are taken with the participation of populations and local communities' (Article 3(a)). It contains further articles that elaborate on this.[30] The 2001 FAO treaty states that the right to participate in national-level decision-making regarding plant genetic resources is fundamental to realising Farmers' Rights[31] while the 1989 ILO Convention[32] recognises the right of indigenous people to decide their own development priorities 'as it affects their lives, beliefs, institutions and spiritual well-being'.[33]

In terms of this essay, it is helpful to identify certain specific approaches that have been proposed to ensure the participation of indigenous and local communities in relation to these and other instruments. This may help to clarify the nature of the measures parties to the ICHC might take in fulfilling their obligation under Articles 2(1), 11(b) and 15.

In relation to Article 8(j) of the CBD, the following broad approaches are identified:

- Establishing local-specific systems for classifying knowledge and procedures for acquiring and sharing it, based on customary law.
- Recognising the importance of addressing the needs not only of the community but also of its members.
- Ensuring free prior informed consent for access to, acquisition and use of knowledge.
- Establishing mutually agreed terms (MATS) for the above and in planning and management of the resource, reflecting mutual respect and understanding.

- Full and equal participation and partnership in planning and management.
- Creating local implementation and incentive measures.
- Establishing access and benefit-sharing agreements (ABS).
- The right of non-disclosure of confidential information.
- The right to review research and authorise its dissemination and community or joint ownership of copyright on publications based on traditional knowledge research.

An FAO report related to the 1994 *Convention to Combat Desertification* (CCD) notes 'of prime importance is the participation of the local people' and makes the following proposals:

1. Institutional, legislative and infrastructure constraints should be eliminated to facilitate the co-management of development and collective community decisions.
2. A variety of technological models and decision-making tools should be provided to cope with local diversities.

A non-governmental document, the *Mataatua Declaration* (1993) on the *Intellectual and Cultural Property (ICP) Rights of Indigenous Peoples*, makes certain recommendations that may also be worth considering in the context of this discussion:

- Indigenous communities should define their ICP for themselves.
- Development of a Code of Ethics for external users when recording their traditional knowledge.
- Prioritising the establishment of indigenous education, research and training centres to promote traditional knowledge.
- Developing and maintaining customary practices for the protection, preservation and revitalisation of ICP.
- Assessment of existing legislative and institutional structures for their effectiveness in protecting ICP.
- Establishing an appropriate body with mechanisms for managing, safeguarding and consulting on ICP (Blake 2001: 66; O'Keefe 1995).

Finally, of course, one can also find models from within existing UNESCO practice in relation to the proclamation of *Masterpieces of Oral and Intangible Heritage* (1998–2005) and the 1972 *World Heritage Convention*. These should be taken account of since both address the issue of community involvement in cultural heritage management and related areas.

The guidelines for candidatures for the proclamation of Masterpieces contain several useful points which are, in brief:

- A candidature file must be prepared as far as possible by persons belonging to the communities concerned or, at least, have the guaranteed participation of members of the community (Paragraph 11).
- In preparing candidature files, the right of access of the community to its own ICH and protection of the custodians of the tradition (i.e. confidentiality of data) should be guaranteed (Paragraph 13).
- The jury, in its evaluation, should focus *inter alia* on the involvement of the community and recognised practitioners of the tradition in the action, revitalisation and protection plan (Paragraph 18).
- Where the bodies referred to in the candidacy are not 'directly representative of the community concerned or the performers/practitioners and/or custodians' of the ICH in question their 'support and collaboration' must be clearly demonstrated (Paragraph 24 (a)).
- The action plan should include, as far as possible, 'substantial and active participation from the community concerned or the performers/practitioners and/or custodians' of the ICH in question 'in the design and application of strategies and mechanisms aimed at safeguarding and preserving' it (Paragraph 24 (b)).

Further relevant considerations might be: measures taken to raise the awareness of members of the community concerned of the importance of safeguarding the ICH concerned; the benefits to be derived by the community concerned from the safeguarding measures; the measures taken within the local community for safeguarding ICH; and the existence of local democratic structures that can ensure full participation.

Over 30 years of experience of implementing the 1972 WHC has provided certain examples of cultural properties that are managed with the active participation of local/indigenous communities, of which Uluru in Australia is probably the best-known example (Simmonds 1997). The 2005 version of the Operational Guidelines to the 1972 WHC also includes certain references to community involvement and participation in the process of nomination and management planning. It notes (UNESCO 2005: 110) that an effective 'management system' depends on the type and needs of the property nominated and 'may vary according to different cultural perspectives, the resources available and other factors'. It may incorporate traditional practices and should demonstrate 'a thorough shared understanding of the property by all stakeholders' and 'the involvement of partners and stakeholders' (2005: 111). In relation to candidacies for cultural landscapes, 'nominations should be prepared in collaboration with and with the full approval of local communities' (Annex 3 at paragraph 12).

The operational guidelines also set out the Global Strategy for World Cultural and Natural Heritage of which 'the primary goal is to ensure that the necessary skills are developed by a wide range of actors for better implementation of the Convention'. This signals a crucial element in ensuring participation and community involvement in the various aspects of safeguarding – capacity-building in the communities in order to equip them to undertake these roles effectively.

Implementing the ICHC – how to ensure community involvement

Role of the Intergovernmental Committee for Safeguarding ICH

One of the main tasks of the Intergovernmental Committee for the Safeguarding of the Intangible Cultural Heritage ('the Committee')[34] during its early sessions is to draw up the first set of operational directives for the Convention which will govern the operation and implementation of the ICHC during its early years. Given the innovative nature – in the cultural heritage field, at least – of the requirement that parties ensure the participation and active involvement of communities and groups in various aspects of safeguarding and managing ICH, it will be a significant challenge to the Committee not only to identify such communities and groups, but also to define the exact nature of this participatory approach.

The first session of the Committee was held in Algiers on 18–19 November 2006 and this was mainly concerned with administrative and procedural matters.[35] An extraordinary meeting of the Committee was then held in May 2007.[36] At this meeting, several decisions concerning the Convention's implementation were taken of direct significance to the role of communities, groups and individuals in identifying and safeguarding ICH. These included drawing up criteria for inscription in the List of ICH in Need of Urgent Safeguarding and in the Representative List and drafting criteria for the accreditation of non-governmental organisations. This meeting also requested that the Secretariat prepare for the General Assembly of State Parties some preliminary draft operational directives for the implementation of Article 18 (dealing with 'Programmes, projects and activities for the safeguarding of the ICH'). This is also an area in which the involvement of cultural communities can be understood to be desirable.

It is still early days in terms of both the Convention's operation and the Committee's deliberations on its operational directives to give any specific indication as to how the involvement of communities required by Articles 11(b) and 15 will work in practice. In order to support the Committee in its work of drafting the Convention's directives, UNESCO held a series of expert meetings between 2004 and 2006 that dealt with some of the more difficult issues of implementation. Three meetings that dealt with questions of direct relevance to this essay concerned: the establishment and management of national inventories of ICH (under Article 12)[37]; developing criteria for listing ICH[38]; and the use of the terms 'community', 'group' and 'individual' and how the involvement of communities and groups in the process of identifying, inventorying and safeguarding ICH can be ensured by parties.[39] Clearly, the latter is the most directly relevant although the former, given the relationship between Articles 11(b) and 12, is also important. These meetings were organised with a view to providing the Committee with an initial basis to work from and the views of the participants cannot be taken as reflecting those of parties. However, they do give a useful indication of some of the important questions that need to be addressed in considering the role of communities under the ICHC and some possible directions in which Articles 11(b) and 15 may be implemented by parties.

The 2005 expert meeting on inventory making recognised that there is a general lack of institutional basis for this activity in member states, exacerbated by a limited availability of financial and human resources. It is one of the major national safeguarding measures proposed in the 2003 Convention (Article 12) and the expert meeting identified a need to develop systematically, or continue to develop, accessible inventories in most countries. International exchange of experience on making inventories of ICH was also seen as very important. Insufficient awareness at both the community and political levels of the importance of ICH and the need to ensure that it is effectively identified and inventoried was also identified as a crucial issue to address. Capacity-building and expanding of capacity in this area, both among government officials and at community level, are therefore key to fulfilling the Convention's obligations in this area, along with education and awareness-raising measures. Since the 2003 Convention places a heavy emphasis on the *representative* character of intangible cultural heritage, the involvement of the communities concerned in its identification, inventorying and safeguarding[40] was also stressed.

An expert meeting was held in Paris in 2005 on defining the criteria for inscription of ICH on the Representative List. The identification of suitable criteria is dependent on the way in which ICH is defined in the Convention as well as on the broader objectives of the listing mechanism. Given the way in which the definition in Article 2(1) very explicitly links ICH to the cultural community (group or individual) that creates, maintains and transmits it and for whom it is an essential element in construction of cultural identity, the selection criteria for inscription will have to reflect this connection. For this reason, the Paris meeting took the recognition of ICH by communities, groups and, in some cases individuals, as part of their cultural heritage as one of three bases from which to develop a set of criteria. This became the first of six specific criteria developed by the meeting, and one of four 'intrinsic' criteria. Further 'extrinsic' requirements were also suggested by this meeting, including that ICH for inscription should be submitted following the participation of the community, group or, if applicable, the individuals concerned at all stages of identification, definition, documentation and nomination.

The Committee, at an Extraordinary Session in China in May 2007 then proposed its own criteria for inscription on the Representative List.[41] Specific reference to identification by the cultural community (group or individual) as part of their cultural heritage was dropped and subsumed into a general reference to the requirement that it 'constitutes intangible cultural heritage' as defined in Article 2(1). This is a drawing back from the more explicit requirement of community identification and reflects a desire on the part of states to be the primary actors in defining national cultural heritage elements of any kind. There is clearly a potential for tension here between the state and the cultural communities that will need to be addressed. However, the wording of the requirement for 'the widest possible participation of the community ... individuals concerned and with their free, prior and informed consent' for the nomination process is unequivocal.

The expert meeting held in Tokyo in 2006 drafted definitions of the key terms and drafted some guidelines on the implementation of provisions relating to community involvement in inventorying and safeguarding ICH. The definitions produced by this meeting were as follows[42]:

- *Communities* are networks of people whose sense of identity or connectedness emerges from a shared historical relationship that is rooted in the practice and transmission of, or engagement with, their ICH.
- *Groups* comprise people within or across communities who share characteristics such as skills, experience and special knowledge, and thus perform specific roles in the present and future practice, re-creation and/ or transmission of their intangible cultural heritage as, for example, cultural custodians, practitioners or apprentices.
- *Individuals* are those within or across communities who have distinct skills, knowledge, experience or other characteristics, and thus perform specific roles in the present and future practice, re-creation and/or transmission of their intangible cultural heritage as, for example, cultural custodians, practitioners and, where appropriate, apprentices.

These definitions met with some criticism from certain parties, which is inevitable with such an extremely sensitive issue, but they do represent an attempt to define terms that have hitherto been used without any exact meaning, albeit with strict reference to ICH. As such, they reflect the expertise of those who work in the field of ICH as well as practitioners and are crafted specifically with the 2003 Convention in mind. It is quite possible that the Committee will choose either to ignore them or to substantially re-work them in drafting their operational directives. However, the Committee cannot ignore that a *Glossary* of some key terms had been prepared by a previous expert meeting in 2002 and that these had been generally accepted by the Intergovernmental Meeting of Experts that negotiated the ICHC. They included[43]:

- *Community* – 'People who share a self-ascribed sense of connectedness. This may be manifested, for example, in a feeling of identity or common behaviour, as well as in activities and territory. Individuals can belong to more than one community'.
- *Cultural community* – 'A community that distinguishes itself from other communities by its own culture or cultural design, or by a variant of the generic culture. Among other possible extensions, a nation can be a cultural community'.
- *Culture* – 'The set of distinctive spiritual, material, intellectual and emotional features of a society or social group, encompassing, in addition to art and literature, lifestyles, ways of living together, value systems, traditions and beliefs'.

There are certain specific points that we can propose in addition that might be helpful when making any further attempts at defining these terms. Beyond the need to define a 'cultural community' in terms of its relationship to its ICH, it can also be defined in terms of the spaces in which the ICH occurs and the community exists. Moreover, the community in question must be a viable one in order to rule out revival of 'folklorised' practices by others who do not belong to that community. Communities must not be viewed as monolithic, but the existence of variation both within and between them should be accepted. For example, some members may be knowledge holders while others have lost their knowledge and some may identify with a specific practice while others reject it. This acceptance of dissent within the community is an important point that serves also to protect the rights of individual community members when they are in conflict with those of the wider group (Sunder 2001). Equally, a community may be a small group or operate as a political 'hypercommunity' and may operate within one geographical region or exist trans-nationally and as a diaspora – taking ICH as the starting point can help in identifying the latter. What must always be born in mind is that the choice as to how we define community membership can have serious social, political and economic impacts on individuals and groups within the state (N'Diaye 2006).

The guidelines prepared by the Tokyo meeting (2006) for ensuring community involvement in inventorying and safeguarding ICH were fairly detailed. They recommended that parties should create appropriate institutional arrangements, *inter alia*, for evaluating the effectiveness of traditional safeguarding systems for inventorying ICH, drawing up inventories of ICH and developing safeguarding policies. They should also establish advisory bodies, comprising cultural practitioners, researchers, NGOs, civil society, local representatives and relevant others, for the purpose of consultation on inventorying and safeguarding ICH. Local support teams including community representatives, cultural practitioners and others with specific skills and knowledge in training and capacity building should also be set up to assist in inventorying and safeguarding specific cases of ICH.

The meeting also proposed a method for inventorying ICH that includes certain specified steps, several of which emphasise the central role of the community and community representatives in this endeavour. For example, in the identification of the ICH present on their territory, parties should identify and inform all relevant stakeholders as well as identify representatives of the communities and groups to ensure the involvement of the community in the process. They should obtain free and prior informed consent from the cultural community for their ICH to be inventoried and establish procedures, if possible in the form of protocols, to ensure an ethical relationship between stakeholders. Lastly, they should respect customary practices governing access to the ICH. Many of these approaches echo demands made in the Mataatua Declaration (1993) cited above.

Some issues relating to community participation and involvement

As noted above, by entering into the area of community (and group) participation and 'active involvement' in the safeguarding and managing of ICH, including its actual identification, the ICHC is navigating relatively uncharted waters and faces some complex and difficult questions. These new legal parameters created by the ICHC will have a significant impact on the formulation and implementation of national policies in the cultural heritage field (Arantes 2007). As Albro (2007) asks in relation to the ICHC and the 2005 *Convention on Diversity of Cultural Expressions* (that also makes reference to participation) – 'how do UNESCO's conventions help to configure the extent and limits of heritage participation and for whom?' The following section attempts to address these and other questions raised by the references to community participation in the 2003 ICHC, but recognises that it is very early in terms of the Convention's operation to be definitive on these matters.

A fundamental point to make is that the relationship between the community and the ICH resource is vital to this and needs to be clarified before further steps can be taken. This is not simple given that the potential for conflict exists here both within and between cultural communities over who should identify and manage the resource. Moreover, communities are not static and unchanging but rather are fluid entities, and it is not always clear what this relationship is or who practised a certain ritual or held certain knowledge (Deacon *et al.* 2004: 42). This then brings into play the question of who should represent the community and, as Arizpe points out (2007), the cultural 'gate-keepers' in a community can play either a positive role in safeguarding ICH or a negative role in repressing it. It is therefore crucial that the relationship between a community and its ICH – the extent of which may vary according to the ICH in question – needs to be carefully defined at the start of negotiating the identification and management of an ICH element.

When writing about participatory development approaches, Alkire (2004) notes that external actors such as experts and government officials (who may well be the same people) have a role to play in supporting informed community participation by providing information, countering local patterns of domination and supporting democratic approaches and handing over decision-making to local people. As Sen argues (2004), the local community may face difficult decisions concerning preserving old and traditional forms of living, but at considerable economic cost to themselves; what is crucial is that people have the ability to participate in public debate on matters concerning ICH safeguarding. Hence, the effective functioning of local democracy is essential to the success of this process. This shows that fully implementing this aspect of the ICHC will present many parties with a great challenge. This challenge is made greater by the fact that there is no clear consensus on the exact meaning and extent of 'participation' even in the relatively better explored area of participatory development. If, for example, it implies the meaningful involvement of local and cultural communities it could range anywhere from simple information dissemination to project planning and the facilitation of people's own initiatives (Albro 2007).

Identifying who 'owns' the heritage management process is also very important since it is not uncommon for CRM professionals to regard the community participation approach as 'belonging' to them. To avoid such pitfalls, clear ground rules need to be established as to how the different actors should work together in the tasks of defining, inventorying and managing the ICH as well as when this is to be done solely by the community and when professionals can assist in this. Involvement of the community at the start of this process is essential so that they have a sense of ownership and will co-operate fully in later safeguarding and management measures. It should also be recognised that there may be a multiplicity of stakeholders in such cases all of whom need to be taken into account. For example, the identification of and safeguarding the Moussem of Tan-Tan in Algeria involved women and men, tribal leaders, local politicians, intellectuals, artists, government officials and specialists (Skounti 2006).

A complicating factor here is that the very act of identification and safeguarding of ICH itself can have unintended or unexpected side effects. An example of this was given during the expert meeting on inventory making (UNESCO 2005) and it illustrates the potentially negative effect of drawing a cultural community's attention to an element of its ICH. Here, a previously unknown traditional dance performed during a village festival in Bulgaria was documented and the dance then became increasingly ornamented and enriched until it had become transformed into something completely different. A counter-example given during the expert meeting in Tokyo in 2006 was that of the Kung San in South Africa whose cultural community feel ashamed of their own culture and do not transmit it to younger generations (Manetsi 2006). In such a case, raising awareness of the value of their ICH could well contribute greatly to its chance of continuing and being transmitted to the next generation.

The new national policy approach required under the ICHC will create a fundamental shift in the relative position of the governmental agencies involved in heritage preservation, particularly vis-à-vis the local communities' new role in identifying what should be officially regarded as heritage. The significance of this should not be underestimated since it has, up until now, been the prerogative of the state to decide which cultural items to include within the domain of 'official culture', representing as it does the public interest (Arantes 2007). As Deacon *et al.* note (2004: 11), including ICH within the national culture or heritage provides opportunities to democratise the process by which we give value to heritage, giving a larger role to local people especially in the developing world. Arantes (2007) points out that this shift of authority is reflected in the inclusion of 'cultural reference' in Brazil's heritage legislation as 'a legitimate source of value to be taken into account in the identification and proclamation of a cultural item as heritage'. This has the effect of giving cultural communities a much stronger position with regard to this process.

There is therefore a need to build a state/community partnership that is both bottom-up and top-down, with the role of government seen as being primarily a supportive one (in terms of finances and expertise). However, such a partnership is not easily constructed and this process will involve complex and often difficult negotiations in which 'cultural mediators' that are both internal and external to the cultural communities will play an important intermediary role (Arantes 2007). These cultural mediators may include: community representatives, office bearers and cultural custodians; technical and administrative personnel of government institutions; independent experts and political activists involved in the institutional practices; and entrepreneurs seeking to develop business opportunities related to the cultural resource. Moreover, any state-level interventions concerning ICH will directly impinge on social and cultural processes taking place within cultural communities. State-sponsored measures to safeguard ICH therefore raise questions concerning the role of the state in regulating social relations.

We can already identify some successful examples of instances where communities have engaged in heritage conservation initiatives through partnerships with the state. In Mexico, for example, the state established civil associations, neighbourhood councils and 'rural inhabitant' (*campesino*) unions with a view to protecting ancient monuments and conservation zones (López 2002, cited in Deacon *et al.* 2004: 44). In New Zealand, the Maori Heritage Council has been established with community representation and control in order to manage Maori heritage and ensure that sites of Maori interest are protected. It also seeks to mediate any conflicts of interest that may arise over the use of these sites and heritage (Paterson 1999). As Deacon *et al.* (2004) point out, one of the key roles for community/government partnerships is to resolve disputes over the meaning and management of heritage, and such disputes are much more likely to occur in relation to ICH than monumental heritage. It is important for these and similar experiences, where they relate to ICH in particular, to be documented and shared between parties of the ICHC – with the UNESCO Secretariat acting as a clearing-house of best practices – and non-parties as well.

Capacity building locally is anticipated by the ICHC as an important element in facilitating effective community involvement in the safeguarding and management of ICH (Article 14). Florey (2003) describes a project on Malukan languages in eastern Indonesia that illustrates how the partnership between specialists and the community (and to some degree the state) can work (Hinton and Hale 2001). The goals of this project were (a) to facilitate language documentation and maintenance by the community and (b) to promote greater linguistic tolerance among speakers in order to facilitate language transmission and maintenance. As she points out, the goal of community empowerment (through local capacity building) is a common feature of such models that facilitate the ownership and control of languages at the local level (see, for example, Hinton 2002; Hinton and Hale 2001; Thiebreger 1995). Encouraging fieldwork by speakers themselves is important since it provides them with skills essential to language revitalisation and maintenance activities. There are obvious parallels here with projects for safeguarding ICH, especially since languages 'as a vehicle for' ICH already feature as the first domain of ICH set out in Article 2(2) of the ICHC.

Conclusion

The ICHC, then, is a new departure for a cultural heritage Convention and, to some degree, for an international treaty in attempting to provide culturally based protection to a non-material subject.[44] Moreover, the nature of ICH is such that it is people acting as the communities, groups or individuals of the 2003 Convention on whom its very existence is predicated. Unlike a site, a monument or artefact that has a material existence beyond the individual or society that created it (possibly wholly unknown to us today) it is only through its enactment by cultural practitioners that ICH has any current existence and by their active transmission that it can have any future existence. Hence, any actions aimed at its safeguarding must rely heavily on the collaborative efforts and active involvement of cultural communities and their members. This, in turn, requires governments and government institutions to find new forms of operating in the cultural heritage field that are both alien to them and challenging. They need to move away from the traditional top-down approach of governmental cultural heritage organisations where the institutions are acting as custodians of the national cultural patrimony and where decision- and policy-making are the domain of the government and its representatives. In relation to ICH in particular, the cultural community has become a new and significant actor with whom governmental bodies must interact directly and seek to build a partnership.

As this chapter has shown, such a participatory approach is not unprecedented in international law and was called for in Principle 10 of the 1992 Rio Declaration as a fundamental means of achieving sustainable development. It is no accident, indeed, that ICH itself is seen as a basic social resource for finding sustainable forms of development and environmental practices. In international law, it has been in the area of environmental protection that this notion has found its greatest expression, although, as this chapter has sought to show, this has suffered from a lack of clarity as to what form such participation should take, how the communities referred to should be identified and who should be their representatives. In the field of development, quite a lot of work both theoretical and practical has been done in relation to participatory decision-making and management approaches and to addressing the aforementioned uncertainties. There has also been, as seen above, criticism of the participatory development approach that (a) should serve as a warning to those tasked with implementing the 2003 ICHC and that (b) they have an opportunity to try to address in new ways.

The 2003 Convention makes unusually direct reference for an international treaty to the central role that communities, groups and individuals have to play in safeguarding ICH and in its management. The requirement placed on parties to apply participatory approaches in safeguarding and to involve them actively in its management is also unusually explicit. It is, in fact, an explicit recognition that without their active involvement such actions become meaningless or, worse, become an appropriation of this heritage by the government from the control of the community that creates and maintains it. In this sense, the ICHC can be seen to go beyond simply calling for participatory approaches to be used as a 'better' model than other existing ones since, in the case of ICH, there is nothing to safeguard without the enactment of cultural practitioners.

In view of the institutional structure of the Convention, in particular the establishment of the intergovernmental ICH Committee, the opportunity exists for future development of practice in this area. If we look to the parallel example of the World Heritage Committee of the 1972 Convention, we see that it has responded actively to the various challenges and evolution in understanding it has faced over the 30 years of its operation. We can hope for a similar responsiveness in the ICH Committee that is currently preparing the first Operational Directives for the Convention, although the make-up of the Committee and its openness to outside views and opinions will be crucial to this. If its members (and those bodies they consult with) are well chosen for their expertise and include a range of people, including practitioners, as well as government officials, then the chances of a dynamic development of practice in this area will be greater.

At a recent meeting, the Committee took decisions on several issues relevant to community participation/involvement.[45] First, a chapter on 'Participation in the implementation of the Convention' was also adopted as part of a draft set of operational directives for the Convention, with a section on the participation of communities, groups and (if appropriate) individuals.[46] In its Preamble, this section recognises that 'at the core of safeguarding of the intangible cultural heritage are the communities ... that create, maintain and transmit it and are therefore the prime concern of the Convention'. Here, then, is an explicit statement of the centrality of the communities, groups and individuals in achieving the Convention's primary stated purpose. Here, parties 'are encouraged to create a consultative body or a coordination mechanism to facilitate the participation of communities [etc.]' as well as other actions such as community sensitisation and capacity building (at 77). Elsewhere, it is noted that the Committee may invite communities (groups and individuals) to participate in its meetings 'in order to sustain an interactive dialogue and consult them on specific matters', in conformity with Article 8(4) of the Convention.[47] Moreover, in relation to national, subregional and regional programmes, projects and activities for safeguarding ICH (Article 18 of the Convention), the criteria for selection include that the selected programme, project or activity 'has been or will be implemented with the participation of the community, group or, if applicable, individuals concerned and with their free, prior and informed consent'.[48]

In sum, the intergovernmental ICH Committee of the 2003 Convention has an opportunity to inform international law through its practice in relation to participation and community involvement, not only in the narrow field of cultural heritage protection but more widely in any areas such as environmental law in which such notions have become a more common currency. However, it is still very early to anticipate what the Committee will do since, as the experience of the 1972 WHC would suggest, their practice will evolve over the next few years and may well develop into something quite different from what they decide at the early meetings now being held. It is, indeed, this capacity for the practice surrounding implementation of the treaty to evolve that is such an important feature of its model and provides the potential, at least, for it to set an important example.

Notes

1 As of 20 February 2008, there were 90 states parties to the Convention of which 21 are from Africa, 26 from Europe, 18 from Latin America and the Caribbean, 13 from Asia and the Pacific and 12 Arab states. This should be compared with UNESCO's *Convention on Protecting the Underwater Cultural Heritage* (2001) that has still only secured 15 ratifications.

2 *Convention on the Means of Prohibiting and Preventing the Illicit Import, Export and Transfer of Ownership of Cultural Property* (UNESCO, 14 November 1970); *Convention concerning the Protection of the World Cultural and Natural Heritage* (UNESCO, 16 November 1972).

3 For more background on the Convention and its development, refer to: Bedjaoui 2004 and Kurin 2004.

4 The 'intangible cultural heritage' means the practices, representations, expressions, knowledge, skills – as well as the instruments, objects, artefacts and cultural spaces associated therewith – *that communities, groups and, in some cases, individuals recognise as part of their cultural heritage.* This intangible cultural heritage, transmitted from generation to generation, is constantly recreated by communities and groups in response to their environment, their interaction with nature and their history, and provides them with a sense of identity and continuity, thus promoting respect for cultural diversity and human creativity. For the purposes of this Convention, consideration will be given solely to such intangible cultural heritage as is compatible with existing international human rights instruments, as well as with the requirements of mutual respect among communities, groups and individuals, and of sustainable development. (Article 2(1), my emphasis)

5 Although much adapted to avoid, for example, any notions of the 'outstanding' value of heritage listed.

6 The Committee's main functions (as set out in Article 7) are: promoting the objectives of the Convention and encouraging its implementation; providing a guiding role for the establishment of best practices in the field of safeguarding ICH; preparing operational directives to aid states parties in the implementation of the Convention; preparing and submitting to the General Assembly a plan for using the resources of the Fund; establishing criteria for the inscription of ICH on the Lists; inscribing ICH on the basis of these criteria at the request of states parties; and examining requests by states parties for international assistance.

7 World Conference on Cultural Policies (MONDIACULT), Mexico City, 6 August 1982. The Preamble, at para. 6, reads, '[I]n its widest sense, culture may now be said to be the whole complex of distinctive spiritual, material, intellectual and emotional features that characterize a society or social group. It includes not only arts and letters, but modes of life ... value systems, traditions and beliefs'.

8 'People, however, are not self-contained atoms; they work together, co-operate compete and interact in many ways. It is culture that connects them with one another and makes the development of the individual possible. It is in this sense that all forms of development, including human development, ultimately are determined by cultural factors'.

9 To be clarified by the ICH Committee when defining the criteria for inscription of ICH on the Lists.

10 *Convention for the Protection of Cultural Property in the Event of Armed Conflict* (UNESCO, 14 May 1954; with Additional Protocols, 1999); 1970 and 1972 Conventions cited n. 1.

11 The right of peoples to self-determination is expressed in joint Article 1 of the *International Covenant on Civil and Political Rights* (1966) and the *International Covenant on Economic, Social and Cultural Rights* (1966).

12 Under the Treaty of Montevideo (1936) – a sufficient population, control over a territory, the ability to establish political institutions and to enter into relations with other states.

13 Precursor to the International Court of Justice.

14 *International Covenant on Civil and Political Rights* (1966).

15 Convention No. 169 *Concerning Tribal and Indigenous Peoples in Independent Territories.*

16 Art.1(2) refers to 'Self-identification as indigenous or tribal' as a 'fundamental criterion' for this.

17 UN *Declaration on the Rights of Indigenous Peoples* (adopted UN General Assembly, 13 September 2007), online: http://www.ohchr.org/english/issues/indigenous/docs/draftdeclaration.pdf.

18 Article 1 states that: '(1) Each culture has a dignity and value which must be respected and preserved. (2) Every people has the right and the duty to develop its culture'.

19 African Charter on Human and Peoples' Rights (Banjul 1981). Article 22 (1) states: 'All peoples have the right to their economic, social and cultural development with due regard to their freedom and identity ... ' Article 29 notes that: 'The individual shall also have the duty: ... 7. To preserve and strengthen positive African cultural values in his relations with other members of the society, in the spirit of tolerance, dialogue and consultation and, in general, to contribute to the promotion of the moral well-being of society'.

20 Article 5 states unequivocally: 'the right of all groups to their own cultural identity and the development of their distinctive cultural life within the national and international context, it being understood that it vests with each group to decide in complete freedom on the maintenance and, if appropriate, the adaptation or enrichment of the values which it regards as essential to its identity'.
Interestingly, the Preamble refers to 'all peoples and all human groups' and to the right to be different as a right of 'all individuals and groups' while Article 3 makes reference to 'human beings', 'people' and 'groups' in one article.

21 The UN *Convention on Biological Diversity* (1992) and the *International Treaty on Plant Genetic Resources for Food and Agriculture* (FAO 2001), respectively.

22 OAU Model Legislation on Community Rights and Access to Genetic Resources.

23 Primarily, the UN *Convention on Biological Diversity* (1992). Available online at: http://www.cbd.int/convention/convention.shtml and the UN *Convention to Combat Desertification* (1994) online at: http://www.unccd.entico.com/English/text1

24 They read as follows: '3. In order to ensure the sustainability of this process [of safeguarding ICH] governments have the duty to take measures facilitating the democratic participation of all stakeholders' and '7 (iv) Consider that it is appropriate and necessary, within this framework, in close collaboration with the practitioners and bearers of all expressions of intangible cultural heritage, to consult and involve all the stakeholders ... '

25 Final Declaration of the UN Conference on the Environment and Development (UNCED) (Rio de Janeiro, 1992).

26 Principle 10 reads: 'Environmental issues are best handled with the participation of all concerned citizens, at the relevant level. At the national level, each individual shall have appropriate access to information concerning the environment ... and the opportunity to participate in the decision-making processes ... ' Principle 22 reads: 'Indigenous people and their communities, and other local communities, have a vital role in environmental management and development because of their knowledge and traditional practices. States should recognise and duly support their identity, culture and interests and enable their effective participation in the achievement of sustainable development'.

27 UN *Convention on Biological Diversity* (1992), available online at: http://www.cbd.int/convention/convention.shtml

28 Article 8 requires each Contracting Party, as far as possible: '(j) Subject to its national legislation, respect, preserve and maintain knowledge, innovations and practices of indigenous and local communities embodying traditional lifestyles relevant for the conservation and sustained use of biological diversity and promote their wider application with the approval and involvement of the holders of such knowledge, innovations and practices and encourage the equitable sharing of the benefits arising from the utilization of such knowledge'.

29 UN *Convention to Combat Desertification* (1994), available online at: http://www.cbd.int/convention/convention.shtml and the UN *Convention to Combat Desertification* (1994), available online at: http://www.unccd.entico.com/English/text1

30 Article 5 calls on affected country Parties to undertake to '(d) promote awareness and facilitate participation of local populations, particularly women and youth, with the support of non-governmental organizations, in efforts to combat desertification ... '
Article 10 states that national action plans should '(f) provide for effective participation at the local, national and regional levels of non-governmental organizations and local

populations … in policy planning, decision-making and implementation and review of national action programmes … '

31 Article 9(2) reads: ' Parties should take measures to protect and promote Farmers' Rights, such as …

   (c) the right to participate in making decisions, at the national level, on matters related to the conservation and sustainable use of plant genetic resources for food and agriculture'.

32 Both cited in the previous section.

33 Article 7(1) reads: 'The peoples concerned shall have the right to decide their own priorities for the process of development as it affects their lives, beliefs, institutions and spiritual well-being and the lands they occupy or otherwise use, and to exercise control, to the extent possible, over their own economic, social and cultural development. In addition, they shall participate in the formulation, implementation and evaluation of plans and programmes for national and regional development which may affect them directly'.

34 Established under Article 5.

35 First Session of the Intergovernmental Committee for Safeguarding the Intangible Cultural Heritage, Algiers (Algeria), 18–19 November 2006, *Decisions Adopted*. UNESCO Doc.ITH/06/1.COM/CONF.2004/Decisions, 19 November 2006.

36 First Extraordinary Session of the Intergovernmental Committee for the Safeguarding of the Intangible Cultural Heritage at Chengdu (China), 23–27 May 2007.

37 Expert Meeting on Inventorying Intangible Cultural Heritage (Paris, 17–18 March 2005).

38 Expert Meeting on the Criteria for Listing ICH (Paris, 5–6 December 2005).

39 Expert Meeting on Community Involvement in Safeguarding Intangible Cultural Heritage (Tokyo, Japan, 13–15 March 2006).

40 As required by Arts. 12 and 15.

41 Extraordinary Session held at Chengdu (China) on 23–27 May 2007 [UNESCO Doc.ITH/07/1.EXT.COM/CONF.202/Decisions].

42 As drafted at Expert Meeting cited n. 38.

43 Expert Meeting for the Preparation of a Glossary of Intangible Cultural Heritage, 10–12 June 2002. See: van Zanten 2002 and 2004.

44 Of course, the subject matter of intellectual property law – a well-established body of law – is equally non-material in character. However, the aim and approach of IPRs is quite different since they are designed primarily to protect economic (and related moral) interests associated with exploitation of the intellectual property in question.

45 Second Extra-ordinary Meeting of the Committee, held in Sofia on 18–22 February 2008. Decisions taken at this meeting can be found in UNESCO Document: ITH/08/2.EXT/COM/CONF.201/Decisions.

46 Chapter 3.1, para. 75–86 in ibid at pp. 35–7.

47 Idem.

48 Decisions cited n. 45 at p. 31.

Bibliography

Abraham, A. and Platteau, J.-P. (2004) 'Participatory development: where culture creeps in', in V. Rao and M. Walton (eds), *Culture and Public Action*, The International Bank for Reconstruction and Development/The World Bank, Palo Alto: Stanford University Press.

Aikawa, N. (2004) 'An Historical Overview of the Preparation of the UNESCO International Convention for the Safeguarding of the Intangible Cultural Heritage', *Museum International*, 56 (1–2): 137–49.

—— (2007) 'The conceptual development of UNESCO's programme on intangible cultural heritage', in J. Blake (ed.), *Safeguarding Intangible Cultural Heritage – Challenges and Approaches*, Builth Wells: Institute of Art and Law.

Albro, R. (2007) 'The terms of participation in recent UNESCO cultural policy making', in J. Blake (ed.), *Safeguarding Intangible Cultural Heritage – Challenges and Approaches*, Builth Wells: Institute of Art and Law.

Alkire, S. (2004) 'Culture, poverty and external intervention', in V. Rao and M. Walton (eds), *Culture and Public Action*, The International Bank for Reconstruction and Development/The World Bank, Palo Alto: Stanford University Press.

Anaya, S.J. (1996) *Indigenous Peoples in International Law*, Oxford: Oxford University Press.

Arantes, A. (2007) 'Cultural diversity and the politics of difference in safeguarding intangible cultural heritage', in J. Blake (ed.), *Safeguarding Intangible Cultural Heritage – Challenges and Approaches*, Builth Wells: Institute of Art and Law.

Arizpe, L. (2004) 'The intellectual history of culture and development', in V. Rao and M. Walton (eds), *Culture and Public Action*, The International Bank for Reconstruction and Development/The World Bank, Palo Alto: Stanford University Press.

—— (2007) 'The cultural politics of intangible cultural heritage', in J. Blake (ed.), *Safeguarding Intangible Cultural Heritage – Challenges and Approaches*, Builth Wells: Institute of Art and Law.

Bedjaoui, M. (2004) 'The Convention for the Safeguarding of the Intangible Cultural Heritage: the legal framework and internationally recognised principles', *Museum International*, 56 (1–2): 150–5.

Blake, J. (2001) *Developing a New Standard-setting Instrument for the Safeguarding of Intangible Cultural Heritage–Elements for Consideration*, Paris: UNESCO.

Brownlie, I. (1988) 'The rights of peoples in modern international law', in J. Crawford (ed.), *The Rights of Peoples*, Gloucestershire: Clarendon Press.

Capotorti, F. (1976) *Study on the Rights of Persons Belonging to Ethnic, Religious and Linguistic Minorities*, UN Doc. E/CN.4/sub.2/Add.1–7, United Nations.

Cassese, A. (1995) *Self-determination of Peoples: A Legal Appraisal*, Cambridge: Cambridge University Press.

Deacon, H. and Beazley, O. (2007) 'Safeguarding intangible heritage values under the World Heritage Convention: Auchwitz, Hiroshima and Robben Island', in J. Blake (ed.), *Safeguarding Intangible Cultural Heritage – Challenges and Approaches*, Builth Wells: Institute of Art and Law.

Deacon, H., Dondolo, L., Mrubata, M. and Prosalendis, S. (2004) *The Subtle Power of Intangible Heritage*, South Africa: HSRC Publishers.

Douglas, M. (2004) 'Traditional culture–let's hear no more about it', in V. Rao and M. Walton (eds), *Culture and Public Action*, The International Bank for Reconstruction and Development/The World Bank, Palo Alto: Stanford University Press.

Food and Agriculture Organization (FAO) (2001) *International Treaty on Plant Genetic Resources for Food and Agriculture*.

Florey, M. (2003) 'Countering purism: confronting the emergence of new varieties in a training programme for community language workers', in P.K. Austin (ed.), *Language Documentation and Description*, London: Hans Rausing Endangered Languages Project.

Garcia Canclini, N. (1998) 'Cultural policy options in the context of globalization', in *World Culture Report – Culture, Creativity and Markets*, Paris: UNESCO.

Hinton, L. (2002) *How to Keep Your Language Alive*, Berkeley: Heyday Books.

Hinton, L. and Hale, K. (2001) *The Green Book of Language Revitalization in Practice*, San Diego: Academic Press.

International Labour Organization (ILO) (1989) *Convention (No. 169) Concerning Indigenous and Tribal Peoples in Independent Countries*.

Klamer, A. (2004) 'Cultural goods are good for more than their economic value', in V. Rao and M. Walton (eds), *Culture and Public Action*, The International Bank for Reconstruction and Development/The World Bank, Palo Alto: Stanford University Press.

Kurin, R. (2004) 'Safeguarding intangible cultural heritage in the 2003 UNESCO Convention: a critical appraisal', *Museum International*, 56(1–2): 66–77.

Leach, M. (1998) 'Culture and sustainability', in *World Culture Report – Culture, Creativity and Markets*, Paris: UNESCO.

López, E.T. (2002) 'Final Report of the Working Group on Cultural Heritage Comparative Study: Similarities and Differences', presented to INCP-RIPC meeting in Cape Town, 2002. Available online at: http://www.incp-ripc.org/meetings/2002/similarities_e.shtml (Accessed 3 August 2008).

Luxen, J.L. (2000) 'The intangible dimension of monuments and sites', *ICOMOS Newsletter*, March–July.

Manetsi, T. (2006) 'Communities, groups and individuals', unpublished paper presented to UNESCO Expert Meeting on Community Involvement in Safeguarding Intangible Cultural Heritage, Tokyo, Japan, 13–15 March.

N'Diaye, D. (2006) 'Community in the context of UNESCO's Convention on intangible cultural heritage', unpublished paper presented to UNESCO Expert Meeting on Community Involvement in Safeguarding Intangible Cultural Heritage, Tokyo, Japan, 13–15 March.

Niec, H. (ed.) (1998) *Cultural Rights and Wrongs*, Paris: UNESCO Publishing.

OAS (1981) *African Charter on Human and People's Rights* ('Banjul Charter').

O'Keefe, P.J. (1995) 'Cultural agency/cultural authority: politics and poetics of intellectual property in the post-colonial era', *International Journal of Cultural Property*, 4(2): 382–7.

Paterson, R.K. (1999) 'Protecting Taonga: the cultural heritage of the New Zealand Maori', *International Journal of Cultural Property*, 8(1): 108–32.

Posey, D.A. (1998) 'Can cultural rights protect traditional cultural knowledge and diversity?', in H. Niec (ed.), *Cultural Rights and Wrongs*, Paris: UNESCO Publishing.

Prott, L.V. (1988) 'Cultural rights as peoples' rights in international law', in J. Crawford (ed.), *The Rights of Peoples*, Gloucestershire: Clarendon Press.

Sen, A. (2004) 'How does culture matter?', in V. Rao and M. Walton (eds), *Culture and Public Action*, Palo Alto: Stanford University Press.

Simmonds, J. (1997) 'UNESCO World Heritage Convention', *Art, Antiquity and Law*, 2(3): 251–81.

Skounti, A. (2006) 'Preliminary notes', unpublished paper presented to UNESCO Expert Meeting on Community Involvement in Safeguarding Intangible Cultural Heritage, Tokyo, Japan, 13–15 March.

Stavenhagen, R. (1990) *The Ethnic Question. Conflicts, Development and Human Rights*, Tokyo: UN University Press.

—— (1998) 'Cultural rights: a social science perspective', in H. Niec (ed.), *Cultural Rights and Wrongs*, Paris: UNESCO Publishing, Paris, pp. 1–20.

Sunder, M. (2001) 'Cultural dissent', *Stanford Law Review*, 54(3): 495.

Thiebreger, N. (ed.) (1995) *Paper and Talk: a Manual for Reconstituting Materials in Australian Indigenous Languages from Historical Sources*, Canberra: Aboriginal Studies Press.

Thornberry, P. (1991) *International Law and the Rights of Minorities*, Oxford: Clarendon.

United Nations (1966) *International Covenant on Civil and Political Rights.*

Warren, D.M., Slikkerveer, L.J. and Brokensha, D. (eds) (1995) *The Cultural Dimension of Development: Indigenous Knowledge Systems*, London: Intermediate Technology Publications.

World Commission on Culture and Development (1996) *Our Creative Diversity*, Paris: UNESCO.

UNCED (1992) 'Rio Declaration', *Final Declaration of the UN Conference on Environment and Development*, Rio de Janeiro.

UNESCO (n.d.) *Third Medium-Term Plan (1990–1995)*, UNESCO Doc. 25C/4, UNESCO.

—— (1954) *Convention for the Protection of Cultural Property in the Event of Armed Conflict* (UNESCO, 14 May, 1954; with Additional Protocol of 1999).

—— (1966) *Declaration on the Principles of International Cultural Co-operation.*

—— (1970) *Convention on the Means of Prohibiting and Preventing the Illicit Import, Export and Transfer of Ownership of Cultural Property.*

—— (1972) *Convention on the Protection of the World Cultural and Natural Heritage.*

—— (1978) *Declaration on Racial Prejudice.*

—— (1989) *Recommendation on Safeguarding Traditional Culture and Folklore.*

—— (2001) *Guidelines on the Procedure for Submission and Evaluation of Candidature Files*, Paris: UNESCO.

—— (2002) *Intangible Cultural Heritage – a Mirror of Cultural Diversity*, Final Communiqué from the 3rd Round Table of Ministers of Culture ('Istanbul Declaration'), Istanbul, September 2002.

—— (2003a) *Convention for the Safeguarding of the Intangible Cultural Heritage.*

—— (2003b) *Identification and Documentation of Modern Heritage*, World Heritage Papers No.5, Paris: UNESCO World Heritage Centre.

—— (2004) *Linking Universal and Local Values: Managing a Sustainable Future for World Heritage*, World Heritage Papers No.13, Paris: UNESCO World Heritage Centre.

—— (2005) *Report of the Expert Meeting on Inventorying Intangible Cultural Heritage*, Paris, 17–18 March, UNESCO.

United Nations (1966a) *International Covenant on Civil and Political Rights.*

—— (1966b) *International Covenant on Economic, Social and Cultural Rights.*

—— (1992) *Convention on Biological Diversity.*

—— (1994) *Convention to Combat Desertification.*

—— (2007) *Declaration on the Rights of Indigenous.*

Van Zanten, W. (ed.) (2002) *Glossary Intangible Cultural Heritage*, prepared by an international meeting of experts at UNESCO, 10–12 June, The Hague: Netherlands National Commission for UNESCO.

—— (2004) 'Constructing a new terminology for intangible cultural heritage', *Museum International*, 56(1–2): 36–44.

Zakayeva, Z. (2003) 'Women and intangible cultural heritage: an innovative concept', paper presented to *The Role of Women in the Transmission and Safeguarding of Intangible Cultural Heritage*, Sub-regional Meeting held by UNESCO and the Iranian National Commission for UNESCO, Tehran, 24–26 April.

Chapter 4

The authentic illusion

Humanity's intangible cultural heritage, the Moroccan experience[1]

Ahmed Skounti

Introduction

The preservation of heritage has never been embraced with more energy than in today's uncertain times, at a major junction in the history of humanity, marked in particular by a shift in large-scale contacts between societies and by the relentless, consumerist exploitation of the world's resources. A change in the mechanisms which regulate 'production of locality' (Appadurai 1996) heralded this state of affairs. This new awareness also has a price: it is when everything or almost everything collapses around them that people cast around, in their panic, for reference points or markers that will enable them to steady destinies caught up in the storm. It is in such a climate that heritage, be it of sites, objects, practices or ideas, is produced and assimilated into an 'invented tradition' (Hobsbawm and Ranger 1983).

The acquisition of heritage status of intangible or non-material kind has two major implications. On the one hand, it introduces a distortion between the heritage and the locality (and society) that gave birth to it. Heritage status results in a loss of connection with the territory, can be reproduced anywhere on the planet, even if a link with the locality is kept. It enters, through the mobility of people and the merchandising of culture, a circuit now operating on a global or nearly global scale. Today the virtual dimension of the internet emphasises even more the lack of territorial identity of cultural heritage elements. On the other hand, the production of an intangible cultural heritage inevitably requires sacrificing something, that very thing that turns cultural facts into heritage; these facts can no longer be the same, they become other, especially for those who own or perform them. These two dimensions, one intrinsic, the other extrinsic, stem from the meeting of the global and the local, one defining the other and vice versa. A kind of 'authentic illusion' is thus created and lies at the basis of the process of heritage creation.

It is in this context – where local identification is paired with the work of standardisation undertaken notably by UNESCO – that the recognition of intangible cultural heritage operates. It faces multiple local and supra-local challenges which have not yet been the subject of close study. The present article hopes to contribute to this research, by going back to the origins of the take-over of the heritage domain, on a local as well as on an international level. We shall retrace the major stages in the process of identification, of recognition and of rendering visible ('visibilisation') cultural elements which have, in the process, acquired a dual status as identity markers both for local communities and for the heritage of the whole of humanity. I shall draw on my participation in the *Convention for the Safeguarding of the Intangible Cultural Heritage* in 2003 and my engagement, at a local level in Morocco, in defining the intangible national heritage. A critical and constructive analysis of this to-ing and fro-ing between the local and the global should allow us, as much as possible, to understand the creation and the workings of the process of heritage creation at a micro and macro scale. Examples from Morocco, in particular from the Place Jemaâ El Fna in Marrakech and the Moussem of Tan-Tan, declared *Masterpieces of the Oral and Intangible Heritage of Humanity* in 2001 and 2005, respectively, will serve to illustrate this anthropological approach to heritage.

The creation of intangible cultural heritage

What we consider today as heritage was not always so; it becomes heritage through the intervention of a variety of diverse factors. It is not a given from the outset; it is produced, and there are numerous elements at stake in this production. First, there are economic stakes, linked to returns expected from controlling the resource such as business opportunities, job creation, invest-ment, tourism, currency, and so forth. Then there are political stakes since heritage (in its wider sense) is called upon during elections, fuelling compe-tition between groups and individuals to claim chunks of power corre-sponding to the economic weight – real or presumed – of these groups. There are social stakes too, involving the drive by these same groups and individuals to achieve social prestige, 'notability' and symbolic capital all at once. Finally there are cultural stakes which rest on the affirmation of a strong, homogeneous and unchanging identity, sometimes manipulated to mobilise people (see Skounti in press b).

Heritage is, at first sight, intimately linked to a territory, a locality, and the community that occupies it. However, intangible heritage differs from material heritage in that the former is rooted in the locality in real as well as in figurative terms, whereas the latter considers the locality as a dimension without it being subject to it in a definitive or durable way. The complexity of today's world manifests itself through resources that are no longer bound to territories, through the increase in 'translocal' and transnational networks (Appadurai 1996). It is also reflected in the growth in associations between individuals, the increase in migration, the intervention at arms' length by management established in distant locations, the development of channels of international cooperation and the intensification of tourism. The local element is therefore under strong threat, with real but obsolete local communities being overtaken by virtual ones. The latter consist of individuals who depend more on resources that are external to the locality, linked to other individuals through a multiplicity of networks.

Here we take 'local' to mean a territory owned as much individually as collectively by a community. This territory represents both a tangible marker and a material basis, and it is governed by strategies which, under cover of an ideology of synergy, are quite real to the individuals concerned. The heritage contained within, both of the material and intangible kind, is of capital importance as much to the authorities as to groups and individuals. By neglecting it or recognising it, by destroying or protecting it, they attribute a definite importance to heritage, shown in social projects that are sometimes contradictory.

The acquisition of intangible heritage status introduces a distortion between the heritage and the locality and the society that gave birth to it. In a way, heritage loses its territorial identity, loosens its material ties in order to survive. On a number of different levels it renounces, at least in part, its local roots. The internet plays a part in this loss of affinity, in this 'virtualisation' of heritage. There are countless professional or amateur websites, official or informal, blogs and personal pages which give a real visibility to aspects of intangible cultural heritage hitherto inaccessible to most. Yet not all the components of intangible cultural heritage follow the same path, nor have the same destiny. State-wide politics play a major role here, as they produce hierarchies and promote certain types of heritage over others which are often those of minority groups. Political criteria often prevail in a domain where expertise has been lacking for decades, including at an international level. In this respect one may recall that it took a whole generation between the adoption by UNESCO of the *Convention Concerning the Protection of the World Cultural and Natural Heritage* (1972) and the *Convention for the Safeguarding of the Intangible Cultural Heritage* (2003). The delay in recognising the protection of intangible heritage concerns not only nation-states, but the whole of humanity.

The creation of intangible cultural heritage represents also a kind of 'recycling' process, recycling cultural facts which become heritage. Where they were once left to their own fate, transformed or left to disappear, today they are, sometimes, the object of great solicitude. Those engaged, either at an individual or at an institutional level, in this work of identification and recognition are absolutely convinced that they are contributing to protecting as they are a whole number of forms of cultural expression, be they alive or under threat of extinction. They feel they are working for the long-term survival of elements whose initial function has run its term. In the absence of a new function, these elements risk disappearing. However, what these agents do not realise is that these elements of intangible cultural heritage are not, and cannot be, the same ever again: they become other, including to those who own and perform them. Their survival depends on sacrificing something of what contributes to their supposed 'authenticity'. The fact that they are considered as heritage introduces in their midst a new, hitherto unsuspected, dimension. Heritage agents are convinced that these elements are 'authentic', faithful manifestations of what they have always been, timeless. But this is only an 'authentic illusion'. The latter is nevertheless necessary, it even lies at the heart of the process of heritage creation. Belief in the 'authenticity' of the intangible cultural heritage element, its anchoring into a past beyond memory and its immutability justify and reinforce the engagement and the activity of heritage agents. At its most extreme, the authentic illusion is akin to 'inventing tradition' (Hobsbawm and Ranger 1983). A number of cultural manifestations present this aspect today, giving to individuals, groups and societies the strong conviction that they are perpetuating or giving new life to well-rooted traditions. Evidently political regimes, thanks to their monopoly over the media, sometimes make disproportionate use of these *constructions*.

On the other hand there is no *one* intangible cultural heritage, there is a wide spectrum, ranging from the non-material dimension of a material heritage element (site, monument, object) to the most intangible aspect (tale, poem, song, musical note, prayer, scent, perfume, etc.). Furthermore, pure immateriality is a fiction: can something intangible exist? There is obviously a material dimension to every element of intangible heritage: the human brain and body that detain it, the book that retains a trace of it, the audio-visual material that captures its sound or image. Without this material dimension this element could not be shared, would not exist. Our awareness and understanding as human beings relies on this material dimension. We need to apprehend it through one of our senses: sight, hearing, smell, taste, touch, depending on the degree of materiality or immateriality.

Intangible cultural heritage material is both fragile and resilient. Unlike material heritage, which can be destroyed over a very short time (the Buddhas of Bamiyan in Afghanistan being a case in point), intangible heritage survives longer. It outlives by far the span of the lives of those who carry it. Even in the *longue durée*, transcending the generations of individuals who transmit this heritage from one to the other, it never simply disappears. On the contrary, it is transformed, adapted, hidden (sometimes to reappear with more vigour), it retracts or expands depending on circumstances, it scatters the micro-elements that make up this heritage to be incorporated into new, emerging cultural traits, and so forth.

The transcendence of the elements of intangible heritage, compared to that of individuals, allows these elements to have a longer life. They pass from one generation to another, as genes are passed on. The transmission from individual to individual almost mirrors genetic transmission. Sometimes it is even assimilated to the latter: the most successful child is one which we have brought up to resemble us in all respects, including what we master best, our knowledge or know-how.[2] But this sublimation of the same also allows for the capacity to act differently at times of great cultural transitions: a craftsman will tell his son that it is in the latter's interest to have formal education, even though this course of action diverges from the father's mode of transmission, breaks with tradition and most probably with his trade. Break in continuity or continuity in broken times, these are some of the modes of adaptation, of survival or of voluntary and involuntary disappearance of intangible heritage.

Time is an equally important dimension when considering intangible cultural heritage. It appears to be the same when it is never quite the same even for two closely related moments in history. Intangible cultural heritage changes, it is fluid, it is never performed identically, it is at once true to itself and different. This defines its essence, its unity, its specificity. As for authenticity, what characterises intangible cultural heritage is that it does not have one. Its constant 're-creation' (to use a term used by the 2003 Convention, article 2), its differentiated application within a group or society, its diversity of meaning for all and everyone, are at odds with a notion of authenticity conceived as rootedness, faithfulness or fixedness.[3] When today we have to fix it to a material support (iconographic, written, audiovisual or digital) we only make a copy at a given time, because we cannot guess the forms it has taken nor predict those which it will take through time. These different faces of a work, past and future, will perhaps always escape us. Moreover, we may well see the work (musical note, song, dance, literary work, rite, etc.) but we might never know the creative process, particularly if it is a collective work, as is often the case in traditional communities.

Finally, the contemporary forms of 'heritage sensitivity' (Candau 2005: 118) differ from an older attachment to objects, relics, images or buildings belonging to ancestors. This also applies to the elements of intangible cultural heritage. It represents at the same time a difference in scale, given the growth of the heritage phenomenon in the last few decades, and a difference in nature, that is, in motivations and in stakes. The difference in scale is apparent, given the popularity which the heritage of the past enjoys the world over, from the most remote village to the smart offices of UNESCO! The difference in nature is visible in the intrusion of outsiders at a large scale in the relationships between societies and cultures, leading the latter to work towards the preservation of distinction vis-à-vis others and the exploitation of heritage elements in the politics of development, towards tourism for example.

The obstacles which beset identification, protection and promotion of intangible cultural heritage, briefly sketched above, have not prevented nation-states and international organisations from taking a serious interest in these problematic questions. Let us now turn to the macro level, to UNESCO's standardising activity. We shall then present, at a micro level, examples from Morocco, to show all the difficulties, but also all there is to gain from reflecting on the challenges thrown up by action.

From the material to the intangible: A treacherous path

Reflecting on the modes, mechanisms and politics of safeguarding what we call today intangible cultural heritage goes back to the time when the *Convention Concerning the Protection of the World Cultural and Natural Heritage* was adopted by UNESCO at its General Conference in Paris in 1972. Voices were then raised to point out that it was necessary to give humanity's intangible past the attention that it merited. Monumentality, one of the major aspects of the 1972 Convention, soon came under fire, because, from the point of view of a large number of (the then-called) Third World countries, it favoured industrialised nations, particularly Western Europe.[4] The World Heritage List indeed reflects what has, in a French context, justifiably been called 'the monumental abuse' (Debray 1999).

It is only in the second half of the 1980s that this reflexive activity resulted, timidly, in an important document which nevertheless had little impact. The *Recommendation on the Safeguarding of Traditional Culture and Folklore* was adopted on 15 November 1989 by UNESCO's General Conference at its twenty-fifth meeting in Paris. A couple of observations, one conceptual, the other referring to its legal character, must be made on this Recommendation. First, let us consider the notion of 'traditional and popular culture': the notions of 'oral heritage' and 'intangible cultural heritage' were not yet in existence. The Recommendation therefore used the term 'traditional and popular culture', the adjectives reflecting the state of knowledge of the human and social sciences of the time: that is a difficulty in opening up the concept of heritage to embrace the intangible aspect of culture on the one hand, and the imposition of a hierarchy of cultural elements from 'elitist elements' transmitted through formal education to 'popular elements' based on oral traditions on the other. Our second observation concerns the legal status of the Recommendation. A recommendation is defined by UNESCO as an instrument in which:

> the General Conference formulates the general principles and the norms destined to regulate a question at an international level and invites the member states to adopt, in the form of a national law or otherwise, depending on the specific questions treated and the constitutional dispositions of the different member states, measures that aim to implement in the territories under their jurisdiction the principles and norms formulated.[5]

The norms thus recommended to the member states are not subject to ratification. A recommendation, though it is commendably presented in a flexible and supple way, is therefore not mandatory for the member states.

The 1989 Recommendation provides a general framework for the identification and conservation of a form of heritage then called 'traditional and popular culture'. Moreover, the preservation of intangible heritage raises methodological and epistemological questions then not addressed, problems which are to an extent still unresolved today. Protecting intangible heritage also raises complex questions of law, such as the concept of 'intellectual property' which applies in this domain, or the protection of informants or collectors of material. Finally, the Recommendation sets out a number of measures to ensure, through international cooperation, the preservation of expressions from traditional and popular culture.

The Recommendation, however, quickly showed its limitations. Without the mandatory power of a Convention, it had little effect on the conservation of humanity's intangible heritage. It has to be said that expertise in this matter was lacking, among the professionals in the member states as well as among UNESCO's experts. UNESCO consequently started a number of initiatives in favour of this type of cultural heritage. Following this activity, and under the impetus of the Spanish writer Juan Goytisolo who had settled in Morocco and of Moroccan intellectuals, the Division for cultural heritage of UNESCO and the national Moroccan Commission for UNESCO organised an international consultation assembling experts on the conservation of cultural spaces in Marrakech in June 1997. A new concept in cultural anthropology was defined at this meeting: *humanity's oral heritage*. It was recommended, among other recommendations, that an international distinction should be created by UNESCO to promote the 'masterpieces' of such a heritage. As a result of this meeting the Moroccan authorities, supported by many member states, submitted a draft resolution which was adopted by UNESCO's General Conference at its 29th meeting. This resolution was debated by UNESCO's Executive Council in two consecutive sessions (sessions 154 and 155). The Executive Council decided in November 1999 to create an international distinction entitled *Proclamation by UNESCO on Masterpieces of the Oral and Intangible Heritage of Humanity* (hereafter shortened to *Proclamation*).

While preparing an application towards a first proclamation of the Place Jemaâ el Fna as a *Masterpiece of the Oral and Intangible Heritage of Humanity* in 2000–1 and of the Moussem of Tan-Tan in a third proclamation in 2004–5,[6] I was able to experience at first hand the complexity of the concepts put forward by UNESCO's experts when confronted with reality on the ground. In our application, in the section entitled 'Justification for your application' one point is specifically dedicated to the analytical examination of heritage as a 'masterpiece of human creative genius'. What then is a masterpiece? The natural history museum in Lyon addressed this question in an exhibition of 2002. Its designers set apparently simple questions: 'How to define a masterpiece? How to recognise one? Why does an object become a masterpiece?'[7] Without ever answering these questions, they invite the visitor to find his own answers. The exhibition sets side by side objects as different as a contemporary Inuit statue, a Formula 1 racing car seat or an Egyptian sculpture made of black limestone dated to the fifth century BC.

The concept is therefore entirely subjective and it would be pointless to reach a consensus on a definition. This certainly explains why it was called into question by some of UNESCO's member states since 2001, after the first Proclamation was issued. They denounced its elitist character, in a domain where the criteria for distinction of one or another cultural expression is as much a question of taste or of social position than specific to the intrinsic qualities of this expression (see Skounti in press a). It amounts to saying that the distinction of one or other intangible heritage elements is an eminently political decision. Seeing the lists of the first and second proclamations, it is not inappropriate to ask how the criteria adopted by the members of the jury appointed by the Director-General of UNESCO allow progression from a local identification (on the ground) to international distinction (the Proclamation), via national recognition (the decision to apply). The exercise is difficult, and one understands that the jury needs to invoke, in addition to the criteria linked to the content of the heritage element considered, other criteria such as the excellence of its execution or the connection with a cultural 'tradition' as well as other criteria linked to the conservation strategy defined by the agenda of the Proclamation.

Questioning the concept of a 'masterpiece' has, for reasons space precludes to explain here,[8] resulted in the preparation of a new international instrument. UNESCO's General Conference decided, at its 31st meeting in 2001 that a new standardising instrument of mandatory character had to be drafted. UNESCO invited its Director-General to submit a report on intangible cultural heritage as well as a Convention draft project (Resolution 31 C/30, 2 November 2001). At its 164th meeting, the Executive Council decided to invite 'the Director General to convene one or several intergovernmental panels of experts [...] the first to meet in September 2002 in order to define the remit of the draft project of an international convention and to work on the draft of the text' (Decision164 EX/3.5.2, May 2002).

The intergovernmental panel of experts met three times at UNESCO headquarters, the first time from 23 to 27 September 2002, the second time from 24 February to 1 March 2003, and the third time from 2 to 14 June 2003.[9] I was delegated by the Moroccan government to take part in the first and third meetings. A draft *Convention for the Safeguarding of the Intangible Cultural Heritage* was worked out during these three sessions and it was adopted at the organisation's 32nd General Conference in October 2003. The processes involved in drafting the Convention, its problems and the issues at stake were also the subject of a colloquium held in Assilah in Morocco in August 2003, shortly before UNESCO's General Conference adopted the Convention in October of the same year (Internationale de l'Imaginaire 2004). The text, born out of intense, sometimes heated but always constructive, debates departs from the Recommendation of 1989 and the Proclamation of 1999 on a number of issues. Let us mention among them:

● the fact that it is a Convention makes it a mandatory instrument for the member states invited to ratify it;
● the controversial concept of a 'masterpiece' was abandoned in favour of the more appropriate notion of 'intangible cultural heritage';
● national inventories were to form the basis for drawing up lists of intangible cultural heritage;
● UNESCO was to fund the implementation of the Convention.

In summary, some 15 years have elapsed between the *Recommendation on the Safeguarding of Traditional Culture and Folklore* in 1989 and the *Convention for the Safeguarding of the Intangible Cultural Heritage* in 2003. Conceptual developments, changes in methodology and a more determined approach have marked this time. We may however note that the final result does not, on a formal level, differ greatly from the spirit of the World Heritage Convention of 1972. Was it worth waiting so long to adopt an international standardising instrument inspired by a Convention already a generation old? It is true to say that the spirit of the 1972 Convention greatly influenced the 2003 Convention. The members of the expert panel who debated the issues in 2002–3 had it constantly in their mind, even though they did not wish to consider it a source of inspiration, arguing that the two texts belonged to different domains which required their own distinct approaches. But this argument only serves to remind us implicitly of the close ties between material and intangible heritage. The examples from Morocco, to which we shall now turn, illustrate this point very well.

From local to global: two examples from Morocco

In accordance with the Convention of 2003 'the Committee includes in the representative intangible cultural heritage List elements declared "masterpieces of humanity's oral and intangible heritage" before the Convention comes into being' (Article 31). The two elements that Morocco nominated are Place Jemaâ El Fna (Jemaâ El Fna square) in Marrakech and the Moussem of Tan-Tan (fair of Tan-Tan); they figure among 90 such elements covered by this measure worldwide. How did they achieve such distinction? What is at stake today in terms of protection? Our third part will address these questions.

Place Jemaâ El Fna in Marrakech

The identification and consecration of Place Jemaâ el Fna as a masterpiece of the oral and intangible heritage are intimately connected with the programme set up by UNESCO in the wake of the Proclamation. In June 1997 Marrakech hosted a meeting of experts organised jointly by UNESCO, the Moroccan Commission for Education, Science and Culture, and the University of Marrakech. While engaged in discussions over methods of identification and ways of protecting the oral and intangible heritage, the participants could not fail to take notice of this square at the heart of the medina of Marrakech, a place vibrant with cultural activity. It was therefore expected that it should be the subject of the first application made by Morocco. However, its identification at a local level and recognition at a national one owe much to the championing of the square and continued support by an illustrious outsider who had settled in Morocco, the Spanish writer Juan Goytisolo. His writings and personal engagement did much to illustrate the heritage of this square and he chaired the first Proclamation jury convened by UNESCO's Director-General in 2000. The value that Moroccans place on the heritage of this space undeniably passes through Goytisolo's vision. Place Jemaâ El Fna is also relevant because it is at the origin of a distinction made by UNESCO when defining two major characteristics of 'humanity's oral and intangible heritage' according to the Proclamation's official text: the cultural space[10] on the one hand, and the form of cultural expression on the other.

Following the Proclamation of 2001, the question of how to protect the Place Jemaâ El Fna according to the action plan drawn up in Morocco's application needed to be addressed, bearing in mind that there was no precedent for such a project. While we could rely on some experience in the protection of material heritage, we were largely unaware of the difficulties we would encounter when attempting to protect intangible heritage; furthermore we were dealing with an urban space which had been used for centuries as both the container of and the backdrop to this intangible heritage. The French ethnologist Michel Leiris (1950) was right to point out that we should not confuse conservation with protection. The management of Place Jemaâ El Fna came up against two major obstacles.

Place Jemaâ El Fna as container: some stumbling blocks

The square is located inside the medina within the city of Marrakech, close to the Koutoubia mosque and the souks. Together they form a triangle, the living heart of the city. This triangle reflects its three fundamental functions: urban life, sacred space and trade. The square is a space dedicated to transition and urban integration. It is also a space for 'spontaneous' creativity, a space which invites to performance, to music and dance, a space for outdoor eating and refreshment. The 'square' is a triangle prolonged by a long arm which extends eastwards to the Guessabine mosque. It is bounded to the south by the quarters of Riyad Zitoun El Qdim and Arset El Bilk, to the west by the Fhel Zefriti quarter, and to the north by those of Bab Fteuh and the souks. The square is surrounded by shops, cafes, restaurants, hotels and offices.

This space has seen multiple transformations over the centuries. Yet it has always retained an open aspect, set within a broader urban space, the medina. The Place Jamaâ El Fna has been a national monument since 1922 (classified on 21 July 1922) and benefits from a royal edict of 21 July 1922 protecting its artistic qualities. These texts have made it possible to limit the damage around the square, without, however, completely halting it. The building height of 8.5 m prescribed by the first legal document has not always been respected, even though the minarets of the nearby mosques (with the exception of Koutoubia which goes back to the late twelfth century) are not tall. The local authorities have undertaken, following a meeting in March 1999, to remedy this situation, but up to now, no municipal edict has come into being. The same goes for the artistic protection of the neighbourhood of the square, which has seen the growth of 'visual pollution' in the form of disharmonious painted and light signs or inappropriate urban furniture, all put up illegally. The fact that the medina of Marrakech was listed in 1985 as a UNESCO World Heritage site did not change anything. As I point out elsewhere (Skounti 2004), this listing will have contributed to the protection of the urban fabric of the medina (which includes Place Jemaâ el Fna) only *by default*.

Nevertheless, the fact that the square was declared a masterpiece of humanity's oral and intangible heritage has contributed towards realising the urgency of its conservation. The town council has put in place new measures since 2001, within a programme aimed at maintaining and embellishing the city of Marrakech. Though the measures concerning the square have met with varied reactions, it appears that the concerns of an increasing number of citizens are finally beginning to be taken seriously. Regulating the circulation of cars was a welcome measure, though alternative arrangements for transporting elderly, infirm or disabled people out of the sector or towards the medina have not yet been put in place. Moped and bicycle traffic also remains unregulated: this anarchic situation can be dangerous for pedestrians. Nevertheless, pollution from car emissions, which had reached alarming proportions, has been brought down to acceptable levels.

The decision to pave the square can also be seen from different points of view. On the positive side, the aspect of the square, after decades of laying tarmac, is improved. When the agency in charge of water and electricity (Régie autonome de distribution d'eau et d'électricité de Marrakech or RADEEMA) was carrying out repair works in 2002–3, it was possible to observe several layers of tarmac. Unfortunately structures and artefacts (wall fragments and pottery shreds) uncovered during these works could not be examined archaeologically and the opportunity to shed light on the development of the square was therefore lost. Paving with sets – reversible blocks set in a thick layer of sand – appears to have been a positive move overall;

connection to the electricity network was carried out at the same time, which benefited open-air food stalls.

Place Jemaâ El Fna's content: more pitfalls

The square provides a setting for a huge repertory of oral and intangible heritage spectacles for a variety of tastes and people: telling tales, playing music, achieving trances, snake charming, showing monkeys, selling herbs, street preaching, performing acrobatics, magic, fortune telling or reading cards (Skounti and Tebbaa 2005). These customs reflect an art conveyed through the spoken word, gesture, costume, sound, and so forth. They are imbued with a diffuse religious content, expressed more formally in the preaching of morals and wisdom.

As rich as these manifestations of the oral and intangible heritage are, as varied are the geographic, social and cultural origins of its performers. Indeed the imperial town of Marrakech has acted as a magnet for neighbouring populations, be they Arab or Amazigh speaking. Place Jemaâ El Fna thus plays a dual role: that of integration and that of perpetuating cultural specificities. Language reflects such diversity: oral literature, among other forms of expression, is expressed in Berber, in classical Arabic and Moroccan Arabic, in a language that also borrows from other languages such as French, Spanish and English.

The performers' know-how shows perfect mastery of the art of story (re-) telling, seducing the public and jostling for position among pairs, having eliminated unfair competition. This is precisely what makes the value of Place Jemaâ El Fna as a space and as a manifestation of the cultural expressions that take place there.

Several dozen people, mostly male, perform in this space, which accommodates:

- herbalists, henna 'tattoo' artists, fortune tellers, practitioners of traditional medicine;
- performers or *hlaïqia* who offer spectacles of music and song in Berber or Moroccan Arabic, preachers, story tellers, acrobats, animal tamers, and so forth.

The square also provides a space for many traders: sellers of herbs, orange juice, dried fruit, food stall-holders, and so on. The food offered in the 'biggest open air restaurant in the world' allows visitors to sample traditional and modern Moroccan dishes as well as recipes particular to the region of Marrakech, such as the *tanjia* (meat cooked in an earthenware jar set in the ash of a hammam's fireplace) (Skounti and Tebbaa 2005).

A plan of action to safeguard the Place Jemaâ el Fna proposed by the Moroccan state has benefited from funds made available in 2004 by a

UNESCO Japanese deposit fund. It aims to revitalise intangible heritage through a number of measures that promote its owners and preserve their knowledge and know-how. This programme, which was carried out by the Moroccan Ministry of Culture and the UNESCO Bureau in Rabat, resulted in the publication of a bilingual French–Arabic book distributed to the schools of Marrakech and its region. It also resulted in research on the transmission of knowledge and know-how (see Skounti and Tebbaa 2006), and in setting up a school liaison programme which invited story tellers from the square to tell their tales in schools and organised drawing competitions for pupils on the theme of the square. It also aims to preserve the memory of the square through collecting written, iconographic and audio-visual documents and by setting up a travelling exhibition and a website.

If programmes aimed at protecting the urban framework and the material conservation of memory are relatively easy to set up, the social rights of the performers and the transmission of their knowledge and know-how are a completely different ball game. First, it is difficult to channel benefits such as pensions, allowances, health cover, etc. towards performers who operate in a context of urban poverty. It would attract too many people and would harm creativity. Conversely, to limit the number of performers through a system of professional cards risks denying the (relative) freedom of the square to people who have always nourished it with new blood. Any project that aims to set up a system of social rights will come up against this dilemma. Furthermore, such a system implies legal and administrative measures that are difficult to provide, as so many different departments are concerned (culture, social affairs, health, finance ...). Such a question may find a solution in a project, the *Human Living Treasures*[11] set up by UNESCO in the Maghreb region.[12]

UNESCO understands transmission to be the contribution of the person recognised as a 'Human living treasure' in exchange for certain privileges. It is difficult to conceive a single system that would suit all categories of intangible cultural heritage (Skounti 2005). If the art of snake charming, monkey taming or acrobatics can be reasonably easily transmitted, it is much more difficult to guarantee the transmission of tales (a genre which is particularly threatened), or fortune telling, or a comic performance. An elderly story teller might have to take on a much younger apprentice, who would have gone to school and become familiar with modern media (television, video, film, internet ...),[13] with all that this implies in terms of references which would be totally different from those of the master's generation. Fortune telling relies on 'professional secrets', which its practitioners are reluctant to reveal, let alone pass on. Comic spectacles depend on individual performances that are difficult to teach. There are so many 'unique' 'Living human treasures' (such as Charkaoui) that it would be futile to look for a blanket solution for transmission. Some of the square's intangible cultural heritage will have to be sacrificed in order to preserve some elements which a system, in whatever form adopted, may be able to support. For the remainder, our only tools are those that already exist in heritage conservation: archiving, documenting, recording in all possible forms.

Finally, the square will continue to feed the nostalgia of the people of Marrakech. In our meetings, seminars, workshops and informal contacts, many people complained about the 'disappearance' of their square. It is hard not to share their feelings, to sympathise with them, to regret a square that has lost its nature, has been degraded, has vanished. People who have known the square two or three decades ago feel sorrow for a space that has been defaced and yet remains attractive, a space which awakens unfathomable emotions. Looking a bit closer, it becomes clear that the people who, justifiably, express such feelings are thinking about *their* square, the square that they had got to know in the first decades of their life. It will always be thus, as long as the Place Jemaâ el Fna exists. All will depend on our position, on the generation we belong to and on the knowledge we bring to this changing space. Moreover, the square cannot be reduced to the sum of images that individuals who have frequented it or who frequent it now have of it. If one were to adopt a phenomenological approach, the square will exist as long as there are performers able to attract a public, whatever form of entertainment is offered. Taken to its limits, it means that even if the story tellers illustrate their tales with graphic or audiovisual reconstructions, even if computers enhance performances, the square will always live, it will just have to adapt to the conditions of production and reception that a global society throws up. The square is destined to change indefinitely. The challenge for conservation is not the form that performances take, but their survival.

The Moussem of Tan-Tan

At the Moussem of Tan-Tan, matters took a different course. This site was not on the list of cultural spaces or forms of cultural expression that Morocco was intending to present during this decade. In 2004, the Moroccan Ministry of Culture had prepared an application for another moussem, the Moussem of Sidi Hmad Ou Lemghenni, better known as the Moussem of the Betrothal of Imilchil, located in the eastern high Atlas Mountains. It was while preparing this dossier that I was asked, in September of that year, to prepare a new application for the Moussem of Tan-Tan; it all happened within a month and attracted media coverage commensurate with the political will that surrounded its (re)birth.[14] Why was the application changed? The answer is complex, but the decision certainly owes something to a suggestion, in all due forms, by another outsider, Kitin Munoz, a Spaniard born in Sidi Ifni in the Sahara, illustrious adventurer, honorary ambassador of Morocco in Spain and a UNESCO goodwill ambassador. Here we have another example of an outsider's view, which met with a political will to reinvigorate a cultural manifestation that was dying out. The sequence could be reversed, but it seems that a necessary condition of recognition is an outside view.

The site of Tan-Tan is located on the western coastal road used by caravans of traders who travel between Guelmim, Tafnidilt and Tan-Tan in Morocco, Atar in Mauritania, Timbuktu in Mali and Senegal. It is also a meeting point for nomadic people and their herds of dromedaries, sheep and goats in the summer and autumn; it provides shelter from the desert heat, access to the sea, abundant water and grazing. The moussem started as a place of spontaneous, but regular, meeting around a well, located on the edge of the nearby wadi of Ben Khlil where the future town of Tan-Tan, then only a place name, was to grow. According to local tradition the word *tan-tan* has its origins in an onomatopoeia which recalls the drip-drip of water at the bottom of the well.

The gathering of the nomads from the Sahara and other peoples from north-western Africa on the site of Tan-Tan is part and parcel of the nomadic calendar: it fulfils the need for dispersed pastoral populations to meet once a year to exchange, in the widest sense of the term, material and intangible products in an enjoyable atmosphere. Dressed in their finest clothes, they buy, sell, feast, marry, play, sing, dance, recite poetry and tell stories in the *hassanya* language, exchange news, talk about the weather, plants, medicine, rituals, and so forth.

These gatherings have taken the form of a moussem (locally known as an *almouggar*),[15] that is, an annual fair, fulfilling economic, social and cultural functions. These fairs have taken place since 1963, when the first fair was organised to celebrate local traditions and cultural diversity, in a spirit of exchange, meeting and pleasure. The moussem period is, so to speak, the nomads' annual holiday. Clearly for the Moroccan authorities, these gatherings were to be incorporated into the 're-insertion' programme for the western Sahara, under Spanish occupation, which was sealed by the Green March initiated by King Hassan II in 1975. Originally linked to Mohamed Laghdef, a resistant to Spanish colonisation who died in 1960, the Moussem of Tan-Tan gradually became a politico-cultural manifestation. The Moussem could not take place after 1979, because of the conflict between Morocco and the Polisario (a political movement claiming the independence of the Sahara) that lasted between 1976 and 1991. An attempt to revive the Moussem was made in 1982, but it was not to last.

The Moussem of Tan-Tan showcases an assemblage of materials and oral and intangible traditions which represents the intangible heritage of the Hassani nomadic populations who occupy the entire Western Sahara, from Morocco, Algeria, Mauritania, to Mali and Senegal. All participate in creating the identity of this form of cultural expression, the annual nomadic fair; they create the framework and the content, without which the fair would be just an empty shell. Black tents (living spaces), camels (for transport, milk and meat), horses (transport for heads of wealthy families) occupy prominent places, but space is also given to music, to Hassani poetry, to story telling, games, crafts, costume and traditional medicine.

Given the political situation of the Saharan conflict, applying for the Moussem of Tan-Tan to be declared a masterpiece of the oral and intangible heritage was quite evidently a difficult task. Granted, the application was made well after the 1991 cease-fire, but it nevertheless led to protests by the Polisario and its supporters in Algeria, giving rise to a kind of politico-symbolic competition. UNESCO had to exercise great care when considering an application with an explicit political agenda. But the visit to the first revived Moussem by UNESCO's Director-General, Koïchiro Matsuura, accompanied by Prince Moulay Rachid of Morocco and a large delegation of UNESCO ambassadors, as well as numerous journalists from the international press, helped dispel the anxieties of the Moroccan authorities. Yet, it was not all plain sailing. The section of UNESCO charged with intangible cultural heritage kept a tight rein on procedures, requesting further information on several occasions. Without going into details, let us mention one question asked by UNESCO's section, which illustrates very well its apprehensions concerning the inclusion of a politically loaded element of intangible heritage: was the fair rooted in a cultural tradition or was it a creation? Morocco's answer was inspired by the spirit of the Proclamation emphasised by the Convention of 2003, that is, that the elements of intangible cultural heritage are part of a permanent cycle of 're-creation' and that the Moussem of Tan-Tan, interrupted for a while, was revived within a rooted cultural 'tradition'.

The challenge for the Moussem of Tan-Tan is less about the form it takes as it comes back to life after decades of interruption, than about the conservation of the intangible cultural heritage that constitutes its framework. How to nurture among the populations of the region the enthusiasm first shown after its revival? What measures could be put in place to ensure its survival and viability? The management plan proposes a number of points of action. In brief there are two essential points: (i) a fixed date is set to ensure that the fair is held annually, so that it becomes part of the calendar of a population which has become largely sedentary and urban but which hankers after a former way of life; (ii) a strategy aimed at conserving the memory of this cultural element must be drawn up; it has to be based on concrete actions and institutional as well as legal measures which will identify, recognise and value its owners and their knowledge and know-how. Although the Moussem has now been held four times in its new form, the management plan has not yet been applied on the ground. A programme is currently being worked out between the Moroccan Ministry of Culture and the UNESCO Bureau in Rabat and should be implemented this year.

Conclusion

Intangible cultural heritage has recently become one of the major challenges facing the construction of local, regional and national identities. UNESCO has taken up the mantle on an international level and is attempting to find the most appropriate means of securing its safeguard. The *Recommendation on the Safeguarding of Traditional Culture and Folklore* adopted in 1989 soon showed its limitations. Gradually progress was made towards a programme that led to the *Proclamation of Masterpieces of the Oral and Intangible Heritage of Humanity* of 1999. Although this programme has initiated a debate and has led to three proclamations identifying and recognising 90 elements of the intangible cultural heritage, it was found wanting in respect of the inappropriate use of the concept of 'masterpieces' and in its non-mandatory character. UNESCO consequently undertook to prepare a new standardising instrument, the *Convention for the Safeguarding of the Intangible Cultural Heritage* that was adopted in 2003 and came into force in 2006.

UNESCO's standardising activity aims to support and help member states and the communities who own intangible cultural heritage to preserve this heritage, which becomes *de facto* part of the heritage of the whole of humanity. Such a process takes place within a context of ongoing heritage creation; in fact, this process can sometimes trigger or feed the latter. Socio-economic difficulties and cultural changes facing the groups and communities engaged in this process exacerbate a latent malaise, causing confusion and sometimes even anxiety. However, this gradual detachment from what was up to then considered part of one's own identity motivates a new quest for self. This quest is never-ending, giving rise to new hopes and sometimes new illusions. What within a culture (in the anthropological sense of the term) was ripe for new functions or meaning, as it would otherwise disappear, is perceived as cultural heritage worth preserving. Those who act in this sense, whoever they are, act within a *heritage time*, where competition is severe and challenges multiple. An *authentic illusion* is created because these agents are convinced that they are taking possession of, and prolonging, the work of their ancestors, whereas in fact the challenge is not so much the past, but the present and above all the future.

Notes

1 Translated from the original French by Dr Madeleine Hummler.
2 For example, Moroccans say: *'herfet bouk la ighalbouk'* – '[be faithful to] your father's trade [or your likes] will overtake you!'
3 To give an example from a completely different domain, the Islamic habitus is taken as the reproduction of the time of the Prophet. This is a modern phenomenon, part of the contemporary history of Moslem societies or of societies containing communities belonging to this religion. The conviction that they are reproducing the Prophet's precepts, perfectly anchored in the minds of the followers of this movement, is symptomatic of the 'authentic illusion', which occupies us here.
4 While taking part in 2002 and 2003, as a delegate for Morocco, in the sessions working towards the 2003 Convention, it was not rare to hear government experts from southern countries describe the instrument being drafted as a revenge from these countries on the 'monopoly exercised by the North on the 1972 Convention!' The Global Strategy put in place by the World Heritage Committee since 1994 tries to redress this imbalance by a

series of measures aiming to produce, in time, a 'representative and balanced World Heritage List'.

5 See http://portal.unesco.org/fr/ev.phpURL_ID=23772&URL_DO=DO_TOPIC&URL _SECTION=201.html

6 UNESCO proceeded with three Proclamations within this programme in 2001, 2003 and 2005. Morocco filed two applications: one at the first Proclamation, the other at the third. The 2003 Convention includes a provision that allows it to incorporate the 90 *Masterpieces of the Oral and Intangible Heritage of Humanity* in the Representative List (Article 31) which it programmed (Article 16). The way this integration was to proceed was hotly debated at the first extraordinary meeting of the Intergovernmental Committee on ICH, which was convened in Chengdu, China, in May 2007, given the complexity of such a procedure.

7 See website of the French daily newspaper *L'Humanité*: www.humanite.presse.fr/journal/ 2002-02-20.

8 See UNESCO's official documents concerning the drafting of the text on the 2003 Convention. See: www.unesco.org.

9 The second was attended by a member of the Moroccan Delegation to UNESCO.

10 Though they are fewer than the elements recognised as forms of cultural expression, the list of declared masterpieces contains other 'cultural spaces' such as the island of Kihnu in Estonia, the cultural space of Sosso-Bala in Guinea and the district of Boysun in Uzbekistan.

11 A number of countries (Japan, South Korea, the Philippines, Romania, France, Mali, Mauritania) have experimented with this system and made recommendations to UNESCO's other member states. The system consists of identifying persons who detain knowledge and/or know-how within the non-material cultural heritage domain. These persons are recognised by the state during an official ceremony and certain advantages (which vary depending on the state) are conferred in exchange for transmitting knowledge to young apprentices.

12 I was commissioned by the UNESCO Bureau in Rabat and the Moroccan Ministry of Culture to carry out the Moroccan study within this programme. See Skounti (2005), which can be accessed on request to the UNESCO Bureau in Rabat.

13 Juan Goytisolo emphasises the rich links which exist between primary oral traditions and other forms of non-oral information and inspiration in his speech opening the meeting of the First Declaration of *Masterpieces of the Oral and Intangible Heritage of Humanity* (see Tebbaa *et al.* 2003: 11–13).

14 The Moussem of Tan-Tan, known locally as Almouggar Tan-Tan, had not been held in an organised form for two decades. The last moussem took place in 1979 and an unsuccessful attempt was made in 1982, according to local information. In 2004, thousands of inhabitants of the Sahara took part; it was opened by Prince Moulay Rachid, who was accompanied by the Director-General of UNESCO, a delegation of ambassadors from the organisation and other personalities. For moussems in Morocco in general, see Reysoo (1991).

15 This Berber word means literally a meeting, and by extension an annual fair around the grave of a saint.

Bibliography

Appadurai, A. (1996 [2005]) *Après le colonialisme. Les conséquences culturelles de la globalisation* (French translation of *Modernity at Large. Cultural Dimensions of Globalization*, 1996), Paris: Payot and Rivages.

Candau, Joël (2005) *Anthropologie de la mémoire*, Paris: Armand Colin.

Debray, R. (1999) *L'Abus monumental* (Actes des Entretiens du Patrimoine, Palais de Chaillot, Novembre 1998), Paris: Fayard.

Hobsbawm, E. and Ranger, T. (ed.) (1983 [2006]) *L'Invention de la tradition* (French translation of *The Invention of Tradition*, 1983), Paris: Editions Amsterdam.

Internationale de l'Imaginaire (2004) *Le Patrimoine culturel immatériel. Les enjeux, les problématiques, les pratiques*, 17, Nouvelle Série, Paris: Babel, Maison des Cultures du Monde.

Leiris, M. (1950) 'L'ethnographie devant le colonialisme', *Les Temps modernes*, 6ème année, 58: 357–74.

Reysoo, F. (1991) *Pèlerinages au Maroc*, Paris/Neuchâtel: Maison des sciences de l'Homme/Musée d'ethnologie.

Skounti, A. (2004) 'Marrakech: pauvreté versus «élitisation». Processus de patrimonialisation, pauvreté et gestion de la médina', *Patrimoine et Développement durable dans les villes historiques du Maghreb*, Rabat: Bureau de l'UNESCO, pp. 143–56.

—— (2005) unpublished, *Le patrimoine culturel immatériel au Maroc. Promotion et valorisation des trésors humains vivants*, étude réalisée pour l'UNESCO. Rabat: Bureau de l'UNESCO.

—— (in press a) 'La notion de patrimoine culturel immatériel: cas de la Place Jemaâ el Fna (Intervention aux Journées d'étude sur la' *Préservation, revitalisation et promotion de la Place Jemaâ el Fna*, organisées par l'Association Place Jemaâ el Fna Patrimoine Oral de l'humanité, Marrakech, 11–12 October 2004.

—— (in press b) 'Le «local» redéfini par la patrimonialisation. Exemples du Maroc', *L'Altérité et la reconstruction de la société locale*, Colloque international organisé par le Laboratoire d'Ethnologie et de Sociologie comparative de Nanterre, l'Université Hassan II de Mohammedia et le Centre Jacques Berque, Rabat-Mohammedia, 14–22 April 2005.

Skounti, A. and Tebbaa, O. (2005) *Place Jemaâ El Fna. Patrimoine culturel Immatériel de Marrakech, du Maroc et de l'humanité*, Rabat: Bureau de l'UNESCO.

—— (2006) unpublished, 'Etude du profil sociologique des acteurs de la Place Jemaâ El Fna et de la transmission du patrimoine culturel immatériel' (Etude réalisée pour l'UNESCO), Rabat: Bureau multi-pays.

Tebbaa, O., El Faiz, M. and Nadim, H. (2003) *Jemaâ el Fna*, Casablanca: La Croisée des Chemins and Paris: Paris-Méditerranée.

UNESCO (2003) *Convention pour la Sauvegarde du Patrimoine culturel immatériel*.

Chapter 5

Intangible heritage as a list

From masterpieces to representation

Valdimar Tr. Hafstein

Perhaps the most controversial issues in the negotiation of the *Convention for the Safeguarding of the Intangible Cultural Heritage* concerned the creation, designation, and purpose of its lists. The final text provides for three types of lists: a Representative List of the Intangible Cultural Heritage of Humanity, a List of Intangible Cultural Heritage in Need of Urgent Safeguarding, and national inventories of intangible heritage. The first of these, in particular, is a compromise solution reached after intense confrontations between those national delegates who wanted to create a merit-based 'List of Treasures' or 'List of Masterpieces' similar to the World Heritage List, those who would rather have seen an inclusive universal inventory of traditional practices, and those who wanted no list at all. In the final text of the Convention, the provisions for the Representative List are vague enough to postpone this debate until the present time when state parties are revisiting it.

In what follows, I analyse the arguments put forward by delegates in the debate on listing – from incentive and promotion value to divisiveness and hierarchisation – and I argue that in fact these go to the heart of heritage practices, which are always and inevitably selective. The system of heritage, in other words, is structured on exclusion: it gives value to certain things rather than others with reference to an assortment of criteria that can only ever be indeterminate. In this respect, heritage and lists are not unlike one another: both depend on selection, both decontextualise their objects from their immediate surroundings and recontextualise them with reference to other things designated or listed. It is hardly surprising, then, that listing seems constantly to accompany heritage making. Heritage lists fuse aesthetic, ethical, and administrative concerns in a rather unique fashion. They celebrate the virtues of particular populations while fuelling a cultural contest among them. Making a people visible to itself and their practices to the world at large, such lists are ultimately designed to channel funds and attention to the task of safeguarding. Once they have been made and are available for circulation, however, lists tend to take on a life of their own; they can be put to uses quite unlike – even diametrically opposed to – those their creators had in mind. The World Heritage List is a case in point, with tourism gradually taking precedence over preservation as its driving concern and principal context of use. It remains to be seen to what uses the Representative List will be put.

Masterpieces, treasures, irony

As a member of the Icelandic delegation to UNESCO, I observed and took part in the third session of the *Intergovernmental Meeting of Experts on the Preliminary Draft Convention for the Safeguarding of the Intangible Cultural Heritage* that took place in June 2003 (the two previous sessions were held in September 2002 and February 2003). It met in a large conference room in the basement of UNESCO Headquarters at Place Fontenoy in Paris and the task it set itself was to finish the work on this new Convention in order to propose it to UNESCO's General Conference for adoption.[1]

In advance of the June session, the UNESCO Secretariat distributed to delegates a draft that they themselves had negotiated at the previous session (and a smaller intersessional committee had refined between February and June). In one of its articles, this draft Convention proposed to create a 'List of Treasures of the World Intangible Cultural Heritage', or alternatively a 'List of Masterpieces of Intangible Cultural Heritage'. The first paragraph of this article provided that this list should be established, kept up to date, and published in order to 'ensure better visibility of the intangible cultural heritage, to promote awareness of its significance and encourage dialogue' (UNESCO CLT-2003/CONF.206/3, Appendix II: 9).

The trajectory of this idea may be traced to a formal proposal from the Korean Republic in 1993 to establish a UNESCO system of Living Cultural Properties. Later that year, the Executive Board of UNESCO responded with a resolution (UNESCO 142 EX/18) in which it invited member states to establish, where appropriate, a system of Living Human Treasures in their respective territories (UNESCO 2002: 8).[2] The Korean proposal advocated that, as part of this new programme, UNESCO would establish 'its own Committee on Living Human Treasures, whose functions are similar to those of the World Heritage Committee'; that the Committee, once established, would 'institute a World Living Human Treasures List, similar to the World Heritage List'; and suggested that, 'in order to institute this system, a convention on living human treasures may be needed' (UNESCO 142 EX/18: 2).

This comparison to the World Heritage Convention is key for under-standing recent developments in this area within UNESCO. The *Convention Concerning the Protection of the World Cultural and Natural Heritage* (its official title) was adopted by the General Conference in 1972 and has been one of UNESCO's great successes. In terms of the number of states that have signed on to it, the World Heritage Convention ranks second among all interna-tional Conventions; only the *Convention on the Rights of the Child* has more signatories (Engelhardt 2002: 29). The associated World Heritage List has been a great public relations coup for UNESCO and is no doubt what the organisation is best known for in many parts of the world.

Korea's proposed world list of living human treasures was, as their proposal made clear, modelled on the World Heritage List and its associated legal instrument and executive committee. Thus, Korea's proposal was to build on UNESCO's experience with world heritage, apparently in hopes of sharing in its success in that domain. In resolution 142 EX/18, cited above, UNESCO's Executive Board welcomes this proposal and 'expresses a hope that if the national list proves successful, UNESCO could, as a next step, institute a world list' (quoted in UNESCO 2002: 51). Four years later, in 1997, the General Conference adopted a resolution creating that list: the *Proclamation of Masterpieces of the Oral and Intangible Heritage of Humanity*.

Although modelled on the World Heritage List, the Proclamation of Masterpieces paled in comparison: it did not rest on a Convention, was not equipped with an intergovernmental executive committee, and no financial resources were committed to it by member states at the General Conference. Instead, the Proclamation sought legitimacy in the failed 1989 *Recommendation for the Safeguarding of Folklore and Traditional Culture*, relied on an international jury appointed by the Director-General, and was altogether dependent on voluntary contributions for funding. It was, in other words, a relatively weak programme established on a slight foundation (the unsuccessful Recommendation), with questionable authority (a jury appointed by the Director-General rather than an intergovernmental committee elected by member states), and with limited and unreliable resources at its disposal.

In the negotiations that led to the establishment of the World Heritage Convention in 1972, the question of whether to create lists as instruments of the Convention was hotly debated (Titchen 1995: 147–51). The negotiations focused on the creation of a trust fund for conserving the world's outstanding heritage, as an expression of international solidarity in heritage conservation, and not on producing lists of such heritage. In fact, an intergovernmental meeting of experts in 1969 declared that it would not be useful to establish an 'international register' of monuments, groups of buildings, and sites of universal value (although some participants felt that a 'limited list' of immovable heritage in danger would be helpful to 'alert world opinion') (Titchen 1995: 148). The World Heritage List of cultural and natural heritage of 'outstanding universal value' was only added late in the game: in a reversal of its previous opposition and in the face of resistance from some delegations, the United States government threatened to withdraw its support for the Convention unless a World Heritage List was established (Titchen 1995: 150–1; Schuster 2002: 2).

By creating the Proclamation of Masterpieces in 1997, UNESCO's General Conference brought into being the list that Korea had proposed in 1993, although it was by no means equivalent yet to the World Heritage List. The Korean proposal advocated the creation of a committee for this list and it suggested that 'in order to institute this system, a convention on living human treasures may be needed' (UNESCO 142 EX/18: 2). When UNESCO's Director-General, Koïchiro Matsuura, set in motion preliminary work to assess the need for a normative instrument in this field, this seems to have been prompted by the need already identified by Korea to supplement the world list with a committee and a Convention. In his preface to the first Proclamation brochure from 2001, Matsuura explains that the Proclamation programme is the first of 'two complementary and parallel lines of action'. It addresses short-term goals, whereas 'the second, the preparation of a normative instrument for the safeguarding of intangible heritage, has long-term objectives' (UNESCO 2001a: 2). 'In time', the Director-General asserts, 'these two programmes will inevitably become even more effective by their combination' (UNESCO 2001a: 3).[3]

The first Proclamation of the Oral and Intangible Heritage of Humanity was launched with great ceremony on 18 May 2001. Much like the subsequent ones, it received a mixed response. Local media in countries whose cultural traditions were recognised as masterpieces of humanity's heritage ran congratulatory stories. The Proclamation met with less enthusiasm, however, not to say indifference, in other contexts. Thus, it is safe to assume that Cullen Murphy's ironic tour-de-force in the *Atlantic Monthly* ruffled feathers among the Proclamation's proponents. Expressing his initial delight with the initiative and his sense of anticipation while waiting for the first announcement of what, after all, would surely be 'the intangible equivalent of Angkor Wat or the Acropolis, of Tikal or the Taj Mahal', Murphy had found that, '[a]las, the list, promulgated at UNESCO's Paris headquarters, proved to be a little underwhelming'. 'The overall impression', he explains, 'is of a program listing for public television at 3:00 AM'. Happily, however, all was not lost, for UNESCO still had an opportunity to 'inject vitality and ambition into the enterprise' in the second Proclamation of Masterpieces in 2003. Cullen Murphy goes on to suggest 'some candidates of real distinction' to add to the list, including the white lie ('its social utility is hard to overestimate'), the passive voice ('a conceptual space that at some point shelters everyone'), the space between things ('a crucial but intangible component of all relationships'), self-fulfilling prophecies, silence, and irony (Murphy 2001).

Murphy's candidates highlight at least a couple of peculiarities in the Proclamation of Masterpieces. It would be a prejudiced jury that did not concede that irony is indeed a masterpiece of the human spirit. What might disqualify its candidature is that its continued practice is hardly under threat. As such, it fails to constitute heritage for it does not justify intervention. The other factor that stands in the way of irony's proclamation as a masterpiece of the oral and intangible heritage of humanity is that no community or state can claim irony as its own – it is not territorial, and there is no delimited population that identifies with it.[4] Paradoxically, then, irony (and the rest of Murphy's candidates) is too common to be proclaimed as the common heritage of humanity.

Discussing the merits of this programme, a UNESCO administrator explained to me that for a country like Zambia,[5] which is not good at sports nor distinguished in 'high art', the importance of the recognition that the Proclamation of Masterpieces would afford should not be underestimated. The Proclamation gives pride to communities, he emphasised, but it also measures out responsibilities to governments. The Proclamation is not only a list, he stressed, it is also a programme: behind the list is a plan of action for safeguarding the proposed items.

As a mechanism of display, the list of proclaimed heritage parallels various other public spectacles of international scale. It is a recent arrival among a range of instruments by which 'a people is made visible to itself and its virtues celebrated in a way which put them in competition with other nations' (Bennett 2001: 16), much like world exhibitions, the World Cup, and Miss World. It can be characterised as a sort of cultural Olympics (cf. Turtinen 2000: 20–1). In this, it follows the example of the World Heritage List, and like world heritage it is designed to harness national pride in the service of safeguarding (see Turtinen 2006).

In spite of the Director-General's forceful encouragement, the Intergovernmental Meeting of Experts was torn over the question of lists. In this, it resembled its precursor that drafted the World Heritage Convention. Resistance was apparent from the outset and had been voiced in no uncertain terms at the meeting's previous sessions. In fact, a reunion of national UNESCO commissions from the European Union had previously found that 'the Proclamation of Masterpieces … which relies on the establishment of a list, is not a convincing precedent' for a list-based approach to safeguarding intangible heritage (EU National Commissions for UNESCO 2002).

By the time the third session rolled around in June 2003, it had become clear, however, that there was no avoiding the list: a considerable majority of member states seemed to back the creation of lists, in the plural, as central instruments of the Convention. A consensus had been reached at the previous session in February to provide for both national inventories of intangible heritage and an international Register of Intangible Cultural Heritage in Need of Urgent Safeguarding. The precise nature and content of a second international list of a more general nature was, however, still up for debate. Many delegations previously opposed to such a list had now shifted their position to regain diplomatic footing. Some abandoned their resistance altogether, picking instead battles where they stood a fighting chance, while others set out to create a list that would at least be as unobjectionable as possible.

Registers, lists, inventories

On Monday morning, 2 June 2003, as we waited for other delegations to sit down and for the third session of this meeting of experts to begin, the head of the Icelandic delegation, Guðný Helgadóttir, filled me in on the background to the meeting. She explained that the committee was sharply divided between those states that wanted a list of masterpieces, based on the *Proclamation of Masterpieces of the Oral and Intangible Heritage of Humanity*, and other states that preferred to see an inclusive 'register' without reference to aesthetic criteria. Japan spearheaded the former group. I later heard through the grapevine that the Japanese delegation was busy taking other delegates to lunch. All kinds of lobbying and negotiations were taking place behind the well-lit scenes of the meeting room at Place Fontenoy, out of earshot from microphones and multilingual headsets.

Someone had placed a small desk in the foyer that the delegates passed through on their way to the meeting room. On top of the desk lay two large stacks of paper. One contained a proposal submitted by Grenada, Saint Lucia, Barbados, and Saint-Vincent and the Grenadines, for a new article creating an International Register of the Intangible Cultural Heritage, in place of the List of Treasures/Masterpieces foreseen in the draft Convention. The other stack was taller and contained, on four stapled pages, an explanatory note in 50 paragraphs, laying out objections to the List of Treasures/Masterpieces and calling attention to the advantages of this proposal for an International Register.

The Caribbean proposal distinguished itself from the List of Treasures/Masterpieces foreseen in the draft Convention chiefly in that it proposed to do away with the mechanism of selection. Inscription on the International Register of the Intangible Cultural Heritage would, according to this proposal, 'be made at the request of the State Party concerned'. The only conditions for inscription would be technical requirements for 'complete documentation' of the heritage, including a description of any 'national legislation which concerns it', a 'plan of action for its safeguarding', and 'identification of the custodian(s) of this heritage'.

The explanatory note that accompanied the proposal identifies at least three major interrelated problems with the List of Treasures. First, the note argued that the list 'bears such a close resemblance to the World Heritage List that it is difficult to tell them apart'.[6] Second, it claimed that a selective list based on criteria of excellence would be likely to divert the aim of the new Convention, 'its underlying objective becoming inscription on the list rather than safeguarding'. And third, such a list would be 'subjective and elitist', much like the Proclamation of Masterpieces from which it is adopted; 'replacing the term "Masterpiece" with that of "Treasure" does not make it any less so', it asserted, adding that 'selection will always be based on criteria of "exceptional value", regardless of the terms used'. In contrast, the Caribbean alternative – the International Register – would 'not eliminate any form of ICH [intangible cultural heritage] under the criteria of excellence or aestheticism'.

During the coffee break on Tuesday afternoon, a Nordic colleague remarked that the UNESCO secretariat was in favour of a list based on excellence. In his opinion, however, such a list was absurd. 'It is impossible', he explained, 'to take folkdances from Finland, Turkey, and Japan, for example, and say that one is better than the others'. Another delegate from Northern Europe made no secret of his intense dislike for the idea of a List of Treasures, adding that he would prefer to have no list at all, 'but that is not going to happen'. They agreed that, as things stood, the best course of action was to lend support to the Caribbean proposal, the lesser of two evils; it was, at any rate, preferable by far to a merit-based roster of treasures or masterpieces.

There was a great deal of informal diplomatic manoeuvring during coffee and lunch breaks, and no doubt also over white-clothed Parisian dinner tables such as the one the Nordic delegations shared on the evening of the third day, the Wednesday night. Alliances were formed and broken around the issue of lists as well as other controversial issues such as questions of national sovereignty, the role of communities in the Convention, and not least, the proposed Intangible Cultural Heritage Fund, the amount of national contributions to the Fund, and the compulsory or voluntary character of these contributions. Behind the curtains, the stage was set for an elaborately scripted no-holds-barred confrontation.

On Thursday afternoon, having ploughed through preceding articles and come to at least a tentative consensus on the number and composition of committees, we reached the articles in the draft Convention concerning lists. An article establishing national inventories had been adopted in plenary at the previous session, as had the principle of an international Register of Intangible Cultural Heritage in Need of Urgent Safeguarding. The controversy concerned the List of Treasures (or Masterpieces).

The committee's chairman, Mohammed Bedjaoui from Algeria, signalled that it was time to move on to this article and to draft it in such a way that it would at least be acceptable to a majority of delegations. Several states had asked for the floor when Grenada called a point of order, thus halting the proceedings. The Grenadian delegate asked for the Caribbean proposal to be discussed before the articles in the draft Convention; once the committee had revamped the text of the draft Convention and reached a consensus, she explained, the Caribbean proposal would be superfluous.

This intervention brought on another point of order from Japan. The Japanese delegate insisted that the committee confine itself to discussing the draft Convention, otherwise all its work up until this point would have been in vain and no progress would be made. Further points of order followed. There was clamour in the meeting room as the tension grew palpable. In another point of order, a Senegalese delegate spoke out in support of Japan and accused Grenada of obstructing the work of the committee.

The Grenadian delegate expressed her resentment at the accusations made by the delegations of Japan and Senegal: of course the draft Convention was under discussion at this meeting, she conceded, but it was not sacrosanct and surely the delegates were entitled to propose amendments. The Venezuelan delegation followed suit with another point of order, protesting the allegations against Grenada and the other Caribbean states behind the proposal. The Venezuelan delegate raised his voice in a rare display of emotion, exclaiming that the delegates who made these unfair accusations were compromising the cordial atmosphere of the negotiations. I must have looked puzzled, for Guðný Helgadóttir, head of the Icelandic delegation, turned to me with a smile and told me not to take this too seriously, expressions of anger and indignation were simply tools of diplomacy to which delegates occasionally resort. Defusing the tension, chairman Bedjaoui promised the Grenadian delegate that she would, in due course, be given the floor to present the Caribbean proposal. But for now, he declared, 'let us move on for the sake of giving us all the feeling that we are getting something done'.

A debate ensued on the list articles, which degenerated alarmingly quickly into a squabble over vocabulary. In an insightful essay on 'Making a List', J. Mark Schuster notes that 'if one wishes to consider listing as a tool in historic preservation ... one immediately confronts a rather contorted and confusing set of vocabulary: schedules, inventories, lists, classifications, surveys, registers, [and] records'. Each of these terms is polysemic and signifies 'different processes with different implications in the countries in which they are used simultaneously' (Schuster 2002: 3).

Schuster's remarks were certainly borne out at Place Fontenoy. For the better part of the afternoon, one after another, different national delegations spoke out in favour of one of the terms: register, list, or inventory, with yet other terms thrown in on occasion, such as registry and 'relaçion'. One delegate claimed that 'register is the technically appropriate word here', without further explanation, while another complained that 'register' is too formal and implies formalities of 'registration'. An African delegate spoke out in support of the term 'register', because it 'gives importance to the item inscribed on it', while a South American delegate advocated the use of 'inventory' instead, as the term 'register' carries formal implications in copyright law. Just when I thought diplomacy could not get any sillier than this, the South African delegation brought the discussion to a new level of absurdity, stating a preference for the term register, which should be defined thus: 'a register is a listing of intangible cultural heritage in need of safeguarding and forms part of an inventory'.

In a point of order, the Netherlands called for an immediate vote to save time: 'We spent a long time on the relative merits of the terms "register" and "list" in February. We've already spent two hours on this today and it is a simple choice: either we use "register" or we use "list".' Japan spoke out in support of the Netherlands. Others objected that before proceeding to a vote, they needed to understand what the different terms meant, and asked for the indulgence of the Dutch and Japanese delegates. In response, the Netherlands asked a legal adviser from UNESCO who was present to define the difference between a register and a list. The legal adviser made the rather obvious point that 'it really doesn't matter which word you use in this convention; what is important is what you put in that list or register, how it is to be treated, etc'. His answer left the issue unresolved, however, and the delegate from Saint Lucia asked whether questions of terminology could not be deferred until the committee had reached a decision on the content of the article. 'We're repeating the debate from the previous session', she complained in exasperation; 'absolutely everything said now has already been said'. Seizing this as his cue, Bedjaoui closed the session for the day. He announced that the following day we would begin with a presentation of the Caribbean proposal; thus, he effectively called a halt to terminological wrangling for the time being.

How will we determine outstanding quality?

Concealed beneath the astonishing sterility of this debate is a political contention of some importance, though it is easy to lose sight of it amidst the diplomatic charade. At stake is the relationship between the new Convention and the World Heritage Convention. The Argentinean delegate summed it up when he expressed support for the term 'register' rather than 'list', so as, in his words, 'to avoid confusion with the World Heritage List'. Though not all delegates were consistent in their use of the terms, overall the preference for 'list' was aligned with support for the List of Treasures/Masterpieces on the model of the World Heritage List. Conversely, those who preferred the term 'register' were likely to be sceptical of that List and favourably disposed toward the International Register proposed by the four Caribbean island states.

The following day Grenada presented this alternative proposal. In her speech, the Grenadian delegate stressed the inappropriateness of designating certain practices and expressions as treasures or masterpieces of humanity while excluding others:

> The intangible cultural heritage of any group is valuable and precious to them, if only to them. The convention, therefore, should not just recognize intangible cultural heritage of 'exceptional' value.

She emphasised also that this Convention should not be used to compensate for imbalance in the World Heritage Convention and warned that, if that was the idea, the results would surely come as a disappointment:

> Safeguarding should not be a competition. Rich countries have already put money into safeguarding, so what will happen is that their intangible heritage will go on the international list, while developing countries will once again be the losers.

A lively debate ensued and delegations presented arguments for and against the Caribbean proposal. It soon became clear, however, that this was a losing battle; a much greater proportion of those who took the floor spoke out against the proposal than in its favour.[7] Still, several delegates argued for the proposal, while others expressed sympathy for the general idea but stopped short of supporting it because they worried that a universal register would be unwieldy.

A Uruguayan diplomat declared that 'the fundamental objective of this convention is safeguarding cultural heritage as a whole and not registering masterpieces', and the Danish delegate agreed that 'this proposal really captures the true meaning of safeguarding'. Argentina, likewise, warned against 'focusing on safeguarding a few objects, whether we call them masterpieces or treasures', and proposed to add to the Convention 'programs, projects, and activities for the safeguarding of intangible cultural heritage' (this latter proposal was accepted and adopted as Article 18).

Saint Lucia and Barbados rejected the terms treasures and masterpieces on the grounds that they suggested a hierarchy among heritage. The Spanish delegation had previously argued that 'intangible heritage is not a beauty contest', and it now reiterated its objections: 'The experience with the World Heritage List', said the Spanish delegate, 'is that through it hierarchies are established that are hard to justify and it creates tensions in countries whose submissions to the list are not accepted' – this from a delegate whose state (along with Italy) ranks at the top of the world heritage hierarchy, with a greater number of inscriptions on the list than any other country.

Another delegate (whose nationality escaped me, but whose English sounded sub-Saharan African) took a similar position, and expressed his concern with great eloquence:

> How will we determine 'outstanding quality'? This will generate competition where we should have cooperation. The search for masterpieces will draw attention away from endangered intangible cultural heritage, which most requires our attention. *It would be like inviting a noisy dance-band into a hospital!*

The point is, he concluded, that 'masterpieces do not need help'. Comparing the Convention to a hospital, this delegate invoked the moral imperative of conservation in the eleventh hour. Lest the committee lose sight of this imperative in a celebration of heritage highlights, the hospital metaphor is a reminder that safeguarding is a matter of life and death – as is implicit in the concepts of survival and revitalisation.[8] This metaphor is regularly invoked also in connection with the World Heritage Convention, for as art historian Dario Gamboni states, 'in a sense, "world heritage" is an ambulance that follows an army and tries to precede it' (Gamboni 2001: 8).

More delegates, however, spoke out against the Caribbean proposal and rose to defend the List of Treasures/Masterpieces – the 'noisy dance-band'.

Many among them referred to the success of the World Heritage List and the Proclamation of Masterpieces. The Chinese delegate, for instance, noted that the Proclamation had been very successful in China and added, 'the World Heritage List has been a tremendous source of publicity for UNESCO – I don't see why we would want to move away from that'. A Japanese delegate cautioned that 'the registry will be nothing but a huge database and will show no visibility', pointing out that 'in my country alone it is said that there are more than sixty thousand items of intangible cultural heritage; this register would include not only all those but all intangible cultural heritage from all parts of the world!' Skirting past the sheer absurdity of this quantification of heritage, a delegate from Chile concurred that 'the register is about to become a phonebook'. And speaking on behalf of the African group, the delegate from Benin added:

> To refuse to proclaim masterpieces of the intangible cultural heritage of mankind would give a dangerous message: that this Convention is second rate, that it is not as good as the 1972 Convention, and that this is because certain states forced us to do so.

What is beautiful is beautiful. Full stop

The majority of delegates at the meeting dismissed charges of elitism and hierarchisation. Thus, the delegate from Cape Verde was 'not really bothered by this business of masterpieces or treasures because what is beautiful is beautiful. Full stop'. The head of the delegation from the Democratic Republic of Congo likewise said she could not 'see anything wrong with masterpieces and treasures; it's a bit romantic, which is exactly what we want in this convention'. In a confusing intervention, the Dominican Republic's delegate expressed support for 'the brilliant initiative from the delegates from the Caribbean' which she found particularly appealing because 'it is not elitist', but then went on to argue against it based on the claim that 'there are works of human genius that are masterpieces; we must be careful not to trivialize culture by denying this'. 'Unfortunately', the Dominican delegate added, 'the human race has not produced these everywhere, but it is nonetheless very important to recognize them where they have been produced'.

The delegate from Benin protested that the anti-elitist argument did not hold water and made the important observation that 'hierarchy is a fact of history'. 'Every culture always considers some items of heritage above others', he stressed. A Brazilian delegate noted to much the same effect that 'there is a difference between the anthropological view of heritage and the political view of heritage'. In contrast to the descriptive perspective of anthropology, the political view of heritage is premised on the fact that resources are never limitless; or as the Brazilian delegate spelled out, 'we cannot safeguard everything, and this means that we cannot value everything equally'.

These astute remarks underline how central questions and mechanisms of selection are to heritage practices. As folklorist Barbro Klein maintains, 'it is hardly possible to speak of cultural heritage without using the word politics', for cultural heritage comes into existence through a political operation when 'individuals or groups nominate or designate it as such' (Klein 1997: 19; my translation). Through the same operation, a much greater number of traces of the past are bulldozed or left to rot or put to new uses. Heritage making inevitably creates casualties; in the words of Dario Gamboni, 'preservation and destruction are two sides of the same coin'. Heritage, Gamboni explains, 'results from a continuous process of interpretation and selection that attributes to certain objects (rather than others) resources that postpone their degradation' (Gamboni 2001: 9).

The politics of selection thus extend well beyond the composition of the list into the designation of certain things, sites, practices, and expressions as heritage. In fact, heritage making is itself not unlike list-making. In his classic analysis of lists as social and cognitive instruments, anthropologist Jack Goody has noted that lists rely on discontinuity and boundaries, giving whatever is abstracted from ordinary speech and placed on a list a generality that it would not otherwise have, especially if the list is sanctioned by official institutions (Goody 1977: 80–1, 105–6). Much the same applies to heritage, for whatever is so designated is abstracted from its previous context and placed in relation to other things, sites, practices, or expressions also selected into the category of heritage. This category is imbued with authority by individuals and institutions that sanction the selection, and objects inducted into the category are accorded a value of a different and more general kind than any value they previously had. It should come as no surprise, then, that listing shadows heritage making.

A Mexican delegate to the meeting made an important remark that sheds light on this selectivity of heritage. Discussing the obligations of states at the national level, he protested:

> There is a lack of assessment of importance in the text at present. As the text stands now, any communities can demand that their traditions be recognized as intangible cultural heritage. They are both judges and parties. This can cause all kinds of problems, with all communities demanding financial support for their culture and with no way of adjudicating among them, no instrument to assess the importance of the proposed intangible cultural heritage.

What is remarkable here is the acknowledgment that traditions have to be *recognised* as intangible cultural heritage, that they are *proposed* as such but that in order to be given recognition, authorities must *assess* their importance and *adjudicate* among them. Intangible cultural heritage is, in other words, an official seal of approval. It is a filing cabinet in the ministry of culture, and whatever is not recognised and filed there ends instead in the dustbin of history. That is why, as many delegates objected, an international register of heritage without a mechanism of selection is 'not practical' (Vietnam), 'not convenient' (Colombia), and 'too huge for anyone's administration' (Uganda). In fact, the dustbin is perhaps that instrument which effective administration can least do without. A boundless list of everything is not administrable. It is not even a list: lists are distinguished by their boundaries and the discontinuity of their contents from all that they exclude.

The uses of lists

Lists itemise culture. They cannot avoid doing so: enumeration and itemisation is their very essence. Such itemisation is at the heart of the new Convention. Not only are lists the central instruments for safeguarding and promoting intangible heritage at the international level; moreover, the primary obligation that the Convention imposes on states is to draw up comprehensive national inventories of intangible heritage in their territories (cf. Kurin 2004: 71–2).

These lists of intangible heritage artifactualise cultural practices and expressions, decontextualising them from the social relations in which they take place in order to recontextualise them in national inventories with reference to other practices and expressions under the same national government and in international lists with reference to other 'masterpieces' of humanity. As such, listing renders transferable the practices and expressions itemised and singled out for attention. This transferability is a cause for concern; at the meeting in June 2003, the Argentinean delegate expressed this concern with regard to the publication of UNESCO lists of intangible heritage:

> There is a danger in publishing just a list per se, even though it is done with all good intentions: we are giving a shopping list for treasure hunters. In the case of this convention, we might end up with a free catalogue for multinationals who want to appropriate intangible cultural heritage. We are all for transparency, but the problem with it is that sometimes others take advantage of it.

The Argentinean delegate went on to note that 'This is a discussion we also had surrounding the Convention on Sub-Aquatic Heritage', and indeed the allusion to treasure hunters refers to real problems that have been associated with the World Heritage List (cf. Schuster 2002: 14–15, and Gamboni 2001: 8–9). As J. Mark Schuster (2002: 8) has remarked, it is an interesting property of lists in general that 'once someone compiles them others will use them, often not for the purposes for which they were originally intended'. Such purposes can even be diametrically opposed to those intended by the lists' authors; thus, in reprisal for the bombing of Lübeck, Hermann Göring is said to have instructed the Luftwaffe in 1942 to destroy 'every historical building and landmark in Britain that is marked with an asterisk in Baedeker' (Boorstin 1992: 106, quoted in Schuster 2002: 15). These raids became known as the Baedeker Blitz, named for the authoritative German travel guidebook to Britain.

Indeed, another use made of UNESCO heritage lists is tourism. Officially, this is not one of the lists' purposes, but it is nevertheless universally acknowledged as a major motive for inscription. States nominate cultural and natural heritage sites for inscription on the World Heritage List and they nominate traditional practices and expressions for the Proclamation of Masterpieces (or the Representative List that continues it) in the hopes of attracting enlightened tourists who make their own use of these lists, checking them off against their travel plans. Far from being an accidental consequence of listing, increased tourism is expected to give a boost to local economies while guaranteeing the economic viability and survival of places and practices that have lost their former economic raison d'être. Thus, for example, presenting the implications of inscription on the World Heritage List, the Australian Department of the Environment and Heritage asserts 'World Heritage listing has featured in promotions that have resulted in greatly increased tourist visitation from overseas and within Australia' and maintains that local communities could expect 'increases in employment opportunities and income' as a result of listing (Australian Department of the Environment and Heritage, n.d.).

There is nothing suspect about these purposes, which correspond well to a liberal conception of the role of the state in facilitating economic growth. Cultural consumption by tourists is often a major incentive for preservation and helps to generate the necessary resources. Nevertheless, listing comes across as a questionable response specifically to the threat of 'folklorisation' as conceived of by UNESCO: a term used in publications, speeches, and internal documents to characterise the reification and commoditisation of traditional practices for outside audiences (Hafstein 2004). In a sense, folklorisation parallels the danger that tourism can present to World Heritage sites, threatening physical destruction through wear, tear, and erosion (Gamboni 2001: 9). Good intentions aside, the listing of traditional practices and expressions would appear, in fact, to contribute to their 'folklorisation' by bringing them to the attention of tourists and by turning them into tools for local economic recovery. This is perhaps not particularly surprising. Heritage and tourism are indeed collaborative industries, as Barbara Kirshenblatt-Gimblett has suggested, 'heritage converting locations into destinations and tourism making them economically viable as exhibits of themselves' (1998: 151).

The system of heritage

After all the diplomatic manoeuvring and deliberation, the Intergovernmental Meeting of Experts in June 2003 finally settled on a compromise. In spite of their successful rejection of the Caribbean proposal for an International Register of the Intangible Cultural Heritage, Japan and its allies were not able to rally sufficient support for the List of Masterpieces or Treasures. Instead, delegates settled on an instrument that they named the Representative List of the Intangible Cultural Heritage of Humanity. This compromise still makes listing the central international instrument of the Convention and it upholds the principle of selection; gone, however, is the highly charged vocabulary of treasures and masterpieces. What precisely this list will contain and how the selection will be made is unclear; at the time of writing, it is under negotiation in the Convention's executive body, the Intergovernmental Committee for the Safeguarding of the Intangible Cultural Heritage.

UNESCO's heritage lists are a prestigious form of display with wide circulation among powerful actors. In much the same way as museum walls, they are surfaces on which heritage may be so arranged that 'its effects – however they might be construed – will be carried back out into the world and enabled to act on it' (Bennett 2000: 1424, on art museums). The arrangement of intangible heritage on such lists is designed to create state and community practice, channelling resources to its preservation and revitalisation, but also transforming people's relationship to their practices and expressions (see Hafstein 2007).

The UNESCO list effects change not least because it provides an incentive to governments to 'proclaim the richness of their cultural heritage' (James Early, quoted in Kirshenblatt-Gimblett 2006). The *Director-General's Preliminary Report on the Situation Calling for Standard-Setting and on the Possible Scope of such Standard-Setting* in the field of intangible cultural heritage, from 2002, thus stressed the importance of establishing such a list in association with the proposed Convention 'for its driving force for States Parties as proved by the 1972 Convention experience' (UNESCO 32 C/26: para. 7).

From this point of view, then, UNESCO's lists of heritage emerge as a form of argumentation, but one whose powers of persuasion depend on flattery. Much like the Proclamation of Masterpieces, these lists parallel other international spectacles that make a people visible to itself by weighing its virtues against those of other peoples. In so doing, the lists yoke pride to the plough of heritage preservation; or, as the Australian Department of the Environment and Heritage maintains with respect to the World Heritage List, 'listing also cultivates local and national pride in the property and develops feelings of national responsibility to protect the area' (Australian Department of Environment and Heritage, n.d).

In the previous pages, I have presented a key debate in the Intergovernmental Meeting of Experts that drafted the ICHC concerning the use of the list as an instrument of the Convention. This debate, I argue, goes to the heart of heritage practices, which are always predicated upon selection. Safeguarding certain sites or practices under the banner of heritage consumes limited resources and directs those same resources away from other sites and practices. Selection and (inevitably) exclusion are thus structural elements of the system of heritage – its designation, preservation, revitalisation, promotion, display, and so forth. The allocation of resources is a political operation and the same goes, *mutatis mutandi*, for the designation of heritage, intangible or otherwise. The particular criteria on which its designation is premised are of course important, but they never fully account for particular selections: it is never self-evident which particular practice, expression, object, or site is most excellent, outstanding, authentic, or, indeed, representative, for these terms are themselves indeterminate and open to debate.

Heritage as category and the list as instrument are alike in many ways. Both depend on selection; both disembed their objects from previous contexts, rendering them discontinuous in some aspects from their surroundings; and both recontextualise them with respect to other objects similarly selected, according them a generality and value that is derived from the authority of the persons or institutions that sanction the selection. The Representative List of the Intangible Cultural Heritage of Humanity is the outcome of a compromise of sorts between delegations that wanted a List of Masterpieces/Treasures and those who wanted no list at all or else a comprehensive register with no selection. The Representative List accepts selection as a structural element, but rejects excellence as a criterion of selection, in an attempt to get away from hierarchisation and competition among states. However, representativity is even more indeterminate as a criterion of selection, begging the question of what the list and the heritage it designates actually represent. It leaves a great deal of discretion to the Intergovernmental Committee responsible for inscribing intangible heritage on the Representative List.

As defined by UNESCO's Convention and its activities in this field so far, intangible cultural heritage *is* a list. Intangible heritage is a mechanism of selection and display. It is a tool for channelling attention and resources to certain cultural practices and not to others. Intangible heritage is both a dance-band *and* a hospital: a serious enterprise concerned with the life and death of traditions and communities *and* a fund-raising dinner dance party with colourful costumes, glaring spotlights, and rhythmic tunes.

Notes

1 According to the Secretariat Report, 249 participants representing 103 member states took part, in addition to 10 delegates from UNESCO's three permanent observation missions, and representatives from two intergovernmental organisations and five non-

governmental organisations. In fact, no more than half that number of people actually took part and I only noted one NGO ('Traditions for Tomorrow') in the room. It should be noted that official figures count the delegates announced in advance by member states. Nevertheless, I find fascinating how wide the gap is between official reports and what one actually observes at these meetings; I mention the number of participants only to illustrate this point. Reports such as this tend to gloss over conflicts, omit confrontations, downplay disagreements, all the while emphasising points of convergence and insisting on consensus, even in its absence. They are, in fact, instrumental in creating the convergence that they portray as though it had actually taken place. Having observed such discrepancies, one soon learns not to take the official presentation at face value but to read against the grain of these documents. What I gathered from participant observation and personal communications is therefore fundamental to my understanding of the process.

Officially, I attended this meeting in the capacity of an 'expert' on the Icelandic delegation. As such, I was alphabetised by state ('Islande') and sat to the right of the Indian delegates (the Iranians were absent, as were the Iraqis, who did not command a sovereign state at the time). On my right-hand side sat Guðný Helgadóttir from the Ministry of Education and Culture, the head of delegation and the only other delegate in attendance from Iceland. Although there was a microphone on the desk in front of us, I never took the floor during the meeting. Guðný was in charge; I was there at her discretion and by special permission from the Icelandic UNESCO commission, to observe the debate, take my own notes, and draw my own conclusions.

2 Systems of Living Human Treasures were developed primarily in Japan and South Korea, along with the closely related category of 'the intangible cultural heritage'. Japan enacted the Law for the Protection of Cultural Properties in 1950, a comprehensive legislation for heritage conservation that replaced the earlier National Treasures Protection Act from 1929. In 1955, Japanese authorities appointed the first intangible cultural properties along with their 'holders', defined as Living Human Treasures, that is 'those who have mastered or possess exceptional skills in arts and crafts' (UNESCO 2002: 13). Such appointments have since been made annually. The 'holders' are awarded grants, and funds are available to assist them in training disciples and to support public performances and exhibitions. A fifth category was added to the Japanese Law for the Protection of Cultural Properties in 1975, 'Folk-Cultural Properties', comprising both tangible and intangible heritage. In distinction from the Living Human Treasures programme associated with the official appointment of intangible cultural properties and holders, folk-cultural properties are always collective and recognition for them is given only to groups, not to individual 'holders' (UNESCO 2002: 14).

The Republic of Korea's Cultural Property Preservation Law dates from 1962. It is based in part on the revised Japanese model and draws a distinction between four categories of cultural properties: important tangible cultural properties, important intangible cultural properties, folk-cultural properties, and monuments. The first Korean intangible cultural properties were appointed in 1964 together with 'holders' or Living Human Treasures. These latter receive monthly stipends and are in return obliged to train successors and make intangible heritage available to the public at large (UNESCO 2002: 14–15). Living Human Treasures systems were also set up in the Philippines and Thailand in the 1980s. In the USA, the National Endowment for the Arts established National Heritage Awards in 1982 on the model of the Japanese system, 'as a way of honoring American folk artists for their contributions to our national cultural mosaic' (National Endowment for the Arts). In the past one and a half decade, analogous programmes focused specifically on handicrafts were instituted in several countries of Europe, including France, the Czech Republic, and Poland (UNESCO 2002: 16–18).

3 The Director-General is even more blunt in the French version of the brochure, where inevitability becomes full-fledged destiny: 'Il est évident ... qu'à terme, la

complémentarité de ces deux volets est destinée à se resoudre dans leur union' (UNESCO 2001b: 3).

4 Except the English, of course.

5 Zambia is not singled out here because it performs exceptionally poorly at sports or because its artists go completely unrecognised in galleries of great repute, but rather because its standing is fairly typical of poorer countries in these arenas where distinction and money so often go hand in hand.

6 This concern is not without basis; media coverage of the Proclamation of Masterpieces often confuses the Proclamation's list with the World Heritage List, which is of course much better known and highly esteemed. Even peer-reviewed articles in prominent scholarly journals do not seem to understand the distinction between the Proclamation of Masterpieces and the World Heritage List; see 'Masterpieces of Oral and Intangible Culture: Reflections on the UNESCO World Heritage List' by Peter J.M. Nas (2002) in *Current Anthropology*.

7 There was not an official vote, but the secretariat kept a tally of states that took a position for and against the Caribbean proposal; like the text of articles under consideration at any given time, the tally was projected onto a large white screen behind the stage where the chairman, the rapporteur, and the UNESCO secretariat sat:

> *For:* Barbados, Denmark, Dominican Republic, Greece, Iceland, Jamaica, Sweden, and Uruguay.
>
> *Against:* Belgium, Benin, Brazil, Cambodia, Central African Republic, Chile, Colombia, Congo, Democratic Republic of Congo, Ethiopia, France, Honduras, India, Japan, Morocco, Niger, Nigeria, Panama, Philippines, Rwanda, Senegal, Spain, Togo, Turkey, Uganda, United Republic of Tanzania, and Vietnam.

8 A discussion of organic metaphors would take us too far afield, but I have analysed these and their rhetorical uses in folklore scholarship in another essay (Hafstein 2001).

References

Australian Department of Environment and Heritage (n.d.) Implications of World Heritage Listing. Available online at: http://www.deh.gov.au/heritage/worldheritage/pubs/implications.pdf (Accessed 30 June 2007).

Bennett, T. (2000) 'Acting on the social. art, culture and government', *American Behavioral Scientist*, 43(9): 1412–28.

—— (2001) 'Cultural policy. Issues of culture and governance', in F. Snickars (ed.), *Culture, Society, Market*, Stockholm: Bank of Sweden Tercentenary Fund/Swedish National Council for Cultural Affairs.

Engelhardt, R. (2002) 'UNESCO Presentation: Regional perspectives', in *Promotion of the 'Proclamation of Masterpieces of the Oral and Intangible Heritage of Humanity'. Final Report of 2002 Regional Workshop for Cultural Personnel in Asia and the Pacific, Tokyo, Japan, 12–16 March, 2002*, Tokyo: Asia/Pacific Cultural Centre for UNESCO.

EU National Commissions for UNESCO (2002) 'Echanges de vues sur la sauvegarde du pci— Réunion des Commissions nationales pour l'UNESCO de l'Union européenne, 9 et 10 juillet 2002'. Unpublished document.

Gamboni, D. (2001) 'World Heritage: Shield or Target?', *Conservation: The Getty Institute Conservation Newsletter*, 16(2): 5–11.

Goody, J. (1977) *The Domestication of the Savage Mind*, Cambridge: Cambridge University Press.

Hafstein, V. (2001) 'Biological metaphors in folklore scholarship. An essay in the history of ideas', *Arv: Nordic Yearbook of Folklore*, 57:7–32.

—— (2004) *The Making of Intangible Cultural Heritage: Tradition and Authenticity, Community and Humanity*. Unpublished Ph.D. thesis, University of California, Berkeley.

—— (2007) 'Claiming culture: Intangible Heritage Inc., Folklore©, Traditional Knowledge™', in R. Bendix, D. Hemme, and M. Tauschek (eds), *Prädikat 'Heritage'— Perspektiven auf Wertschöpfungen aus Kultur*, Münster: Lit Verlag.

Kirshenblatt-Gimblett, B. (1998) *Destination Culture. Tourism, Museums, and Heritage*, Berkeley: University of California Press.

—— (2006) 'World heritage and cultural economics', in I. Karp, C.A. Kratz, L. Szwaja, T. Ybarra-Frausto, G. Buntinx, B. Kirshenblatt-Gimblett, and C. Rassool (eds), *Museum Frictions: Public Cultures/Global Transformations*, Durham, North Carolina: Duke University Press.

Klein, B. (1997) 'Tillhörighet og utanförskap. Om kulturarvspolitik och folklivsforskning i en multietnisk värld', *Rig*, 1–2: 15–32.

Kurin, R. (2004) 'Safeguarding intangible cultural heritage in the 2003 UNESCO Convention: a critical appraisal', *Museum International*, 221–2: 66–76.

Murphy, C. (2001) 'Immaterial civilization', *The Atlantic Monthly*, 288(2): 20–2.

Nas, P.J.M. (2002) 'Masterpieces of oral and intangible culture: reflections on the UNESCO World Heritage List', *Current Anthropology*, 43(1): 139–48.

Schuster, J.M. (2002) 'Making a list and checking it twice: the list as a tool of historic preservation', *Working Paper no. 14*, The Cultural Policy Centre at the University of Chicago. Available online at: http://culturalpolicy.uchicago.edu/papers.html (Accessed 30 June 2007).

Titchen, S.M. (1995) *On the Construction of Outstanding Universal Value. UNESCO's World Heritage Convention (Convention Concerning the Protection of the World Cultural and Natural Heritage, 1972) and the Identification and Assessment of Cultural Places for Inclusion in the World Heritage List*, Unpublished Ph.D. thesis, Australian National University.

Turtinen, J. (2000) *Globalising Heritage – On UNESCO and the Transnational Construction of World Heritage*, SCORE Rapportserie 2000: 12, Stockholm: Stockholm Center for Organizational Research.

—— (2006) *Världsarvets villkor. Intressen, förhandlingar och bruk i internationell politik*, Acta universitatis stockholmiensis, Stockholm Studies in Ethnology, 1, Stockholm: Stockholms Universitet.

UNESCO (1993) *Establishment of a System of 'Living Cultural Properties' (Living Human Treasures) at UNESCO*, UNESCO Executive Board, 142nd Session, 142 EX/18, Paris: UNESCO.

—— (2001a) *Proclamation of Masterpieces of the Oral and Intangible Heritage of Humanity. Guide for the Presentation of Candidature Files*, Paris: Intangible Heritage Section, Division of Cultural Heritage, UNESCO.

—— (2001b) *Première Proclamation des chefs-d'œuvre du patrimoine oral et immatériel de l'humanité*, Paris: Intangible Heritage Section, Division of Cultural Heritage, UNESCO.

—— (2002) *Guidelines for the Establishment of Living Human Treasures Sytems*, Paris: UNESCO Section of Intangible Cultural Heritage and Korean National Commission for UNESCO.

—— (2003a) *Intersessional Working Group of Government Experts on the Preliminary Draft Convention for the Safeguarding of the Intangible Cultural Heritage Report*, CLT-2003/ CONF.206/3, Paris: UNESCO.

—— (2003b) *Preliminary Draft International Convention for the Safeguarding of the Intangible Cultural Heritage and Report by the Director-General on the Situation Calling for Standard-Setting and on the Possible Scope of such Standard-Setting*, 32 C/26, Paris: UNESCO.

Chapter 6

Lessons learned from the ICTM (NGO) evaluation of nominations for the UNESCO *Masterpieces of the Oral and Intangible Heritage of Humanity, 2001–5*

Anthony Seeger

This chapter describes the experience of the International Council for Traditional Music (ICTM) with the evaluation of the nominations for the UNESCO *Proclamation of the Masterpieces of the Oral and Intangible Heritage of Humanity* (hereafter 'Masterpieces') between 2001 and 2005.[1] There are several reasons for publishing these observations. First, the role of the UNESCO NGOs in UNESCO programme evaluations is not widely understood. Anthropologist Karen Olwig asks:

> How [can] a global organization, operating according to general guidelines, recognize and appreciate the complexity and diversity of the cultural expressions that it seeks to protect. By what criteria can one compare widely different cultural expressions and how does one single out the 'masterpieces of the oral and intangible heritage of humanity' worthy of preservation?
>
> (Olwig 2002: 145–6)

These difficult decisions were not made by the UNESCO bureaucracy acting alone but through the fairly complex consultation process I shall describe. Second, the UNESCO *Convention on the Safeguarding of the Intangible Heritage* replaces the Proclamation of the Masterpieces of the Oral and Intangible Heritage of Humanity with two lists of 'representative intangible cultural heritage' in which the selection and role of the NGOs has not been decided as of this writing. Since those elaborating the operational guidelines for the lists may also be unfamiliar with the roles NGOs played in the Masterpieces proclamations, I hope this chapter can help to guide them in formulating future policies. Finally, scholars and professional organisations like the ICTM can learn some lessons from the described evaluation process that might be useful in their future professional activities and consultancies. It is clear that cultural policy is still under-theorised by scholars (as remarked by Richard

Kurin 2002; Barbara Kirshenblatt-Gimblett 2004, and others). The rapid growth of interest in safeguarding intangible cultural heritage provides ample subject matter both for theoretical reflection and for intelligent action.

I begin with a brief history of the Masterpieces programme and a description of the ICTM. Then I move to a discussion of the process through which nominations were proposed for proclamation as Masterpieces and the procedures employed by the ICTM Secretariat for providing the scientific and technical evaluations. Then I discuss some of the lessons we learned from this process and conclude with observations on the significance of the role of NGOs in the Masterpieces project. I argue that without the evaluations provided by the NGOs the programme would have been far less meaningful and some of the action plans would certainly have been less effective.

I write about this process from the perspective of the ICTM, the NGO that evaluated the largest number of nominations in the programme, since music was involved in so many of them.[2] I served as Secretary-General of the ICTM from 2001 to 2005 and supervised the evaluation of approximately 90 nominations submitted by member states for the second and third round of proclamations (in 2003 and 2005). My predecessor, Professor Dieter Christensen, served as Secretary-General for 20 years and supervised the evaluation of the 2001 round of the masterpieces. I assumed the position in 2001 and supervised the evaluation of the 2003 and 2005 rounds. To the best of my knowledge, no other NGO has described its procedures for evaluating nominations for the Masterpieces project.[3]

The Masterpieces of the oral and intangible heritage of humanity (2001–5)

The origins of the *Proclamations of the Masterpieces of the Oral and Intangible Heritage of Humanity* have been described in a number of publications, probably most cogently by Noriko Aikawa (2004, 2005, this volume), an active participant in many of the events she describes. She places the Masterpieces in the context of a series of UNESCO actions aimed at the recognition and safeguarding of intangible cultural heritage, starting with efforts in the 1970s and 1980s that resulted in a 1989 document, followed by the Masterpieces programme, and concluding with the 2003 *International Convention for the Safeguarding of the Intangible Heritage* (see Kurin 2004 for another nuanced description of the process). While this chapter focuses on certain aspects of the Masterpieces programme, it must be kept in mind that the objectives of the programme extended beyond the Masterpieces programme itself to broader goals regarding intangible heritage within the scope of UNESCO objectives.

The formal objectives of the Masterpieces programme were repeatedly described in UNESCO documents. They were to:

- raise awareness and recognise the importance of oral and intangible heritage and the need to safeguard and revitalise it;
- evaluate and take stock of the world's oral and intangible heritage;
- encourage countries to establish national inventories of the intangible heritage and provide legal and administrative measures for its protection;
- promote the participation of traditional artists and local creators in identifying and revitalising the intangible heritage.

The proclamation encourages governments, NGOs and local communities to identify, safeguard, revitalise and protect their oral and intangible heritage. It also aims to encourage individuals, groups, institutions, and organisations to contribute to its management, preservation, protection and promotion (UNESCO 2001a: 5).

The Masterpieces programme achieved the first objective, raising awareness of intangible heritage, very well. It brought to the attention of many member nations the significance of elements of their intangible cultural heritage. The number of nominations increased over the years, as did the number of masterpieces proclaimed. UNESCO proclaimed 19 Masterpieces in 2001, 28 in 2003, and 43 in 2008, the last round before the programme was replaced by the lists authorised in the new Convention. As Aikawa states 'thanks to the proclamation, all of the member states could see exactly what this intangible heritage consisted of' (2005).

The Masterpieces programme is also rightly credited with creating an environment in which the *International Convention for the Safeguarding of the Intangible Heritage* could be written, approved, and swiftly ratified by the requisite number of member states (Aikawa 2004, this volume; Kurin 2004). Since the programme was inaugurated, many nations have begun inventories of their intangible heritage.

The UNESCO objective of involving artists and tradition bearers in these processes has had mixed results. As I shall describe below, many of the nominations failed to provide evidence of the inclusion of artists and tradition bearers in the planning and realisation of the action plans submitted as part of their nominations. The empowerment of tradition bearers constituted an important policy innovation and had been strongly recommended in a number of documents in the 1990s, among them the Action Plan of the 1999 conference 'A Global Assessment of the *1989 Recommendation on the Safeguarding of Traditional culture and Folklore*: Local Empowerment and International Cooperation' held at the Smithsonian Institution in Washington DC (Seitel 2001: 302–6; see also Aikawa-Faure this volume). Even experienced supporters of local empowerment recognised how difficult it can sometimes be to use it effectively:

> Identifying who speaks for the cultural tradition being safeguarded is no easy task … A cultural community may also be beset by factionalism.

Developing a means of working together is also difficult. There are often great status differentials between public officials and experts on the one hand and the practitioners of the tradition on the other. Bringing community participation into play has been a great challenge for many cultural projects in the past and will continue to be so in the future.

(Kurin 2004: 72)

The Masterpieces programme can also be credited with an international surge in scholarly reflection on intangible cultural heritage programmes in general, of which this volume is a part. Increasing numbers of papers on the Masterpieces programme and the 2003 Convention are being presented at professional meetings (for example the ICTM and the Society for Ethnomusicology have both recently featured this topic) and in print (for example *Museum International* 2004 no. 1–2). The nominations process has also led to some interesting publications. In Brazil, for example, participants in preparing nomination files have presented sophisticated reflections on the process (Sandroni 2005; Carmo 2007; Gallois 2007). This chapter provides another point of reflection on the Masterpieces nominations that has so far been absent – that of an evaluating NGO.

From nomination to proclamation – the process

The Intangible Heritage Secretariat employed very competent people, but they were not experts in all of the traditions being nominated and thus could not evaluate them on qualitative grounds. The use of NGOs for anonymous evaluations also removed the evaluations from the internal politics of UNESCO and reduced pressure on the members of the International Jury as well. The Secretariat did, however, prepare detailed guidelines for creating and evaluating nominations.

The procedure for creating and submitting a nomination was fairly laborious and involved a number of distinct stages. Each member state of UNESCO could submit only one nomination for each round. Submissions required the preparation of a large and complex dossier following a detailed outline developed by UNESCO. The requirements included a written section on the history and current status of the form, documentation to support the claim including bibliographies and discographies, a professional quality video of no more than 10 minutes, additional documentary video, 'irrefutable proof testifying to the agreement of the community or practitioners concerned with the contents of the file', a detailed action plan and budget for preserving the heritage, and a list of five other projected forms of cultural expression to be nominated in future years. In the case of multi-national candidatures, an additional document testifying to the agreement of each member state involved submitting the joint domination. The proposed

Masterpiece also had to be compatible with the ideals of the United Nations and its documents on human rights.

Preparing the nomination files required a considerable amount of time and effort. Some member nations received financial support and technical assistance in the preparation of their files; most did not. More detail is available in the *Guide for the Presentation of Candidature Files* (UNESCO 2001b).

The completed nominations would arrive at the UNESCO office and the UNESCO Secretariat would review them to be sure they were complete. Often they found that some pieces were missing and would request further documentation. In a few cases additional information continued to arrive throughout the evaluation process. The UNESCO Secretariat would then select the appropriate individuals or organisations to evaluate each of the nominations and sent them the nomination files. This process was described a follows:

> Once the entries have been recorded and after the submission of any supplementary documentation, the Secretariat will pass them on to the competent NGOs or other experts designated by UNESCO for expert evaluation. This evaluation, which will be based on the selection criteria approved by the executive board at its 155th session, will take the form of an evaluation report for the recommendation for or against the proclamation of the entry. The report, which will be submitted to the members of the jury, will also focus on an evaluation of the quality of the action plan ...
>
> (UNESCO 2001b: 11)

The NGO evaluations, which usually took several months to complete, were returned to Paris along with the dossiers where they were prepared for review by an 18-member International jury. The jury members viewed the 10-minute video, discussed each nomination, and eventually forwarded to the Director-General of UNESCO a list of candidatures that its members recommended be accepted for proclamation, a list of rejected candidatures, and a list of candidatures which could be revised and reviewed two years later. On the basis of the jury's proposal, the Director-General would proclaim a list of Masterpieces of the Oral and Intangible Heritage of Humanity at a special press conference.

After the proclamation, nations whose intangible heritage was proclaimed to be a masterpiece, could apply to UNESCO for funding to undertake parts of the proposed action plan for safeguarding the proclaimed masterpiece. When their action plans were reviewed for funding, some of the reservations and recommendations of the evaluators and members of the jury could be raised with the country and its action plan modified before being funded and implemented. If the country did not apply for funds, however, there was no further control over how the action plan was implemented.

The ICTM and the evaluation procedures

During the three rounds of the Masterpieces, the majority of the forms of intangible heritage nominated were either musical or mixed forms that included music (for example, musical theatre, or dance). In the 2005 round, the number of other forms of intangible heritage grew, but the majority still had music as an important component. As a result, the ICTM was the NGO in formal consultative relations with UNESCO that received the largest number of nominations to evaluate. Seven other NGOs were consulted (UNESCO 2008).

The ICTM was founded in 1947 in the aftermath of World War II, and is currently an 'NGO in formal consultative relations with UNESCO'. From 1947 to 1981 it was called The International Folk Music Council (IFMC). The stated aims of the ICTM are 'to further the study, practice, documentation, preservation and dissemination of traditional music, including folk, popular, classical and urban music, and dance of all countries' (ICTM 2008). It is a membership-based professional organisation supported by member dues. Its approximately 1,200 members are typically researchers who devote their lives to the detailed study of one or more specific musical and/or dance traditions. In addition to attending the bi-annual ICTM World Conferences, members may participate in 15 study groups dealing with such issues as ethnicity, regional traditions of various kinds, ethnochoreology, and others.

Organisationally, the ICTM is an international organisation with 33 national committees and 37 liaison officers. National committees are usually national organisations selected by the ICTM Executive Board to serve as the committees for their nations. The liaison officers are residents of countries that do not (yet) have national committees. The ICTM maintains a secretariat, which has been hosted in five different countries during its history, and publishes the annual *Yearbook for Traditional Music* and a semiannual *Bulletin*. Back issues of the *Yearbook* may be accessed through Journal Storage (JSTOR).

As Secretary-General, it was my task to select the specialised evaluator for each nomination. This was one of the more challenging steps in the evaluation process. UNESCO stipulated two selection criteria that I was expected to follow: (1) evaluators should not be citizens or residents of the country submitting the nomination because of possible conflicts of interest or pressure; and (2) whenever possible the evaluators should come from the region of the nomination. For example, for a nomination from one country in Latin America, an evaluator from another country in Latin America was preferred, but not required. The ICTM Secretariat had three additional criteria. First, the evaluator had to be someone who had studied the intangible heritage form nominated. Second, he or she had to know the scholars and cultural institutions in the country in order to be able to judge the qualifications of the participants and the action plans. Third, he or she had to be available to do the evaluation quickly and complete it within the deadlines established by UNESCO – approximately 90 days.

I began my selection of evaluators by reviewing the nomination files and then consulting the ICTM network of specialists about the most appropriate evaluators. Once I decided which specialist(s) would be appropriate for a given case, it was my job to contact them, convince them to do the evaluation, and to answer any questions they had about the process. Not all the evaluators were members of the ICTM – I used the knowledge of the field and its practitioners of national committees and liaison officers, the Executive Board, and scholars whose work I knew, in order to recruit qualified individuals as broadly as possible. Sometimes it would take a while, but I eventually would find an evaluator I judged to be qualified according to both UNESCO and ICTM criteria.[4]

Once selected, we sent each evaluator the files we had received from UNESCO along with a detailed letter paraphrasing the sometimes hard-to-understand instructions that UNESCO provided for the evaluation of the nominations. Scholars unfamiliar with the vocabulary and rhetorical style of UNESCO had difficulty understanding the instructions and the reasons for following a specific format in their reports. Our letter assisted those who read it carefully, but not all did so. Following considerable correspondence and reminders we would eventually receive the evaluations, edit them into a format that would be easily comparable among the different reports, write a required 1–2 page summary of the report, and send them to the UNESCO secretariat in Paris.[5]

Most of the evaluators were not native speakers of English and editing was quite time-consuming. We were careful not to change the meaning of the evaluations we received, but did have to edit many of the evaluations to facilitate their use by the International Jury and also their translation into French or English. We discovered that the necessity of translation required more than usual attention to clarity in the original language. During this entire process, additional documents would appear for certain nominations and we would send them to the evaluators if they had not yet completed their evaluations. If we already had received the evaluation, we would communicate the substance of the new information and ask if that might change the overall evaluation. If so, we sent them the documents to examine in detail; if not, we added them to the nomination file. Overall, this was a very time-consuming process.

Confidentiality was very important to the evaluators. When we edited the evaluations for UNESCO we also carefully removed every trace of the identity of the evaluator from the document. The evaluations were all submitted in the name of the ICTM and signed by the Secretary-General. Only the ICTM Secretary-General, his assistant, and a few UNESCO officials knew the names of the evaluators. The reason for the secrecy should be obvious. Since the evaluators have to reside outside the country but research an art form within the nominating country, their ability to get visas, research support, and even the trust of local officials and tradition bearers could be adversely affected should they be identified with a negative evaluation. In other cases, however, especially where the evaluations were positive and the intangible form was proclaimed a masterpiece, the evaluators have asked whether they could allow their role to be revealed. Dr Rieks Smeets, Head of the Section of Intangible Cultural Heritage at UNESCO during those years, replying to a question about whether the process could be written about, said that he had no objection to people writing about the Masterpieces programme as long as they did not identify the nominations that were not proclaimed. He felt the countries that submitted nominations not proclaimed to be Masterpieces would be embarrassed by the publicity regarding the nomination.[6] In this chapter, I have chosen to identify neither the nations nor the evaluators in my examples, since I do not believe that to be necessary for my objectives.

The evaluations were expected to be between 8 and 10 pages in length (some needed shortening; few needed lengthening). They had to address specific issues under specific headings that, on occasion, were repetitive. I tried to maintain the structure requested by UNESCO so that the evaluations could easily be compared across a given subject heading. For example, even though the answer to Section 22-a 'demonstrate its outstanding value as a masterpiece of the human creative genius' was somewhat redundant with Section 22-e 'demonstrate excellence in the application of the skill and technical qualities displayed' each was answered separately. In addition to answering the qualitative questions about the Masterpiece and the action plan that accompanied it, each evaluator provided a final recommendation to the International Jury to approve, reject or request revision of the nomination. Although there were always a few evaluators who had difficulty meeting the timeframe established by UNESCO and the ICTM, we would eventually send all evaluations to Paris and then to the International Jury.

The 18-member International Jury has been described both in print (Nas 2002: 139) and on the UNESCO website (UNESCO 2008). When the jury met to make its own evaluation of the nominations and propose a selection of them to the Director-General of UNESCO for proclamation as Masterpieces, the Secretary-Generals of the evaluating NGOs were requested to attend the four-day meeting of the jury in a non-voting advisory capacity. In 2001, the Secretary-Generals presented verbal summaries of each evaluation to the jury. In 2003 and 2005, the Secretary-Generals were there more in an informational capacity. If the jury had questions about aspects of the written evaluation, the Secretary-General was there to respond, but did not otherwise speak. This meant I had to be familiar with all the nominations and evaluations, although in most cases the ICTM evaluations were written clearly enough that no questions arose.

The members of the jury were given an opportunity to review the summaries and the entire dossiers in advance of their meeting. At the meeting, the jury would view the 10-minute professional-quality video on the nomination and then discuss the suitability of the form of intangible heritage and the action plan proposed to safeguard it. The jury made extensive use of the NGO evaluations, but was in no way obligated to follow their recommendations. Often, when they voted to propose a given nomination for proclamation, they would note the reservations expressed by the NGO regarding the action plans and asked that they be considered by UNESCO should the country request funding to implement the action plan. At the end of four intense days, the jury would have reviewed all of the nominations and prepared a list of recommended nominations for proclamation.[7] The following day, the Director-General of UNESCO would hold a well-attended news conference and announce the nominations that he had selected. In general, the Director-General followed the recommendations of the international jury.

The economics of the evaluations

The funding for the UNESCO Masterpieces programme was largely extra-budgetary for UNESCO – most of the funding came from a gift to support the programme in the Intangible Heritage unit. These funds provided grants to assist some nations in the preparation of the nominations; it paid for the expenses of the evaluation process; and it paid for part of the implementation of some of the action plans.

It may be helpful to describe the financial arrangements under which the evaluations were made. The ICTM received approximately US$2,000 for each evaluation. This amount had to pay for all its expenses. We had argued that the evaluators should be well paid for their work, since they were required to undertake the project quickly, to employ knowledge acquired over a lifetime, and to pay for the expenses they incurred during evaluation (library, telephone, fax, translation, etc.). No money was allotted for travel as there was usually not enough time for it and the specialists were chosen for their knowledge of the form.[8] In 2003, each evaluator received US$1,500 for his or her evaluation; the other $500 was used to pay an assistant and for express courier deliveries, telephone calls, faxes, airplane fare to attend the international jury meeting, and other expenses. In view of the costs incurred in the 2003 round, evaluators in 2005 were paid $1,200 and the rest was used for the Secretariat's expenses. I felt this was still a reasonable honorarium for evaluating the nomination – one that reflected the status and knowledge of the evaluators and compensated them for the time they devoted to the task. I did not evaluate any of the nominations myself, nor did I receive a salary from the ICTM for the work – my university supported my work as Secretary-General and gave me one course release to allow me to devote my time to the work of the Council.

Eleven lessons learned from the evaluations

Many of the nominations were well conceived and well executed, with cogent action plans. Other nominations were flawed in concept and had poorly designed action plans. Here are 11 lessons that we learned by evaluating the nominations, organised under the headings 'nominations', 'action plans' and 'ICTM evaluators'.

The nominations

There were some general features of the nominations submitted by the member nations that are worth noting.

1   The influence of nationalism. Many of the intangible heritage forms nominated by member states had some form of geopolitical and/or nationalist importance to the nominating country. Dominant groups within a nation often nominated their own traditions, not those of minority groups within their nations (although it is important to note that there were important exceptions to this generalisation). Although many forms of cultural heritage are shared across national boundaries, joint nominations were quite rare – nations preferred to claim the masterpiece as their own. In some cases, the UNESCO secretariat would intervene to encourage a joint nomination of a shared cultural heritage; in other cases that was politically or practically impossible. This problem would only be apparent if you understood the cultural geopolitics of the region and were a specialist in the intangible heritage form and its international distribution.

2   Incompetence in the preparation of the nominations. Nominations were prepared by different organisations in different countries. Many of the nominations were prepared by people and institutions apparently unfamiliar with the intangible heritage traditions they were nominating. It was surprising how often qualified specialists and research institutions within the nominating country were neither consulted in the preparation of the dossier nor in the development of the action plan. The writers' ignorance of the intangible form was clear if one knew the form but otherwise not necessarily obvious. In one case, for example, most of the master musicians whose names appeared on a list of living musicians were in fact already deceased. Bibliographies were often very incomplete, and many omitted all reference to scholarship by foreign scholars. The institutions involved in the action plans were often inappropriate to the intended objectives of the plan itself. These problems would only be apparent if you knew the individuals and institutions of the country as well as the details of the intangible heritage form and its practitioners.

3   'Cultural cleansing' and reduced cultural diversity. There were repeated instances of what I call 'cultural cleansing' and 'intentional cultural forgetting' in descriptions of the heritage and in the action plans. In many parts of Europe, for example, Rom (Gypsy) musicians were important participants in individual rites of passage such as marriage for most non-Rom, even though they suffered centuries of discrimination. Rom provided most of the music, and sometimes other services, in these rituals. The Roma peoples were not mentioned in most descriptions of the heritage forms nominated and were replaced in action plans by other groups, for example urban semi-professional troupes of dancers and musicians under the supervision of a choreographer. In other parts of the world, members of different religions who were involved in parts of each other's cultural heritage were similarly unmentioned in the descriptions and in the action plans for the safeguarding of the heritage traditions of which they were a part. This would not be noticed except by those familiar with the detailed history of a given heritage form.

4   Human rights. Some proposals failed to meet the criteria of the United Nations Declaration of Human Rights. In one example, materials submitted with the nomination included songs in the proposed heritage form that praised convicted war criminals and celebrated war crimes. Unless one understood the language of the songs, this would have passed unperceived in the nominations process.

The challenge of preparing action plans

Action plans were often more difficult to prepare than the nominations. Although there were certain problems with the objectives and description of the forms of intangible cultural heritage nominated, there were even more problems with the action plans submitted to safeguard that heritage. These weaknesses could be instructive in the future.

5   It was difficult to involve local practitioners in action plans. UNESCO required the involvement of local practitioners and culture bearers in the preparation of the nominations and action plans but this was often poorly demonstrated. The idea of involving local practitioners and culture bearers in developing projects in the Masterpieces programme was, as I described earlier, a fairly new one. It went against the pattern of national policies developed from the top (Ministry of Culture) down that is found in many countries today. In spite of very specific instructions, many action plans failed to meet the UNESCO requirements. In some cases, the required documents showing the culture bearers agreement were entirely lacking. In other cases, groups or individuals were called 'culture bearers' who were not the individuals or groups that actually carried on the traditions.

6   The gap between stated intentions and programme budgets. There was
    often a large gap between the stated involvement of the tradition bear-
    ers in a project and the details of the budget submitted with the action
    plan. In many cases, most of the money went to bureaucrats and scho-
    lars; rarely were funds provided to the artists and tradition bearers for
    things they required or for their participation in the project (in some
    cases it was as little as 10%). For example, even when all members of
    the planning group were required to attend a meeting, the scholars and
    bureaucrats would be budgeted to receive *per diems* and the local artists
    were expected to participate without remuneration. I do not mean to
    suggest that tradition bearers should always receive money, but the
    social and economic inequality of the parties in the action plans was
    often reproduced in specific details of the project budgets. These pro-
    blems would be difficult to evaluate without detailed knowledge of
    both the tradition bearers and the institutions in a given country.

The NGO evaluations

The ICTM was not perfect either. In all fairness and honesty, it is important
to reflect on the shortcomings of the NGO evaluation process.

7   Lessons can be learned from my experience selecting the evaluators. It
    was clear to me that the most knowledgeable scholars about a given
    tradition were often living or working in the nominating country. In
    many countries around the world, scholars devote most of their atten-
    tion to traditions within their nation's boundaries. Very often scholars
    in other countries in the region knew little about the traditions of their
    neighbours. Each country focused on its own traditions. The second
    most knowledgeable scholars were thus often located in nations with a
    history of colonial expansion whose scholars studied the traditions of
    other countries. Neither UNESCO nor I wanted to use these scholars to
    the exclusion of regional scholars, but sometimes I could find no other
    alternative once the in-country scholars had been eliminated.
8   Another, related, problem was language and communications. Not all
    scholars in the world were capable of reading the extensive documenta-
    tion in English or French in the nomination file, or of writing their
    evaluation in French or English. Although I told evaluators that they
    could have their evaluations translated before sending them to us, lan-
    guage difficulties were certainly one of the limiting factors in the eva-
    luation process. Another limitation was that I had to be able to contact
    the evaluator. In some countries there is little internet, there are very
    few telephones, and international couriers do not deliver. The evaluators
    who lived in such countries took much more of our time than almost all
    of the other evaluators put together, largely because of the difficulties of

communication with them. We were working under tight deadlines. If I could not reach a fully qualified evaluator after several attempts, I would have to select another.[9]

9   There was a possible bias of the evaluators in favour of the intangible traditions whose nominations they reviewed. The evaluators had spent most of their professional lives studying the forms that were being proposed for proclamation as Masterpieces. They were often strongly in favour of such a designation because they felt the art form was a masterpiece and they knew many of the artists who performed it.[10]

10   Since the ICTM evaluators knew the local situations very well, they often were quite critical of the action plans yet conflicted about criticising them. They felt that if they criticised the action plans too severely, the heritage form might not be proclaimed a masterpiece. This was a subject about which I had many long discussions with evaluators as they worked on their reports. Often the evaluators wrote suggestions for improving the action plans into their evaluations – we subsequently attached these as appendices.

11   The International Jury was comprised of eminent people who had a limited amount of time and a large number of applications to review.[11] They also had to develop and implement their own guidelines for their evaluating procedures. Even though they worked hard, and many jury members had already gone through the nominations in some detail before the meeting started, they had to make their decisions based largely on a 10-minute video, the NGO evaluations, additional information solicited from the NGO Secretary-Generals present, and a relatively short discussion among themselves. In most cases, they relied quite heavily on the video and the NGO evaluations. Members of the jury also had very important things to say about the nominations based on their own knowledge, experience, and scholarship.

Conclusions

This chapter has described the consultative role of the ICTM, which provided the technical and scientific evaluations of many of the nominations of intangible heritage for the UNESCO *Proclamation of the Masterpieces of the Oral and Intangible Heritage of Humanity* between 2001 and 2005. After describing the procedures, I presented 11 issues raised in the process from which we might draw some lessons.

The first set of issues revolves around representation and diversity. It is very important for future programmes to curb nationalist efforts to celebrate forms of intangible heritage as if they are found exclusively within a nation's borders. It should be possible to celebrate and safeguard traditions that are deeply meaningful for the citizens of a country even if they are not exclusively found there. In this era, when large numbers of migrants and refugees carry with them intangible heritage to places distant from where they were born, it is very important not to reify the link between a tradition and a nation-state. It is also important that the nomination process openly confront issues of cultural diversity within forms of cultural heritage. When different groups participate in an event (as when Rom participate in non-Rom weddings), that diversity should be recognised and maintained in safeguarding efforts. Promoting intangible heritage should not result in the reduction of prior cultural diversity.

The second set of issues arises from inadequacies in the actions plans that accompanied the nominations. Not only did the preparers of the action plans often fail to present suitable proposals for safeguarding the heritage, but scholars have confessed that it is difficult to do. Barbara Kirshenblatt-Gimblett writes: 'Safeguarding requires highly specialized skills that are of a different order from the equally specialized skills needed for the actual performance of Kutiyattam or Bunraku or Georgian Polyphonic song' (2004: 55). I recommend that there be some careful follow-up studies of those action plans that have been implemented as part of the Masterpieces programme. Because so much prior documentation of these traditions is available in the nominations files and because the action plans were presented and also critiqued during the evaluation process, follow-up studies could be extremely useful for learning what sometimes works and what sometimes does not. In this area, we need to learn from our mistakes as well as our successes. As Kurin has written, 'The ethnographic literature documents many cases in which well-intentioned efforts to help actually harmed local traditions' (Kurin 2002: 145). I also recommend that the original evaluators of the nominations be involved in the evaluation of the action plans, whenever possible.[12]

The third set of issues revolves around the selection of the evaluators by the NGO and their possible bias in favour of the heritage forms whose nominations they evaluate. Some of this will be improved by the passage of time – global communications will probably continue to improve, translation programmes may improve, and UNESCO language policies may change. I am not especially concerned about the possible bias of the scholars in favour of the heritage form nominated – UNESCO provided clear guidelines for the criteria to be used to make that determination. In preparing for future evaluations, however, it would be important to continue to require evaluators to be very specific about why they recommend a certain heritage for listing.

On a more general level, this chapter has demonstrated the importance of involving NGOs in the evaluation of nominations submitted to UNESCO. I have tried to make the process more transparent for those unfamiliar with it. I have also emphasised how important detailed and somewhat detached knowledge of traditions and the contexts in which they are performed can be for successfully evaluating a nomination. If the nominations for the

Masterpieces had not been evaluated by qualified members of the ICTM, some UNESCO Proclamations could have promoted nationalism and cultural hegemony without the knowledge of those who made the proclamation. The jury would not have known when the most knowledgeable specialists within nominating countries were being ignored in favour of politically expedient or powerful groups that knew little of the tradition and thus had few effective ideas of how to safeguard it. Traditions celebrating ethnic and/or religious discrimination and 'cultural cleansing' could have been proclaimed Masterpieces. Many weaknesses in the action plans would have gone unnoticed and important recommendations for improving action plans would not have been made by those familiar with the heritage tradition and its practitioners.

Along with the skill and tact of the UNESCO Secretariat and the probity and thoughtfulness of the International Jury, the careful work of the ICTM lent credibility to the proclamation of a form of intangible heritage as a masterpiece. I hope that those developing the procedures for nominating elements of the intangible heritage to the lists named in the *Convention for the Safeguarding of the Intangible Cultural Heritage* will recognise the importance of the expertise to be found in the membership of the international NGOs that are part of the UNESCO network.

The Masterpieces programme was a step on a path from a flawed 1989 resolution to the 2003 *Convention on the Safeguarding of the Intangible Heritage*. Creating lists has been criticised as 'the most visible, least costly, and most conventional way to "do something" – something symbolic – about neglected communities and traditions' (Kirshenblatt-Gimblett 2004: 57). This criticism is somewhat unjust. For many practitioners whose arts were proclaimed Masterpieces, the results of the programme could be very tangible and often positive. At the international level, the Masterpieces programme sensitised many countries as to the significance of their intangible heritage. With different degrees of effectiveness, they began to undertake inventories, prepare dossiers, and train specialists in administering intangible cultural heritage.

With the passage of the 2003 Convention, creating lists becomes less important than the other activities required by the Convention. Nevertheless, I believe the involvement of international NGOs in deliberations on national programmes and the representative lists would be very beneficial. What their role will be under the Convention is not yet defined (Zanten 2008), but their usefulness and probity should be clear from this description of how the ICTM evaluated the nominations for the *Proclamation of Masterpieces of the Oral and Intangible Heritage of Humanity*. As nations and organisations expand their efforts to shape and safeguard intangible heritage, I believe it is extremely important that international NGOs and their networks of specialists continue to be active participants in the process.

Notes

1 An earlier version of this chapter was delivered at the ICTM Colloquium on Intangible Cultural Heritage in Canberra, Australia, on 17 February 2008. I am grateful to the participants for their helpful comments and suggestions.

2 In the 2005 round, for example, there were 64 nominations. The ICTM evaluated 32 of them, followed closely by the International Social Science Council, which evaluated 25. Three other NGOs provided around 15 evaluations. Eleven nominations were evaluated by more than one NGO.

3 Peter J.M. Nas refers to his participation in the 2001 round of evaluations as Secretary-General of the International Union of Anthropological and Ethnological Sciences, but he does not describe the way the evaluations were prepared (Nas 2002: 148).

4 Not all NGOs were apparently as broadly consultative in their approach as the ICTM. I overheard a criticism of one NGO where the Secretary-General had written more than one evaluation himself and the evaluators overall were not a diverse group. The ICTM made a consistent effort to involve scholars from many countries in the evaluation process.

5 This process required a great deal of e-mail exchange with the evaluators, especially to clarify points that were unclear in their evaluations. It also required considerable editorial skills. I gratefully acknowledge the contributions of Megan Rancier (2003) and Kathleen Noss Van Buren (2005) in the evaluation process. Without Kelly Salloum, who administered the office of the Secretariat, the ICTM could not have accomplished the tasks at all.

6 Dr Smeets is a linguist and scholar by training. He repeatedly emphasised the importance of scholarship, of the NGOs, and spoke to the membership at one of the ICTM World Conferences. His stance on the open discussion of the procedures is another example of his commitment to transparency and scholarly understanding, tempered by diplomacy.

7 Olwig (2002: 146) notes that six of the 19 masterpieces proclaimed in the first round were from nations represented on the 18-member board; the percentage was much lower in ensuing years. The members of the jury were not representing their countries but rather had different kinds of expertise that they could bring to bear on the nominations. When nominations from their own countries were reviewed in 2003 and 2005, they left the room until the deliberations were over.

8 This is different from the procedures used for archeological sites, which I understand usually involved a visit to the nominated site. The difference reflects the specifics of research on intangible cultural heritage. The ICTM evaluators usually needed only access to a library, a telephone or e-mail, and their own usually considerable experience.

9 It was impossible to know why I was not getting responses in some cases. Scholars often spend considerable amounts of time away from their offices, and I could not be sure those I could not reach would return before the deadline had passed and had to move on.

10 A number of authors raise the issue of how 'Masterpieces' can be distinguished from other forms of intangible heritage (for example Olwig 2002: 146). The UNESCO requirements for evaluation required very specific evaluations of the excellence, depth of tradition, and status of being an 'endangered' form. Many nominations met these criteria and when they did so, the evaluators often agreed. The more difficult part of the evaluations usually revolved around the action plans.

11 The summary report on the three rounds of the Masterpieces gives the names, brief bios, and photographs of the jury members (*Brochure of the Masterpieces of the Oral and Intangible Heritage of Humanity* available on the UNESCO website).

12 Since the former evaluators would be studying the implementation of the action plans of heritage that had been proclaimed as a masterpiece, the need for confidentiality would probably be less important. Their familiarity with the form and the agencies involved might be very helpful in evaluating the results of the safeguarding efforts.

Bibliography

Aikawa, N. (2004) 'An historical overview of the preparation of the UNESCO International Convention for the Safeguarding of the Intangible Cultural Heritage', *Museum International,* 56(1–2): 137–49.

——— (2005) '30 years of reflection and commitment for safeguarding intangible heritage', edited videotaped interview on *Second Proclamation of Masterpieces of the Oral and Intangible Heritage of Humanity,* CD-ROM, UNESCO.

Carmo, R.A.M.L. (2007) 'As contribuições dos estudos etnomusicológicos para as políticas de salvaguarda do patrimônio imaterial', in *Anais do XVII Congresso da Associação Nacional de Pesquisa e Pós graduação em Música-ANPPOM,* Rio de Janeiro: ANPPOM.

Gallois, D. (2007) 'Os Wajãpi' ('The Wajãpi' a paper on the impact of the 2003 proclamation on the Wajãpi Indians of Brazil) presented at the seminar 'Memória das Culturas' ('Memory of Cultures'), Instituto de Estudos Brasileiros, Universidade de São Paulo, São Paulo, Brazil, 29 November 2007.

ICTM (2008) *International Council for Traditional Music.* Available online: http://ictmusic.org/ICTM/ (Accessed April 6 2008).

Kirshenblatt-Gimblett, B. (2004) 'Intangible heritage as metacultural production', *Museum International,* 56(1–2): 52–64.

Kurin, R. (2002) 'Comment on Peter M. Nas, masterpieces of oral and intangible culture, reflections on the UNESCO World Heritage List', *Current Anthropology,* 42(1): 144–5.

——— (2004) 'Safeguarding intangible cultural heritage in the 2003 UNESCO Convention: a critical appraisal', *Museum International,* 56(1–2): 66–76.

Nas, P.J.M. (2002) 'Masterpieces of oral and intangible culture, reflections on the UNESCO World Heritage List', *Current Anthropology,* 42(1): 139–43 and 147–8.

Olwig, K.F. (2002) 'Comment on Peter M. Nas, masterpieces of oral and intangible culture, reflections on the UNESCO World Heritage List', *Current Anthropology,* 42(1): 145–6.

Sandroni, C. (2005) 'Questões em torno do dossiê do samba de roda', in A. Falcão (ed.), *Registro e Políticas de Salvaguarda Para as Culturas Populares,* Rio de Janeiro: IPHAN/CNFCP [Série Encontros e Estudos; 6], pp. 45–53.

Seitel, P. (ed.) (2001) *Safeguarding Traditional Cultures: A Global Assessment of the 1989 UNESCO Recommendation on the Safeguarding of Traditional Culture and Folklore,* Washington DC: Center for Folklife and Cultural Heritage, Smithsonian Institution.

UNESCO (2001a) *First Proclamation of the Oral and Intangible Heritage of Humanity,* Paris: UNESCO.

——— (2001b) *Proclamation of Masterpieces of the Oral and Intangible Heritage of Humanity, Guide for the Presentation of Candidature Files,* Paris: UNESCO.

——— (2008) *Proclamation of the Masterpieces of the Oral and Intangible Heritage of Humanity* (2001–5). Available online at: http://www.unesco.org/culture/ich/index.php?pg=00103 (Accessed April 6, 2008).

Zanten, W. Van (2008) 'Report to the Executive Board February 17, 2008', a memorandum prepared for the ICTM Executive Board meeting in Canberra, Australia, in February 2008.

Part 2

The material politics and practices of the intangible

Chapter 7

Following the length and breadth of the roots

Some dimensions of intangible heritage

Dawson Munjeri

Introduction

This chapter is premised on the assumption that since October 2003, when member states of UNESCO unanimously adopted the *Convention for the Safeguarding of the Intangible Cultural Heritage* (ICHC), any serious discussion of intangible heritage must be influenced by this Convention. Hailed as marking 'a decisive point in the comprehension of the concept of heritage' (Vinson 2004: 4–6), in both conception and execution the ICHC was meant to usher in the era in which intangible heritage would be recognised as integral to cultural identity, cultural diversity, human creativity, human rights and sustainable development (Preamble: para. 2 and 3). The Convention provides a series of safeguards against 'grave threats of deterioration, disappearance and destruction of the intangible cultural heritage' (Preamble: para. 4); those threats include the process of globalisation and social transformation.

The Convention reflects the determined efforts by the international community to comprehensively define the notion of intangible cultural heritage and its many manifestations. The parameters, definitions and applications of intangible cultural heritage are severally and collectively premised on the recognition that communities, in particular local and Indigenous communities, play a critical role in the production, safeguarding, maintenance and recreation of the intangible cultural heritage (Preamble para. 7 and *inter alia* Articles 2.1, 11–14). In that context, the definition of intangible cultural heritage encompasses those practices, representations, expressions and knowledge 'that communities, groups and, in some cases, individuals *recognize as part of their cultural heritage*' (Article 2 (1), emphasis added). If implemented to the letter and spirit, this morally-driven Convention, should, as Mohamed Bedjaoui, the Chair of the Intergovernmental Experts Group entrusted with drafting the Convention says, 'provide this "poor relation of culture" (intangible cultural heritage) with the legal framework to find a set of universally accepted principles for comprehending situations' (Bedjaoui 2004: 150). Ideally, such an outcome should result in intangible cultural heritage playing a role of 'reconstruction of truly humane humanism in a kingdom without exile for all' (Bedjaoui 2007: 1–2).

The moral imperative would ultimately rectify the imbalances created and perpetuated by an array of Conventions that were targeted at tangible heritage.[1] The main beneficiaries there were those societies steeped in materialist or 'monumentalist' traditions and that are mainly in the developed 'North'. Societies whose heritage was mostly 'immaterial' were mostly in the 'South'. The 'Expert meeting on the "Global Strategy" and thematic studies for a representative World Heritage List', appropriately pointed out that 'living cultures and especially the "traditional" ones with their depth, their wealth, their complexity and their diverse relationships with their environment, figured very little on the [World Heritage] List' (WHC-94/ CONF.003/INF. 6: 3–4). The issues of balance, representation and credibility thus became more than a moral issue but *inter alia* of justice, geopolitics and averting a 'clash of civilisations'. As Mr Koichiro Matsuura, the Director-General of UNESCO (himself a Japanese national of the 'South'), put it:

> As I delved deeper into this issue, I came to recognize that through its exclusive focus on the tangible cultural heritage and natural sites, most of which was located in the 'North' – the 1972 Convention [and other cultural conventions] was unable to deal adequately with the living cultural expressions of the 'South'. Since becoming Director-General of UNESCO in November 1999, I have sought to rectify this situation.
>
> (Matsuura 2004: 4)

The underlying message of this chapter is that, notwithstanding these good intentions, the weaknesses of those conventions on tangible cultural heritage may yet be replicated with respect to the intangible cultural heritage. The current trend, as reflected in some pronouncements and actions, points to that negative prospect. There is some serious disconnection in the interpretation of the purpose, meaning and the application of intangible cultural heritage. All parties and stakeholders may be reading from the same script, but their interpretation is much influenced by the *interests* of the *actors*, and the *issues* at stake. These issues are defined in the context of the historical, temporal, spatial, socio-economic, geo-political environments and from varying perspectives and vantage points, hence the incongruity characterising the debate on intangible cultural heritage. Using case studies, this chapter illustrates how these historical, socio-cultural, legal, economic and geo-political dictates are having an influence that cyclically affects the conceptual, theoretical and political constructs in the spatial realm of the local, national, regional and global.

A systems approach to intangible cultural heritage

Munyaradzi Manyanga (2004) narrates his experiences as a site manager at an archaeological site known as Ntaba zika Mambo in the Matebeleland North province in Zimbabwe. The site was declared a national monument in 1952 because of its significance as a centre of a sixteenth–seventeenth-century Rozvi Mambo civilisation. It is located on a private property (Meikles Holdings) and administered under the provisions of the *National Museums and Monuments of Zimbabwe, Act 25/11*. Under *Act 25/11,* and because the land is 'private property', access to the site is highly restricted, while the Act also does not permit unauthorised practices, excavations and 'distortions of the cultural landscape' (Manyanga 2004: 3).

However, the 1990s witnessed 'the revival of living traditions' and Andrew Moyo, a traditional spiritual leader, together with his spiritual group, 'invaded' the site for the express purpose of conducting rituals. These practices entailed clearing part of the site, constructing a shelter and a granary, the latter to store grain required for ritual ceremonies. At the behest of their ancestors, the social and spiritual values of the site emboldened them to defy *Act 25/11* and the civil law on property rights. Both sets of laws emphasised the importance of the physical heritage as 'property'. This legal framework in Zimbabwe does not refer to intangible heritage. The conflict between the two stakeholders was essentially one of the important factors attached to values: the tangible versus intangible and their placing in the hierarchical order. Were the actions of the group, as Manyanga asks, 'a desire to revive their past traditions through the spiritual consultation of the Mambo shrine or is this coupled with a desire to repossess their ancestral land and have a share of it?' (1999: 13). In essence, is empowerment inherent in spiritual heritage synonymous with empowerment and entitlement to tangible heritage? In the case of Ntaba zika Mambo, after protracted discussions, a compromise was reached whereby the party valuing the essentially tangible was given powers over the tangible heritage while the party interested in the spiritual heritage obtained access to the intangible asset for the purpose of practising their tradition. According to Manyanga, this win–win situation resulted in 'the revival of these living traditions at the site and that has enhanced the value of the site' (Manyanga 1999: 7). Its utilisation as a spiritual site by the people who had a direct link to the heritage enhanced the cultural and religious values of the site; simultaneously the national legal framework, which protects tangible heritage, has been enhanced by local communities who now respect the physical attributes of the site and help protect it. This is a lucid demonstration that tangible heritage can indeed be an expression of underlying norms and values (the intangible dimension). The Ntaba zika Mambo equally illustrates that there is a symbiotic relationship between the tangible and the intangible (Bouchenaki 2004: 8).

As the chief executive officer of National Museums and Monuments of Zimbabwe (NMMZ), in September 1991, the author received a letter from the local community around the Great Zimbabwe world heritage site, which read, in part:

> We feel it is necessary to tell you *what pains us most* with regards to the keeping of our African traditional customs and with particular reference to Great Zimbabwe ... There used to be one major sacred gathering at sacred places. All this is no longer taking place. *The people who look after them* [NMMZ] *do not know how to practise these traditions.* All they do is follow government instructions. ... When independence came, we Africans took control [of Zimbabwe and] the traditional leaders celebrated because they felt we could now practice our customs and traditions. The traditional leaders soon discovered that our [Black] government was equally tough in preventing the traditional customs from being practiced. *Our ancestral spirits* both senior and junior are not happy with what the Government is doing. *What pains us most is that no one is allowed to practice the customs.*
>
> (Manwa *et al.* 1991, emphasis added.)

The circumstances surrounding the complaint are essentially similar to those at Ntaba zika Mambo; they relate to the enforcement of *Act 25/11*. In the case of Great Zimbabwe, the situation was compounded by the inscription of the site onto the UNESCO World Heritage List in 1986, as the stricter provisions of the *Convention Concerning the Protection of the World Cultural and Natural Heritage, 1972* (World Heritage Convention) and its Operational Guidelines were applied. This Convention focuses on physical heritage, however, the bygone Great Zimbabwe civilisation was intrinsically linked to the spiritual traditions of that civilisation, in that Great Zimbabwe was a major centre of the Mwari deity. Great Zimbabwe was and continues to be considered by many Zimbabweans as the centre of their historical cultural identity, hence the naming of the country after the site. As Alison Johnson points out, such World Heritage sites are singled out for qualities attributed by national governments and the international community (2006: 121). This can result in conflict between the universal values for which the place is listed and the values that are important for the local communities. The ceremonies carried out at Great Zimbabwe by local communities and elders are not the reason why the site is on the World Heritage List. The site is on that List because of its spectacular tangible attributes, in particular the monumental dry stone architecture and engineering skills used by the site's builders.

This case introduces another dimension of dealing with intangible heritage. Where the stakes are high, and where the intangible heritage is more than just of local significance, the political dimension comes to the fore. In the case of Great Zimbabwe the issue was only resolved when high-level political directives permitted customary practices as long as they did not negatively affect the heritage properties. On 9 January 2004, traditional chiefs drawn from all over Zimbabwe convened at Great Zimbabwe to celebrate this victory. In 2005, the site was the venue for the ceremonial reburial of the freedom fighters that died in the war of liberation (1966–80) which culminated in the independence of Zimbabwe. Thus yet another layer of meaning was added to the patina of spiritual values: the site as the source of the liberation spirit. However, there is tension for those wishing to access the site for spiritual purposes, between the NMMZ which is the *de facto* and *de jure* authority in terms of *Act 25/11*, which relates to the tangible heritage, and the traditional authorities, who hold similar authority with respect to the spiritual heritage. A resolution was possible when both policies accepted that what Manwa *et al.* refer to as, 'what pains us most with regards to the keeping of our African traditional customs' could be achieved within the rule of law (1991). It was essentially a mutual acceptance by all that 'intangible cultural heritage must be seen as a broader framework within which tangible heritage takes on its shape and significance' (Bouchenaki 2004: 8).

The above cases also demonstrate the very strong attachment of communities to their traditions and customs. The community actors in the Ntaba zika Mambo case are primarily driven by the interest in reviving their tradition, and secondarily in resuscitating the values that are inherent in the bygone Rozvi Mambo dynasty. The legitimacy of their cause is morally premised while the focus is on safeguarding their heritage through practising and transmitting it. In this way, intangible cultural heritage plays a central role in the cultural identity of the people and enactment is central. Significantly, as Manyanga stresses, in this case, 'religious prayer groups rarely claim ownership of physical entities of the monument but seek permission to fully utilize it as their place of consultation and for it not to be desecrated' (Manyanga 2004: 7).

However, while the actors at Ntaba zika Mambo are primarily spiritual authorities, the signatories to the 'Letter to the Authorities' were led by Chief Zephaniah Charumbira who was powerful both at the local and national levels. At that time, he was a Senator in the House of Assembly and the President of the Zimbabwe Council of Chiefs. Drawn from different clans and backgrounds, the focus of the community was to ensure not only the recognition of their rights to the intangible heritage in terms of both access and control. They were equally concerned with the physical fabric embodying the spiritual heritage. This came out clearly in an anonymous letter (later traced to one of the aforementioned signatories) that was published in the 'Letters to the Editor' column of the daily newspaper, *The Herald* on 24 June 1994. Signed 'Very Concerned', it in part reads:

We are concerned at the state of affairs at Great Zimbabwe. The decision by the Government [sic. NMMZ] to engage the French to rebuild the ruins are [sic] *stupid and ill-advised. They should have consulted us the elders of the area* but we were treated like outsiders. What do the French know about Great Zimbabwe or even the National Museum people? Absolutely nothing except patches of its history.

I understand that one wall which they had built with cement [sic] collapsed *showing the supernatural power of the spirits*. If something meaningful is to be done to reconstruct the ruins then the elders have to do it after brewing appeasement beer. We must follow our tradition if we want to prevent their collapse.

(*The Herald*, 24 June 1994: 9 emphasis added)

The background to this letter was the decision of the NMMZ to preserve the site using scientifically approved international conservation standards and techniques. The dry stone architecture of the site has always presented many problems in terms of conservation and so expertise has sometimes been sourced globally, in this case from Loughborough University (UK) not from France.

The bottom line is that 'Very Concerned' expressed the strong attachment of the local community to their heritage. Use of 'cement' desecrates the dry stone nature of the architecture and concomittantly pollutes the spiritual heritage because lime-based cement is a 'foreign body'. The important message is that the physical fabric is subordinate to the intangible and so any remedial action to the physical component of the heritage must be initiated and controlled by the spiritual realm using the traditional and spiritual custodians of the site and their designated skilled personnel. It is these local communities who are endowed with the traditional knowledge that can save this heritage because the others know 'absolutely nothing'. As the ICHC underlines, it is this traditional knowledge that must be recognised because it plays an important role in the production, safeguarding, maintenance and recreation of intangible cultural heritage (Preamble: para. 7). The Great Zimbabwe community is also demonstrating that spiritual purity is a factor of physical purity and that, in the tiered system, the sacred and intangible values reign supreme (Manyanga 2004: 7). So supreme are these values that they embolden the local community to challenge the decision of the national government as 'stupid' and 'ill-advised'.

The two cases also illustrate that intangible cultural heritage is a factor of the local, domestic and international laws. Heritage laws, at least in most Southern African countries, have not adequately accommodated the intangible dimension of heritage. The legal regime is thus an important determinant in the matrix of relationships surrounding intangible heritage. As it is 'in an ongoing process that began with colonization in Southern Africa and has continued undiminished by the attainment of political independence, local communities have experienced alienation from their cultural heritage' (Ndoro 2005: 15).

In both cases (Ntaba zika Mambo and Great Zimbabwe), the local communities are non-resident. While living in close proximity to the sites, these communities were physically removed from their ancestral lands during the colonial era, and nothing has changed in the post-colonial period. Co-existence between the 'official' heritage authorities and traditional heritage authorities is by way of *quid pro quo* arrangements. Physical possession is retained by the 'formal authorities', while the traditional authorities gain the spiritual possession. It is an issue of balancing the temporal with the spiritual and the profane with the sacred.

The ICHC definition of intangible cultural heritage includes practices, experiences, knowledge and skills that communities recognise as part of their cultural heritage. However, the degree and extent of dependence on those customs, traditions and practices is relative. There are those manifestations of intangible cultural heritage that are essential for providing basic physiological human needs. There are other manifestations that are not of a life-sustaining nature. The Zimbabwe cases belong to the latter manifestations, while the case below illustrates instances where intangible cultural heritage practices, knowledge and skills are a *sine qua non* for the survival of some communities.

On 8 August 2007, the Kenyan newspaper, *The Daily Nation* carried a news item titled, 'Gripe of Ogieks now forced into modernity'. The opening lines read:

> Honey and dogs are all an *Ogiek* man needs to get himself a wife. Uncommon as it may look, *Ogieks* have for years shunned the conventional lifestyle and have stuck with customs and practices that enabled them to blend with nature.
>
> But that cultural practice is now facing challenges [threats] after the ethnic group was evicted from government forests paving the way of intermarriage with other tribes that prefer cows and cash as bride price.
>
> (Odunga 2007: 3–4)

The item relates to a Kenyan Indigenous community of hunters/gatherers known as the Ogieks (or Okiek), but disparagingly referred to by other ethnic groups as '*Dorobo*', a term derived from the Maasai term *il torobo*, which means 'a poor person who has no cattle and has to live on hunting and gathering' (Bernstein 1973: 47). For centuries, the Ogieks dominated the central highlands of Kenya, but they have gradually been squeezed out by other tribes, colonial settlers and in the postcolonial era by pastoral and agricultural communities. The introduction by the colonial government of game and forest laws saw the criminalisation of the Ogieks. The *Forest Act* and *Wildlife Conservation Act* had a multiple effect, the Ogieks were evicted from their traditional lands in order to 'conserve forests' (Migingo 2004). The 1937/38 Kenya Land (Carter) Commission systematically sought to concentrate them into White farms as 'squatters' or in the Forestry Department labour camps. In addition, by replacing indigenous forests with exotic conifer plantations which produced 'totally sterile, unproductive plantations useless for either bees or wild animals' (Kamau 2000), the traditions and customs of the Ogiek were undermined. Some of them were forced into arable farming and livestock keeping and intermarried with other ethnic groups, a practice the Ogieks strongly resent: 'Our daughters nowadays sneak into neighboring villages and in the process [regrettably] marry men from neighboring tribes who could present cattle as bride price' lamented one elder Ng'etich (Odunga 2007: 3). Despite these pressures, the Ogieks remained 'untamed'. To the European farmers, foresters and administrators these Ogieks were a 'tiresome problem' and 'elusive' uncountable people lacking a recognisable hierarchical structure, resistant to tidy organisation (Yeoman 1993: 3).

Key to their survival was their dependence on the indigenous forests out of which they eked a living and from which they drew inspiration. They became well known for their 'astonishing technical expertise in their special arts of hunting and bee-keeping and having a most unusual sensibility in relation to their forests and creatures which inhabit them' (Kamau 2000).

It was traditional knowledge borne out of acute powers of observation and profound respect for wildlife and natural history. According to the anthropologist Huntingford, the Ogieks 'only killed to meet their domestic needs and [hunted] predominantly only those species with buoyant populations such as warthog and tree hyrax' (1955: 602). What was true in 1955 remains true today, as testified by the present generation of Ogieks. Samuel Laldin speaking to *The Daily Nation* had this to say: 'During our stay in the forest we used to conserve the forest and would not allow anyone to cut trees for charcoal or any other purpose. ... We knew trees were homes for bees and destroying them meant that flowers which are the source of nectar could be ruined as well' (Odunga 2007: 3–4). In their deposition to the Njonjo Land Commission (tasked to settle the land issue in Kenya), the Ogieks' submission was that:

> Our history has shown that we are environmentally friendly, our land tenure system is also environmentally friendly. ... Members of Parliament [we] are asking [you] to help us to live in our ancestral land and *retain our human and cultural identities as Kenyans of Ogiek origin.* We the Ogieks likes [sic] living in isolation where flora and fauna provides [sic] with psychological comfort.
>
> (Ogiek submission 2000: Appendix, emphasis added)

The message that runs through this is the strength of tradition in holding societies together and as a stamp of cultural identity. As Nader and Bakhtiar appropriately point out:

> There is nothing more timely today than the *truth* which is timeless that the message that comes from tradition and is relevant now because it has been relevant at all [time] in traditions. Such a message belongs to a now which has been, is and will ever be present. To *speak of tradition is to speak of immutable principles* of their application to different moments of time and space.
>
> (Nader and Bakhtiar 1975: xi, emphasis added)

In the case of the Ogieks, that *truth* includes the timelessness of a tradition that had developed a complex rights-based organisational system centred on different local lineages. To outsiders, these were people 'lacking a recognizable hierarchical structure, resistant to tidy organization'. It is such non-community-framed misconceptions that impact negatively on intangible cultural heritage. Commenting on the nomadic way of life in Mongolia, Jacques Legrand notes the same misconceptions with respect to nomadic pastoral systems. He rightly notes that the general perception of nomadism is focused on mobility, but 'reducing nomadism to mobility is a major obstacle to understanding nomadism' (Legrand 2006: 60–1). This reductionism results in failure to understand that 'mobility is subordinate to dispersion and irregularity and mastery of irregularity is the central feature of nomadism' (2006: 61). Nomadism, he argues 'is the entire set of elements which develop peculiar social relationships and institutions along the path that is at once technical, social, political and historical' (Legrand 2006: 62–3).

Similarly, the truth about the Ogiek tradition is that their complex rights-based organisational structure did not extend to the exclusive use of territory for residence or hunting by the owning lineage. A lineage could bequeath the honey-collecting rights to other persons or lineages. This involved legal compensations, bride-price payment or outright purchase in those zones where there were no animals (Blackburn 1974: 146, cited in Kamau 2000). The Ogiek community, like the communities at Great Zimbabwe and Ntaba zika Mambo, was not a threat to the physical landscape, and the issue of land ownership does not arise. On the other hand, the centrality of honey in Ogiek culture means that without honey, and the conditions necessary to obtain it, the very existence of the Ogieks is threatened. Honey is the dowry, and is used for multiple purposes: *Sosomek* honey for curing flu and for the quick development of children's teeth; *Ngunuk* honey for curing diarrhoea, and the bees themselves have stings that are an appropriate substitute for injections. As the 69-year-old N'getich testifies, 'I have a natural phobia for injections since I have never been injected since I was born. Few stings from bees in the forest could heal some diseases' (quoted in Odunga 2007: 3). The issues here are of an existential nature vis-à-vis those at Ntaba zika Mambo and Great Zimbabwe.

It is against this background that the Ogieks have, though pacifists, but faced with threats to their intangible heritage, a *sine qua non* condition for their survival, continued the struggle that began in the 1930s. Constant efforts to remove them and integrate them in other communities continue to be resisted. When in 1989 the Nakuru District Commissioner tried to transfer them to West Mau, an estimated 90 per cent refused and those who left under duress returned. Those recently evicted from Kipkurere, Cerengony, Kelboi and Tinderei forests in Nandi South and Uasin Gishu districts continue the resistance because they want to go back to the forests to live normal lives. However, in the view of the Rift Valley Provincial Commissioner 'having land was not the only sure way to a successful life and instead [he] asked the "squatters" to explore other income generating activities" (Odunga 2007: 3). The Commissioner is also quoted as saying 'water catchments, land under forest cover and the general ecosystem must be *safeguarded* against any form of depletion. Therefore it's absolutely necessary to conserve our forests' (Odunga 2007: 3, emphasis added). A classic case of what Ali Mazrui describes: 'Western culture introduced into Africa a kind of ecological apartheid, explicitly designating certain areas exclusively for animals and others for human beings' (1986: 54). The Ogieks do not contest the importance of forests; the Ogieks actually have strained relationships with other communities who they blame for encroaching into the forest and introducing agriculture (Bie and Matokwe 2007: 4).

The case further highlights the real definition of 'communities' and the role they play in intangible cultural heritage. The Ogieks typify entirely eco-based ethno-communities for whom the ICHC could have been primarily meant to safeguard, and before it the UN *Convention on Biological Diversity, 1992* (CBD). The latter emphasises the important role of Indigenous communities and their traditional knowledge and innovation for the sustainable development of natural resources and preservation of biological diversity. It is about the preservation of ways of life and knowledge of the holders of traditional cultural practices. Article 8(j) of the CBD implores Contracting Parties 'to respect, preserve and maintain knowledge, innovations and practices of local communities that embody traditional lifestyles relevant for conservation and sustainable use and to promote their application'. The Ogieks are a classic example of communities who are at the centre of intangible heritage. They are the vortex that perpetuates the continuation of traditions, customs and practices. It is these communities that the human rights dimension of the ICHC targets, and why that dimension is given preeminence by its placing in the second paragraph of the Preamble to the Convention. The Ogiek's case is above all testimony that 'survival of the intangible cultural heritage much more than any other aspect of cultural heritage depends on the survival of the way of life of a community or a group and their economic viability' (Blake 2006: 25).

It is this critical message that underpins the ICHC. Regrettably, it is only those at the centre that seem to view it that way. For them, it is not an issue of 'To whom it may concern', but one that concerns them most. The centre versus the periphery in a scenario of concentric circles of relative dependence on the intangible environment is central to the discourse on intangible cultural heritage. This is succinctly captured in the observations of the Vanuatu delegate to the Intergovernmental Experts meeting on the ICHC who remarked that what makes intangible cultural heritage unique is that it targets the people, groups, and communities that enact the intangible cultural heritage while other conventions target the products. It is a view that resonated with the participants from many developing countries, in particular in Sub-Saharan Africa. The Ogieks' case also shows that the term 'community' conjures in some minds ascription of certain rights – Blake (2006) uses the term 'special rights'; however, to be consistent with paragraph 2 of the Preamble, it becomes not a question of special rights but of human rights.

The Ogieks' case is but a total manifestation of the definition of intangible cultural heritage (ICHC Article 2(i)):

> practices, representations, expressions, knowledge, skills – as well as the instruments, objects, artefacts and cultural spaces associated therewith – that communities, groups and, in some cases, individuals recognize as part of their cultural heritage. This intangible cultural heritage, trans-mitted from generation to generation, is constantly recreated by com-munities and groups in response to their environment, their interaction with nature and their history, and provides them with a sense of identity and continuity, thus promoting respect for cultural diversity and human creativity.

It emphasises the point stressed by Richard Kurin, that this 'definition assumes that intangible cultural heritage is articulated with the social pro-cesses and other aspects of life. *It cannot be isolated from the larger constellation of lifestyles nor de-articulated from a broader world of ecological, economic, political and geographic interactions*' (Kurin 2007: 12, emphasis added).

The Ogieks owe their very existence to traditions and customs that define their way of life. It is not the possession of land as the physical asset *per se* that is at issue. In both the Zimbabwean and Kenyan cases, however, land is important as a medium through which intangible values are expressed, its inner meaning is the core of traditions and customs which transcend all else. It is what Indigenous Australians refer to as 'country', which is the 'Indigenous view of the cultural and natural landscape of the Indigenous people' (Sullivan 2004: 53). What is this concept of country?

Country is a place that gives and receives life. People talk about country in the same way they would talk about a person: they speak to country, sing to country, visit country, worry about country, feel sorry about country. People say that country knows, hears, smells, takes notice, takes care, is sorry or happy. … Because of this richness, country is home and peace, nourishment for body, mind and spirit.

(Rose 1996: 7–8, quoted in Sullivan 2004: 53)

The Ogieks are not after 'country' as a physical manifestation and physical possession. They want the landscape as a medium to perpetuate their way of life. As already mentioned: 'Significantly rights do not extend to the exclusive use of territory for residence of hunting by the owning lineage. A lineage could even bequeath the honey collecting rights to other persons or lineages' (Blackburn 1974: 146). The debate that surrounded the drafting of the ICHC, and one that continues to preoccupy the Intergovernmental Committee for the Safeguarding of the Intangible Heritage, relates to the connotations of 'community' and ascription of special rights to them as a 'community'. This is because states are looking narrowly at the physical manifestation of 'rights' and that is why to them the term 'community' carries much 'baggage'. As such, they see it as a 'slippery slope towards the recognition of collective rights in contradiction to human rights law that ascribes rights to individuals' (Blake 2006: 24). It is this failure to comprehend the deeper meaning of intangible heritage, which typically triggers the reaction of the Provincial Commissioner of the Rift Valley, whose response to the Ogieks' persistent requests for them to return to their home, the forest, is: 'Land was not the only sure way to a successful life' and so the 'squatters' 'must explore other income generating activities' (Odunga 2007: 3). That is certainly a wrong answer to an unasked question. Material wealth is not the issue.

A seemingly irreconcilable situation could be resolved if only the two sets of actors realised they had everything in common in terms of interests over the issue of the natural resources and physical terrain. In the view of the Rift Valley Commissioner, 'water catchments, land under forest cover and the general eco-system must be safeguarded against any form of depletion therefore it is absolutely necessary to conserve *our forests*' (emphasis added). It is a message that ironically resonates with that of the Ogieks, who unlike the Commissioner, cannot survive without the forests and therefore have a vested interest in conserving the forests threatened not only by the actions of the encroaching agriculturalists, but by the official policies that replace indigenous floral species with exotic conifers. The solution lies in better defining and broadening the meaning of 'our forests', putting emphasis on inclusion rather than on exclusion of the other actors and their interests. It also lies in bringing into a symbiotic relationship the eco-system and the ethno-systems based on Indigenous knowledge. That way the accumulated knowledge becomes the foundation for future generations to develop their own under-standing of both the cultural landscape and human relationships (Brown Weiss 1989: 2–4).

For this to happen, the knowledge systems must be removed from the periphery and brought to the centre, bringing the community from the margins to the core. As aptly put by one delegation to the first extraordinary session of the Intergovernmental Committee for the Safeguarding of the Intangible Cultural Heritage (IGCSICH), 'Communities are the main differ-ence between tangible and intangible heritage' (Draft Summary Record IGC SICH 2007: 8). Christopher Wulf (2005), using a number of cases that relate to rituals (festivals, marriage, birth and death rites, etc.), demonstrates that successful performance of a ritual depends on the individual's 'body arrangement' and how it relates to other participants. Rituals are only suc-cessful where there is empathy in terms of ideas, practices, beliefs, traditions and shared values that create group identity. Therefore, character and con-tinuity are bound up with the corporeality of the community. The body has to be 'inscribed' within a certain society and culture which has been shaped by these processes (relationships) and which itself simultaneously creates social and cultural processes (Wulf 2005: 86–8). Herein lies the importance of both inter-generational and intra-generational transmission of knowledge. Through that process, solidarity is established as each generation receives a cultural legacy from the past, holds it in trust, and passes it to future gen-erations (Brown Weiss 1989: xxviii). Wulf shows that through the perfor-mance character of rituals, the rituals themselves help create the community and cultural identity. This applies not only to rituals, but also to all other manifestations detailed in Article 2.2(a) of the ICHC.

The community itself becomes a phenomenon and mechanism whose continuity is sustained by the intangible heritage that is enacted. While the community creates intangible heritage, that creation replicates itself in turn giving life to the continuation of the community. It is a cyclical and con-tinuous phenomenon and process premised on community-based knowledge and hence the importance of ensuring that it is the community's responsi-bility to safeguard this invaluable intangible resource:

> Loss of knowledge, whether through an initial failure to conserve exist-ing knowledge, through lack of maintenance or through a failure to gather it when it is available represents an impoverishment of the knowledge of future generations.
>
> (Brown Weiss 1989: 262)

It is against a background of such truisms that one finds it incomprehensible that four years after the adoption of the ICHC, there is still debate on an acceptable definition of 'community', and on whether or not, and to what extent, the community's consent should be sought when considering what constitutes intangible cultural heritage. At the first extraordinary session of the Intergovernmental Council for the Safeguarding of Intangible Cultural Heritage 'the Chairperson recalled that many different views on how to interpret communities' existed (first Extraordinary Session 2007: para. 57 and 125). How then can the Convention be implemented if the debate follows this trend? The NGO 'Traditions pour Demain' (Traditions for Tomorrow) succinctly puts it: 'The Convention clearly gives communities a central role in the recognition and safeguarding of intangible cultural heritage. *They (communities) are indeed the keystone.* ... [and] are at the forefront of the concern of the Convention and a vital stakeholder regarding its implementation' (Traditions pour Demain 2007: 2, emphasis added). Regrettably, as the NGO adds: 'Although the community participation issue has been discussed since the first session of the Intergovernmental Council Meeting in Algiers 2006, only minor progress has been made' (Traditions pour Demain 2007: 2). Intangible heritage experts have noted that some interests 'resent having to cede anything to communities' (Kurin 2007: 16). It has become an issue of the dynamics of power, about the centre versus the periphery, and an issue of who occupies which space in the hierarchy. The issue of defining 'community' should have been concluded when the Experts on Community Involvement painstakingly came up with a succinct, apolitical and practical definition of community, based on realities. Community, 'a network of people whose sense of identity and connectedness emerges from a shared relationship that is rooted in practice and transmission of or engagement with intangible cultural heritage' (UNESCO UIHS/ACCU 2006: 7 and 9). With some amplification and refinements that should have ended the debate. The 'search' is still on because, in the view of some states, time is needed to see 'how the Committee wishes to view "community"' (1st Extraordinary Session (para. 57)). Commenting on the debate on the *Convention on the Protection and Promotion of the Diversity of Cultural Expressions*, Alan Riding said, 'Try turning this seemingly straightforward idea into an international treaty however and things soon become complicated. Why? The reason is simple: behind the idealistic screen of cultural diversity, *weighty, economic and political issues are at stake*' (Riding 2005: 2, emphasis added). This is essentially the same issue with respect to 'community'. As Blake argues 'the issue of safeguarding intangible cultural heritage is by its nature controversial since it can be achieved only through recognition of the central role communities play in its creation and safeguarding' (2006: 35).

The Great Zimbabwe, Ntaba zika Mambo and Ogieks cases suggest the utility of the UIHS/ACCU definition. The cases that follow illustrate, however, that the stakes can even be higher.

In order to coincide with the 176th session of the UNESCO Executive Board, the Ministry of Culture of China held an exhibition at UNESCO Headquarters in April 2007. Titled, 'Festival of China's Intangible Cultural Heritage' the exhibition showed the significant role intangible cultural heritage has played in China for a period of over 5,000 years. In the preface to the published catalogue of the exhibition, the Minister of Culture, Sun Jiazheng, underscored the fact that it is a 'national development strategy to protect China's intangible cultural heritage'. The recurrent theme of the catalogue is 'the splendor of Chinese civilization, nation, bravery and innovation':

> China's intangible cultural heritage is the symbol of the Chinese nation, the precious source for fostering the self identity of the Chinese nation, the solid basis for promoting unity of nationalities and safeguarding the unification of the country as well as the important force of unifying all peoples.
>
> (Ministry of Culture, PRC 2007: 30)

Simply put, safeguarding intangible cultural heritage is synonymous with safeguarding the unity of the People's Republic of China. Through intangible heritage, China's 56 ethnic groups are united to achieve 'the great revitalization of the Chinese nation'. In effect, the present resurgent economic growth, and China's developing role as a global power, is a factor of its intangible cultural heritage 'manifesting the diversity of China and diversity of world culture displaying its distinctive ethnic features'. Above all it is:

> The valuable treasure of all humanity and enjoys a high prestige in the treasure house of the world culture. Its mode of thinking, values, principles and its ideas can provide valuable reference for the international community to realize the ideal of equal exchanges, harmonious existence and common development.
>
> (Ministry of Culture, PRC 2007: 31)

The exhibition catalogue shows how this has been achieved and how this momentum will be sustained. A closer look at one genre of cultural expression – the Chinese opera – reveals how it can be achieved. The Chinese traditional opera is 'a synthesis of literature, music, dance, acrobatics and fine arts' (Ministry of Culture, PRC 2007: 28). All these components give it a Chinese identity. It is, however, a Chinese opera composed of 'Ethnic operas' such as the Dai, Peking (Han), Tibetan, Zwang, Bai and Dong operas. These ethnic operas have local variants featuring regional dialects, music etc. Min, Jueju, Qinqiang and Chuanju are some such examples (Ministry of Culture, PRC 2007: 28).

What can be said of opera equally applies to other expressions such as acrobatics, artisanship, and so forth. The linkage between the local, provincial and the national ensures consistency and unity of the country's cultural expressions. It is clear what the centre is and its locus. The whole is made greater than the sum of its parts, through the Chinese government drawing up the rules and regulations to provide guidance, and to be an effective guarantee for the protection of the intangible heritage. The central principle is 'Government leadership, social participation, clarification of duty and responsibilities, combination of forces as well as long-term planning. Implementation by steps, integrating priorities with emphasis on effectiveness and efficiency' (Ministry of Culture, PRC 2007: 43).

In this way, China has been able to produce huge compendia of Chinese folk songs, Chinese opera, Chinese folk dance, Chinese Quyi amongst others. Given impetus by the ICHC, four Ministries including the Ministry of Culture and Finance launched the 'Project of Protecting Folk and Ethnic Culture in China', which will run until 2020, promoting the protection of Chinese ethnic and folk culture 'in a scientific, rational and orderly fashion' (Ministry of Culture, PRC 2007: 43). The setting up in July 2005 of the 'Opinions of the General Office of the State Council on strengthening the safeguarding of China's intangible heritage'; will ensure China is well poised to implement the 2003 Convention. By May 2006, experts drawn from all sectors involved in intangible heritage had drawn up a list of national masterpieces that was promulgated by the government (Ministry of Culture, PRC 2007: 44–7). It is evident that intangible cultural heritage plays an important role in nation building, as do the economy, foreign policy and exchange systems that disseminate this intangible heritage globally. The community at local level for example, through the local varieties of opera, generates and laterally propagates this heritage. Provincial and national structures then propagate this knowledge vertically into the unified national co-ordinating organs, which since March 2005 feed into the 'Opinions of the General Office of the State Council on strengthening the Safeguarding of China's Intangible Cultural Heritage'. All this is presented on the global stage through travelling operas, exhibitions and so forth.

After World War II, Japan set up a programme that offered government recognition and support to those traditions that embodied its national cultural patrimony. The programme was a reaction to fears that modernisation would erase the national identity of Japan (Kurin 2004: 67–8). It is notable that it was only in 1992, 20 years after the coming into being of the World Heritage Convention (1972), that Japan ratified this Convention. Contrast this with the fact that Japan was the third State Party to the ICHC: 'This gave the movement towards a Convention an added boost, especially given the appointment of the Japanese diplomat, Koichiro Matsuura, as Director-General of UNESCO' (Kurin 2004: 68). Matsuura himself says:

> As soon as I arrived at UNESCO in 1999, I made the safeguarding of intangible cultural heritage one of the priorities of the organization. Indeed I felt it was urgent to act to preserve the fragile heritage that was often under threat of extinction and which had not until then enjoyed sufficient sustained attention from our organization.
>
> (Matsuura 2006: 2)

Japan has played a leading role in the adoption of the ICHC and accelerated its ratification particularly in the developing countries. Within Japan itself, under the *Law for Protection of Cultural Property*, there are two major categories of intangible cultural heritage. Intangible Cultural Property (ICP) relates to techniques, music and other similar expressions. The state plays a central role in identifying the tradition to be preserved. After this first step, 'holders' of that tradition are then identified. These holders (community) may seek formal designation and support (including financial) and 'successor training'. The second category of intangible heritage is Intangible Folk Cultural Property (IFPC) which embraces local religious rites, festivities and so forth. The first step in its safeguarding is the reverse order to the first category. That is, 'Confirmation or determination of practitioners or preservers of the tradition' come first followed by steps to identify the tradition (Cang 2007: 46–50).

What determines the national strategy is the nature and components of intangible heritage. In the case of ICP, the state takes a prominent role in identifying the tradition or techniques, such as pottery, because they 'have an existence apart from their practitioners' (Cang 2007: 48). The logic in this case is to inventory and safeguard that which may not have an ascribed community responsibility. With respect to IFCP, religious, rites and festivities and so on these, 'have to be practiced and performed to exist' (Cang 2007: 48) and the role of the national government working through local governments is to identify those practitioners who will ensure the survival of the tradition, and the state works with them. There are, however, situations and traditions where local and national authorities determine the course and action. Voltaire Garces Cang gives an example of one such state-sponsored intangible cultural heritage expression. This is the Matsuuri festival which has been 'tirelessly promoted by local and national governments as "quintessentially" Shinto traditional Japanese practice and though newly minted at times, it is given a traditional form and attached to historical, local, political, social and religious organization' (Cang 2007: 53–4). In this way, 'Japan has created a system for selecting and identifying a tradition of heritage which it deems significant for its own patrimony and no less for its identity' (Cang 2007: 53). However, it is important that community is at the centre of safeguarding systems.

For instance, one of the brands of Matsuuri is called Gujo Odori, which is a festival for the dead. It takes place in mid-July of each year when the procession starts from the Old Town Hall of Gujo city: 'Every year the politicians outnumber the shrine representatives [by] at least 10:1' (Cang 2007: 46). Cang makes an interesting observation, that illustrates the importance of 'community'. Though there are long traditions that could fall into the government categorisation and obtain national protection, 'they do not need protection from decline' because they have 'fanatical followers and supporters who will ensure their longevity'. These 'keepers of the heritage have become so established and entrenched that even the national law and its regulations on intangible cultural heritage in Japan have become irrelevant' (Cang 2007: 54). Be it in Zimbabwe, Kenya, Japan or China, this message underscores the truth that the community, when defined in terms of its ownership of its heritage, is the guarantor for sustainability of that heritage. Despite the many threats, particularly those posed by urbanisation, modernism and tourism, the tradition of 'Processional Giants and Dragons' practised in Belgium (Ath, Mons, Brussels) and France (Tarascan, Cassel, etc.) dating back to the fourteenth century, remains robust. This is so because intangible heritage is underwritten by the principle of intergenerational equity, which is the responsibility of generations to inherit and pass on that heritage to succeeding generations. It is this 'temporal solidarity and responsibility in space and time' (Brown Weiss 1989: xxviii) that is the guarantor of heritage. Further, intangible cultural heritage cannot retain its designation or survive 'if it is appropriated by others who are not members of the community whether they be government officials, scholars, artist etc' (Kurin 2007: 12).

It is in this context that this chapter has sought to demonstrate that intangible heritage does not survive under overly interventionist and or restrictive conditions. Some examples of intervention are a reaction to the phenomenon of globalisation, and in other cases are 'reminiscent of early anthropology which was driven by the condition that [to be safeguarded] primitive cultures must be documented' (Brown 2005: 48). Freeing rather than freezing the conditions under which intangible cultural heritage exists and operates is the best safeguard for intangible cultural heritage. Such conditions are best set by the communities that generate and perpetuate that heritage; the alternative is to encapsulate and in the process smother this dynamic phenomenon known as intangible cultural heritage.

I can only conclude by concurring with Kurin that the significance of the 2003 ICHC lies in the fact that it

> shifts both the measure and onus of safeguarding work to the cultural community itself. Intangible cultural heritage is not preserved in States' archives or national museums. It is preserved in communities whose members practice and manifest its forms. If the tradition is still alive, vital and sustainable in the community, it is safeguarded.
>
> (2007: 12–13)

Notes

1 These are: *Convention for the Protection of Cultural Property in the Event of Armed Conflict (1954); Convention on the Means of Prohibiting and Preventing the Illicit Import, Export and Transfer of Ownership of Cultural Property (1970); Convention Concerning the Protection of the World Cultural and Natural Heritage (1972); Convention on the Protection of the Underwater Cultural Heritage (2001).*

Bibliography

Bedjaoui, M. (2004) 'The convention for intangible cultural heritage: the legal framework and universally recognized principles', *Museum International,* 56(221–2): 150–5.

—— (2007) *The Intangible Heritage Messenger n°5.* Paris: UNESCO, pp. 1–2.

Bernstein, J.I. (1973) *Maasai and Iioikop: Ritual Aspects and Their Followers,* unpublished M.A. Thesis. University of Wisconsin.

Bie, B. and Matokwe, T. (2007) '4000 evicted Ogieks want to return to their forest homes', *The Daily Nation,* 28 June, Kenya, Nairobi.

Blackburn, R.H. (1974) 'The Ogiek and their history', *Azania,* volume 9, Nairobi: British Institute of Eastern Africa.

Blake, J. (2006) *Commentary on the UNESCO 2003 Convention for the Safeguarding of the Intangible and Cultural Heritage,* Leicester: Institution of Art and Law.

Bouchenaki, M. (2004) 'Editorial', *Museum International,* 56 (221–2): 6–11.

Brown, M.F. (2005) 'Heritage trouble: recent work on the Protection of international cultural property', *International Journal of Cultural Property,* 12 (1): 40–61.

Brown Weiss, E. (1989) *In Fairness to Future Generations, International Law, Common Patrimony and Intergenerational Equity,* Tokyo: UN University.

Cang, V.C. (2007) 'Defining intangible cultural heritage and its stakeholders: the case of Japan', *International Journal of Intangible Heritage,* 2: 46–55.

Huntingford, G.W.B. (1955) 'The economic life of the Dorobo', *Anthropos,* 50: 602–34.

Draft Summary Record of the First Session of *Intergovernmental Committee for the Safeguarding of the Intangible Cultural Heritage,* Algiers, 18–19 November 2006. *I COM. ITH/06/I.COM/CONF.204/10*

Johnson, A.M. (2006) *Is the Sacred for Sale?* London: Earthscan.

Kamau, J. (2000) *The Ogiek: the Ongoing Destruction of a Minority Tribe in Kenya, an In-depth Report.* Available online at: http://www.ogiek.org/report (Accessed 1 September 2007).

Kurin, R. (2004) 'Safeguarding Intangible Cultural Heritage in the 2003 UNESCO Convention, a critical appraisal', *Museum International,* 56 (221–2): 66–77.

—— (2007) 'Safeguarding intangible cultural heritage: key factors in implementing the 2003 Convention', *International Journal of Intangible Heritage,* 2: 10–20.

Legrand, J. (2006) 'Society systems and value systems: nomadic cultures as a means and actors of dialogue', in S. Waushape (ed.), *Cultural Diversity and Transversal Values: East-West dialogue on Spiritual and Secular Dynamics,* Paris: UNESCO and International Centre for Japanese Studies.

Manwa, A.T., Charumbira, Z., Chivanhu, N.J., and Mutogwepi, C. (1991) Letter to the Authorities responsible for Great Zimbabwe, Nemwana Growth Point (Masvingo), 19 September, unpublished.

Manyanga, M. (1999) 'The antagonism of living realities: archaeological and religion, the case of Manyanga (Ntaba zika Mambo), National Museums of Zimbabwe', *Zimbabwea,* 6: 10–14.

—— (2004) Intangible cultural heritage and the empowerment of local communities: Ntaba zika Mambo revisited, unpublished paper, History Department, University of Botswana, Gaborone.

Matsuura, K. (2004) 'Preface', *Museum International,* 56 (221–4): 4–5.

—— (2006) 'Preface', in R. Smeets (ed.), *Masterpieces of the Oral and Intangible Heritage of Humanity. Proclamations 2001, 2003, and 2005,* Paris: UNESCO.

Mazrui, A.A. (1986) *The Africans: A Triple Heritage,* Boston: Little, Brown and Co.

Migingo, R. (2007) Historic ICT for Ecoliving–Ogiek Community History. Available online at: http://www.blog.onevillage.tv/?p=25 (Accessed 1 September 2007).

Ministry of Culture of the Peoples Republic of China (PRC) (2007) *Festival of China's Intangible Cultural Heritage*, Beijing: Ministry of Culture.

Nader, A. and Bakhtiar, L. (1975) *The Sense of Unity in the Sufi Tradition in Persian Architecture*, Chicago: University of Chicago Press.

Ndoro, W. (2005) *The Preservation of Great Zimbabwe: Your Monument Our Shrine*, Rome: ICCROM.

Odunga, D. (2007) 'Gripe of Ogieks now forced into 'modernity'", *The Daily Nation*, Nairobi, 8 August.

Ogiek community submission before the Njonjo Land Commission (2000) in Kamau, *The Ogiek: the ongoing destruction of a minority tribe in Kenya, an in-depth report*. Available online at: http://www.ogiek.org/report (Accessed 1 September 2007).

Riding, A. (2005) 'A global culture war pits protectionists against free traders', *International Herald Tribune*, 3 February, p. 2

Smeets, R. (2006) *Masterpieces of the Oral and Intangible Heritage of Humanity. Proclamations 2001, 2003, and 2005*, Paris: UNESCO.

Sullivan, S. (2004) 'Local involvement and traditional practices in the world system', in R. Smeets and E. Merode (eds), *Linking Universal and Local Values: Managing a Sustainable Future for World Heritage*, Paris: UNESCO World Heritage Centre.

Summary Record of the First Session of *Intergovernmental Committee for the Safeguarding of the Intangible Cultural Heritage, 2COM ITH/07.2 & 2COM/CONF. 203/3 23–26 May 2007.* Chengdu (China) 31 July 2007.

Traditions pour Demain (2007) 'Community participation in the 2003 UNESCO Intangible Heritage Convention'. *Online Posting.* Available e-mail: tradi@fgc.ch (25 November 2007).

UNESCO (1972) *Convention Concerning the Protection of the World Cultural and Natural Heritage*, Paris: UNESCO.

—— (2003) *Convention for the Safeguarding of the Intangible Cultural Heritage*, Paris: UNESCO.

UNESCO Intangible Heritage Section (UIHS) and Asia Pacific Cultural Centre for UNESCO (ACCU) (2006) *Report on the Expert Meeting on Community Involvement in Safeguarding Intangible Cultural Heritage: Towards the Implementation of the Convention for the Safeguarding of Intangible Cultural Heritage*, 13–15 March 2006, Paris and Tokyo.

—— (2007) *The Intangible Heritage Messenger 5*, February.

United Nations (1992) *Convention on Biological Diversity.*

'Very Concerned' (1994) 'Letters to the Editor', *The Herald* [Harare], 24 June, p. 9.

Vinson, I. (2004) 'Editorial', *Museum International,* 56(221–22):6–11.

WHC-94/CONF.003/INF.6: (1994) Expert Meeting on the 'Global Strategy' and thematic studies for a representative world heritage list, Paris: UNESCO World Heritage Centre.

Wulf, C. (2005) 'Crucial points in the transmission and learning of intangible heritage', L. Wong (ed.), *Globalization and Intangible Cultural Heritage: International Conference*, 26–27 August 2004, Tokyo, Paris: UNESCO & UN University.

Yeoman, G. (1993) 'High altitude forest conservation in relation to Dorobo people', in Kamau, J. (ed.), *The Ogiek: the Ongoing Destruction of a Minority Tribe in Kenya, an In-depth Report*. Available online at: http://www.ogiek.org/report (Accessed 1 September 2007).

Chapter 8

Deeply rooted in the present[1]

Making heritage in Brazilian quilombos

Mary Lorena Kenny

Heritage is often assumed to be the uncontested residue of static traditions. Yet, according to David Lowenthal, heritage 'clarifies the past by infusing it with present purposes' (1998: xv). In other words, as current social and political landscapes shift, so do the ways in which people think about themselves and their relationships with the past, what is considered authentic and valuable, and the means and justifications for its preservation. Thus, analysing heritage as a process in the present allows for a more dynamic understanding of cultural production. This reconfiguration of heritage is a key observation for the argument developed in this chapter, which posits heritage as an important tool for interpreting and practising a new legal and ethno-racial classification: remanescente de quilombo. Here, the importance of negotiating and, ultimately, controlling the meaning and value of heritage is directly related to control over territorial rights legislated by the 1988 Brazilian Federal Constitution, Article 68. As such, there is no fixed remanescente heritage. The content and practice of what it means to be a remanescente community, or descendent community of ex-slaves or fugitive slaves (quilombos), are heterogeneous and shift with location, political aspirations, and social and economic relations, where race, ancestry, memory, and place are differentially employed to construct, maintain, and communicate a specific sense of heritage. The form that remanescente heritage takes, what is protected, preserved, or showcased, is thus negotiated and influenced by a variety of actors, agencies, and ideas that expand beyond the community. These may include international and state agencies, NGOs, religious groups, politicians, academics, artists, and social movements, all of which mediate what is considered valuable and worth preserving, who it is preserved for, what is at risk of disappearing, and how it should be made available for future generations (Ortiz 1988: 164; Tamaso 2006). Therefore, notions of heritage, race, identity, and authenticity are not so understanding of the social and political construction – and ultimate plasticity – of remanescente heritage.

Recent policies produced to address the rights of 'minorities' have continued to shape the discourses, materials, and practices that *remanescentes de quilombos* use to communicate their relationships with the past. The notion of 'rights' and legal protection for Brazil's 'founding groups' provides a different vision of social relations and access to resources, leading to new questions, and new ways of seeing oneself in relation to the past and future. By interpreting, remembering and commemorating, groups challenge and redefine authoritative heritage and their 'place' in the world. The construction and practice of heritage, then, is an inherently political act. To examine some of the complexities of heritage in quilombos, or maroon communities, I draw from field research carried out in Santa Luzia, in the northeastern state of Paraíba, where two communities were recently federally recognised as quilombo descendent communities: a rural community recognised in 2004, and an urban extension recognised in 2005. The rural community, formed in 1860, is located 26 kilometres up a mountain, and today consists of 120 people. Its urban extension is made up of family members who have migrated to the urban zone. Together they are engaged in stimulating cultural (identity work), political (collective territory rights), and economic production through heritage tourism.

Remanescente heritage and collective memory

Memory work is a key component in creating remanescente heritage. It is linked to larger issues, processes, and discourses that recognise marginalised populations as 'without history' (Young 2000: 1). By linking history with memory, the 'silent' histories, outlawed practices and censured memories of those long seen as *not having history*, such as blacks, Indigenous people, women and homosexuals, take their place as important creators and heirs of history. For Brazil, this silent history is inevitably tied up with its importation of the enslaved, which began in 1530 and did not cease until 1888, as the last country to abolish slavery. Over the course of this 300-year period, Brazil imported more slaves than any other country in the Western hemisphere. Here, the urgency of making audible a silenced history is clear, given that 75% of the enslaved brought into Brazil died in the first three years, leaving few authors to tell their stories (Santos 2005). It was at this time that the term *quilombo* emerged, used by the Portuguese *Conselho Ultramarino* (Overseas Council) in 1740 to define a settlement with five or more runaway slaves (Kent 1973). The Portuguese term 'quilombo' derives from the Kikongo (Bantu) term referring to troops, military unit or warrior society that supplied captives in exchange for European goods (Abreu Funari cited in Reis and Gomes 1996: 29). Quilombos are also called *mocambos* (from the Kimbundu *mú kambu*, meaning hideaway) and individual members are called *quilombolas*, *calhambolas* or *mocambeiros* (Reis and Gomes 1996). Quilombos also formed throughout Latin America and the Caribbean. In Colombia and Cuba, they are called *palenques* (enclosure), in Venezuela *cumbes*, in Jamaica, Suriname, and the southern USA they are referred to as *maroons*, and in Haiti and other French Caribbean islands *marrons* (Carvalho *et al.* 1996). The term 'maroon', comes from the Spanish term *cimarrón*, and was used on the island of Hispaniola (today Haiti and the Dominican Republic) to refer to cattle that had run away. By the early sixteenth century, it connoted fierce, wild, and unbroken, and was used to refer to runaway slaves (Dawson 2002).

Until recently, federal recognition as a community with quilombo origins relied exclusively on an archaeological paradigm, which required groups applying for recognition and land titles to prove continued occupation (prior to 1888, the end of slavery and up to 1988, when the new Constitution was written) and provide evidence of communal land use (Fonseca de Castro 2006). These criteria evolved from early studies of quilombos (primarily Palmares, a multi-ethnic settlement with an estimated population of 30,000 that survived for over a hundred years, 1604–1716), which described them as sites of cultural resistance, socialist in organisation and without internal conflict (Arruti 2006: 73). This model, which relies upon an unproblematised notion of 'quilombos', is inappropriate for communities as *living historical patrimony*, as it tends to freeze communities in time, anchoring them to specific locations, and excising them from the political, social, and ecological forces that continue to shape change throughout Brazil (Arruti 1997: 27; Andrade and Treccani 1999: 36). Moreover, this model fails to take into account the varied ways in which black communities are, or are not, 'seen' in different regions.

The historian David Lowenthal aptly captures the complexity of relying upon official documents for historical accuracy with his statement that 'Truth is a chameleon and its chroniclers fallible beings' (1998: 119). Indeed, as Richard Price reminds us, 'We cannot forget that almost everything written about Palmares was written by their enemies' (cited in Reis and Gomes 1996: 53). Implicit in colonial documents is the notion that quilombos were a threat to public security (Oliveira 1996: 231–2) due to assaults, robberies and insurrections. Oral history has been a valuable resource for modifying the historical record and weakening the exaggerated power elites claimed to have had by showing that they were unaware of native leaders and resources, or even the presence of nearby quilombos. Studies show that quilombos were composed from a variety of groups (Indians, poor white people, military deserters) with a variety of languages, and do not distinctly differentiate 'African cultures' (Price 1988/89: 90). Their formation and disintegration were shaped by the economy (sugar, coffee and gold), demographics, nature and type of threat (Indigenous, military), defence (weapons, inaccessibility) and means of survival (information, goods, subsistence) (Reis and Gomes 1996; Price 1988/89). Some engaged in significant trade with nearby Portuguese and Indian settlements. Others were located in areas that were forgotten, or of little market value, not only because the land was unproductive, but because of the mere presence of blacks (Carvalho *et al.* 1996; Leite and Mombelli 2005: 47). Some acquired land through donation or inheritance (Mattos 2005); others received land in exchange for labour or remained on abandoned land (Almeida 2002: 63; Schmitt *et al.* 2002: 3). Most of these transactions were informal arrangements between slaveholders and ex-slaves, carried out without any legal registration or protection.

Barbara Fields, referring to ex-slaves in the USA, illustrates the unstable nature of freedom with her observation that 'Liberty was not a fixed condition, but a moving target' (1985: 193). To rely on official documents and material artefacts as proof of quilombo ancestry was the equivalent of putting a 'straight jacket' onto black history, as invisibility has been their survival (Almeida 2002: 63). In the sertão, until the mid-nineteenth century, the rural poor were in many ways off the radar of authoritative control, intervention and classification, primarily because the state lacked the resources for exercising control in this mostly unsettled area (Arruti 2006: 172–3). Area census reflect the 'limitations, silences, opacity and discursive consistency' (Gomes 2004: 740) of this invisibility, which allowed poor farmers to craft subsistence and commercial agriculture (as well as own slaves) on small plots of land (Falci 1995). In a detailed study of the historical and social construction of a remanescente community in the state of Sergipe, Arruti (2006: 168) argues that naturalising state and religious census of black and Indigenous communities, without a concurrent contextualisation of the means, motives, organisation and limits of such information, produces a skewed, if not erroneous, portrait of black and Indigenous history. Census takers also defined populations as mixed or assimilated, rendering extinct Indigenous groups and resulting in the loss of land (Arruti 2006: 58). In other areas, the incursion of large landowners in the sertão for cattle raising in the mid- to late 1800s, and the difficulty in proving ownership of land after the Land Laws of 1850 (blacks and Indians could not be land owners), resulted in the annexing of Indigenous and black farming communities, officially absorbing them as landless renters. Shifts in the structure of landholding (sesmarias, fazendas) rearranged not only how black communities were categorised, but also their social organisation, subsistence, recreation, and memory (Arruti 2006: 237). Today, both the lack of official documentation and the *absence of memory* among such groups are asserted as evidence that black or Indigenous communities are non-existent, and have no claim to land based on ancestry or continued occupation. By contrast, taking account of oral histories among these groups can unveil the complicated and diverse ways in which both the enslaved and ex-slaves acquired land, as well as diverse means of survival in areas structured by economic and racial inequity.

Lawyers, anthropologists and black activists responeded to this narrow definition for recognition. They discussed the historical practices and policies that rendered black communities 'invisible' and challenged the notion that an objective definition of 'remanescentes of quilombos' could be operationalised. They pressed for a 'resemantisation' of the classification, arguing that pre-conceived criteria such as biology (pigmentation), colonial documents, or archaeological evidence failed to capture the complexity of movement and memory among Afro-descendants. Rosario Linhares, the national coordinator of the quilombo descendents project at the Palmares Cultural Foundation (FCP), advocated amplifying the term to include any black community, in both urban and rural areas, *independent of the means by which the community was formed*. In effect, then, this would include those *without* a quilombo past that *appeared to be the residue of a system of slavery or contemporary inequities*, especially in areas with disputes over land (Linhares 2006). Indeed, why focus only on those who were able to flee and form quilombos, when, as Almeida (2002: 61) argues 'There were those that dreamed of fleeing and could not; those that fled and were recaptured; those that couldn't flee because they helped others to flee and their role was to stay'? However, while a broadened idea of self-identification has been taken up and codified at governmental levels, particularly with the 2003 government decree 4887/art.2, (Rocha 2005: 97), an 'expert report' by an anthropologist is still required in cases where there are land disputes.

Although remanescentes share ancestors, relatives, rituals and socio-economic status with their rural neighbours, as *ethno-racial* political subjects, they insert experiences that had previously been 'airbrushed out of history' (Kundera 1980, cited in Cohen 2001: 243). Arruti (2006: 28) refers to this as a 'historical revisionist boom' concerning the history of slavery and race relations in Brazil, as it problematises the notion of a syncretic nation of Europeans, Indians and Africans. Through the memories of Afro descendents, benign descriptions of slavery, popularised by social historian and anthropologist Gilberto Freyre since the 1940s, are being rehistoricised, rupturing the 'pact of consensus' within this narrative (Santos 1996: 220). Freyre popularised the notion that Brazil's racial mixture produced a social world significantly different to the institutionalised segregation and racial tensions in the USA (under the Jim Crow laws) and South Africa (under apartheid) (Bastide and Fernandes [1959] 1971: 229–68). One of his most important and polemical works, *The Masters and the Slaves* (Freyre 1946), painted a unilateral and sentimentalised portrait of sugar cane plantation life where everyone 'knew their place' in a harmonious social order, without violence or rebellion (Oliven 1982; Ortiz 1988: 36). A natural syncretism was assumed to have occurred between Portuguese colonisers and enslaved Africans and Indians. This, it was argued, was due to their proximity (as wet nurse, or nanny), the high ratio of men to women, and a particular Portuguese cultural/psychological preference for 'dark, sensual, women' that brought white overseers and their sons into contact with compliant, enslaved women (Freyre 1959). The received 'common sense' view of racial and cultural harmony that Freyre asserted has since been discredited by historiography showing high mortality, runaways, rebellions, revolts, and suicide, as well as the estimated

3,524 quilombos (in 24 different states), attesting to significant resistance to a 'benign' system of slavery.

The current legal classification 'remanescente' shapes collective memories in various ways. The notion of a community homogenously and horizontally passing on memories of its 'origins' is problematised when memory is juxtaposed intergenerationally, and with other developments and changes. Access to financial resources through the Palmares Cultural Foundation, new discourses concerning the rights of minorities, and communal access to land foment radically different generational narratives. At age 83, Dona Rita remarked: 'I still don't understand what this quilombola stuff means'. Yet, for her granddaughter, this identity is the axis, or central core of meaning, for describing her work making clay pots, her relationship with her family, and her social and spatial location in the 'urban quilombo'. The label is embedded in every conversation she has with outsiders, making a statement not only about the political reality of *who she is* as a resident of the urban zone, but also about her *roots* and her physical and metaphorical quilombo origin 26 kilometres up a steep and rocky mountain. According to bell hooks, the politics of belonging point 'to experiences that may no longer be an actual part of one's life but is a living memory shaping and informing the present' (1989: 158). For others, 'collective memory' is rooted in key events (when we got electricity in 1997), life passages (when the community leader died, when the family migrated to Rio), or a specific period (drought of 1997), that significantly influenced who they were, their relations with other community members, as well as the ways they thought about themselves in relation to 'outsiders'. The creation, form, and expression of collective memory, then, depend on the ways individual, family and community experiences are reinterpreted through the current lens of remanescente, which in turn shape what it means to be a remanescente in this context. The recent engagement with social, political, and economic institutions *as remanescente* further anchors remanescente heritage by institutionalising (in school, community events, political rallies) *who they are*. These new multi-stranded relationships continue to shape attitudes, practices, and memory in relation to earlier historical experiences.

Memory reflects experiences and social relations, but memory also shapes daily life and the ways in which people think about social relations, transforming contemporary lifeways and objects into sites of memory. The notion of the intangibility of the tangible is instructive here (Smith 2006). Although material artefacts are privileged as stable manifestations of culture that can be protected and preserved, their meaning, value, purpose and utility are actually more plastic and contested, shifting as political strategies and notions of community incorporate these objects as tools of memory. For example, almost all women from Talhado make clay pots. This is interpreted as a trait passed on from their 'African' ancestry. This is disputed by historians and anthropologists who state that this practice has indigenous, not

African, origins. Yet for women from Talhado, it is something that they have 'always done'. Until recently, Talhado was located outside of the circuits of local power and clientelistic relations, relying on family (the community) rather than public aid or charity from wealthy patrons and politicians. The making, selling, and trade of pots for food, although an economically fragile enterprise, has helped to keep families afloat and has supported local festive and other (birth, death, marriage) rituals. The narrative of African origins, then, is strengthened not with evidence that enslaved persons continued this practice in the Americas, as community members deny having slaves as ancestors. Rather, it 'takes hold' through the very process of making the pots *as remanescentes*, toughened by the *strength* needed to gather the clay and pound it into a powder with heavy wooden sticks, the *talent* and *patience* to mould and cut it into forms, the *muscle* to smooth it for hours with stones, and the *vigour* that is needed to withstand intense heat when fired (in a large oven fed with wood and topped by broken pieces of clay). The pots are made in the same way they were a century ago, and the women have resisted all attempts to mechanise this process, even though it would make the process less arduous and time-consuming. The reproduction of this heritage is interpreted as a vital, living link to the past, now shaped by contemporary political classifications that discharge benefits based on minority status. The memories of earlier generations were more closely related to a script of 'family', reinforced through racial, class and geographic endogamy, while later, through becoming a remanescente, memory is shaped by engagement with public agencies and bureaucratic institutions. The expression of their material heritage, then, is not consistent or linear (based on an objective 'past'), but uneven, multilayered and fragmented, like the softened pots arranged in the large brick oven, being hardened into 'tangible' material goods.

This heritage is interpreted by some as slippery, indicating those from Talhado as fake quilombo descendents because the story of their origin is inconsistent, contradicts official history, and is without material evidence. Although federally recognised as remanescentes since 2004, many deny having enslaved persons as ancestors. They identify as people who were 'always there', like Indigenous peoples, and mark out slaves as a different race, or type of people (see Carvalho *et al.* 1996 for a similar case). The meaning of 'slave-descendent' in this context requires an examination and analysis of the connections between experiences, beliefs and practices, and the ways these are manifested in contemporary social relations. Being called a 'negro from Talhado' was, and continues to be, derogatory and stigmatising. There is also the lingering fear that slavery could be reinstituted. A colleague working on a public health campaign in a remanescente community in Pernambuco told me that blood samples were required in order to test for the prevalence of Chagas disease. The women with whom she had previously conducted oral histories feared the 'taking of their blood'. They saw her as a threat, as she had information about their history as slaves or slave descendents. They accused her of being in partnership with the government to reinstitute slavery, and were convinced that the test and analysis of their blood was a way to discover who the 'real' slaves were. Here, memory structures perception, not from evidence that others were being carted away as slave descendents, but that this *could* happen, fomented by the sentiment that their bodies (or blood) were being used for profit, a common-sense logic that expresses fear of exploitation and conspiracy. Such sentiments are common where intergroup disparities are extensive (Gordillo 2002: 34).

Memory among remanescentes, then, is crafted from a palimpsest of historical, political, social and economic relations. Tourism operators, large landowners, the state, academics and NGOs tend to interrogate remanescente heritage by searching for narratives related to slavery as the 'chosen' collective memory, or single, overriding classification for the black experience (Matory 2005: 288). Yet this shadows the complexity of history and processes of memory making. According to Almeida (2002: 77), mandating proof or emphasising that one is a 'leftover' of slavery (through ancestry, blood ties, common origin, culture) controls blacks by forcing them to adhere to objectified notions of 'who they are' (Arruti 1997: 17). Residents of the Mocambo quilombo told Arruti that their liberty ended and slavery (servitude) began not because of their *raça*, race, but due to their loss of land to large landowners in the 1800s (2006: 243). In the Rio das Rãs quilombo, residents describe the history of their settlement as pre-dating any colonial presence or occupation. They were autonomous free 'settlers', not fugitive slaves occupying someone else's land (Carvalho *et al.* 1996: 127–63). By claiming their own history through memory, remanescentes challenge dominant narratives and common ways of 'reading' and interpreting experience. They give new meanings to race, ethnicity, and heritage; meanings significantly more complex than colour or ancestry.

Identity, place, and commemorating heritage

The institutionalisation of remanescente and access to land are vital tools for shaping ethnogenesis, the resignification of identity through a discourse of multiculturalism and diversity, black alterity, and a place-based (quilombo) culture (Hill 1996; French 2006: 351). The 'settling of accounts' through reparations in the form of land titles and the creation of a institutionalised racial/ethnic category was not created by the 1988 Constitution. Rather, it is the result of years of activism in *terras de preto, comunidades negras rurais* and *mocambos* (Almeida 2005: 17; Arruti 2006: 56) – places historically zoned by racial, ethnic, economic, and political exclusion. It builds on the political movements of the 1960s and 1970s that widened debates concerning the exigencies of the *povo* (proletarians, exploited workers, rural and urban poor, anyone of low status and any group victimised by the state), whose concerns were homogenised by the political left as originating in class conflict, rendering ethnicity insignificant. Since the *abertura* (the gradual process of redemocratisation after a 20-year military dictatorship) in the mid-1970s, and the development of a new constitution in 1988, numerous NGOs and other grassroots associations fomented the notion of the 'right to have rights ... and created *identities* where previously only undifferentiated men and women existed in their own deprivation' (Paoli and Telles 1998: 66). Rural farmers, factory workers, Indigenous peoples, women, homosexuals, the physically disabled, elderly and *sem terra* (landless workers movement), as well as those seeking environmental protection, were all motivated by this new social and political space extending cultural, social and economic rights to the 'excluded' through idioms such as multiculturalism, minority and ethnicity.

Spaces are made into places by attributing meaning through shared experiences, lifestyles, and rituals, creating a sense of belonging (Lovell 1998). According to Tuan (1974), one's 'location' (gender, age, race/ethnicity class, religion) produces varied memories and meanings tied to places. These same categories are also exclusive, marking where one *does not belong* through a range of physical and discursive controls such as gated communities (Douglas 1991: 289). The boundaries and politics of belonging, then, are inventions that require continued analysis.

Although there are no templates for *who remanescentes are* or *what they should be,* place is a useful tool for defining and delimiting the boundaries of remanescente as racial alterns in the sertão (Arruti 1997: 30). The conflicts, negotiations, meanings, practices and boundaries of space re-imagined as *black* with the acknowledgment of Afro-descendents as the 'legitimate owners' of territory (Arruti 1997: 22) are radical deviations from a national assimilast ideology that has dominated relations with the state, the media, and international aid agencies since the 1930s. Although the status, stability, occupancy and classification of rural black communities has shifted significantly in the sertão, place remains a key emblem for remembering, experiencing and practising heritage among remanescentes. Collective memory (fugitive or ex-slaves), cultural practices (making clay pots), ideology (racial discrimination), academic and media studies (isolated culture) and heritage tourism (commodified space) are all framed by the geoimaginary of quilombo. Legislating collective territorial rights for *remanescentes* resulted not only in a major reorganisation of land ownership, but a radical shift in the way residents of rural communities were categorised in relation to place. This process manifests itself in a way similar to those who have, 'reimagined themselves as Indians' (Warren 2001: 98) in order to demand claims to land as an essential anchor for their physical, social, economic and cultural survival. As in the past, present political and economic conditions are reworking relations to place and memory. Remanescentes provokes antagonism (and envy) by those who resent them for acquiring land titles without having to

purchase the land. The 'non-ethnic' poor, for example, criticise remanescentes for capitalising on a fake (meaning political, not cultural) identity
in order to access land: 'Why is it that only slave descendants get land? I'm
sem terra [landless] too', is a common statement made by their poor, rural
neighbours, and by those who must exit in areas demarcated as quilombo
territory.

Remanescentes who have come down the mountain from Talhado have
settled within two peripheral neighbourhoods, where they have formed
'urban quilombos'. Local discourse refers to these areas as 'our favelas' and
isolates social problems as originating in these communities. Social and
spatial distance from these 'bad' blacks, who are perceived as violent criminals, drunks and illicit drug users, occurs through a discursive biological/
geographical/racial paradigm that attributes such traits to a predisposition
originating in *self-imposed* intergenerational social, racial, and spatial isolation from those 'in the city' (code for white, civilised, articulate, hard-work-
ing, church-going). Their voluntary isolation (unassimilation) is reinforced
by their lack of participation in legitimate expressions of black identity
and heritage, such as the celebration of the Irmandade de Nossa Senhora
do Rosario, a public performance that gains currency because it is funded
and shared by powerful local whites. Irmandades are 'ethnic'/religious associations that own or support churches, and provide a variety of social and
material aid (such as burial funds) for blacks since the eighteenth century.
The absence of those from Talhado from this ritual denies the notion of a
shared history, thrusting doubt onto their claims as remanescentes. Local
discourse, referring to Talhados as isolated, unassimilated, and impenetrable,
further shapes the meaning, value and legitimacy of their heritage. Cunha
(1998: 241) makes the point that in Brazil, popular culture has historically
been identified as culture among subalterns that bridges the social and spatial divide between the *morro* (slum dwellers, poor, black) and the *asfalto*
(paved streets, wealthy, white). The lack of participation of 'those' blacks
from Talhado is no different than the social distance, spatial exclusion, and
networks that separate the poor, mostly dark-skinned persons living in the
peripheral 'urban quilombo' from the lighter-skinned, well-to-do residents of
the town centre.

Remanescentes and heritage tourism

In 2005, a joint UN, World Tourism Organization, and Ministry of
Tourism declaration asserted tourism as key for alleviating poverty (Blake *et
al.* 2005: 2). The Minister of Culture, Gilberto Gil, and the World Bank,
endorsed culture as an 'instrument for citizenship and social inclusion'
(Brazzil Magazine 2004) and the 'driving force behind human development'
(Ministry of Culture 2006). Gil specifically privileged economically marginal
communities and people as those with the most 'cultural assets' (Gil 2005).

An ambitious and extensive inter-agency plan called the 'Living Culture Program' (LCP) encouraged the production and preservation of culture through 'non-hierarchical' cultural 'beacons' expected to stimulate cultural production through 'social acupuncture' (Ministry of Culture 2006: 16–20). Providing financial support to 'tradition bearers' in exchange for performing, providing workshops and teaching others their craft, is a necessary condition for the continuity of 'cultural assets' (IPHAN 2000 cited in Tamaso 2006). For example, Griôs (from the French term Griots), as masters of oral tradition, receive financial support, which indirectly supports the 'preservation' of this cultural practice (Fonseca 2003: 72).

Although there is a long tradition of commodifying culture for a non-local, wider audience through tourism and the sale of crafts, culture is increasingly seen as a magic bullet for development and poverty eradication (Falcão 2001; Yúdice 2003: 156; Edelman and Haugerud 2005: 2). The absence of state welfare often leaves 'culture' as a scaffold for weak schools, a vehicle for solving racial tension and tackling problems such as crime and unemployment, and a prompt for reducing structural inequities and enhancing one's well-being and self-esteem (Yúdice 2003: 156). Economists assert the positive impact of cultural tourism as a development scheme through employment, diffusion of crafts, music and food, which allegedly pave the way for social, political and economic inclusion, although there is little systematic evidence to support this (Blake *et al.* 2005). Despite this, heritage tourism has been proposed as a significant alternative for generating income in remanescente communities and ameliorating the vestiges of structural and racial violence. It also plays an important role in performing identity by utilising the discourses, performances, and material practices of 'resistance to globalisation', marked by 'authenticity', as a strategy for gaining public recognition (Smith 2006: 6). As national *patrimônio*, quilombos usher in a level of attention that had been absent since the communities were formed. Some sites federally recognised as quilombos garner symbolic and political prestige as valued national cultural assets, income through heritage tourism, as well as attention from academics, journalists, and the World Bank, and opportunities for travel as quilombo representatives, etc. The consequences, however, are not necessarily consistent with *quilombismo,* an idiom and metaphor developed by Afro-Brazilian writer and politician, Abdias do Nascimento (1980), for interpreting and *responding to* the social, political, and economic exclusion of Afro-Brazilians. The effectiveness in highlighting local heritage and generating tourism tends to be dominated by reified notions of 'African culture' (aesthetic, colourful performances, capoeira, Candomblé). While these garner currency as heritage, they obscure continued forms of racial discrimination and structural inequity.

The current 'place' of remanescentes, for example, is the result of colonialism, slavery, and other forms of structural violence (Ferguson 1992).

However, the symbolic and economic capital of heritage in Talhado increases in direct relation to its loss of complexity. As with many heritage sites in the USA, it is more important to 'charm' than 'frighten' tourists (Young 2000: 135). *Depoliticized* folklore, scripted as 'African survivals', is emphasised rather than the 'collective memory' of marginalisation. This emphasis on residual Africanisms indicates their 'resistance', and is disseminated as a clear cultural difference from their sertanejo neighbours. Moreover, it acts as a marker of authenticity, facilitating access to resources as remanescentes, which is grounded in their resistance to slavery, capitalism and globalisation. However, it simultaneously shadows the equally authentic, but less exotic, conditions in this neglected community. Thus, while remanescentes appear to have 'resisted' globalisation because they make clay pots – a 22-step process without mechanisation – and live in homes made of *taipa* (clay and sticks) without electricity, water, or sanitation, they also wear the latest fashions, blast the latest pop music, have sophisticated mobile phones, satellite dishes, and have built a chapel. Because of this, many visitors to Talhado say they feel 'deceived' because the population is not that *different* from other rural communities in the area. They are disappointed that the local they were expecting to find (primitive, unassimilated, isolated, animistic) is significantly less exotic than they were led to believe, framed by a discourse of isolation, fugitive slaves and residual Africanisms. Their culture is 'invented', and their authenticity questioned by those whose definition of authenticity relies on fixed, stereotypical traits, although what a 'slave descendent' looks like in the twenty-first century is rarely articulated. Usually any indication of modernity, such as owning or knowing how to operate a DVD player, or wearing contemporary fashions, dismisses them as 'racial charlatans' (Warren 2001). Visitors to Talhado find instead what the area has *authentically* become – a desperately poor rural community with modern forms of consumption and urban social problems. As Yúdice (2003: 12) argues, this celebration of 'tolerable' folklore among those 'poor in material goods but rich in spirit' is a 'carnivalisation of injustice', in which the illusions of an integrated nation are drawn upon while at the same time glossing over gross inequities (Carvalho *et al.* 1996; Maio 1996: 179). Quilombismo, then, is a call to racialise inequity, or what bell hooks (1991: 147) calls the 'politicization of memory that distinguishes nostalgia, that longing for something to be as once it was, a kind of useless act, from that remembering that serves to illuminate and transform the present'. To *quilombolizar* means becoming political subjects by radically reworking history through memory, and becoming your own expert through autonomous self-expression, freed from representation by others (see also Bhabha 1990: 311; Spivak 1993; Said 1994). It is an idiom for articulating the 'lingering cruelty' of inequity, not a geoimaginary of a bounded, place-based, and fossilised African heritage (Winter 1995). It means *taking one's place* rather than being put *in their place* (Cunha 1998: 229).

Conclusion

Although now classified by the state as remanescentes, the meanings, benefits and discontents of this classification continue to be expressed both in the visual and tangible heritage of ceramics, and in the less visible spatial, political and discursive boundaries that shape 'us' and 'them'. Remanescente heritage is manifested both in the tangible houses made of clay and sticks on a mountaintop, as well as the intangible resources of memory, as discriminated persons, in their reliance on family (community), in their talent as potters, and in their historical narrative as descendents of 'settlers', not slaves. The active use of this intangible heritage continues to define social relations with non-remanescentes, and shape their 'place' in public life as political subjects.

In 1937, the *Serviço do Patrimônio Histórico e Artístico Nacional* (SPHAN) was created as the federal institution responsible for 'interpreting and guarding the cultural values of the nation' (Fonseca 1997: 121). The first of its kind in Latin America, SPHAN was responsible for generating an inventory of 'culture' that reflected a 'national ethos'. This interpretation of 'artistic and historical value with national merit' prioritised the aesthetic and material vestiges of elite, Portuguese, Catholic, colonial Brazil in Minas Gerais, Pernambuco, Rio de Janeiro and Bahia. However, Fonseca, in her analysis of the construction of heritage in Brazil, makes the point that Mario de Andrade's *manifesto,* or outline of the goals of SPHAN was significantly more elaborate and advanced for its time, recognising the value of intangible cultural heritage long before UNESCO's Convention (1997: 110). Rodrigo Andrade, the first director of SPHAN, advocated the importance of 'democratising culture' by documenting, disseminating and protecting popular, Indigenous and Afro-Brazilian culture (knowledge, songs, dances), as they were least likely to have material remains as part of their past (Fonseca 1997: 111). He believed in the value of cultural heritage as an educational tool, and supported community museums with community members as curators. This was a radical shift and amplification of the notion of national heritage for the 'masses' as defined and managed by elites. Nonetheless, the mechanisms for carrying out Andrade's ideals were never realised, and the processes of registration continued to rely on material definitions of heritage (Fonseca 1997: 115; Williams 2001: 67). Fonseca makes the point that even during the 1960s, with the widespread politicisation of cultural activity related to civil and economic rights, a dogmatic definition of popular culture was dominated by the political left. Only culture produced through *conscientização*, critical reflection (a term and method developed by Brazilian educator Paulo Freire), was considered 'true' popular culture (Ortiz 1988: 162; Fonseca 1997: 149).

Today, the *Instituto do Patrimônio Histórico e Artístico Nacional* (Institute of National Historic and Artistic Heritage, IPHAN), under the Ministry of Culture, is responsible for *tombamento,* the identification, registration, preservation, restoration, diffusion and protection of heritage that has 'national relevance for the memory, identity and formation of Brazilian society' (IPHAN 2000). This idea of national relevance expands beyond monuments and churches to include 'living culture' (rites, memory, handicrafts) (Fonseca 1997: 181). Despite the emphasis on culture as dynamic, dominant discourses of heritage continue to rely on the notion of authenticity. Celebrations, places and other forms of cultural expression harness authenticity currency if they appear to be preserved from the homogenising effects of globalisation (Harvey 1993). It is interesting that the forms of cultural expression valued as most authentic are those that apparently have *not* been affected by colonialism or capitalism, yet are the very peoples and places that have been most profoundly affected by these processes.

In the sertão, heritage tourism is seen as a way to steer the area towards its never-ending voyage of 'integration into the national development of Brazil' (Lima 1998: 65). This sets high expectations, especially where 25% of the population live on less than two dollars a day and 13% live on less than one dollar a day (World Bank 2005). Melding heritage tourism with development in quilombos offers an inherent paradox. This is because the symbolic and economic capital afforded authenticity, in this case, African survivals, isolates these practices as located outside of history and not coeval with development. In other words, residents must remain 'in their place' in order to be seen as successfully resisting globalisation and maintaining their culture, despite this place having never been a bounded, homogeneous or static anchor for identity. Places like Talhado are improbable places for heritage tourism, not because they lack guesthouse, infrastructure, monuments, or commercial establishments, but because the 'African heritage' they want to market is not evident. It has to be welded on, like prosthesis (Nora 1989). Shifts in laws and land use, agricultural production, and the labour market brought the landless into the area and daily sends them out, fomenting demographic, political and personal changes in perspective and aspirations. As in other rural communities throughout Brazil, young people see themselves as 'on the move' rather than 'tied to the land', revising their agrarian 'heritage' and their memories of place.

The idea that heritage reflects the consensual meanings and values of a functionally integrated and homogenous 'community' is a notion with little basis in practice. 'Collective memories' as a descendent of slaves do not embrace everyone, and many are sceptical about the numerous promises and projected beneficial outcomes as remanescente, most of which are yet to be realised. One 70-year-old resident did not hesitate in expressing her suspicion and outrage that 'outsiders' associate with remanescentes for personal and professional gain:

> Politicians, journalists, students, artists, researchers have all benefited from cashing in on [our] past. They come and go. So many people show

up that no one even bothers to look up from what they are doing any- more. Why do they look for us? Why do they always want to talk about slavery, but not things that will help this community?

Dona Rita's comments provide an acerbic critique of the 'gaze' (Urry 1990), whether in the form of the 'search for origins' (O'Dwyer 2002: 35), the pressure to conform to or reproduce cultural forms as 'African', or identify as a slave descendant. By challenging 'one-sided' views of history, rejecting received, composite notions of who they are, and who they are not, rema- nescentes are crafting their own heritage through memory, identity and material practices. To identify or reimagine oneself as a remanescente, embedded in the notion of rights, does not rule out mining for traces of African heritage, if that is the shape that their memories take. The primary importance is the right to memory at all, and to have those memories valued and documented. The charges of charlatanism, and the significance of being a descendant of slaves, are part of the dialogic and contested nature of heritage. It is a continually crafted portrait drawn from the meaning, values, common interests, contradictions, silences, transformations and rein- terpretations of the past. In some locations, the meaning given to rema- nescente heritage is corralled by land disputes, in others, by the deeply entrenched social and spatial distance between 'those blacks from the mountain' and residents of the urban zone. Overall, 'visible', material heri- tage, such as the granting of land titles to communities that originated as quilombos, 120 years after the end of slavery, is the exception rather than the rule, with only 82 out of 1,000 federally recognised communities being granted land titles as of 2008. The invisibility or exclusion of Afro-descendant heritage is not something of the past, but something that requires con- tinuous vigilance.

Notes

1 Title phrase from article by Véran (2002).

Bibliography

Almeida, A.W.B. de (2002) 'Os quilombos e as novas etnias', in E.C. O'Dwyer (ed.), *Quilombos: Identidade étnica e Territorialidad,* Rio de Janeiro: ABA/FGV.
—— (2005) 'Nas Bordas da Política Étnica: os quilombos e as políticas sociais', in I.B. Leite, L.F. Cardoso e Cardoso and R. Mombelli (eds), *Territórios Quilombolas: Reconhecimento e Titulação das Terras (O Boletim Informativo do NUER),* Florianópolis: NUER (Núcleo de Estudos sobre Identidade e Relações Interétnicas da UFSC).
Andrade, L. and Treccani, G. (1999) *Terras de Quilombo,* in Laranjeira, R. (ed.), *Direito Agrário Brasileiro Hoje,* São Paulo LTr.
Arruti, J.M.A. (1997) 'A emergência dos "remanescentes": notas para o diálogo entre indígnenas e Quilombolas', *Mana,* 3: 7–38.

——— (2006) *Mocambo: Antropologia e História do processo de formação quilombola*, São Paulo: Universidade do Sagrado Coração and ANPOCS.

Bastide, R. and Fernandes, F. (1959 [1971]) *Brancos e negros em São Paulo*, São Paulo: Campanhia Editora Nacional.

Bhabha, H. (1990) 'Dissemination: time, narrative, and the margins of the modern nation', in H.K. Bhabba (ed.), *Nation and Narration,* London: Routledge.

Blake, A., Arbache, J.S., Teles, V. and Sinclair, T. (2005) 'Tourism and poverty alleviation in Brazil'. Available online at: http://www.un.br/cet/noticias/Adam_Blake.pdf (Accessed 25 November 2006).

Brazzil Magazine (2004) 'Brazil wants culture as basic human right', *Brazzil Magazine.* Available online at: http://www.brazzil.com (Accessed 27 August 2004).

Carvalho, J.J.D., Doria, S.Z. and Adolfo Neves de Oliveira, J. (1996) *O Quilombo do rio das Rãs: Histórias, Tradições, Lutas,* Salvador: Universidade Federal da Bahia.

Cohen, S. (2001) *States of Denial: Knowing about Atrocities and Suffering,* Massachussetts: Blackwell.

Cunha, O.M.G.D. (1998) 'Politics of identity in Brazil', in S. Alvarez, E. Dagnino and A. Escobar (eds), *Cultures of Politics, Politics of Cultures. Re-Visioning Latin American Social movements,* Colorado: Westview.

Dawson, D.C. (2002) 'Treasure in the terror: The African cultural legacy in the Americas', Available online at: http://www.nku.edu/~freddomchronicle/OldStieArchive/archive/issue3/ (Accessed 30 December 2002).

Douglas, M. (1991) 'The idea of a home: a kind of space', *Social Research,* 58: 287–307.

Edelman, M. and Haugerud, A. (2005) *The Anthropology of Development and Globalization,* Oxford: Blackwell.

Falcão, J. (2001) 'Patrimônio Imaterial: Um sistema sustentável de Proteção', *Tempo Brasileira,* 147: 163–80.

Falci, M.B.K. (1995) *Escravos do Sertão,* Teresina: Fundação Cultural Monsenhor Chaves.

Ferguson, B. (1992) 'Tribal warfare', *Scientific American,* 266(1): 108–13.

Fields, B.J. (1985) *Slavery and Freedom on the Middle Ground: Maryland During the Nineteenth Century,* New Haven: Yale University Press.

Fonseca, M.C.L.F. (1997) *O Patrimônio em Processo: Trajetória da Política Federal de Preservaçao no Brasil,* UFRJ: Ministry of Culture, IPHAN.

——— (2003) 'Para além da pedra e cal: por uma concepçãoampla de patrimônio cultural', in R. Abreu and M. Chagas (eds), *Memória e patrimônio: ensaios contemporaneos,* Rio de Janeiro: DPandA.

Fonseca de Castro, A.H. (2006) 'Quilombos: comunidades e patrimônio', IPHAN. Available online at: http://www.revista.iphan.gov.br (Accessed 25 May 2006).

French, J.H. (2006) 'Buried alive: Imagining Africa in the Brazilian Northeast', *American Ethnologist,* 33: 340–60.

Freyre G. (1946) *The Masters and the Slaves: A study in the Development of Brazilian Civilization,* New York: Alfred A. Knopf.

——— (1959) *New World in the Tropics: The Culture of Modern Brazil,* New York: Alfred A. Knopf.

Gil, G. (2005) Oral presentation, Columbia University, School of International Affairs.

Gomes, F.D.S. (2004) 'Slavery, black peasants and post-emancipation society in Brazil (nineteenth century Rio de Janeiro)', *Social Identities,* 10: 735–56.

Gordillo, G. (2002) 'The breath of devils: memories and places of an experience of terror', *American Ethnologist,* 29: 33–57.

Harvey, D. (1993) 'From space to place and back again: reflections on the condition of postmodernity', in J. Bird (ed.), *Mapping the Futures: Local Cultures, Global Change,* London: Routledge.

Hill, J.D. (1996) *History, Power, and Identity: Ethnogenesis in the Americas, 1492–1992*, Iowa City: University of Iowa Press.

hooks, b. (1989) *Talking Back: Thinking Feminist. Thinking Black*, Toronto: Between the Lines.

—— (1991) *Yearning: Race, Gender, and Cultural Politics*, London: Turnaround.

IPHAN (2000) 'Registro do Patrimônio Imaterial: Dossiê final das atividades da comissão e do Grupo de Trabalho Patrimônio Imaterial', IPHAN. Available online at: http://www. iphan.gov.br (Accessed 30 August 2006).

Kent, R.K. (1973) 'Palmares: An African state in Brazil', in R. Price (ed.), *Maroon Societies: Rebel Slave Communities in the Americas*, Garden City, NY: Anchor-Doubleday.

Leite, I.B. and Mombelli, R. (2005) 'As Perícias antropológicas realizadas pelo NUER e as lutas por reconhecimento e Titulação das Terras de Quilombos', in I.B. Leite, L.F. Cardoso e Cardoso and R. Mombelli (eds.), *Territórios Quilombolas: Reconhecimento e Titulação das Terras*, Florianópolis: NUER (Núcleo de Estudos sobre Identitade e Relações Interétnicas da UFSC).

Lima, N.T. (1998) *Um Sertão chamado Brasil*, Rio de Janeiro: IUPERJ/UCAM:Revan.

Linhares, L.F.D.R. (2006) 'Comunidade negra rural: um velho tema,uma nova discussão', NEAD. Available online at: http://www.nead.org.br (Accessed 25 April 2006).

Lovell, N. (1998) 'Introduction', in N. Lovell (ed.), *Locality and Belonging*, London: Routledge.

Lowenthal, D. (1998) *The Heritage Crusade and the Spoils of History*, Cambridge: Cambridge University Press.

Maio, M.C. (1996) 'A questão racial no pensamento de Guerrerio Ramos', in M.C. Maio and R.V. Santos (eds.), *Raça, Ciência e Sociedade*, Rio de Janeiro: Fiocruz.

Matory, J.L. (2005) *Black Atlantic Religion: Tradition, Transnationalism, and Matriarchy in the Afro-Brazilian Candomblé*, Princeton: Princeton University Press.

Mattos, H. (2005) 'Remanescentes de Quilombos: Memory of slavery, historical justice, and citizenship in contemporary Brazil', unpublished paper presented at the 'Repairing the Past: Confronting the Legacies of Slavery, Genocide and Caste', The Gilder Lehrman Center's Seventh Annual International Conference, Yale University, New Haven, CT, October 27–29, 2005.

Ministry of Culture (2006) *Living Culture. National Culture. Education and Citizenship Program*, Brasília: Ministry of Culture.

Nascimento, A.D. (1980) *O Quilombismo: Documentos de uma Militáncia pan-Africanista*, Petrópolis: Vozes.

Nora, P. (1989) 'Between memory and history: Les Lieux de Mémoire', *Representations*, 26:7–25.

O'Dwyer, E.C. (ed.) (2002) *Quilombos-Identidade Étnica e Territorialidade*, Rio de Janeiro: ABA/FGV.

Oliveira, J., Adolfo Neves de. (1996) Reflexão Antropológica e Prática Pericial *O Quilombo do rio das Rãs: Histórias, Tradições, Lutas*, Salvador: Universidade Federal da Bahia.

Oliven, R.G. (1982) 'As metamorfoses da cultura Brasileira', in R.G. Oliven (ed.), *Violência e Cultura no Brasil*, Petrópolis: Vozes.

Ortiz, R. (1985) *Cultura brasileira e identidade nacional*, São Paulo: Brasiliense.

—— (1988) *A Moderna Tradição Brasileira*, São Paulo: Brasiliense.

Paoli, M.C. and Telles, V.D.S. (1998) 'Social rights: conflicts and negotiations in contemporary Brazil', in S. Alvarez, E. Dagnino and A. Escobar (eds.), *Cultures of Politics, Politics of Cultures: Re-Visioning Latin American Social Movements*, Colorado: Westview.

Price, R. (1988/89) 'Resistance to slavery in the Americas: Maroons and their communities', *Indian Historical Review*, 15:71–95.

Reis, J.J. and Gomes, F.D.S. (1996) *Liberdade por um Fio: História dos quilombos no Brasil*, São Paulo: Companhia das Letras.

Rocha, M.E.G.T. (2005) 'O Decreto No 4887/2003 e a Regulamentação das Terras dos Remanescentes das communidades dos quilombos', in I.B. Leite, L.F. Cardoso e Cardoso and R. Mombelli (eds.), *Territórios Quilombolas: Reconhecimento e Titulação das Terras*, Florianópolis: NUER (Núcleo de Estudos sobre Identitade e Relações Interétnicas da UFSC).

Said, E. (1994) *Culture and Imperialism*, London: Vintage.

Santos, J.R.D. (1996) 'O Negro Como Lugar', in M.C. Maio and R.V. Santos (eds), *Raça, Ciência e sociedade*, Rio de Janeiro: Fiocruz.

Santos, M.S.D. (2005) 'Representations of black people in Brazilian museums', *Museum and Society*, 3:51–65.

Schmitt, A., Turatii, M.C.M. and Carvalho, M.C.P. (2002) 'A Atualização do conceito de quilombo: Identidade e Território nas definições Teóricas', *Ambiente and Sociedade*, Ano V:1–6.

Smith, L. (2006) *Uses of Heritage*, London: Routledge.

Spivak, G. (1993) 'Can the subaltern speak?', in P. Williams and L. Chrisman (eds.), *Colonial Discourse and Post-Colonial Theory*, Hemel Hempstead: Harvester Wheatsheaf.

Tamaso, I. (2006) 'A expansão do patrimônio: novos olhares sobre velhos objetos, outros desafios', *Série antropologia*, 390, Brasilia. Available online at: http://www.unb.br/ics/dan/Serie390empdf.pdf (Accessed 14 May 2008).

Tuan, Y.-F. (1974) *Topophilia: A Study of Environmental Perception, Attitudes, and Values*, Englewood Cliffs, NJ: Prentice Hall.

Urry, J. (1990) *The Tourist Gaze: Leisure and Travel in Contemporary Societies*, London: Sage.

Véran, J.F. (2002) 'Quilombos and land rights in contemporary Brazil', *Cultural Survival Quarterly*, 25(4): 20–5.

Warren, J.W. (2001) *Racial Revolutions: Antiracism and Indian Resurgence in Brazil*, Durham: Duke University Press.

Williams, D. (2001) *Culture Wars in Brazil: The First Vargas Regime, 1930–1945*, Durham: Duke University Press.

Winter, J. (1995) *Sites of Memory: Sties of Mourning: The Great War in European Cultural History*, Cambridge: Cambridge University Press.

World Bank (2005) 'World country brief: Brazil', World Bank. Available online at: http://www.worldbank.org (Accessed 30 April 2005).

Young, J. E. (2000) *At Memory's Edge*, New Haven: Yale University Press.

Yúdice, G. (2003) *The Expediency of Culture: Uses of Culture in the Global Era*, Durham: Duke University Press.

Chapter 9

The UNESCO *Convention for the Safeguarding of the Intangible Cultural Heritage* and the protection and maintenance of the intangible cultural heritage of indigenous peoples

Henrietta Marrie

Introduction

The cultures, languages and heritages of Indigenous peoples are threatened globally. If language loss is taken as an indicator of the loss of a people's intangible cultural heritage (as embodied in their folklore, oral traditions and expressive arts), it has been predicted that the world will lose one-third of its remaining languages by the end of the twenty-first century. In this chapter, a review and an assessment are made of the *Convention for the Safeguarding of the Intangible Cultural Heritage* (ICHC) in terms of what its provisions contain that will help Indigenous peoples to gain a measure of protection for their intangible cultural heritage. This, under the Convention, includes their oral traditions, languages, performing arts, social practices, traditional knowledge and practices concerning nature and the universe, and traditional artisanship. Of particular importance is the extent to which Indigenous peoples themselves are empowered by the Convention to effectively protect and maintain their own intangible cultural heritage and to participate in the Convention's processes. The relative strengths and weaknesses of the ICHC are also assessed against other standard-setting international instruments and processes that can be used to provide a measure of protection for the intangible cultural heritage of indigenous peoples, particularly in relation to their languages and traditional knowledge such as the United Nations *Declaration on the Rights of Indigenous Peoples* (adopted by the United Nations Human Rights Council in June 2006) and ILO *Convention (No. 169) Concerning Indigenous and Tribal Peoples in Independent Countries.* Reference is also made to the relevance and effectiveness of the suite of intellectual property laws overseen by the World Intellectual Property Organization (WIPO) and particularly the deliberations of the WIPO Intergovernmental Committee on Genetic Resources, Traditional Knowledge and Folklore regarding the development of a *sui generis* law for the protection of traditional knowledge. Other international environmental treaties and processes, such as the *Convention on Biological Diversity*, the *International Treaty on Plant Genetic Resources for Food and Agriculture* (the 'Seed Treaty') and the UN *Convention to Combat Desertification*, are also examined to provide a comparative perspective on what measures are currently being taken that can enable the maintenance and survival of aspects of the intangible cultural heritage of Indigenous peoples. Before reviewing the ICHC, and placing it within the context of other instruments, it will be useful to summarise its key features.

The UNESCO Convention for the Safeguarding of the Intangible Cultural Heritage: *Purposes, definitions, administrative provisions and mechanisms*

The General Conference of UNESCO in the preamble to the Convention considered, *inter alia*, 'the importance of the intangible cultural heritage as a mainspring of cultural diversity and a guarantee of sustainable development', 'the deep-seated interdependence between the intangible cultural heritage and the tangible and natural heritage', and that intangible cultural heritage has 'the invaluable role ... as a factor in bringing humans closer together and ensuring exchange and understanding among them'. The General Conference also recognised in the preamble that 'the processes of globalization and social transformation ... also gives rise, as does the phenomenon of intolerance, to grave threats of deterioration, disappearance and destruction of the intangible cultural heritage, in particular owing to a lack of resources for safeguarding such heritage'.

Article 1 of the Convention states its purposes as being:

(a)   to safeguard the intangible cultural heritage;
(b)   to ensure respect for the intangible cultural heritage of the communities, groups and individuals concerned;
(c)   to raise awareness at the local, national and international levels of the importance of the intangible cultural heritage, and of ensuring mutual appreciation thereof;
(d)   to provide for international cooperation and assistance.

For the purposes of the Convention, Article 2.1 defines the 'intangible cultural heritage' to mean:

... the practices, representations, expressions, knowledge, skills – as well as the instruments, objects, artefacts and cultural spaces associated therewith – that communities, groups and, in some cases, individuals recognize as part of their cultural heritage. This intangible cultural heritage, transmitted from generation to generation, is constantly recreated by communities and groups in response to their environment, their interaction with nature and their history, and provides them with a sense of identity and continuity, thus promoting respect for cultural diversity and human creativity. For the purposes of this Convention, consideration will be given solely to such intangible cultural heritage as is compatible with existing international human rights instruments, as well as with the requirements of mutual respect among communities, groups and individuals, and of sustainable development.

In further clarifying the above definition, Article 2.2 provides that 'intangible cultural heritage' is:

> ... manifested inter alia in the following domains:
> (a) oral traditions and expressions, including language as a vehicle of the intangible cultural heritage;
> (b) performing arts;
> (c) social practices, rituals and festive events;
> (d) knowledge and practices concerning nature and the universe;
> (e) traditional craftsmanship.

The term 'safeguarding' is defined in Article 2.3 as meaning:

> ... measures aimed at ensuring the viability of the intangible cultural heritage, including the identification, documentation, research, preservation, protection, promotion, enhancement, transmission, particularly through formal and non-formal education, as well as the revitalization of the various aspects of such heritage.

With regard to the administration of the Convention, the state parties to the Convention comprise the General Assembly of the Convention, which meets every two years (Article 4), while Article 5 establishes an Intergovernmental Committee for the Safeguarding of the Intangible Cultural Heritage (IGICHC), comprised initially of representatives of 18 state parties, elected by the General Assembly and increasing to 24 once the number of the state parties to the Convention reaches 50. Now that there are more than 50 state parties to the Convention, state parties' representation on the IGICHC has increased to 24.

The safeguarding of the intangible cultural heritage is primarily a national responsibility, and in accordance with Article 11, each state party shall:

> (a) take the necessary measure to ensure the safeguarding of the intangible cultural heritage present in its territory;
> (b) among the safeguarding measures referred to in Article 2, paragraph 3, identify and define the various elements of the intangible cultural heritage present in its territory, with the participation of communities, groups and relevant non-governmental organizations.

In addition, pursuant to Article 12:

> To ensure identification with a view to safeguarding, each State Party shall draw up, in a manner geared to its own situation, one or more inventories of the intangible cultural heritage present in its territory. These inventories shall be regularly updated.

Other measures for safeguarding are also identified in Article 13 to ensure the safeguarding, development and promotion of the ICH within its territory by each state party. These measures are:

(a)   adopt a general policy aimed at promoting the function of the intangible cultural heritage in society, and at integrating the safeguarding of such heritage into planning programmes;

(b)   designate or establish one or more competent bodies for safeguarding of the intangible cultural heritage present in its territory;

(c)   foster scientific, technical and artistic studies, as well as research methodologies, with a view to effective safeguarding of the intangible cultural heritage, in particular the intangible cultural heritage in danger;

(d)   adopt appropriate legal, technical, administrative and financial measures aimed at:

   (i)   fostering the creation or strengthening of institutions for training in the management of the intangible cultural heritage and the transmission of such heritage through forums and spaces intended for the performance or expression thereof;

   (ii) ensuring access to the intangible cultural heritage while respecting customary practices governing access to specific aspects of such heritage;

   (iii) establishing documentation institutions for the intangible cultural heritage and facilitating access to them.

Education, awareness raising and capacity building are key components of any safeguarding strategy. Under Article 14, each state party shall endeavour, by all appropriate means to:

(a)   ensure recognition of, respect for, and enhancement of the intangible cultural heritage in society, in particular through:

   (i)   educational, awareness-raising and information programmes, aimed at the general public, in particular young people;

   (ii) specific educational and training programmes within the communities and groups concerned;

   (iii) capacity-building activities for the safeguarding of the intangible cultural heritage, in particular management and scientific research; and

(iv) non-formal means of transmitting knowledge;

(b) keep the public informed of the dangers threatening such heritage, and of the activities carried out in pursuance of this Convention;

(c) promote education for the protection of natural spaces and places of memory whose existence is necessary for expressing the intangible cultural heritage.

Concerning participation, Article 15 states that:

Within the framework of its safeguarding activities of the intangible cultural heritage, each state party shall endeavour to ensure the widest possible participation of communities, groups and, where appropriate, individuals that create, maintain and transmit such heritage, and to involve them actively in its management.

The Convention provides additional measures for safeguarding the ICH at the international level through the publication of a Representative List of the Intangible Cultural Heritage of Humanity to be established by the Intergovernmental Committee (Article 16) as well as a List of Intangible Cultural Heritage in Need of Urgent Safeguarding (Article 17); selection and promotion of national, subregional and regional programmes, projects and activities, taking into account the special needs of developing countries (Article 18); international cooperation and assistance to include, *inter alia*, the exchange of information, joint initiatives, and the establishment of a mechanism of assistance to state parties (Article 19); and the establishment of a fund for the Safeguarding of the Intangible Cultural Heritage (Article 25). State parties are also required to submit to the Intergovernmental Committee periodic reports on the legislative, regulatory and other measures taken for the implementation of the Convention (Article 29).

The Convention, in accordance with its Article 34, entered into force on 20 April 2006. By December 2007, 87 state parties had become signatories (that is, ratified, accepted, approved or acceded) to the Convention with 69 having actually ratified it.

The UNESCO *Convention for Safeguarding Intangible Cultural Heritage* and Indigenous peoples

The Convention was established primarily because 'no binding multilateral instrument as yet exists for the safeguarding of the intangible cultural heritage' (Preamble) and existing international agreements, recommendations and resolutions concerning the cultural and natural heritage need to be effectively enriched and supplemented by means of new provisions relating to the intangible cultural heritage' (Preamble). While it is the case that there are no other binding multilateral instruments for safeguarding intangible cultural heritage, given the extremely precarious state of this component of the heritage of Indigenous peoples and their communities, the general tone of this Convention and its provisions fall way below that of the two bench-mark instruments by which it can be evaluated, namely, the United Nations *Declaration on the Rights of Indigenous Peoples* (DRIP) and ILO *Convention (No. 169) Concerning Indigenous and Tribal Peoples in Independent Countries* (ILO Convention 169). There are also other international instruments, which include the suite of intellectual property conventions administered by the World Intellectual Property Organisation (WIPO), the *Convention on Biological Diversity* (CBD), the *International Treaty on Plant Genetic Resources for Food and Agriculture* (ITPGRFA) – the so-called 'Seed' Treaty, and the United Nations *Convention to Combat Desertification in those Countries Experiencing Drought and/or Desertification, Particularly in Africa* (UNCCD), which offer stronger protections to particular components of Indigenous intangible cultural heritage.

Given that most of the world's cultural diversity is borne by Indigenous peoples and their communities and that they are, with the exception of refugees, the most politically and culturally disempowered group of peoples in the world, it is difficult to understand why they should be so overlooked in this Convention. Issues surrounding the protection of what can broadly be referred to as Indigenous traditional knowledge have been on the agenda of a number of UN specialised agencies (such as WIPO, United Nations Development Program, United Nations Conference on Trade and Development, the Food and Agriculture Organisation, the World Health Organization and the Working Group on Indigenous Populations of the (formerly) Commission on Human Rights Subcommission on the Protection and Promotion of Human Rights) as well as regional organisations such as the Organization of American States, the African Union and the African Intellectual Property Organization, for over a decade. The most ready explanation is that Indigenous peoples were not included in the negotiation processes, either by having direct representation (for example, through the Working Group on Indigenous Populations or the UN Permanent Forum on Indigenous Issues), or by having Indigenous representation in the national delegations sent to negotiate the Convention. The word 'indigenous' occurs only once in the Convention – in the Preamble where the General Conference of UNESCO 'recogniz[es] that communities, in particular indigenous communities, groups and, in some cases, individuals, play an important role in the production, safeguarding, maintenance and recreation of the intangible cultural heritage, thus helping to enrich cultural diversity and human creativity'.

In the ensuing analysis, the legal status of the various kinds of international instruments should be borne in mind. Declarations, principles and guidelines, for example, have no binding legal effect. Nevertheless, these instruments have an undeniable moral force, and provide practical guidance to states in their conduct – the *Universal Declaration of Human Rights*, for example. The value of such instruments rests on their recognition and acceptance by a large number of states, and, even without binding legal effect, they may be seen as declaratory of broadly accepted principles within the international community. Conventions, covenants, treaties and protocols that come under the purview of the UN and its organisations, however, are legally binding for those states that ratify or accede to them.

Aspects of intangible cultural heritage not covered by the Convention

The central issue for Indigenous peoples regarding the protection of their cultural heritage and intellectual property is the lack of an international system that provides recognition to and promotes a holistic approach to such protection. The current fragmented and piecemeal approach sees the protection of some components, such as biodiversity-related medicinal and agricultural knowledge, being actively promoted, while languages, for example, as the fundamental vehicle for the broad spectrum of traditional knowledge and creative expression, are almost totally neglected. This Convention, at best, offers only selective protection for ICH at the international level through the mechanism of the Representative List of the Intangible Cultural Heritage of Humanity (RLICHH). Article 16 states:

1. In order to ensure better visibility of the intangible cultural heritage and awareness of its significance, and to encourage dialogue which respects cultural diversity, the Committee, upon the proposal of the States Parties concerned, shall establish, keep up to date and publish a Representative List of the Intangible Cultural Heritage of Humanity.
2. The Committee shall draw up and submit to the General Assembly for approval the criteria for the establishment, updating and publication of this Representative List.

This list will provide an important guide as to what the Intergovernmental Committee and ultimately the General Assembly of the Convention consider to be the kinds of examples of ICH appropriate for the list – a reference guide, as it were – and therefore important as much for what is included as for what is not. State parties are expected, under Article 12, to draw up their own inventories, and these may well be much more comprehensive and include examples of the ICH not represented in the RLICHH. The Convention also provides for the establishment of a List of Intangible Cultural Heritage in Need of Urgent Safeguarding (Article 17). Adding an endangered Indigenous language to this List would set an important precedent.

In dealing with any processes that affect their lives, Indigenous peoples are particularly concerned that: (i) they are consulted, and can participate and drive such processes to the fullest extent possible; and (ii) their essential rights to their traditional territories, to maintain their lifestyles and retain their cultural identities are not interfered with. Concerning consultation and participation, the *Declaration on the Rights of Indigenous Peoples*, in Article 18, states:

> Indigenous peoples have the right to participate in decision-making in matters which would affect their rights, through representatives chosen by themselves in accordance with their own procedures, as well as to maintain and develop their own Indigenous decision-making institutions

Article 6.1 of the ILO Convention 169 is even more explicit:

> In applying the provisions of this Convention, Governments shall:
> (a) Consult the peoples concerned, through appropriate procedures and in particular through their representative institutions, whenever consideration is being given to legislative or administrative measures which may affect them directly;
> (b) Establish means by which these peoples can freely participate, to at least the same extent as other sectors of the population, at all levels of decisions-making in elective institutions and administrative and other bodies responsible for policies and programmes which concern them;
> (c) Establish means for the full development of these peoples' own institutions and initiatives, and in appropriate cases provide the resources necessary for this purpose.

Concerning participation, Article 15 of the ICHC states that:

> Within the framework of its safeguarding activities of the intangible cultural heritage, each State Party shall endeavour to ensure the widest possible participation of communities, groups and, where appropriate, individuals that create, maintain and transmit such heritage, and to involve them actively in its management.

However, much will depend on the kinds of processes and bodies (for example, statutory boards, committees, etc.) that state parties establish to safeguard their intangible cultural heritage; the extent to which Indigenous peoples are represented and are able to participate in decision-making; and the extent to which they are able to participate in the safeguarding measures implemented, including all those mentioned in Articles 11–14 (see above).

The intangible cultural heritage referred to in Article 2.1–2 of the ICHC can be loosely translated to mean the 'intellectual heritage' of a people, that is, the knowledge and know-how they possess about all aspects of their culture. This covers the many aspects of Indigenous cultures critical to Indigenous cultural identity: language, knowledge (including sacred knowledge) of territory and natural resources (and how to sustainably use and manage them), customs (including customary law and governance), religious/spiritual/sacred knowledge and practices, social and kinship structures, educational practices, and so on. Loss of control of or the diminution of any of these components of Indigenous intellectual heritage invariably erode a sense of identity. While the definition of the 'intangible cultural heritage' given in the Convention is very broad, the test of what is considered worthy of safeguarding will ultimately be those items/components of this heritage entered into the inventories established and maintained by the state. For example, a critically endangered Indigenous language might be excluded while the threatened knowledge and techniques of how to make a unique basket of one of the last traditional weavers and speakers of that language may be digitally recorded in detail for posterity and be entered on the list for safeguarding. Cost considerations can also never be far from mind: the costs of maintaining a language (especially if it is going to be taught in the classroom) and the effort and commitment necessary far exceed those of digitally recording the techniques of basket-weaving. Besides, such a recording would admirably support the display of such a basket in a museum exhibition, and would enable others to learn the techniques to make such a basket, whether or not they are from that culture. But the loss of a language?

While the definition of what constitutes 'intangible cultural heritage' is very broad, it is also very vague and imprecise if we read it with the critical components of Indigenous intellectual heritage in mind, and is unlikely to resonate much with the Indigenous peoples whose intangible cultural heritage is in such dire need of safeguarding. For example, it is estimated that some two-thirds of the world's languages (some reports go as high as 90%) – and these constitute languages largely spoken by Indigenous peoples – could become extinct by the end of the twenty-first century (Maffi 1999). Yet the Convention appears to define language more in terms of its value as 'a vehicle of the intangible cultural heritage' (Article 2.2(a)) rather than as a distinct and unambiguous category – 'domain' in the Convention's terminology – of the intangible cultural heritage and marker of cultural diversity. A further example: a body of Indigenous customary law (or particular aspects of it), governance, economic systems (based on barter, exchange and reciprocity), and social and kinship structures could conceivably be covered by 'social practices' (Article 2.2(c)); sacred knowledge, spiritual and religious traditions may be considered as 'rituals' (Article 2.2(c)) or as 'knowledge and practices concerning nature and the universe' (Article 2.2(d)). Similarly, the land-based 'customs, traditions and land tenure systems', referred to in DRIP Article 26.3, might also be covered by 'social practices' and/or 'knowledge and practices concerning nature and the universe'. This might also be applicable for safeguarding the huge bodies of traditional ecological and medicinal knowledge that enable Indigenous peoples to live and maintain their own particular lifestyles, customs and traditions. Such imprecise definitions play into the hands of those assimilationist governments that have no particular interest in safeguarding Indigenous ICH.

The Convention's mechanisms *vis-à-vis* other standard-setting instruments that can be used to protect the intangible cultural heritage of Indigenous peoples

While there are a number of human rights instruments that contain provisions protecting individuals' rights to culture, religious freedom, use of own language, etc., their wording is general in nature. Such provisions can be found, for example, in the *International Convention on the Elimination of All Forms of Racial Discrimination* (Article 5(e)(vi)) and the *International Covenant on Economic, Social and Cultural Rights* (Article 15). Article 27 of the *International Covenant on Civil and Political Rights*, however, is more explicit and states:

> In those States in which ethnic, religious or linguistic minorities exist, persons belonging to such minorities shall not be denied the right, in community with the other members of their group, to enjoy their own culture, to profess and practice their own religion, or to use their own language.

The two instruments that deal with and more comprehensively articulate the rights of Indigenous peoples, and are therefore seen as the standard setters, are the United Nations *Declaration on the Rights of Indigenous Peoples* and International Labour Organization's *Convention (No. 169) Concerning Indigenous and Tribal Peoples in Independent Countries* (ILO Convention 169).

United Nations Declaration on the Rights of Indigenous Peoples

This Declaration contains a number of standard-setting provisions expressed as rights, that if put into effect by nation-states whose territories also encompass those traditionally inhabited by Indigenous peoples, would provide a high level of 'safeguarding' of what are, in effect, components of Indigenous intangible heritage. While there is no particular Article identifying intangible cultural heritage per se and thus distinguishing it from other forms of cultural heritage, there are a number of Articles that incorporate components of intangible cultural heritage as defined in the

UNESCO Convention (these include Articles: 8, 11, 12, 13, 14, 16, 18, 20, 24, 26, 31, 34, 39, 41, 42 and 43). For example, if the 'domains' of the ICH listed in Article 2.2 of the Convention are taken into account, then the domain of 'oral traditions and expressions, including language as a vehicle of the intangible cultural heritage' finds elaboration in Article 13.1 of the Declaration whereby:

> Indigenous peoples have the right to revitalize, use, develop and transmit to future generations their histories, languages, oral traditional, philosophies, writing systems and literatures, and to designate and retain their own names for communities, places and persons.

Under Article 13.2, states shall take effective measures, *inter alia*, to protect this right.

Performing arts, another 'domain' listed under Article 2.2(b) is covered by Article 11.1 of the Declaration:

> Indigenous peoples have the right to practice and revitalize their cultural traditions and customs. This includes the right to maintain, protect and develop the past, present and future manifestations of their cultures, such as archaeological and historical sites, artefacts, designs, ceremonies, technologies and visual and performing arts and literature.

> Article 31.1: Indigenous peoples have the right to maintain, control, protect and develop their cultural heritage, traditional knowledge and traditional cultural expressions, as well as the manifestations of their sciences, technologies and cultures, including human and genetic resources, seeds, medicines, knowledge of the properties of fauna and flora, oral traditions, literatures, designs, sports and traditional games and visual and performing arts. They also have the right to maintain, control and develop their intellectual property over such cultural heritage, traditional knowledge, and traditional cultural expressions.

Like Article 13.2 (above), Article 13.2 calls for states to take effective measures to implement Article 31.1

ILO Convention (No. 169) Concerning Indigenous and Tribal Peoples in Independent Countries

Adopted on the 27 June 1989 by the General Conference of the International Labour Organization, ILO Convention 169, since entering into force in September 1991, has generally been seen as the standard-setter for the recognition of the rights of Indigenous peoples while the negotiations for a Declaration on the Rights of Indigenous Peoples were taking place. Article 2, for example, states:

3. Governments shall have the responsibility for developing, with the participation of the peoples concerned, co-ordinated and systematic action to protect the rights of these peoples and to guarantee respect for their integrity.
4. Such action shall include measures for:
    (b) Promoting the full realization of the social, economic and cultural rights of these peoples with respect to their social and cultural identity, their customs and traditions and their institutions.

Article 4.1 provides that special measures should be adopted for safeguarding, *inter alia*, the cultures of Indigenous and tribal peoples, while Article 28.3 expressly requires that 'Measures shall be taken to preserve and promote the development and practice of the indigenous languages of the peoples concerned'.

ILO Convention 169 also contains a number of other provisions that equate with 'domains' of the ICH laid out in the ICHC, such as Article 5 in reference to 'social practices, rituals and events' (Article 2.2(c)), Article 5 states that:

In applying the provisions of this Convention:
(a) The social, cultural, religious and spiritual values and practices of these peoples shall be recognized and protected, and due account shall be taken of the nature of the problems which face them as groups and as individuals;

And Article 8:

1. In applying national laws and regulations to the peoples concerned, due regard shall be had to their customs or customary laws.
2. These peoples shall have the right to retain their own customs and institutions, where these are not incompatible with fundamental rights defined by the national legal system and with internationally recognized human rights. Procedures shall be established, whenever necessary, to resolve conflicts which may arise in the application of this principle.

ILO Convention 169, in Article 23.1, specifically refers to the kinds of activities, knowledge and technologies particularly associated with subsistence living, which would fall within the 'domains' of 'knowledge and practices concerning nature and the universe' and 'traditional craftsmanship' – Article 2.2(d) and (e) of the ICHC:

Handicrafts, rural and community-based industries, and subsistence economy and traditional activities of the peoples concerned, such as hunting, fishing, trapping and gathering, shall be recognized as important factors in the maintenance of their cultures and in their economic self-reliance and development. Governments shall, with the participation of these peoples and whenever appropriate, ensure that these activities are strengthened and promoted.

ILO Convention 169 has been ratified by 17 states (since January 2003), 13 of which are Latin American countries with large Indigenous populations.

Intellectual property instruments and the safeguarding of the intangible cultural heritage of Indigenous peoples

In essence, Intellectual Property Rights (IPR) are designed to protect the commercial rights and interests of the holders/creators and prevent or compensate for illicit use, misappropriation, or exploitation of such rights, rather than for promoting the maintenance and longevity of particular forms of cultural or intellectual expression or endeavour. The bundle of rights protected as intellectual property covers copyrights, patents, designs, trademarks, trade secrets, plant breeders' rights, and geographic indicators/appellations of origin. The relatively temporary protections afforded to such rights, measured in decades, as opposed to cultural traditions that often span millennia, make them singularly unsuited for the long-term safeguarding of ICH, but nevertheless they can through direct remedial actions and establishment of legal precedent, afford protections for certain components of Indigenous ICH.

There is considerable (on-going) debate about the relevance, compatibility and appropriateness of using a system of IPR designed to protect particular forms of intellectual property evolving out of Western cultural, intellectual, scientific and technological traditions and practices and now being universally applied through the intellectual property treaties administered by WIPO, and also enforced through the World Trade Organization, to protect different components of Indigenous cultural heritage including ICH. Both the CBD, through decisions of the Conference of the Parties (COP) regarding the implementation of Article 8(j), and WIPO, through its Intergovernmental Committee on Intellectual Property and Genetic Resources, Traditional Knowledge and Folklore continue to deliberate the extent to which Western-style IPRs are effective in providing protection to Indigenous traditional knowledge and other expressions of ICH, with WIPO taking the lead agency role. Both agencies are also assessing whether or not a special *sui generis* treaty should be devised to particularly provide protection to traditional knowledge and other forms of traditional cultural expression. Needless to say, Indigenous peoples evolved their own diverse systems of customary laws to protect certain forms of knowledge, particularly sacred and secret knowledge, customs and traditions and would prefer to have such systems officially recognised. Many countries with large Indigenous populations (such as the Philippines, India, Ecuador, Peru, Nicaragua, Costa Rica) and realising, perhaps in response to the CBD, that traditional environmentally/ecologically related knowledge and practices, that is, traditional ecological knowledge (TEK), in particular represents a huge economic asset, have passed domestic laws (in effect *sui generis* laws) giving greater protection to Indigenous ICH. Other countries, such as Australia and Canada, encourage 'their' Indigenous peoples to use standard forms of IPRs, particularly copyright, to protect items of cultural expression. Both of these countries have expended considerable resources to help Indigenous people and their communities negotiate the IPR system. In Australia, there has been a series of 'land-mark' cases that have brought relief to Indigenous plaintiffs over breaches of copyright in relation to artworks, demonstrating to some extent that the IPR system can work for Indigenous peoples. The biggest drawback to the IPR system may not so much be the laws themselves, but Indigenous ignorance of them, how they can be accessed and applied, and the expenses involved. For example, while copyright law has been applied to protect Indigenous artworks, and Indigenous peoples in Australia and Canada have developed some understanding of it, the other forms of IPRs, such as patents, plant breeders' rights and trademarks have rarely, if ever, been used.

Contractual methods for the safeguarding of the intangible cultural heritage

Another form of protection of ITK can be sought through contractual means embedding basic principles of prior informed consent, mutually agreed terms and equitable benefit sharing. These are favoured by many countries when access to genetic resources for commercial and research purposes is being sought, for example, in accordance with Article 15 of the CBD, and which has given rise to the *Bonn Guidelines on Access to Genetic Resources and Fair and Equitable Sharing of the Benefits Arising out of their Utilization* adopted by the COP at its sixth meeting held in The Hague in April 2002 (COP to the CBD Decision VI/24A, para. 3). The guidelines provide important and useful advice to governments and other interested parties regarding, *inter alia*, basic principles, elements and procedures for establishing a system for prior informed consent that would enable Indigenous peoples to protect their interests in relation to outside parties wishing to access traditional knowledge regarding particular traditionally used species. The guidelines could also be usefully referred to in relation to matters affecting access to Indigenous ICH.

International environmental instruments

There are two environmental Conventions that offer high standards for the protection of particular components of ICH that essentially relate to traditional TEK, the domain of ICH, which most closely relates to the 'knowledge and practices concerning nature and the universe' (ICHC Article 2.2(d)). These are the CBD and the United Nations *Convention to Combat Desertification in those Countries Experiencing Drought and/or Desertification, Particularly in Africa* (UNCCD), although other environment-related Conventions, such as the UN *Convention on Wetlands (Ramsar Convention)*, have established processes and work programmes which involve respect for, maintenance and application of TEK. A third instrument, the ITPGRFA – the 'seed treaty' – also contains important provisions protecting the rights of traditional farmers.

With respect to the CBD and UNCCD, the argument here is the 'use it, or lose it' principle whereby both Conventions adopt a practical rather than rights-based approach to the protection and maintenance of TEK. Within this argument the parties to these Conventions have essentially recognised the strong connection between cultural and biological diversity, that the world's indigenous peoples and local communities (who are essentially Indigenous peoples) inhabit, conserve and sustainably use critical regions of the world's biodiversity. In addition, in order to conserve this biodiversity, the traditional inhabitants of those regions should be encouraged, empowered and resourced to maintain their traditional lifestyles relevant to the conservation and sustainable use of this biodiversity. In this regard, the decisions of the COP to the CBD regarding the establishment of work programmes, rules for Indigenous participation and involvement under observer status, and the establishment of the Ad Hoc Working Group on Article 8(j) are important precedents for the engagement of Indigenous peoples in the implementation of the CBD. Within this paradigm, the valuable service in the cause of the conservation of biological diversity performed by Indigenous peoples through the continued application of their traditional knowledge and customary practices to the natural resources found on their traditional territories and thus enabling the maintenance of their traditional lifestyles, is tantamount to their cultural survival. In other words, this enables the survival (or safeguarding) of many other 'domains' of their ICH, such as 'oral traditions and expressions, including language as a vehicle for the intangible cultural heritage', 'performing arts', 'social practices, rituals and festive events' and 'traditional craftsmanship' (ICHC Article 2.2(a)–(c), and (e)), which are all, in essence, based around relationships with their traditional country and use of its resources.

Convention on Biological Diversity

The CBD was opened for signature on 5 June 1992 at the United Nations Conference on Environment and Development (the Rio 'Earth Summit'), and entered into force on 29 December 1993. By the end of 2002, 187 countries had become parties to the CBD, and of those 168 had ratified the Convention. In the preamble to the CBD, the contracting parties recognise:

> ... the close and traditional dependence of many indigenous and local communities embodying traditional lifestyles on biological resources, and the desirability of sharing equitably benefits arising from the use of traditional knowledge, innovations and practices relevant to the conservation of biological diversity and the sustainable use of its components.

While the CBD adopts the term 'indigenous and local communities embodying traditional lifestyles relevant for the conservation and sustainable use of biological diversity' and which is unacceptable to many Indigenous peoples, the CBD nevertheless delivers many benefits critical to the survival of Indigenous peoples and their cultures. In geo-political terms, the term 'Indigenous peoples', as it has largely evolved over the last three decades (roughly corresponding to the establishment of the Commission for Human Rights Working Group on Indigenous Populations), generally refers to those Indigenous peoples of the New World who were colonised by European powers (i.e., in the Americas, Southeast Asia, the Pacific and Oceania) and who total around 600 million people. The term 'local communities' has largely been adopted by sovereign countries like Russia, China and India, and in Africa, to identify and describe their own ethnically and culturally diverse populations who are also, for the most part, indigenous to their regions. Most of these local communities comprise most of the world's traditional farmers and number about 1.4 billion people (FAO 1998: 25). Thus the 'indigenous [peoples] and local communities' referred to in Article 8(j), combined, make up roughly one-third of the world's population.

The CBD contains a number of important provisions protecting the TK interests of Indigenous peoples. Article 8, which generally addresses the in situ conservation of biological diversity, states that:

> Each Contracting Party shall, as far as possible and as appropriate:
> (j)   Subject to its national legislation, respect, preserve and maintain knowledge, innovations and practices of indigenous and local communities embodying traditional lifestyles relevant for the conservation and sustainable use of biological diversity and promote their wider application with the approval and involvement of the holders of such knowledge, innovations and practices and encourage the equitable sharing of the benefits arising from the utilization of such knowledge, innovations and practices.

Article 10: Sustainable Use of Components of Biological Diversity, contains an important provision regarding the importance of customary uses of biological diversity within the parameters of conservation and sustainable use, thus laying a foundation for the continuance of cultural practices and traditions of Indigenous peoples on their traditional estates. Under Article 10:

Each Contracting Party shall, as far as possible and as appropriate:
(c)   Protect and encourage customary use of biological resources in accordance with traditional cultural practices that are compatible with conservation or sustainable use requirements.

Two other Articles dealing with the exchange of information and technical and scientific cooperation essentially place Indigenous traditional knowledge on a par with scientific knowledge and expertise in the implementation of the CBD. The parties also affirmed this at their third meeting in Buenos Aires, Argentina, in 1996, in the Preamble to Decision III/14 whereby:

The Conference of the Parties,
Recogniz[es] that traditional knowledge should be given the same respect as any other form of knowledge in the implementation of the Convention.

With regard to the exchange of information, Article 17.2 states that:

exchange of information shall include exchange of results of technical, scientific and socio-economic research, as well as information on training and surveying programmes, specialized knowledge, indigenous and traditional knowledge as such and in combination with the technologies referred to in Article 16, paragraph 1. It shall also, where feasible, include repatriation of information.

And Article 18.4 regarding technical and scientific cooperation states that:

The Contracting Parties shall, in accordance with national legislation and policies, encourage and develop methods of cooperation for the development and use of technologies, including indigenous and traditional technologies, in pursuance of the objectives of this Convention. For this purpose the Contracting Parties shall also promote cooperation in the training of personnel and exchange of experts.

United Nations Convention to Combat Desertification in those Countries Experiencing Drought and/or Desertification, Particularly in Africa

The UNCCD was adopted in June 1994, and entered into force on 26 December 1996. The UNCCD makes no specific reference to 'Indigenous people(s)' but uses the term 'local populations'. However, there are specific references to 'traditional and local knowledge', 'technology', 'know-how' and 'practices', as contained, for example in Article 17: Research and Development:

1. The Parties undertake, according to their respective capabilities, to promote technical and scientific cooperation in the fields of combating desertification and mitigating the effects of drought through appropriate nation, subregional, regional and international institutions. To this end, they shall support research activities that:

    (c) protect, integrate, enhance and validate traditional and local knowledge and know-how and practices, ensuring, subject to their respective national legislation and/or policies, that the owners of that knowledge will directly benefit on an equitable basis and on mutually agreed terms from any commercial utilization of it of from any technological development derived from that knowledge.

And in Article 18, Transfer, Acquisition, Adaptation and Development of Technology:

2. The Parties shall, according to their respective capabilities, and subject to their respective national legislation and/or policies, protect, promote and use in particular relevant traditional and local technology, knowledge, know-how and practices and, to that end, they undertake to:

    (a) make inventories of such technology, knowledge, know-how and practices, and their potential uses with the participation of local populations, and disseminate such information, where appropriate, in cooperation with relevant intergovernmental and non-governmental organizations;
    (b) ensure that such technology, knowledge, know-how and practices are adequately protected and that local populations benefit directly, on an equitable basis and as mutually agreed, from any commercial utilization of them or from any technological development derived therefrom;
    (c) encourage and actively support the improvement and dissemination of such technology, knowledge know-how and practices or of the development of new technology based on them; and
    (d) facilitate, as appropriate, the adaptation of such technology, knowledge, know-how and practices to wide use and integrate them with modern technology, as appropriate.

International Treaty on Plant Genetic Resources for Food and Agriculture

The ITPGRFA was adopted by the 31st session of the Food and Agriculture Conference on 3 November 2001, and entered into force on 29 June 2004. Currently there are 116 parties signatory to the Treaty. This Treaty is important for the recognition it gives to the role of particularly traditional farmers in conserving and improving crop and other species fundamental to world food security. Generally characterised as 'resource-poor', the estimated number of traditional farmers is around 1.4 billion, the majority of whom are women. In the Treaty, the contracting parties have affirmed that:

> ... the past, present and future contributions of farmers in all regions of the world, particularly those in centres of origin and diversity, in conserving, improving and making available these resources, is the basis of Farmers' Rights,

and also that:

> ... the rights recognized in this Treaty to save, use, exchange and sell farm-saved seed and other propagating material, and to participate in decision-making regarding, and in the fair and equitable sharing of the benefits arising from, the use of plant genetic resources for food and agriculture, are fundamental to the realization of Farmers' Rights, as well as the promotion of Farmers' Rights at national and international levels.

These rights are specified in Article 9:

1   The Contracting Parties recognize the enormous contribution that the local and indigenous communities and farmers of all regions of the world, particularly those in centres of origin and crop diversity, have made and will continue to make for the conservation and development of plant genetic resources which constitute the basis of food and agriculture production throughout the world.
2   The Contracting Parties agree that the responsibility for realizing Farmers' Rights, as they relate to plant genetic resources for food and agriculture, rests with national governments. In accordance with their needs and priorities, each Contracting Party should, as appropriate, and subject to its national legislation, take measures to protect and promote Farmers' Rights, including:

   (a)   protection of traditional knowledge relevant to plant genetic resources for food and agriculture;

(b)　the right to equitably participate in sharing benefits arising from the utilization of plant genetic resources for food and agriculture; and

(c)　the right to participate in making decisions, at the national level, on matters related to the conservation and sustainable use of plant genetic resources for food and agriculture.

3　Nothing in this Article shall be interpreted to limit any rights that farmers have to save, use, exchange and sell farm-saved seed/propagating material, subject to national law as appropriate.

General considerations on the effectiveness of the *Convention for Safeguarding Intangible Cultural Heritage*

While the ICHC is the only binding multilateral instrument available for the safeguarding of the intangible cultural heritage – or intellectual heritage – its effectiveness for safeguarding this heritage of Indigenous peoples depends on a number of factors. These include:

a)　Knowledge of the Convention itself – and this is also true of other UN instruments and processes. Too often little or no information about UN treaties and their processes filters down to Indigenous peoples, even though these instruments are directly relevant to their interests. Also while it is one thing to know about their existence and what governments are doing about them (whether to ratify or not, resources allocated to implement them, participatory mechanisms for indigenous peoples, etc.), it is quite another matter on how indigenous peoples can use them to their own best effect (e.g., by using reporting mechanisms, case studies, lobbying at Convention meetings, gaining NGO observer status, participation in specialised bodies set up under the Convention, using the UN Permanent Forum on Indigenous Issues, and so on).

b)　It will only be effective in those countries that have ratified the Convention. Countries with diverse populations of Indigenous peoples, such as Australia, Canada and the USA, have not signed on to the Convention, so the Convention will be of no benefit to Indigenous peoples in those countries.

c)　The number of ratifications. If the Convention is ratified by relatively few countries (such as is the case with ILO Convention 169 where only 17 countries have ratified) it will diminish its stature and the amount of resources available for its implementation. By contrast, the *Convention on Biological Diversity* has been signed by 187 countries and the *Convention to Combat Desertification* has 191 signatories.

d)　Respective capacities of states parties to implement the instrument with regard to, for example, the quality of domestic legislation; constitutional implications of federal systems of government; human, technical and financial resources to implement and administer laws and policies (e.g., with regard to protection of Indigenous languages), and so on. It is also the nature of even legally binding instruments that they contain much 'soft' wording. The language of such instruments is always respectful of the sovereign status and rights of nation-states, tempered with such phrases as 'as far as possible and as appropriate' (for example, CBD Article 8), 'subject to national legislation and policies', which enables considerable lee-way in the manner and extent to which state parties fulfil/implement their obligations.

e)   Consultative and participatory structures to include Indigenous representation at both national and international levels. With regard to the ICHC Convention, such participatory mechanisms should include observer status for Indigenous peoples' representatives, membership in national delegations, participation in ad hoc working groups, and so forth.

f)   Definitional interpretation (e.g., further clarification of definitions of what constitutes ICH, which may evolve over time in terms of what is inscribed on the RLICHH).

g)   Implementation through the decisions of the General Assembly regarding, for example, establishment of special bodies such as, ad hoc working groups, experts advisory committees, and clearing house mechanisms for the exchange of information, among others.

h)   Consideration of a (de facto) hierarchy of international treaty commitments in accordance with national priorities (heritage issues generally rank lower than national commitments to upholding trade and intellectual property laws). Such considerations also flow on to the assignment of resources (human and financial) to enable attendance/participation in Convention meetings (a huge issue for the economically least-developed states and the small island developing States of the Pacific and the Caribbean – especially given the number of UN bodies and processes in which countries are expected to participate).

Promoting Indigenous participation in the implementation of the Convention

While the ICHC Convention appears to provide little of direct comfort to Indigenous peoples for the safeguarding of their intangible cultural heritage, it should also be remembered that this is a 'young' Convention, only coming into force in April 2006, and many of its processes and procedures are still to be established. It is therefore extremely important that Indigenous peoples through their representative bodies (including the UN Permanent Forum on Indigenous Issues) and with the support of 'their' national governments, lobby for direct representation and participation in these processes and procedures. In this regard, the CBD, although it contains no provisions explicitly requiring that, in the terminology of the Convention, 'indigenous and local communities embodying traditional lifestyles' be involved in the

Convention's processes, has nevertheless established some important precedents for such involvement through the decisions of the COP.

While the General Assembly of the States Parties is the 'sovereign body' of
the ICHC (Article 4.1), the Intergovernmental Committee for the
Safeguarding of the Intangible Cultural Heritage (established under Article 5)
has the major responsibility for implementing the Convention. Functions of
the Committee include 'prepar[ing] and submit[ting] to the General
Assembly for approval operational directives for the implementation of this
Convention' (Article 7(e)). To ensure their participation in the implementation
of the Convention, Indigenous peoples would want to ensure that their
appropriate representative bodies could apply for 'observer status' to enable
them to attend, in a non-voting capacity, meetings held under the
Convention. In accordance with Article 23.5 of the CBD, the UN Permanent
Forum on Indigenous Issues, along with any other specialised agencies of the
UN has 'automatic' observer status, and can therefore be represented at
meetings of the CBD. While there is no equivalent provision in the ICHC,
the Intergovernmental Committee, nevertheless, pursuant to its powers
regarding adoption of its own Rules of Procedure (Article 8.2; cf. CBD,
Article 23.3) may enable agencies like the United Nations Permanent Forum
on Indigenous Issues (UNPFII) to regularly attend its meetings and those of
its governing body, the General Assembly. The Intergovernmental Committee
also has the power to establish 'whatever ad hoc consultative bodies it deems
necessary to carry out its task' (Article 8.3). The COP to the CBD, using its
powers under Article 23.4(g), by its Decision III/14, para. 7, established an
intersessional process – in the first instance a 5-day workshop, and subsequently, by Decision IV/9, para. 1, an Ad Hoc Open-ended Inter-Sessional
Working Group (Working Group on Article 8(j)) – to advance further work
on the implementation of Article 8(j) and related provisions to which representatives of Indigenous communities were explicitly invited to participate.
Further, the COP in Decision IV/9, para. 2, decided that the Working
Group on Article 8(j) should be composed of parties and observers, 'including,
in particular, representation from indigenous ... communities embodying
traditional lifestyles relevant to the conservation and sustainable use of biological
diversity *with participation to the widest possible extent in its deliberations in
accordance with the rules of procedure*' (emphasis added). Irrespective of whether
or not it establishes some form of ad hoc consultative body to enable Indigenous
representatives to provide input on the safeguarding of Indigenous ICH, the
Intergovernmental Committee nevertheless, has the authority, under Article
8.4 to 'invite to its meetings any public or private bodies, as well as private
persons, with recognized competence in the various fields of the intangible
cultural heritage, in order to consult them on specific matters'. This, of
course, can include indigenous public or private bodies and individuals.

While the CBD, under Article 23.5 also enables any other relevant governmental or NGO bodies or agencies – in addition to UN agencies – to be an

observer and participate at a meeting of the COP, subject to the rules of procedure, the Intergovernmental Committee, under Article 9.1 of the ICHC Convention, arguably has stronger powers to invite and accredit 'non-governmental organizations with recognized competence in the field of the intangible cultural heritage to act in advisory capacity to the Committee'. It is also the role of the Intergovernmental Committee to 'propose to the General Assembly the criteria for and modalities of such accreditation' (Article 9.2). Thus, to ensure maximum involvement in the implementation of the ICHC Convention, Indigenous peoples, through their national governments and representative bodies, and the UNPFII, need to be as active as possible during these early years of the establishment of the processes for its implementation to ensure their voice is being heard and that they can forge a role within the Convention to ensure that their ICH can be properly safeguarded.

Conclusion

Ultimately, it will be national and sub-national governments through their national constitutions, laws and policies that will determine the extent to which Indigenous ICH within their jurisdictions will be safeguarded. The ICHC, assuming that its many references to 'communities' also includes 'Indigenous communities', provides standards for community participation and involvement, capacity building, research, documentation, and so forth, that if faithfully implemented in national laws and policies (the process of ratification), then the Convention can provide comprehensive safeguarding for Indigenous peoples' ICH. To ensure that they also participate at the international level in the administration, decision-making processes and implementation of the ICHC, Indigenous peoples will also need to lobby 'their' national governments, use their own representative organisations, and the UNPFII to strive for similar levels of involvement that have been achieved, for example, under the CBD processes.

Bibliography

Food and Agriculture Organization (FAO) (1998) *The State of the World's Plant Genetic Resources for Food and Agriculture*, Rome: FAO.
—— (2001) *International Treaty on Plant Genetic Resources for Food and Agriculture*, Rome: FAO.
International Labour Organization (ILO) (1989) *Convention (No. 169) Concerning Indigenous and Tribal Peoples in Independent Countries*.
Maffi, L. (1999) 'Linguistic diversity', in D.A. Posey (ed.), *Cultural and Spiritual Values of Biodiversity: A Complementary Contribution to the Global Biodiversity Assessment*, Nairobi, Kenya: United Nations Environment Programme.
UNESCO (2003) *Convention for Safeguarding Intangible Cultural Heritage*.
United Nations (1963) *International Convention on the Elimination of All Forms of Racial Discrimination*.
—— (1966a) *International Covenant on Economic, Social and Cultural Rights*.

—— (1966b) *International Covenant on Civil and Political Rights.*

—— (2007) *Declaration on the Rights of Indigenous Peoples.*

United Nations Environment Programme (UNEP) (1971) *Ramsar Convention on Wetlands.*

—— (1979) *Convention on Migratory Species.*

—— (1992) *Convention on Biological Diversity.*

—— (1994) *Convention to Combat Desertification in those Countries Experiencing Drought and/or Desertification, Particularly in Africa.*

Chapter 10

Indigenous curation, museums, and intangible cultural heritage

Christina Kreps

Fifteen to 20 years ago, few curators working in an American museum housing Native American collections would have questioned their right to open and handle the contents of a sacred medicine bundle, to put an Iroquois false face mask on display, or to mount an exhibition without consulting representatives from the source community. These were the taken-for-granted, exclusive roles and responsibilities of curators working within professional guidelines and ethics of the time. However, as museums have been making efforts to become responsive to the needs and interests of their diverse constituencies, especially minority and Indigenous communities, they have become more inclusive of diverse perspectives and sensitive to the rights of people to have a voice in how their cultures are represented and their heritage curated. Today, collaboration between museums and source communities and the co-curation of collections and exhibitions has become commonplace in many museums (see Peers and Brown 2003). These activities have also inspired the development of more culturally relative and appropriate approaches to curatorial work (see Kreps 2008).

Collaboration and co-curation has also revealed how many Indigenous communities have their own curatorial traditions, or ways of perceiving, valuing, handling, caring for, interpreting, and preserving their cultural heritage. What we have learned is that just as museums are diverse in the multiple voices, perspectives, and identities they represent so too are approaches to curation and cultural heritage preservation.

While the recognition of Indigenous or non-Western approaches to curation has become *de rigueur* in some mainstream museums, Western-based and professionally oriented museological theory and practice continues to dominate the museum world. Indigenous curatorial traditions and approaches to heritage preservation are unique cultural expressions. As such, they should be recognised and preserved in their own right as part of a people's cultural heritage. They also, however, contribute to world, cultural diversity and have much to contribute to our understanding of museological behaviour cross-culturally, in addition to the formulation of new museological paradigms.

The growing awareness of Indigenous curation coincides with increased discussion within the international museum community on the place of intangible cultural heritage (ICH) in museums. The discourse has been heightened since the United Nations Educational Scientific Cultural Organization (UNESCO) adopted the *Convention on the Safeguarding of the Intangible Cultural Heritage* in 2003. Much of the discussion has focused on how museums can supplement their conventional tasks of curating and preserving tangible culture (objects and collections) with activities devoted to curating and preserving intangible, living cultural expressions (performing arts, skills, knowledge, and practices). If the intention is to more fully integrate ICH into museums rather than merely add it on to existing curatorial activities, greater attention needs to be given not only to what is curated, but also to how it is curated.

In this chapter, I examine how aspects of Indigenous curation are both a form of intangible cultural heritage as well as means of safeguarding it. I also discuss the suitability of the Convention for the promotion of Indigenous curation in museums. Of special interest is how recognition of Indigenous curation and the importance of ICH mark a shift in museological thinking and practice from a focus on objects and material culture to a focus on people and the sociocultural practices, processes, and interactions associated with their cultural expressions. Taken together these current museological trends and the Convention indicate how concerns over cultural and human rights are increasingly being addressed in museums and global public culture (see Galla 1997; Karp *et al.* 2006).

Indigenous curation

The term 'Indigenous curation' has entered museological discourse in recent years as a way to denote non-Western models of museums, curatorial methods, and concepts of cultural heritage preservation (see Kreps 1998, 2003a, 2007; Stanley 2007). This complex of cultural expressions can be collapsed into what I refer to as 'museological behaviour' which includes the creation of structures and spaces for the collection, storage, and display of objects as well as knowledge, methods, and technologies related to their care, treatment, interpretation and conservation. Museological behaviour also encompasses concepts of cultural heritage preservation or conceptual frameworks that support the transmission of culture through time. The recognition of Indigenous curation acknowledges that while the idea of the museum as a modern, public institution dedicated to collection, preservation, display, and interpretation may be Western in origin, museological behaviour is an ancient, cross-cultural phenomenon.

Indigenous models of museums and curatorial methods may be easily recognised in some cultures. However, in others it may be necessary to look for evidence of museological behaviour embedded in larger cultural forms and systems, such as vernacular architecture, religious beliefs and practices; social organisation and structure (especially kinship systems and ancestor worship); artistic traditions and aesthetic systems; and knowledge related to people's relationships and adaptations to their natural environment.

Indigenous models of museums may be found in vernacular architectural structures or spaces, such as Pacific Islander meeting houses or New Guinea *haus tumbuna*, which are often used to store and display sacred and ceremonial objects. They also can serve as centres for teaching younger generations about their people's history, culture, arts, and spiritual beliefs (see Mead 1983; Dundon 2007; Haraha 2007; Welsch 2007). As Simpson has suggested, contemporary museums in the Pacific are not necessarily new or foreign concepts in the region, but extensions of older traditions (1996: 107).

Throughout the course of my research in Indonesia over the years, I have come across many examples of architectural forms designed for the storage and safekeeping of valuable goods and cultural materials. For example, while conducting research in villages in East Kalimantan in 1996, I observed how the Kenyan Dayak rice barn (*lumbung*) is not only a structure in which rice is stored, but also family heirlooms such as ceramic jars, gongs, drums and brassware. I also learned that certain measures are taken to preserve contents that can be seen as preventive conservation measures. For instance, rice barns are generally located outside the village on high ground to protect them from fires and the river's seasonal flooding. Certain architectural features, such as thatched roofing, movable awnings and vents, which control interior temperature and regulate airflow, function as a technologically and environmentally appropriate means of 'climate control'. Techniques for 'pest management' are also evident in the rice barns' architecture. An ingenious and effective means of preventing rodents from entering the rice barn is the placement of curved wooden planks or discs at the top of piles that support the structure. In the high heat and humidity of equatorial Borneo, mould and bacterial growth are a big problem. Villagers slow the growth of moulds by smoking peppers inside the rice barn and using charcoal as a dehumidifier. All of these preventive conservation measures are part of curatorial traditions that represent knowledge and skills dedicated to the care and protection of specially valued things.

The word curator is derived from the Latin word *curare*, which means 'to take care of'. If we think of curators as caretakers and guardians of culture, we can see how certain individuals in many societies, such as priests, ritual specialists, shamans, and elders, are curators. Indigenous curators may possess specialised knowledge on the care and treatment of certain types of objects, and are entrusted with keeping these objects safe on behalf of a community, family, or clan. This responsibility is often socially sanctioned and grounded in customs, traditions, and systems of social organisation (see Kreps 1998, 2003a, 2003b; Sullivan and Edwards 2004).

Indigenous curatorial methods may be intended to protect the spiritual as well as material integrity of objects. These practices reflect a particular community's religious and cultural protocols pertaining to the use, handling, and treatment of certain classes of objects. Collaboration between museums and Native American communities in the USA has illuminated how these objects are differently perceived and how they should be curated. Several museums and organisations have established guidelines and procedures for curating culturally sensitive, ceremonial and sacred objects, such as the Association of Art Museum Directors' *Report on the Stewardship and Acquisition of Sacred Objects* (2006), the Smithsonian National Museum of the American Indian's 'Culturally Sensitive Collections Care Program' (see Sullivan and Edwards 2004), and the Minnesota Historical Society's *Caring for American Indian Objects. A Practical Guide* (Ogden 2004). Such publications and programmes provide guidance on how to appropriately store, handle, and treat culturally sensitive and sacred items. This is because every tribe has its own methods of 'traditional care', and cultural protocol, making consultation essential to integrating Indigenous curatorial practices into museum practices. As noted in one National Museum of the American Indian (NMAI) publication:

> The manner in which certain objects are stored may be important to the Native community. For example, some tribes prefer certain objects to be placed according to one of the cardinal directions, others to be handled only by women or only by men, others to be fed regularly, others to be handled regularly, and so forth.
>
> (NMAI 2004: 138)

In many museums, culturally sensitive and sacred objects are separated from general collections and stored with access restricted to certain tribal members such as elders, religious leaders, 'faith keepers', and so on. In some cases, objects have been removed from sealed containers or plastic since they are spiritual entities imbued with a life force and need to breathe. Conrad House, Navajo, was dismayed to find masks stored in plastic when he visited one museum, as described in the following passage:

> At the museum, I saw a number of sacred masks covered up with plastic. In our way, this is wrong. The masks have to breathe because there's energy in them – in the Navajo way, they're alive. You can't suffocate them or they'll be angry in time to come.
>
> (House 1994: 95)

The periodical smudging and feeding of objects has also become acceptable practice in some museums. The Cultural Resource Center of the NMAI has a room specifically designated for these ceremonies. Culturally sensitive and sacred objects have also been removed from public display in exhibitions and publications in many museums (see Rosoff 1998; Flynn and Hull-Walski 2001; Clavir 2002; Kreps 2003a; Ogden 2004; Sullivan and Edwards 2004).

These practices illustrate how Native American interpretations of the meanings and values of objects stand in sharp contrast to how they are perceived and valued in museums. To most Indigenous people, objects are not just scientific specimens or works of art. They are also family heirlooms, symbols of rank and status, sacred materials necessary for the perpetuation of religious beliefs and practices, or documents of a community's history and heritage. Objects stand for significant traditions, ideas, customs, social relations, and it is the stories they tell, the performances they are a part of, and the relationships among people and between people and places that are more important than the objects themselves (see Clifford 1997 and Fienup-Riordan 2003). The process of creation and an object's function also may be more highly valued than the object (West 2004).

The above examples show how Indigenous models of museums and curatorial practices are tangible expressions of the intangible, or rather, ideas about what constitutes heritage, how it should be perceived, treated, passed on, and by whom. They exemplify holistic approaches to heritage preservation that are integrated into larger social structures and ongoing social practices. The concept of *pusaka*, common among many ethnic groups in Indonesia, is one such approach to cultural heritage that takes both tangible and intangible forms. Moreover, pusaka has worked to protect and preserve valuable cultural property and transmit cultural knowledge and traditions through the generations.

The word pusaka is generally translated into English as 'heirloom'. However, it takes on a wide range of meanings in the Indonesian language. Soebadio, in the book *Pusaka: Art of Indonesia* (1992) states that one Indonesian dictionary lists three separate definitions for the word pusaka:

> 1) something inherited from a deceased person [analogous to the English word inheritance]; 2) something that comes down from one's ancestors [analogous to heirloom]; 3) an inheritance of special value to a community that cannot be disposed of without specific common descent [analogous to heritage in the sense of something possessed as a result of one's natural situation or birth].
>
> (1992: 15)

Tangible forms of pusaka include things like textiles, jewellery, ornaments, weapons, ceramics, beads, dance regalia, land, ancestor figures and houses. Intangible cultural expressions such as songs, dance dramas, stories or names can also be considered pusaka. Virtually anything can be regarded as pusaka, although not everything that is inherited is pusaka nor are objects created to be pusaka. An object or entity becomes pusaka in the course of its social life. As one Indonesian curator/anthropologist, Suwati Kartiwa, explains, pusaka are social constructs, and it is the meaning a society gives these objects, not anything innate in the objects themselves, which makes them pusaka (1992: 159).

So, like cultural heritage in general, the meanings and values assigned to particular pusaka are socially and culturally constructed and contingent on specific contexts and circumstances. Because pusaka is a social construct, it is more appropriate to think of it in terms of social relationships because pusaka emphasises, expresses or defines relationships within a society (Martowidkrido 1992: 129).

Different cultural groups throughout Indonesia have their own categories of pusaka and ways of assigning value and meaning to it. Hence, they may have their own, particular notions of what constitutes their heritage and approaches to its preservation. They may also have their own protocol regarding who is responsible for looking after the pusaka, or its curators. In one group it may be a village headman, in another a shaman or a priest, and yet in another a member of a royal court. Curatorial work in this context is a social practice that is deeply embedded in larger social structures and processes that define relationships among people and their particular relationships to objects (Kreps 2003b).

These examples of Indonesian and Indigenous models of museums, curatorial practices and concepts of heritage demonstrate how different cultures have their own curatorial traditions and ways of preserving aspects of their culture, which, in themselves, are part of people's cultural heritage. Additionally, they illustrate how approaches to cultural heritage protection and curatorial traditions are products of specific cultural contexts, and are culturally relative and particular.

Indigenous curation is being recognised and openly embraced in some quarters, but it is still a relatively new phenomenon to many in the professional museum world. The body of literature on Indigenous curation remains relatively small given the volumes devoted to the study of Indigenous arts and artefacts. It is ironic that anthropologists, curators, art historians, and collectors have historically taken an interest in non-Western materials, but have not, until recently, turned their attention to the study of how source communities have curated these materials despite the fact that curatorial practices are also part of culture. As I have previously maintained (Kreps 2003a), this lack of attention can be attributed to an ideology that locates the invention of the museum and the development of museological practices firmly in the West. Western, scientifically based museology has been the primary context and referent for our thinking and practice. Because of the hegemony of Western museology, it is difficult for many to imagine museological behaviour expressed in alternative forms.

The hegemony of Western museology has contributed to two phenomena that have worked to undermine or erase Indigenous curatorial traditions, and paradoxically, the preservation of people's cultural heritage. The first is the global spread and reproduction of Western-oriented museum models, the second is a reliance on expert-driven, top-down, and standardised professional museum training and development (see Kreps 2008).

Some members of the professional museum community resist the promotion and application of Indigenous curatorial methods because they believe them to be too closely tied to religious beliefs, and therefore, in conflict with the secular, scientific character of museums. Others consider Indigenous curatorial practices technologically inferior, and believe their use compromises a museum's ability to properly care for and save valuable art and artefacts. However, collaboration between Indigenous communities and museums has shown that the recognition and use of Indigenous curatorial techniques should not compromise the integrity and value of standard, professional museum practices. Instead, traditional methods can be combined with professional practices to maximise choices on how to better and most appropriately curate cultural materials. Co-curation opens channels for the exchange of information, knowledge and expertise and the development of new museological paradigms.

Indigenous curation as intangible cultural heritage

Indigenous curatorial traditions, such as Native American approaches to the care and handling of sensitive materials discussed above, fit the definition of intangible cultural heritage because they consist of practices, knowledge systems, skills and instruments that function to transmit culture and are part of people's cultural heritage. According to the Convention, intangible cultural heritage is defined as:

> the practices, representations, expressions, knowledge, skills – as well as instruments, objects, artefacts and cultural spaces associated therewith – that communities, groups and in some cases individuals recognize as part of their cultural heritage. This intangible cultural heritage, transmitted from generation to generation, is constantly recreated by communities and groups in response to their environment, their interaction with nature and their history, and provides them with a sense of identity and continuity thus promoting respect for cultural diversity and human creativity.
>
> (Article 2.1, Definitions)

The Convention also includes in its definition of ICH objects, artefacts and cultural spaces that are associated with manifestations of ICH and goes on to state:

> Intangible cultural heritage is manifested in oral traditions, including language; performing arts (traditional dance, music, and theatre); social

practices, rituals, and festive events; knowledge and practices; and traditional craftsmanship

(Article 2.2, Definitions)

As previously discussed, Indigenous curatorial traditions can be both a form of intangible cultural heritage as well as a measure for its safeguarding, for example, as seen in the Indonesian concept of pusaka and the Kenyan Dayak rice barn (lumbung). Under the Convention, 'safeguarding' means:

> measures aimed at ensuring the viability of the intangible cultural heritage, including the identification, documentation, research, preservation, protection, promotion, enhancement, transmission (particularly through formal and informal education) as well as revitalization of the various aspects of such heritage.

(Article 2, 3, Definitions)

One of the primary purposes of the Convention is to raise awareness and appreciation of ICH and foster the conditions under which it can survive. Consequently, the focus is on helping sustain living cultural traditions, practices, and processes instead of just collecting and preserving cultural products. The Convention also establishes a fund for the Safeguarding of Intangible Cultural Heritage that can be drawn on to support such efforts. Furthermore, the Convention supports international cooperation and assistance, especially in the areas of research, documentation, education, and training (Article 21). An important requirement of the Convention is that local communities and the 'culture bearers' themselves are involved in identifying their ICH and developing and implementing measures for its safeguarding, although it also institutes 'standard-setting' objectives.

The different articles under each section of the Convention outline safeguarding measures in detail, as well as the role and responsibilities of state parties or signatories to the Convention. One of the primary means for safeguarding ICH is the creation of national inventories of ICH and lists, such as the Representative List of the Intangible Cultural Heritage of Humanity and the List of Intangible Cultural Heritage in Need of Urgent Safeguarding. Listing and lists are to play a major role in ensuring better visibility of ICH, increasing awareness of its significance, and encouraging dialogue that respects cultural diversity.

The 2003 Convention is the fifth legal instrument adopted by UNESCO over the past 30 years for the protection and safeguarding of world cultural heritage. The *Convention Concerning the Protection of World Cultural and Natural Heritage*, adopted in 1972, concentrated on identifying and protecting tangible cultural heritage, defined as monuments, architectural works, monumental sculpture and painting, archaeological sites, and natural features thought to be of outstanding universal value in the fields of history, art and science. Thus, its focus is on protecting the products of human creativity and ingenuity predominantly of the past. It also favoured what can be seen as 'classical' works produced by 'great civilisations'. In contrast, the 2003 Convention shifts attention to safeguarding the knowledge, skills, and values behind tangible culture, concentrating on the people and social processes that sustain it. In addition to demonstrating a heightened concern for protecting living culture expressed in popular and folkloric traditions, it also acknowledges how these traditions are of value to local communities, and in particular, communities that can be characterised as marginal vis-à-vis dominant cultures, such as those of Indigenous peoples (see Kurin 2004).

Intangible cultural heritage and museums

Since the Convention was adopted in 2003, there has been a great deal of discussion within the international museum community on the role of museums in safeguarding ICH. The International Council of Museums (ICOM), a division of UNESCO, has been a particularly strong voice in advocating ICH. Many articles on the topic have appeared in its publications, most notably, *ICOM News*, the organisation's newsletter, as well as its journal, *Museum*. Intangible Cultural Heritage was also the theme of ICOM's 2004 tri-annual conference in South Korea. In a 2003 piece in *ICOM News*, Amar Galla states that:

> ICOM strongly supports UNESCO's efforts towards the safeguarding and promotion of intangible heritage, and stresses the importance of inputs from professional bodies like ICOM ... The UNESCO Convention is a significant first step in renewing our relation to cultural heritage, by promoting integrated approaches to tangible and intangible heritage.
>
> (2003, n.p.)

It is logical that museums should play a prominent role in promoting ICH and the aims of the Convention since museums have long been devoted to curating and preserving cultural heritage, albeit mostly in tangible forms. But the curation of ICH is not an entirely new role for museums. Many museums around the world have been doing this all along, such as community-based and Indigenous museums where language and literature programmes, dance and musical performance, festivals and ceremonial gatherings take place on a regular basis (see Simpson 1996; Stanley 2007). There are also examples of museums and cultural centres where Indigenous approaches to curation have always been integral to their purpose and functions. The Makah Cultural and Resource Centre on the Makah Indian Reservation in the state of Washington, for example, is concerned with documenting and preserving Makah etiquette associated with the objects in its possession. Staff and tribal members see this as a way of preserving the sensibilities, memories, and emotions of Makah histories (Erikson *et al.* 2002: 177).

The Makah and other examples described above underscore how Indigenous curation cannot be isolated or detached from their larger cultural contexts. This ethos is beginning to take hold in mainstream museums as more and more curators are coming to realise that their job is not only to take care of objects, but also relationships between objects and people. As Richard Kurin of the Smithsonian Institution in Washington, DC testifies:

> Some anthropologists in the museum world are making the shift from curating collections of objects to curating the systems, and the people, that produce them. Anthropologists have long recognized a moral responsibility to the people with whom they work. And they long recognized that their study or curating of some small abstraction of the studied culture is dependent upon a much larger system. Rather than curate dead or captured specimens of a culture, are increasingly concerned with the living larger whole.
>
> (1997: 93)

This trend represents a turn toward the social and cultural dimensions of curatorial work. It signals how museums today are being defined more in terms of their relationships and responsibilities to people than to objects, collections, and tangible culture. In this light, museums are becoming key agents and arenas for the appreciation, promotion, and safeguarding of intangible cultural heritage.

These trends are also in keeping with the emergence of what Eileen Hooper-Greenhill calls the 'post-museum', which counters many of the premises and practices of the 'modernist' museum born in the nineteenth century (Hooper-Greenhill 2000: 152). Hooper-Greenhill contends that the post-museum will 'retain some of the characteristics of its parent, but it will re-shape them to its own ends' (Hooper-Greenhill 2000: 152). Regarding the place of objects and collections in museums, she asserts that the post-museum will place more emphasis on their use rather than on accumulation and that intangible heritage will also receive greater attention (Hooper-Greenhill 2000: 152).

In the post-museum, curatorial authority is shared among the museum, community members, and other stakeholders whose voices and perspectives contribute to the production of knowledge and culture in the museum through partnerships that celebrate diversity. As Hooper-Greenhill states, 'Knowledge is no longer unified and monolithic; it becomes fragmented and multivocal' and 'much of the intellectual development of the post-museum will take place outside the major European centres which witnessed the birth of the modernist museum' (2000: 153).

The Convention and paradox of cultural heritage preservation

Like the post-museum, the *Convention on the Safeguarding of the Intangible Cultural Heritage* can be seen as a break from modernist paradigms of cultural heritage preservation in which concepts of heritage were lodged in material things, and heritage resources were curated and managed largely by experts. In contrast, the Convention advocates sharing curatorial authority by emphasising the central role of local communities and the 'cultural bearers' themselves in safeguarding their own cultural heritage. In this sense, it recognises the cultural right of people to have greater control over and a say in how their cultural heritage is treated. Of special significance is how the Convention celebrates the cultural expressions of people who historically have been marginalised and disenfranchised, such as Indigenous and minority peoples. While these principles and guidelines can be seen as considerable advancements, the Convention's suitability for promoting Indigenous curation in museums is debatable due to the problematic nature of the safeguarding measures it recommends.

As discussed earlier, one of the main measures for safeguarding ICH proposed in the Convention is the creation of inventories and lists, such as the Representative List of the Intangible Heritage of Humanity and the List of Intangible Cultural Heritage in Need of Urgent Safeguarding. Some question the logistics involved in creating such inventories and lists, and see their creation as a 'vast exercise in information management' (Brown 2005). Especially disconcerting is how the 'rescuing' mission behind the List of Intangible Cultural Heritage in Need of Urgent Safeguarding echoes the sentiments behind nineteenth-century 'salvage ethnography'. There are also some who believe this effort will divert limited resources from nurturing environments that enable traditional music, dance, artisanship, knowledge, and so forth, to survive.

Barbara Kirshenblatt-Gimblett (2006) critically examines the concept of world heritage and the instruments and measures designed to protect it. She is concerned with 'how valorization, regulation, and instrumentalization alter the relationship of cultural assets to those who are identified with them, as well as others' (Kirshenblatt-Gimblett 2006: 162). Ultimately, such processes create a paradoxical situation in which the diversity of cultural assets and those who produce them are subsumed under the umbrella of humanity and world heritage.

Kirshenblatt-Gimblett labels Conventions and lists as well as the heritage enterprise itself as 'metacultural artifacts'. Of special interest is:

> how the process of safeguarding, which includes defining, identifying, documenting and presenting cultural traditions and their practitioners, produces something metacultural. What is produced includes not only an altered relationship of practitioners to their art but also distinctive artifacts such as the list ...
>
> (Kirshenblatt-Gimblett 2006: 171)

In cases where Indigenous curatorial knowledge is in danger of being lost, documentation and archiving may be welcomed, but documentation and listing raise a number of issues and concerns. For one, this process may inadvertently undermine the integrity of Indigenous curation by isolating or detaching practices from their cultural whole and making them fit criteria outlined in the Convention. Herein lies one of the more contradictory aspects of the Convention as a mechanism for supporting Indigenous curation. One of the ultimate goals of the Convention is to protect world cultural diversity and promote diversity as a universal value, yet the methods used in the archiving and documenting process in themselves can lead to the standardisation and homogenisation of practices that are inherently varied, and governed by specific cultural protocol. The universality principle inscribed in the Convention is especially problematic because it implies that one people's cultural heritage is the heritage of humanity and is thus part of a public cultural commons. As Kirshenblatt-Gimblett points out, 'when culture becomes the heritage of humanity, the presumption is open access' (2006: 185). This premise is unacceptable to many Indigenous communities that find the public nature of museum collections and curatorial work disturbing. For some, the concept of collecting objects to be seen, studied and cared for by outsiders is inconsistent with tribal traditions. Certain objects can only be seen, touched, or used by specific members of the community, such as men or women, elders. Parker states that 'the fact that public collections exist is a source of social problems in Indian communities' (1990: 37).

Peter Jemison, Seneca, further explicates the problem:

> The concept in the white world is that everyone's culture is everyone else's. That is not really our concept. Our concept is there were certain things given to us that we have to take care of and that you are either part of it or you are not part of it.
>
> (Jemison, quoted in Parker 1990: 37)

Given these issues, listing is not a culturally appropriate measure for safeguarding Indigenous curation, nor does this strategy represent a significant departure from previous heritage preservation tactics, such as the World Heritage List that was a product of the 1972 Convention. Perhaps, as Kirshenblatt-Gimblett suggests, the value of listing and more so the Convention, rests primarily in the symbolic realm:

> The list is the most visible, least costly, and most conventional way to 'do something' – something symbolic – about neglected communities and traditions. Symbolic gestures such as the list confer value on what is listed, consistent with the principle that you cannot protect what you do not value.
>
> (2006: 170)

Despite its limitations and contradictions, the Convention has stimulated an international dialogue on the role of ICH in museums, and thus, has opened avenues for the exploration of Indigenous curation as ICH on theoretical and practical levels. It has expanded the notion of what constitutes heritage and could similarly be used to broaden ideas of what constitutes 'safeguarding' as well as the measures for that safeguarding. The promotion of Indigenous curation in museums as both a form of ICH plus a means of safeguarding could liberate museums from their traditional role as custodians of tangible, static culture to stewards and curators of intangible, living, dynamic culture. In the words of Dr Nguyen Van Huy, former director of the Vietnam Museum of Ethnology:

> presenting intangible cultural heritage requires the museum to develop new skills, knowledges, and methodologies; subjects of study and for presentation are no longer simply objects and artifacts, but living people and living culture. This calls for further research and capacity-building, closer relationships with local communities, and available staff and funding for these activities.
>
> (2003, n.p.)

On the one hand, the Convention contains elements of older heritage preservation models that were largely about documenting and making lists, but on the other hand, it represents a departure by placing emphasis on supporting conditions necessary for cultural reproduction. The museum is one arena in which Indigenous curatorial practices can be encouraged and kept alive, allowing for further research on such practices in addition to the creation of innovative museological approaches:

> The museum itself has become a fieldsite – a place for cross-cultural encounter and creative dialogue. A more inclusive and muti-perspectivist approach to material in museum collections is crucial in illuminating the multiple meanings of specific objects as well as the complex processes involved in their production, collection and interpretation. Working with members of source communities provides an opportunity for developing productive relationships and collecting contemporary material for future generations.
>
> (Herle 2003: 204–5)

Conclusion

The 2003 *Convention on the Safeguarding of the Intangible Cultural Heritage*, as opposed to earlier instruments, acknowledges that our conceptualisation of heritage, like culture in general, is an ever evolving process expressed in multitudinous forms. The work being done today in museums with source communities is clear evidence of how museums are key sites for the promotion and safeguarding of intangible cultural heritage. However, it is only through sustained critical analysis and reflexive practice that our concepts of heritage can be continually revised, and safeguarding measures appropriately applied:

> Cultural processes (like heritage curation) are inherently particular and particularizing, so we should not expect the application of a global policy to have the same results in all situations.
>
> (Handler 2002: 144)

Acknowledgements

Research for this essay was conducted while I was a Fellow of the Rockefeller Foundation funded Institute 'Theorizing Cultural Heritage' at the Smithsonian Center for Folklife and Cultural Heritage during the summer of 2005. I want to thank colleagues at the center for giving me the opportunity to participate in the Institute, especially Dr Richard Kurin, Dr Peter Seitel, Dr Frank Proschan, Dr Richard Kennedy, Carla Borden and James Early. I am also grateful to Nancy Fuller of the Smithsonian Center for Museum Studies for her abiding support and guidance. This essay is a revised version of 'Indigenous Curation as Intangible Cultural Heritage: Thoughts on the Relevance of the 2003 UNESCO Convention', first published in 2005 in *Theorizing Cultural Heritage*.

References

Association of Art Museums Directors (2006) *Report on the Stewardship and Acquisition of Sacred Objects*, New York: New York.

Brown, M. (2005) *Safeguarding the Intangible*. Available online at: http://www.culturalcommons.org/comment (Accessed 26 July 2005).

Clavir, M. (2002) *Preserving What is Valued: Conservation and First Nations*, Vancouver: University of British Columbia Press.

Clifford, J. (1997) *Routes: Travel and Translation in the Late Twentieth Century*, Cambridge, MA: Harvard University Press.

Dundon, A. (2007) 'Moving the centre: Christianity, the longhouse, and the Gogodola Cultural Centre', in N. Stanley (ed.), *The Future of Indigenous Museums. Perspectives from the Southwest Pacific*, New York and Oxford: Berghahn Books.

Erikson, P., Ward, H. and Wachendorf, K. (2002) *Voices of a Thousand People. The Makah Cultural Research Center*, Lincoln and London: University of Nebraska Press.

Fienup-Riordan, A. (2003) 'Yu'pik elders in museums; fieldwork turned on its head', in L. Peers and A. Brown (eds), *Museums and Source Communities: A Routledge Reader*, New York and London: Routledge.

Flynn, G. and Hull-Walski, D. (2001) 'Merging traditional Indigenous curation methods with modern museum standards of care', *Museum Anthropology*, 25(1): 31–40.

Galla, A. (1997) 'Indigenous peoples, museums, and ethics', in G. Edson (ed.), *Museum Ethics*, New York and London: Routledge.

—— (2003) 'Frequently asked questions about intangible heritage', *ICOM News* (4): n.p.

Handler, R. (2002) 'Comments on Masterpieces of Oral and Intangible Culture', *Current Anthropology*, 43(1): 144.

Haraha, S. (2007) 'The Papua New Guinea National Museum and Art Gallery as a modern *haus tumbuna*', in N. Stanley (ed.), *The Future of Indigenous Museums. Perspectives from the Southwest Pacific*, New York and Oxford: Berghahn Books.

Herle, A. (2003) 'Objects, agency and museums: continuing dialogues between the Torres Strait and Cambridge', in L. Peers and A. Brown (eds), *Museums and Source Communities: A Routledge Reader*, London: Routledge.

Hooper-Greenhill, E. (2000) *Museums and the Interpretation of Visual Culture*, New York and London: Routledge.

House, C. (1994) 'The art of balance', in R. West (ed.), *All roads are Good. Native Voices on Life and Culture,* Washington, DC: Smithsonian National Museum of the American Indian.

Karp, I., Kratz, C.A., Szwaja, L., Ybarra-Frausto, T., Buntinx, G., Kirshenblatt-Gimblett B. and Rassool, C. (eds) (2006) *Museum Frictions: Public Cultures/Global Transformations*, Durham, North Carolina: Duke University Press.

Kartiwa, S. (1992) 'Pusaka and the palaces of Java', in H. Soebadio (ed.), *Pusaka: Art of Indonesia.* Singapore: Archipelago Press.

Kirshenblatt-Gimblett, B. (2006) 'World heritage and cultural economics', in I. Karp, C.A. Kratz, L. Szwaja, T. Ybarra-Frausto, G. Buntinx, B. Kirshenblatt-Gimblett and C. Rassool (eds), *Museum Frictions: Public Cultures/Global Transformations*, Durham, North Carolina: Duke University Press.

Kreps, C. (1998) 'Museum-making and Indigenous curation in Central Kalimantan, Indonesia', *Museum Anthropology*, 22(1): 5–17.

—— (2003a) *Liberating Culture: Cross-Cultural Perspectives on Museums, Curation, and Cultural Heritage Preservation*, New York and London: Routledge.

—— (2003b) 'Curatorship as social practice', *Curator,* 46(3): 311–23.

—— (2007) 'The theoretical future of Indigenous museums', in Stanley, N. (ed.), *The Future of Indigenous Museums. Perspectives from the Southwest Pacific,* New York and Oxford: Berghahn Books.

—— (2008) 'Appropriate museology in theory and practice', *International Journal of Museum Management and Curatorship*, 23(1): 23–41.

Kurin, R. (1997) *Reflections of a Culture Broker. A View from the Smithsonian*, Washington, D.C.: Smithsonian Institution Press.

—— (2004) 'Safeguarding intangible cultural heritage in the 2003 UNESCO Convention: a critical appraisal', *Museum,* 56(1–2): 66–77.

Martowidkrido, W. (1992) 'Heirlooms of the outer islands', in H. Soebadio (ed.), *Pusaka: Art of Indonesia*, Singapore: Archipelago Press.

Mead, S. (1983) 'Indigenous models of museums in Oceania', *Museum,* 35(3): 98–101.

National Museum of the American Indian (NMAI) (2004) 'National Museum of the American Indian: culturally sensitive collections care program and repatriation procedures', in L. Sullivan and A. Edwards (eds), *Stewards of the Sacred*, Washington, DC: American Association of Museums in cooperation with the Center for the Study of World Religions, Harvard University.

Nguyen, Van Huy (2003) 'Intangible cultural heritage at the Vietnam Museum of Ethnology', *ICOM News* (4): n.p.

Ogden, S. (ed.) (2004) *Caring for American Indian Objects. A Practical and Cultural Guide*, St. Paul, MN: Minnesota Historical Society.

Parker, P. (1990) *Keepers of the Treasures: Protecting Historic Properties and Cultural Traditions on Indian Lands*, Washington, DC: National Park Service, United States Department of the Interior.

Peers, L. and Brown, A. (2003) *Museums and Source Communities: A Routledge Reader*, New York and London: Routledge.

Rosoff, N. (1998) 'Integrating Native views into museum procedures: hope and practice at the National Museum of the American Indian', *Museum Anthropology*, 22(1): 33–42.

Simpson, M. (1996) *Making Representation: Museums in the Post-Colonial Era,* New York: Routledge.

Soebadio, H. (1992) 'Introduction', in H. Soebadio (ed.), *Pusaka: art of Indonesia*, Singapore: Archipelago Press.

Stanley, N. (ed.) (2007) *The Future of Indigenous Museums. Perspectives from the Southwest Pacific,* New York: Berghahn Books.

Sullivan, L. and Edwards, A. (eds) (2004) *Stewards of the Sacred*, Washington, DC: American Association of Museums in cooperation with the Center for the Study of World Religions, Harvard University.

UNESCO (2003) *Convention for the Safeguarding of Intangible Cultural Heritage.*

Welsch, R. (2007) 'The transformation of cultural centres in Papua New Guinea', in N. Stanley (ed.), *The Future of Indigenous Museums: Perspectives from the Southwest Pacific*, New York: Berghahn Books.

West, R. (2004) 'The National Museum of the American Indian. Stewards of the sacred', in L. Sullivan and A. Edwards (eds), *Stewards of the Sacred*, Washington, DC: American Association of Museums in cooperation with the Center for the Study of World Religions, Harvard University.

Chapter 11

Intangible cultural heritage

Global awareness and local interest

Amanda Kearney

Introduction

In this chapter, I present an overview of emerging global discourse concerning intangible cultural heritage (ICH). I posit current legislative arrangements are in their infancy and yet to engage adequately with the complexities that interlace distinctions and connections between tangible and ICH and the capacity for ICH to be owned exclusively. For the vast majority of indigenous peoples, existing legal arrangements concerning their heritage remain under the control and definitional power of the state, rather than the distinct Indigenous nations that own, enact and assert these heritages in specific cultural terms.[1] Focusing on the United Nations *Convention for the Safeguarding of the Intangible Cultural Heritage* (ICHC) this chapter problematises aspects of current engagements with Indigenous people's ICH, identifying and critiquing the power imbalances generated by international and state-defined legislation and Conventions concerning aspects of ICH.

Recognising the political frame in which discourses of ICH have emerged and are maintained is imperative to this discussion. This reveals a discursive relationship between global trends of new environmental ethics, ecophilosophy and ecofeminism, and international interest in sustainable practices and ideologies as embodied in Indigenous or alternative knowledge systems. There is a dilemma in state control and direction over the very terms on which Indigenous knowledge systems and ICH are defined, perceived and safeguarded into the future. In line with this assertion I argue that fundamental shifts in epistemologies surrounding intangible and tangible cultural heritage must occur, highlighting the extent to which knowledge and heritage inform group and individual cultural identity, and mark cultural autonomy and distinctiveness. This chapter complicates existing discussions of ICH, while making recommendations for a shift in the discourse about such heritage. This complication can inform a range of academic discussions of tangible and intangible heritage, Indigenous knowledge systems and intellectual property.

Theorising ICH

Heritage is most commonly taken to denote that which we, as humans, value or 'what we wish to pass on to future generations' (Deacon *et al.* 2004: 7). It denotes performative cultural resources (Brown 2005: 41), including dance, song, language, oral traditions and knowledge systems, monumental constructions, archaeological sites, material culture and ideology. These reflect a time depth to cultural expressions that draws connections between ancestors, contemporaries and descendants, making such expressions fundamental to cultural identity and cultural distinctiveness. To designate some of this as *intangible* is to signal the ephemeral components of culture or performative culture (Deacon *et al.* 2004).

Existing definitions of intangible heritage trace their roots to earlier incarnations of non-physical heritage and folklore (Blake 2000, Brown 2005). The evolution of intangibility as a form of recognised cultural heritage tracks a legacy of earlier associations implicating invisibility, immateriality, incorporeality, and disconnection. There is a psychology associated on the one hand with materiality and tangible cultural heritage and on the other, intangibility and intellectual cultural heritage. The immediacy of built and tangible heritage is appealing because it takes recognisable form; discernable, and therefore knowable. The universality that is accorded material and built culture resonates within anthropology and archaeology, as linked to a world of form and function, whereby the form tells of, or reveals the function. When challenged to engage with the immaterial, function is often overlooked or assumed accessible only through the acquisition of certain forms of insider knowledge to unlock the world of intangible meanings that underscore performative culture. Such levels of engagement require suspension of dominant cultural understandings and knowledge structures, and full recognition of cross-cultural values and knowledge systems. Such practices rarely mark the point of engagement between dominant state powers and Indigenous communities or nations.

Jean-Louis Luxen, former Secretary-General of the International Council on Monuments and Sites, suggested that 'the distinction between physical heritage and intangible heritage is ... artificial' (UNESCO 2000: 4). The alternate view is that intangible heritage gives meaning to the tangible; therefore making the tangible subsidiary (Deacon *et al.* 2004: 10). 'All tangible heritages therefore have intangible values associated with them, but not all intangible heritages have a tangible form' (Prosalendis 2003 cited in Deacon *et al.* 2004: 11). Theorising this somewhat confusing distinction requires a phenomenological approach to heritage. The immediate and long-term position offered by a phenomenological approach is that 'being' in the most immediate tangible form of the human body and consciousness creates all possible perception and thus creates all potentials for tangible and intangible cultural expressions (see Merleau-Ponty 1962; Crossley 1994). Such a position renders distinctions of tangible and intangible almost redundant as the only imperative status of tangible is held by the human actor and agent, as physical embodiment of culture and heritage. Through this 'being', human heritage is always and at once tangible and intangible. 'Being', as human existence, prefaces all, thus stressing the intimacy between perceptual subjects (people) and perceptual objects (heritage). A phenomenological approach views heritage as an embedded concept that cannot be disengaged from the world and people around it, while establishing distinguishing links between the perceptual subject and their distinct and owned perceptual objects. As Crossley (1994: 14) wrote, because the observer (human actor) and the observed (heritage) are relationally constituted and the relationship is an embodied one: 'I am part of the spectacle that I see. I have a visible (embodied) presence in the world that I see and this visible presence is integral to my perception'.

The ultimate intangible is human consciousness, or what some cosmologies define as the human soul, the very substance of psychological engagements with human 'being', the most intriguing, yet unimaginable aspect of the human condition. In some cosmologies, the 'soul', while disembodied at death, can retain tangible expression among the living. In many cultural contexts, the 'soul' or 'spirit' of the deceased can manifest in other physical forms. In Australian Indigenous epistemologies the 'soul' or 'spirit' of the deceased never departs from the land, but continues to reside as a spiritual presence, embodied by non-human animals, the elements, and natural phenomena (Langton 2002). The consciousness that surrounds this creates the parameters of cultural identity and heritage, yet carries the legacy of intangible slipperiness, and indescribability. It is perceived, at its best, to be ethereal, evanescent, and essential, but at its worst; abstract, elusive and vague. Most commonly deemed as that which cannot be seen or perceived through the senses, intangible cultural elements are often defined through their incorporeality. In phenomenological terms, this separation cannot exist. As such, any discussion of intangibility implicates tangibility (of the body): a most basic, yet complex realisation.

Full engagement with heritage on these terms draws on a psychology that underscores notions of tangibility and intangibility. Each concept carries a legacy of associated meaning and triggers varied intellectual and emotive responses that are fundamental to how we perceive and value different expressions of cultural identity. The comprehension and valuing of different cultural expressions are at the very core of cultural heritage legislation worldwide. The determination of what constitutes heritage is part of a global dialogue, largely supported and facilitated by UNESCO's Culture Sector. Legislative arrangements at the international level reinforce the fact that the value and future of human heritage is very much on the global agenda. This agenda is equally preoccupied with salvaging and safeguarding cultural diversity, as it is the promotion of sustainable living practices and environmental ethics in the twenty-first century.

Global consciousness and cultural heritage

Globalisation now stands as the 'devil' of the twenty-first century, capable of threatening any 'communities' sense of its own authenticity' (Deacon *et al.* 2004: 7). It is regarded for its capacity to appropriate and inventory information from a range of cultural contexts for inclusion within the public domain of global awareness and consciousness (Brown 2005: 40). One part of this global consciousness includes environmental and ecological ethics and criticism of worldwide market economies. These heavily critique ecological thoughtlessness, while drawing from what are perceived to be alternative, largely Indigenous, knowledge systems in their aims to mirror, and promote sustainable living practices, while increasing awareness of and moral sensitivity to our relations with the non-human world (Barry 1999: 201). Brown (2005: 46) has described the threat of globalisation in the following terms: 'the gap between data on the one hand and wisdom on the other is the crux of the conflict between Information Societies [global community] and folkloric ones [Indigenous community]'. Others have argued that there is potential for Indigenous peoples to 'find a sense of unity and common purpose' through the 'formation of global economic, social and political networks' (Smith and Ward 2000: 3). Virtual global networks of this kind are now enabled by information technology tools, which some have argued can be refined and extended to enable Indigenous communities to preserve and protect their unique cultures, knowledge and artefacts while supporting traditional protocols and facilitating better cross-cultural communication and understanding (Hunter 2005; Nakata and Langton 2005).

The emergence of environmental movements and ecophilosophy is characterised by deep thinking in ecological engagements with the world around. Environmental problems have become part of everyday existence for people worldwide. With this comes an awareness of shifts in terrestrial, marine, and atmospheric environments, depletions and extinctions. Increased awareness of these problems has given rise to a variety of popularly based responses collectively referred to as the environmental movement (Fox 1995: 4), or more specifically as ecophilosophy, green consciousness, and ecofeminism (Fairweather 1993; Leahy 2003).[2] These movements strike down critique on the body of Western culture for its anthropocentrism (Plumwood 2002). The 'West', held to be the basis of global power, is characterised by a human centeredness that only voluntarily engages with the 'natural world', cementing a separation between the human and non-human worlds (White 1967; Fox 1995: 5–6). This is unlike the 'East', which is held to conceive of nature in a contemplative-intellectualist and supremely connected sense (White 1967; Said 1978; Fox 1995: 5–6). This view has been powerfully reinforced for decades, and in its contemporary form the dualism is more commonly upheld between Western – global, developed and colonial knowledge systems and Indigenous – local, marginalised, developing and colonised knowledge systems (Langton *et al.* 2005).

Global movements resisting anthropocentric value systems openly identify Indigenous cultural consciousness as the key to a connected, contemplative and sustainable relationship with the natural world (Berkes 1999). In line with globalisation's capacity to threaten any community's sense of its own authenticity, such willingness to engage with Indigenous knowledge and ICH must be met with scepticism and wisely critiqued. In a discussion of Australian environmentalism, Frawley (1999: 265) has traced the emergence of 'green vision' to the permeation of 'Aboriginal conceptions of the land' into European Australian consciousness. Further to this point, he (1999: 288) stated that 'many non-Aboriginal Australians have also begun to develop an affinity with the landscape, to think themselves into country and in turn are better able to appreciate Aboriginal environmental knowledge'. One cannot help but reflect on the lowly status of land rights and human rights for Indigenous Australians when speaking of such knowledge sharing and appreciation.

Environmental knowledge, Indigenous knowledge, and folk knowledge all fall within the rubric of ICH. The dominant frame shaping discussions of global sharing and awareness of ICH and Indigenous knowledge systems has been set by UNESCO. In line with and led by UNESCO's example, state party members worldwide have adopted the terminology intangible cultural heritage into legislative vernacular, initiating a global interest in the potential range and scope of cultural expressions contained by the human body and mind. In fact, such is the emphasis on UNESCO-derived working definitions of ICH that few alternative elocutions exist. The UNESCO definition of ICH is, 'the practices, representations, expressions, knowledge, skills, as well as the instruments, objects, artefacts and cultural spaces associated therewith, that communities, groups and, in some cases, individuals recognize as part of their cultural heritage'.[3]

The inclusion of wider ranging notions of heritage signals a radical broadening of the heritage field. It marks a desire to move beyond Eurocentric understandings of property, heritage and ownership, and highlights the interconnectedness of ICH, knowledge systems and intellectual property. Prior to the early 1980s, cultural property was taken to denote the portable artworks and monuments of human groups (Brown 2005: 40). The ethnocentric tone of such heritage definitions and descriptions maintained a distinction between tangible human heritage and intellectual traditions or knowledge systems. Discussions of ICH have universally challenged this and increasingly work towards more holistic understandings. This marks a 'growing doubt in the universality of Western notions of property and widespread recognition that culture cannot be reduced to an inventory of objects without marginalizing its most important features' (Brown 2005: 41). As Brown (2005: 40) has identified, human rights activists, and Indigenous rights activists in particular, have challenged propositions that cultural heritage and property are entirely dependant on materiality. Much of the desire to assert such intangible rights and values is bound up in fights for cultural autonomy, self-determination and intellectual property rights among Indigenous and minority groups worldwide.

Entertaining the possibility that human landscapes are composed of more than physical spaces and tangible markers of human presences and engagement is certainly not a new development in heritage discussions. The notion of ICH has been engaged for some time but what remains a grey area is how to recognise, legislate and promote multiple forms of heritage on culturally relative terms. More recent interest in ICH is expressed in worldwide heritage legislation, the parameters of which have been partially set by UNESCO's 2003 *Convention for the Safeguarding of the Intangible Cultural Heritage* (ICHC). The Convention is the product of several years of discussion and consultation over legal provisions governing cultural property and the definitional parameters of cultural heritage (see chapters Part 1, this volume). A key step in this legislative process was the adoption of the *Recommendation on the Safeguarding of Traditional Culture and Folklore* in 1989. As a recommendation, this suggested practical provisions for dealing with ICH. It represented a benign option to safeguarding culture and folklore, as it lacked any demand for binding commitments from the international community. As Deacon *et al.* (2004: 17) have astutely observed,

> Key criticisms of the Recommendation were that it could recommend to but not oblige states to implement protective mechanisms, and that it failed to ensure that control over intangible heritage management and benefits remained with the communities who owned that heritage.

Ongoing discussions concerning the 1989 Recommendation brought the 'shift to a higher legal gear' and the drafting of the *Convention for the Safeguarding of the Intangible Cultural Heritage.*[4] As a Convention this meant the principles and laws were to be binding on signatory states. The Convention, which entered into force on 20 April 2006, following its ratification by 30 member states, provides a more detailed text on the nature and legal parameters of ICH (UNESCO 2003). However, the extent to which criticisms of the earlier Recommendation have been tackled and resolved remains unclear, particularly in regard to control over management and benefits derived from safeguarding ICH. While proponents of the Convention praise it, others, such as Brown (2005: 48) have identified a 'salvage' undertone and remain unconvinced that the Convention necessarily offers a better alternative, stating that:

> The policy [Convention] is oddly reminiscent of early anthropology, which was driven by the conviction that primitive cultures should be documented in their entirety ... because their extinction was inevitable.

The discipline long ago concluded that documentation has only a modest role in the preservation of culture.

The Convention is primarily concerned with recognising ICH in the face of globalisation and social transformations worldwide. Despite the apparent limitations associated with it, attention to the intangible expressions of culture runs much deeper than earlier dealings with cultural heritage in which protection and documentation were dominant themes; a legacy of the before it's too late approach to Indigenous cultures. As Rose (2004: 66) reflected, there has been a tendency, particularly in anthropology, to view Indigenous people and their cultures in terms of imminent or recent extinction. The offshoot of this has been a preoccupation with salvage and documentation of cultural practices, knowledge and objects, in which the value of the living came down to what information they can offer 'concerning a past that the anthropologists assumed in advance would be discontinuous with their future' (Rose 2004: 67). The 2003 Convention appears committed to moving away from crystallising manifestations of ICH, and aims to correct this practice by addressing the role of repository communities, and by building awareness in younger generations of the importance of ICH (UNESCO 2003).

The Convention identifies vulnerability inherent in ICH within the modern world system, tracing this to the fact that, for the most part, intangible cultural expressions are transmitted orally and cross-generationally. It aims to foster the appropriate conditions for these transmissions to continue, providing guidelines for state parties to submit proposals for the safeguarding of ICH, which are then considered in terms of the Convention's criteria (UNESCO 2003). It is on the basis of proposals submitted by state parties, and in accordance with criteria defined by the UNESCO Committee, that a selection is made to 'promote national, sub-regional and regional programmes, projects and activities for the safeguarding of the heritage' (UNESCO 2003).

In a review of the subtle power of intangible heritage, Deacon *et al.* (2004: 11) have asserted, 'investigating intangible heritage as a concept helps us to review and expand the notion of heritage as a whole, we need to develop new ways of safeguarding intangible resources, which may improve existing management practices for tangible heritage'. However, the questions remain, who constitutes 'us' and on what terms and for whose benefit are intangible cultural expressions to be safeguarded? In any discussion of ICH, at a legislative level, issues of ownership, cultural autonomy, self-determination, and human rights must be taken into account. All forms of cultural heritage are necessarily owned by human groups, distinct cultural entities that politically, socially and economically assert the very right to create and know this heritage. State parties, if not the owners of such heritage, should not be overwhelmingly empowered to determine the process by which ICH is defined, categorised and safeguarded.

State involvement in the determining and safeguarding of ICH is the foundation of the UNESCO Convention. The power relations reinforced by state party membership to UNESCO significantly influence existing heritage legislation, and the role of state members in the safeguarding of ICH (Brown 2005: 44). In itself state involvement in heritage legislation and safeguarding represents the 'movement of cultural elements from the politically weak to the politically strong' (Brown 2005: 44). The politically weak are Indigenous, minority or diasporic people living within dominant or colonial state frames or across marginal landscapes. The extent to which the ICHC facilitates formal and internationally binding recognition of Indigenous knowledge systems, performative culture and cultural autonomy remains to be seen, particularly when balanced alongside the view that 'respect is notoriously difficult to guarantee by legislative means' (Brown 2005: 44). Further to this point, any notion that Indigenous knowledge must be recorded by outsiders to ensure its survival in contemporary settings is in complete opposition to the appeals of Indigenous nations and communities to autonomously govern cultural and knowledge systems into the future (Brown 2005: 48).

The overriding authority of state parties versus that of communities in possession of ICH is expressed in Articles 11, 12 and 13 of the Convention.[5] Involvement and protection of the cultural rights of the community practising ICH are noted in Articles 11 and 13, with brief mention of community participation and respect for customary practices governing access to specific aspects of heritage. The terms 'practising community' or 'holding community' reflect some acknowledgement of ownership of ICH. Beyond this, ownership of ICH is not explicitly addressed throughout the text of the Convention. In a discussion of this, Deacon *et al.* (2004: 42) proposed, 'exclusive community ownership over heritage is both philosophically problematic and difficult to prove'. Further, Deacon *et al.* (2004: 42) argued that, 'ownership of an intangible heritage resource is not the same as ownership of a thing or a place'. Such an argument has its roots in the psychology of the intangible. It is the legacy of abstraction, that positions ICH as elusive, incapable of being seen and immaterial that impacts on the capacity to understand ICH as owned, culturally guarded and exclusive. The notion that only that which can be seen, namely 'thing' or 'place', as physical expressions of culture can be owned as legal property falls short of recognising a discreet community's or nation's right to control and manage all forms of their cultural heritage. In this regard, notions of ownership that appeal to a discourse of European legal praxis must also be abandoned, for they serve no great justice within Indigenous cultural contexts. European legal discourse is too often incapable of distinguishing the powerful relationships that inform ownership, control, and meaning of ICH in Indigenous political and cultural arenas (see for instance Langford 1983; Fourmile 1989; Dodson 1994). Article 15 of the Convention is the only hint at efforts to remedy this oversight and power imbalance. It reads:

> Within the framework of its safeguarding activities of the intangible cultural heritage, each State Party shall endeavour to ensure the widest possible participation of communities, groups and, where appropriate, individuals that create, maintain and transmit such heritage, and to involve them actively in its management.

The need to recognise exclusive ownership of ICH is imperative for any legislative effort that engages with the cultures, homelands and knowledge systems of Indigenous people worldwide. In line with this, Maori Chief Sir Tipene O'Regan (1987: 145), asserted: 'New Zealand's past belongs to all New Zealanders – but first it is ours!'. Langford (1983: 1) and Dodson (1994: 5 cited in Smith 2004: 16) have echoed similar sentiments, giving voice to Indigenous demands for recognised ownership of their past and heritage in Australia. For Langford (1983: 1) it is a case of Indigenous Australians owning their past; of asserting an exclusive right to their culture and heritage. Thus, it is also about control and resisting outsider efforts of appropriation and the colonisation of Indigenous knowledge. Similarly Dodson reflected on the violation of Indigenous Australians' 'sovereign right to control' their lives. For Dodson, at the core of this violation is the regulation of Indigenous people's rights to cultural expression. State mechanisms to control constructions and expressions of indigeneity in Australia have manifested in legislative efforts aimed at controlling individual lives and group identities, such as policies of assimilation, child removal, and land rights legislation. This has also involved control over the means by which Indigenous Australians make and remake their cultures and themselves (Dodson 1994: 5 cited in Smith 2004: 16). ICH is an ultimate symbol of culture and identity and through expressions of language, medicine, learning systems, oral traditions, spirituality, symbols, designs, ecological methods, music, and song it is maintained on discreet cultural terms for future generations. While the UNESCO Convention claims to recognise and address Indigenous (as well as 'Eastern') concepts of intangible cultural heritage, Indigenous resistance to state efforts of control over this, and appropriation of knowledge, persist (see Marrie, this volume). This resistance is grounded in the view that ICH, like Indigenous knowledge, is holistic. 'It cannot be compartmentalized and cannot be separated from the people who hold it. It is rooted in the spiritual health, culture, and language of the people and is a way of life' (Longley Cochran 2004). Beyond this 'it gives credibility to the people' (Longley Cochran 2004).

The UNESCO Convention, like other instruments developed to identify, protect and manage cultural heritage, is formulated and administered by state and global powers. State parties are responsible for taking the necessary measures to identify ICH and to ensure the safeguarding of ICH. Bestowing ultimate discretionary power onto the state renders Indigenous owners of ICH mere stakeholders. The state stands to control ICH, and challenge the exclusivity of Indigenous ownership. The making of public meaning and national identity has long been drawn from the display and representation of Indigenous cultural heritage (Kaplan 1994), and as such, heritage legislation is a site of contested identity and rights (Smith 2004: 17). The use of cultural heritage to assert identity, ethnicity and ownership of the past to the exclusion of others is located within the context of past and present sociopolitics (Smith 2004: 16–26). Under such conditions,

> cultural identity ... may become, as the anthropologist Simon Harrison has observed, a scarce resource to be defended as another form of property, either personal or collective. Heritage, the retrospective expression of culture, is likewise transformed into a highly politicised commodity
>
> (Brown 2005: 43)

Internationally, Indigenous people are lobbying for the right to determine what constitutes their ICH, to administer the mechanisms for safeguarding, developing and promoting ICH and to control any research methodologies and investigations that purport to protect this heritage (see Battiste and Youngblood Henderson 2000; Brascoupe and Mann 2001; Longley Cochran 2004). Currently, in Australia, there are a number of Indigenous, community-based cultural initiatives in place. These seek to illuminate and protect Indigenous knowledge systems and cultural heritage, by way of language maintenance, the use of new technologies in cross-generational knowledge sharing, land and sea management programmes, cultural and healing centres. Some are formally supported by the Australian government, through financial provisions, however the vast majority are supported through local Indigenous councils. Few of these efforts, despite their clear commitment to the safeguarding of cultural heritage, fall within legal range of existing Australian heritage legislation. The Australian government's failure to ratify UNESCO's ICHC renders the Convention useless for Indigenous Australians seeking to safeguard and manage their ICH (see Connolly 2007). I propose that non-ratification of the Convention reflects an ongoing homogenising of Indigenous identity in Australia, and this contributes to an undermining of Indigenous self-governance, autonomy and cultural distinctiveness in individual Indigenous communities. The prevailing political view of indigeneity in Australia is one of pan-Aboriginality in which individual groups are subsumed into the nation's whole, the mechanisms of which maintain a climate of authorial and cultural dispossession. For ratification of this Convention to occur, the Australian government would have to undergo a significant ethical and ideological makeover. To engage with Indigenous people as a population made up of many distinct languages and cultural practices that are governed by discreet bodies of Indigenous knowledge, would mean the acknowledgement of cultural autonomy. This would signal an important step in setting the stage for individual group-based negotiated processes to formally recognise and secure Indigenous heritage, knowledge, intellectual and cultural property rights on terms set by the cultural group themselves. Ratification of this and a number of other United Nations' Conventions would place the Australian State on an international stage of scrutiny, allowing for global commentary on its treatment of Indigenous people, and its human rights record.

In Australia, it is this lack of adequate legislative arrangements that has created the impetus for autonomous, localised projects that reflect and reinforce Indigenous knowledge systems and governance principles. For example, the Yanyuwa, Indigenous owners of land and sea in the southwest Gulf of Carpentaria, northern Australia, are one of many Indigenous communities activating the means to record and transmit distinct cultural knowledge or ICH. Over the past few decades the Yanyuwa have actively sought to document the intangible cultural expressions, knowledges and intimacies associated with spiritually powerful places across their homelands (Bradley 1988; Bradley *et al.* 1992, 2003, 2006; Kearney and Yanyuwa Families 2005; Kearney and Bradley 2006). Through these efforts they have shared and exchanged knowledge within their own community and also with outsiders, both Indigenous and non-Indigenous. For the Yanyuwa, ICH is governed by rights to possess certain forms of knowledge and responsibilities to share and withhold certain forms of information in particular contexts. All of this is mediated through community-defined programmes of ICH management. Since the 1980s this community has engaged in various forms of research and recording with linguists, anthropologists, archaeologists, ethnomusicologists, filmmakers and lawyers. Collaborative projects involving members of the community have included the documenting and drafting of a Yanyuwa dictionary, compilation of an Indigenous atlas detailing the intricacies of their homelands, recording song and dance, drafting and presenting land claim evidence, filming documentaries and establishing a community website. More recent efforts include a collaborative project drawing together Yanyuwa knowledge of their homelands and ancestors, and new technologies of visual-digital representation.[6] These are consciously aimed at increasing the rate of cross-generational knowledge sharing, encounters with homelands and maintenance of Yanyuwa identity and cultural distinctiveness, and do so on culturally defined terms, far beyond the scope of any existing national heritage legislation or international Conventions.

The Yanyuwa are not alone in the pursuit of programmes to support, safeguard and manage ICH and distinct knowledge systems. According to Neitschmann (1994: 225–42), in 1994 there were between 5,000 and 8,000 internationally unrecognised Indigenous nations that predate and continue to resist the spread of the modern state. Today these nations correspond to an estimated 370 million Indigenous people worldwide. At the same time, some 192 international states continue to occupy, suppress and exploit many of these nations (United Nations 2007). It is in this context that resistance to cultural dominance, annihilation or ethnic homogeneity is enacted. By way of recording, documenting, information sharing and enacting of cultural practices and knowledges, Indigenous groups and nations safeguard their ICH through autonomous means (Smith and Ward 2000). Within this context, UNESCO's Convention represents but one formal means to engage with ICH, and represents an opportunity to develop and reinforce national laws and policies concerning ICH. However, the Convention does not necessarily engage well with the intimacies and complexities that link tangible and intangible cultural expressions. One part of this failure is the tendency to view ICH as a 'universal heritage of humanity'. This issue has been addressed by Blake (2002: 12), who rightly identified 'an unresolved contradiction in international law between the "universal" approach to protection and one that recognizes the special interest of a State, people or group to a particular element'. While this remains a critique levelled at the UNESCO World Heritage Convention, the ICHC has been upheld for its capacity to move beyond universality and accommodate localised concern over the safeguarding of ICH. In early discussions over the development of an instrument for the safeguarding of ICH, the following point was made:

> What is vital is that the potential contradictions of that position are taken into account and it is advisable to make reference to intangible heritage as a 'universal heritage of humanity' in the Preamble as a justification for protection but to avoid its use within the definition itself. In this way the specific value that this heritage has for the community is safeguarded while the need for its international protection on the grounds of preserving cultural diversity is underlined.
>
> (Blake 2002: 12)

Acknowledging 'cultural rights as culture specific' is a resounding theme throughout the text of the Convention, however, state party members to UNESCO maintain control over those processes that concern the identification and safeguarding of ICH with no specific mandate to formally or legally recognise Indigenous rights to exclusive ownership and control over such ICH (see Blake 2002: 5). The status of Indigenous nations or communities, as holders of ICH, is not sufficiently defined throughout the text of the Convention nor are provisions explicitly spelt out to accommodate Indigenous rights to the exclusion of the state. Therefore, the state retains ultimate discretionary power in the pursuit of safeguarding mechanisms. This fact alone maintains elements of universality and upholds a system that supports an obliteration of local rights in preference to state and global interests.

For the Convention to have meaning or provide reasonable protections for Indigenous people's ICH it needs to be capable of addressing localised needs, be flexible in its delivery of culturally appropriate mechanisms of safeguarding, and go beyond securing the interests of state parties. Without this, the Indigenous knowledge systems that underscore ICH will continue to be positioned as mere alternatives to a 'Western', paternal logic of safeguarding. In the context of state and global power Indigenous resistance movements and cultural maintenance projects are too often rendered powerless or appropriated for the interests of the state. As it currently stands, the UNESCO Convention (2003) continues to empower the state, by leaving it at the discretion of dominant power structures to initiate efforts of safeguarding ICH.

To support the aspirations of Indigenous communities, national heritage legislation and policy and international instruments need to be aligned with projects of Indigenous self-governance and self-determination. There is an essential bond between self-governance and self-determination as both are fundamental to the recognition and assertion of Indigenous rights. The right to determine the nature of ICH is about the right to define one's cultural identity and place in the world today. Indigenous people worldwide are resisting state efforts to define this identity and place and efforts to subvert their systems of knowledge and law. Speaking passionately of this resistance, Yanyuwa elder Annie Karrakayn (in Bradley and Yanyuwa Families 2007: 46), stated:

> Everyone in this country, black and white follows white law. If we make a mistake off to court and might be jail, but white people have no respect, they do not care. We Yanyuwa people are not equal partners on our own country, we are low down and the white people are high up ... how is that?

Management of ICH should ensure or create opportunities for culturally meaningful negotiations between Indigenous peoples and heritage agencies, and culturally aware and sensitive management protocols adopted. Part of this involves the designation or establishment of one or more competent bodies for the safeguarding of ICH in its territory. Reflecting existing management structures in Indigenous communities, best practice would have the responsibility lie with Indigenous governing bodies or community groups of elders and young people, and the promotion of studies and research methodologies that reinforce Indigenous autonomy and collaborative links, with agendas being set, defined and redefined on Indigenous terms. These are daunting yet necessary complexities for policy-makers (Brown 2005: 41). Legislation, instruments and Conventions that require direct engagement with the Indigenous owners of ICH are more likely to communicate something of value to Indigenous people and increase the likelihood of culturally appropriate mechanisms for defining, safeguarding and valuing ICH. Legislation that positions Indigenous people as more than just stakeholders can champion the value of localised, rather than global and national benefits that take precedence. A global or national approach, which prioritises state or global community concern for the safeguarding of ICH disempowers the vast majority of Indigenous and minority groups, by denying them the authority, cultural rights and power to define and control cultural heritage as consisting of their past, present and future identities.

Conclusion

'The category of intangible heritage encourages the recognition of formerly marginalised forms of heritage' (Deacon *et al.* 2004: 11). The ICHC rightly identifies vulnerability inherent in ICH within the modern world system, tracing this to the fact that, for the most part, intangible cultural expressions are transmitted orally and cross-generationally. Current global trends of new environmental ethics and ecophilosophy are largely responsible for international and state interest in sustainable practices and ideologies as embodied in Indigenous or alternative knowledge systems and ICH. This interest encourages collective consciousness of human heritage, and is expressed in legislative arrangements such as UNESCO's ICHC. There are a number of complexities in collective claims to human heritage and knowledge systems. First and foremost, cultural internationalism, as facilitated by global consciousness, has the power to override local and Indigenous claims to self-determination and cultural autonomy. Second, it undermines the legal and intellectual property rights that are involved in a cultural group's exclusive possession of ICH.

Intangible cultural expressions can be owned and culturally distinct, for they are located and found within contexts of distinct languages, homelands and cultural systems. The knowledge systems that underpin ICH, as made up of oral traditions, song, verbal and nonverbal communications, power and authority, relationships and kinship, ceremony and ritual performance are discreet and owned by individuals, families and entire communities. Resistance to cultural and ethnic homogeneity is foremost for Indigenous groups worldwide, and cultural maintenance projects that involve all aspects of heritage are an imperative part of this. As suggested here, international heritage instruments would benefit from a return to localised interests, in which the lives and intangible cultural expressions of Indigenous peoples are safeguarded for the direct and primary benefit of those peoples. This requires policy changes and an epistemological rethink of the manner in which human heritage is defined and required to fit within state-defined categories that ultimately express themselves through heritage legislation.

Acknowledgements

This paper has benefited from the professional support of John Bradley, Liam Brady, Ian McNiven and Lynette Russell at Monash University. I also wish to thank the Yanyuwa community. It is through learning of their law and culture that I have come to appreciate the profound connections between people and their heritage.

Notes

1 I adopt the term 'state' to refer to self-governing political entities. This usage is interchangeable with 'country' and is aligned with the United Nations' definition of 'state parties'.
2 Ecofeminism proposes an alliance between feminism and environmentalist movements. It draws an alliance between women's oppression within patriarchal power regimes and environmental crisis. This, like ecophilosophy and green consciousness, echoes the desire for a more ethical position of connectedness between people and the environment (Leahy 2003).
3 UNESCO, 'Text of the *Convention for the Safeguarding of Intangible Cultural Heritage*'. Available online at: http://www.unesco.org/culture/ich/index.php?pg=00022 (Accessed 28 August 2007).
4 UNESCO, 'Legal responses by the international community at UNESCO'. Available online at: http://www.portal.unesco.org/culture (Accessed 17 March 2006).
5 The authority of state parties is outlined in the following extracts from Articles 11, 12 and 13 of the Convention:

> Article 11 reads:
> (b) among the safeguarding measures referred to in Article 2, paragraph 3, identify and define the various elements of the intangible cultural heritage present in its territory, with the participation of communities, groups and relevant nongovernmental organizations.
> Article 12 reads:
> 1. To ensure identification with a view to safeguarding, each State Party shall draw up, in a manner geared to its own situation, one or more inventories of the intangible cultural heritage present in its territory.
> Article 13 reads:
> To ensure the safeguarding, development and promotion of the intangible cultural heritage present in its territory, each State Party shall endeavor to:
> a) adopt a general policy aimed at promoting the function of the intangible cultural heritage in society, and at integrating the safeguarding of such heritage into planning programmes;
> b) designate or establish one or more competent bodies for the safeguarding of the intangible cultural heritage present in its territory;
> c) foster scientific, technical and artistic studies, as well as research methodologies, with a view to effective safeguarding of the intangible cultural heritage, in particular the intangible cultural heritage in danger;
> d) adopt appropriate legal, technical, administrative and financial measures.
> UNESCO, 'Text of the *Convention for the Safeguarding of Intangible Cultural Heritage*',
> op. cit.

6 This is a collaborative project involving the Li-wirdiwalangu Group of Yanyuwa Elders, John Bradley, Amanda Kearney and Tom Chandler of Monash University.

Bibliography

Barry, J. (1999) *Environment and Social Theory*, London and New York: Routledge.
Battiste, M. and Youngblood Henderson, J. (2000) *Protecting Indigenous Knowledge and Heritage: A Global Challenge*, Saskatoon, Canada: Purich Publishing Ltd.
Berkes, F. (1999) *Sacred Ecology: Traditional Ecological Knowledge and Resource Management*, Philadelphia: Taylor & Francis.
Blake, J. (2000) 'On defining the cultural heritage', *International and Comparative Law Quarterly*, 49: 61–85.

—— (2002) 'Developing a new standard-setting instrument for the safeguarding of intangible cultural heritage: elements for consideration'. Available online at: < http://unesdoc.unesco.org/images/0012/001237/123744e.pdf > (Accessed 30 July 2008).

Bradley, J. (1988) *Yanyuwa Country: The Yanyuwa People of Borroloola Tell The History of Their Land*, Melbourne: Greenhouse Publications.

Bradley, J., Holmes, M., Norman, D., Isaac, A., Miller, J. and Ninganga, I. (2006) *Yumbulyumbulmantha ki-awarawu (All kinds of things from Country) Yanyuwa Ethnobiological Classification*, Monograph series of the Aboriginal and Torres Strait Islander Studies Unit Research Report Series 6, Brisbane: University of Queensland Press.

Bradley, J., Kirton, J. and the Yanyuwa Community. (1992) 'Yanyuwa Wuka: language from Yanyuwa country', Unpublished document.

Bradley, J. and Yanyuwa Families. (2007) 'Barni-Wardimantha Awara: Yanywua Sea Country Plan, Unpublished document.

Bradley, J., Yanyuwa Families and Cameron, N. (2003) *Forget About Flinders: An Indigenous Atlas of the Southwest Gulf of Carpentaria*, Canberra: Australian Institute of Aboriginal and Torres Strait Islander Studies.

Brascoupe, S. and Mann, H. (2001) *A Community Guide to Protecting Indigenous Knowledge*, Ottawa, Canada: Department of Indian Affiars and Northern Development, Research Affairs Directorate.

Brown, M. (2005) 'Heritage trouble: Recent work on the protection of intangible cultural property', *International Journal of Cultural Property*, 12:40–61.

Connolly, I. (2007) 'Can the World Heritage Convention be adequately implemented in Australia without Australia becoming a part to the Intangible Heritage Convention?', *Environmental and Planning Law Journal*, 24(3):198–209.

Crossley, N. (1994) *The Politics of Subjectivity: Between Foucault and Merleau-Ponty*. Aldershot, Brookfield: Avebury.

Deacon, H., Dondolo, L., Mrubata, M. and Prosalendis, S. (2004) *The Subtle Power of Intangible Heritage*, South Africa: HSRC Press.

Dodson, M. (1994) 'Towards the exercise of Indigenous rights: policy, power and self-determination', in P. Poynton (ed.), *Aboriginal Australia: Land, Law and Culture*, London: Institute of Race Relations, pp. 65–76.

Fairweather, P. (1993) 'Links between ecology and ecophilosophy, ethics and the requirements of environmental management', *Austral Ecology*, 18(1):3–19.

Fourmile, H. (1989) 'Who owns the past? – Aborigines as captives of the archives', *Aboriginal History*, 13(1–2):1–8.

Fox, W. (1995) *Towards a Transpersonal Ecology: Developing New Foundations for Environmentalism*, Devon, UK: Green Books.

Frawley, K. (1999) 'A green vision', in K. Anderson and F. Gale (eds), *Cultural Geographies*, Sydney: Longman Australia, pp. 265–94.

Hunter, J. (2005) 'The role of information technologies in Indigenous knowledge management', in M. Nakata and M. Langton (eds), *Australian Indigenous Knowledge and Libraries*, Canberra: Australian Academic and Research Libraries, page number.

Kaplan, F. (ed.) (1994) *Museums and the Making of 'Ourselves': The Role of Objects in National Identity*, London and New York: Leicester University Press.

Kearney, A. and Bradley, J. (2006) 'Landscapes with shadows of once living people', in B. David, B. Barker and I.J. McNiven (eds), *The Social Archaeology of Indigenous Societies*, Canberra: Aboriginal Studies Press, pp. 182–203.

Kearney, A. and Yanyuwa Families. (2005) *An Ethnoarchaeology of Engagement: Yanyuwa Country and the Lived Cultural Domain in Archaeology*, unpublished thesis, The University of Melbourne.

Langford, R. (1983) 'Our heritage, your playground', *Australian Archaeology*, 16:1–6.

Langton, M. (2002) 'The edge of the sacred, the edge of death: sensual inscriptions', in B. David and M. Wilson (eds), *Inscribed Landscapes: Marking and Making Place,* Honolulu: University of Hawaii Press, pp. 253–69.

Langton, M., Ma Rhea, Z. and Palmer, L. (2005) 'Community-oriented protected areas for Indigenous peoples and local communities', *Journal of Political Ecology*, 12:23–50.

Leahy, T. (2003) 'Ecofeminism in theory and practice: women's responses to environmental issues', *Journal of Interdisciplinary Gender Studies*, 7(1):106–25.

Longley Cochran, P. (2004) *Ethical Guidelines for the Use of Traditional Knowledge in Research and Science*. Adapted from the Traditional Knowledge Research Guidelines of the Council of Yukon First Nations. Available online at: < http://www.ed.psu.edu/icik/2004Proceedings/section8-cochran.pdf > (Accessed 8 January 2008).

Merleau-Ponty, M. (1962) *Phenomenology of Perception*, trans. C. Smith, London and New York: Routledge and Kegan Paul.

Nakata, M. and Langton, M. (eds). (2005) *Australian Indigenous Knowledge and Libraries*, Canberra: Australian Academic and Research Libraries.

Neitschmann, B. (1994) 'The fourth world: nation versus states', in G. Demko and W. Wood (eds), *Reordering the World: Geopolitical Perspectives on the Twenty-First Century*, Boulder, Colorado: Westview Press, pp. 225–42.

O'Regan, T. (1987) 'Who owns the past? Change in Maori perceptions of the past', in J. Wilson (ed.), *From the Beginning: The Archaeology of the Maori*, Auckland: Penguin Books, pp. 141–5.

Plumwood, V. (2002) 'Decolonising relationships with nature', *PAN* 2:7–30.

Prosalendis, S. (2003) *Input at the Workshop on Intangible Heritage*, Cape Town: HSRC.

Rose, D.B. (2004) *Reports from a Wild Country: The Ethics of Decolonisation*, Sydney: UNSW Press.

Said, E. (1978) *Orientalism*, New York: Random House.

Smith, C. and Ward, G. (2000) *Indigenous Cultures in an Interconnected World*, St Leonards: Allen & Unwin.

Smith, L. (2004) *Archaeological Theory and the Politics of Cultural Heritage*, London and New York: Routledge.

UNESCO (2000) *Report of the Bureau of the World Heritage Committee 24th Session 26 June – 1 July*, Paris: UNESCO.

—— (2003) *Convention for the Safeguarding of Intangible Cultural Heritage.*

—— (2007) United Nations Member States. Available online at: http://www.un.org/members/list.shtml (Accessed 5 September 2007).

United Nations (2006) 'United Nations list of member states'. Available online at: http://www.un.org/members/list.shtml (Accessed 5 September 2007).

White, L. (1967) 'The historical roots of our ecologic crisis', *Science*, 155:1203–7.

Part 3

Reflecting on the intangible

Chapter 12

A critique of unfeeling heritage

Denis Byrne

Introduction

Those of us who have pushed for recognition of 'the intangible' in heritage work are also those who tend to stress the 'cultural' in cultural heritage. We try to resist the tendency of heritage discourse to reduce culture to things, we try to counter its privileging of physical fabric over social life (for example, Byrne 1995, Byrne in press). The UNESCO *Convention for the Safeguarding of Intangible Cultural Heritage* (2003) seems to us to be a mixed blessing. While it has the potential to bring more focus to the social dimension of heritage it seems also to want to regard social practices, skills and traditions as the equivalent of heritage objects, places or landscapes.

The Convention (Article 2.1) defines intangible heritage as the 'practices, representations, expressions, knowledge and skills' (e.g., musical instruments and artworks) present in a culture, along with 'instruments, objects, artefacts and cultural spaces associated therewith' (for example, sites of ritual, workshops for art production). The Convention's call for the documentation of intangible heritage is likely to face challenges from those Indigenous groups who do not want their intellectual property documented on the grounds that, once documented, its ownership too easily passes out of their hands. In any case, the Convention's call for signatory states to prepare inventories of the intangible heritage present in their territories prefigures a task of 'staggering' proportions (Brown 2003), one that would surely be impossible to ever achieve in any comprehensive manner. In fact, though, the Convention's intent appears not to be comprehensive so much as selective and hierarchical. The programme for Proclaiming Masterpieces of Oral and Intangible Heritage instituted by UNESCO in 1998 implies that, like the World Heritage List, its concern is with the exceptional. Also, the absence of a review process for items of intangible heritage on the World Heritage List implies that intangible values are fixed and immutable rather than fluid and socially determined (Beazley 2006: 5). All of this is suggestive of the reification or thingification of culture (Taussig 1992: 84).

Already, however, the Convention is being taken by some heritage practitioners as giving tacit support to the position that 'the tangible can only be interpreted through the intangible' and that 'tangible and intangible heritage are two sides of the same coin' (Gonçalves and Deacon 2003). They seem to share, as I do, Smith's (2006: 56) concern regarding a tendency by many heritage agencies and practitioners to think of tangible and intangible heritage 'as two separate things', two distinct types of object, place or landscape. I agree with Smith (2006: 56) that 'heritage' only comes into being via the discourse of heritage and to this extent heritage, being by nature discursive, is always intangible.

Archaeology's subject matter is mostly buried under the ground and even when remains are present on the surface they are often obscured by vegetation. The matter of detectability is important for archaeologists, as are the processes of decay and taphonomic processes, all of which play a role in deciding what parts of the material past are recoverable. As an archaeologist working in the heritage field I have long been conscious that in addition to the questions of what survives and what is recoverable there is the question of what, in any given political and social climate, will be given attention. For me, then, the words tangible and intangible have a somewhat different connotation to what has been discussed above.

'Heritage' is a certain way of knowing archaeological objects and sites, a certain way of drawing attention to them, of bringing them forward and valorising them. What though of the objects and sites that are *not* brought forward in this way? I have argued elsewhere (Byrne 2007: xi) that the selectivity of heritage discourse can serve to bury or efface certain places at the same time as it reveals and celebrates certain others. Nowhere has this been as true as in relation to the archaeological traces of the Cold War. In the following section I consider the case of mass graves belonging to the era of the Cold War since these sites and the way people relate to them have much to teach us, I believe, about the nature of intangibility. I then look at some of the ways that people remember and commemorate past events 'behind the scenes' as it were. In certain cases this constitutes a kind of counter-heritage in which places are commemorated *despite* official heritage discourse.

The industrial-scale recording of archaeological sites that occurs in the course of environmental impact assessment in some cases results in the inventorying of thousands of sites in a manner that sheds little or no light on history. The obsessive focus on the recording and salvage of archaeological material makes it appear that it is present behaviour, in the form of lucrative archaeological survey and excavation routines, rather than past behaviour that is the object of the exercise. What is so often eclipsed is the humanity of people in the past. Archaeological objects and places are potential contact points in a transaction in which past lives become real to us by drawing upon our own subjective experience of life in the present. Archaeology's focus on the technologies and economics of the past, along with heritage practice's focus on physical fabric as an end in itself, both act to dehumanise the past. Our insistence upon taking an objective or quasi-objective stance as researchers denies the potential to engage as feeling beings with past people (Hamilakis 2002).

In a recent article, Sally Ann Ness (2005) describes the manner in which, in the interests of manufacturing short-term 'paradise' experiences, destination tourism resorts effect a rupture with the pre-existing reality of the sites where they are constructed, as well as with the surrounding physical and social reality of the landscapes surrounding them, which can be considered a form of violence. The result is a deformation of place (2005: 135). I suggest that the approach to heritage conservation that treats materiality as an end in itself similarly effects a deformation of place. The excision of the material past from its social context, past and present, hollows it out and deforms it. What you are left with are things minus feeling.

The grievous dead

Consider the case of what Kwon refers to as the 'grievous dead' (2006). A great many of the monuments that comprise the modern world's tangible heritage were created to commemorate those who have died in war or in various national causes or as heroes on the side of justice. What, however, of the millions of victims of war, colonial violence and state violence who have gone uncommemorated. As a case study in the way that the traces of catastrophe can be rendered invisible, I turn to the events of 1965 in Bali. In the midst of the Cold War, an alleged coup attempt by communists in Jakarta on 30 September 1965 was followed by a repressive counter-coup by the Indonesian military in the course of which somewhere in the vicinity of half a million communists, alleged communists, and their associates were killed in Java, Bali, North Sumatra, and Borneo in late 1965 and early 1966 (Cribb 1990a). The death toll on Bali is thought to have been around 100,000 (Robinson 1995). Bodies were thrown down wells or buried in mass graves and the landscape of what many Westerners since the 1920s had come to regard as the quintessential island paradise was 'pock-marked with the blackened shells of former settlements' (Cribb 1990b: 241). It was a landscape of 'blackened areas where entire villages had been burnt to the ground' (Vickers 1989: 170).

The events of 1965 in Bali constituted a traumatic event of enormous proportions. The killings were also instrumental in establishing the new government of General Soeharto in Indonesia. Soeharto maintained an iron grip on power in Indonesia for the following three decades, banning any public mention of the killings let alone any public mourning for those who had died. A generation of Indonesians who had witnessed the events of 1965 were silenced by fear, while a subsequent generation, in the words of Ann

Stoler (2002: 646), was 'schooled with purged history books and with access only to book-stores immaculately emptied of ways of making sense of the world into which they were born'. Fear and censorship combined to render the events unmentionable. For a foreigner living in Bali in the early 1990s there was not only this complete absence of public reference to the events of 1965 but also an absence of any readily visible trace of them in the landscape (Byrne 2007: 84–5).

We might well ask, from an archaeological standpoint, how it is that the physical imprint of a catastrophe be so muted. What, for instance, happened to the sites of those burnt villages in Bali? Had the remains been demolished and recycled? Had the sites been resettled by people who, perhaps living with a sense of guilt at having benefited from the misfortune of others, added their silence to the general silence? Catherine Merridale (1996) posits something of this nature having occurred during and after the famine of 1933 in Russia. 'Untold numbers' benefited from that famine, whether by appropriating the land or chattels of the dead or by resettling abandoned villages (Merridale 1996: 12). She suggests that this helps explain why 'there was no public outcry against the blatant official denial' that a famine had occurred.

In cases where Balinese villages had not been burned, were the wooden houses simply dismantled and removed? There is mention of this happening in 1965, near Jakarta, where the houses of victims were taken apart and transported elsewhere, with nothing remaining of certain villages 'except stripped trees and gardens' (McKie 1969: 94). Built without nails or screws and with only pegs locking the joinery together, the portability of many old-style wooden houses in Southeast Asia is well known (Waterson 1990: 78).

'Suppressing memories is one thing but erasing them is quite another'. These words were penned by James Miles (quoted in Mirsky 1997: 33) in reference to the tread-marks left by tanks in June 1989 on a street leading into Tiananmen Square. The marks had been mostly smoothed away but years later, if you listened carefully, you could still hear the faint hum produced by the tires of your car passing over the indentations. This graphic, almost poetic, instance of the potential of archaeological traces to speak in the midst of politically imposed silence might come as something of a relief after considering the modern state's facility with censorship. But while suppression can operate via censorship it can also mobilise archaeological traces for its own purposes. In Indonesia, Robert Cribb (1990b: 9) found it 'a little puzzling' that in the years after 1965–66 there had been no reports of mass graves being discovered in Indonesia. He speculated that while their locations were known locally the sites were avoided by new construction projects. He mentioned 'sporadic accounts' from Central Java of rice fields no longer tilled because they concealed mass graves. Anyone who happened to come upon such a place, he observed, would 'think carefully' before reporting it (Cribb 1990b: 10). In such situations, is it not merely the public mention of certain past events that is proscribed? Must the archaeology of these events also remain 'unnoticed' by those who continue to live in the local landscape? Or is it more complicated than that? In Indonesia under Soeharto, it appears the authorities actually banked on the assumption that people *would* notice, knowing as they did that the noticing kept alive a fear that in turn produced compliance. We should never underestimate the subtlety of people's relationship with the material past as they manoeuvre around it in the course of their everyday lives.

The silence of the Balinese landscape regarding the question of mass graves resonates with our inability in Australia to identify the sites where Aboriginal people were massacred on the nineteenth-century pastoral frontier. While there have been calls for memorials to be erected at Aboriginal massacre sites, the problem is that of the hundreds or thousands of places where the killings took place only a mere handful are recorded on maps. The location of some others are known in a very general way, for instance as having occurred somewhere along a certain river or creek. The haze that has settled over the specifics of these events might simply be put down to 'memory decay' except that we know that the killers of these people normally took care to burn or otherwise dispose of the bodies. And, as Henry Reynolds (1987: 59, 61) points out, while the killers often boasted of their deeds in private conversation there was a code of silence which kept information from circulating to outsiders. At a local or personal level the massacres may have been committed to memory – apparently to the extent that the perpetrators were often haunted by their deeds later in life – but they took measures to prevent these events becoming a subject of public memory and to prevent the sites being available for commemoration.

For an example of the exercise of discretion in relation to such absences it is difficult to go past Norman Lewis's (1995) account of his experience in East Timor in the 1970s, in the years immediately after the Indonesian invasion of the former Portuguese colony. Lewis had been staying with some nuns at a small mission in the village of Venilale, in the hills of central East Timor, and had been accompanied on his walks in the surrounding countryside by a young man, a local, who always carried a guitar.

> He was an unobtrusive and diffident presence, tailing along behind at a distance of three or four yards and occasionally twanging urgently on his guitar to draw our attention to some feature of the sinister wilderness through which we were trudging that had sparked off strong emotion … A twang of the guitar might be a signal for the eyebrows to shoot up over widened eyes and the corners of the mouth to droop in a sort of depressed smirk. We followed his eye, wondering what could have happened to provide fury or grief among a largely featureless spread of thickets, cunningly pruned trees, and sallow rocks at this particular spot … Once only were we able to identify the cause of Thomas's

excitement, when a spar of charred wood poked through the under-
growth on a ridge over a shallow valley. This had been a village, but no
more of it remained than the Romans had left of Carthage.

(Lewis 1995: 160–1)

Catastrophic events may be 'buried' by the state's control of official history
but this does not mean they cannot be recuperated by local action. In his
book, *After the Massacre*, Heonik Kwon (2006) studies the circumstances and
aftermath of civilian massacres that took place during the Vietnam War at
Ha My in January 1968 and My Lai in March 1968, both in Central
Vietnam (see also Kwon 2007). Kwon shows how in the 'revolutionary politics' of post-war Vietnam it was only the 'heroes', those who fought against
the French and the Americans, who were publicly commemorated and honoured with monuments. Civilians such as those killed by American and
Korean troops at My Lai and Ha My were left in the mass graves they had
been buried in without their relatives having a chance to enact appropriate
rituals. In Central Vietnam, the whole project of ritual remembrance, of
which ancestor worship is one part, is aimed at integrating the dead into
contemporary society. The spirits of those ancestors in the mass graves
remained outside society. Local people believe that the tragic and horrific
circumstances in which these people died are continuous with the pain these
dead continue to suffer by lying abandoned in mass graves. The living, their
relatives and fellow villagers, owe it to the 'grievous dead' to rescue them
from this horror and 'escape their tragic conditions' (2006: 133) by giving
them proper burial.

At a local level – the level of the family and the village – commemorative
ritual serves to reconstitute the community of the dead by reuniting them in
the landscape of local history where genealogy counts for more than past
politics (Kwon 2006: 162). Looked at in this way, local people work behind
the scenes to repair the damage to community that war and state practices of
commemoration inflict on them. Kwon (2006: 105–8, 113–16) also shows
how in the 1990s in Central Vietnam the activities surrounding the renovation of ancestral and village temples, destroyed during the war and in the
second half of the 1970s by the communist state, often reunited those who
had been on the opposite side of wartime politics.

Mass graves constitute a somewhat extreme case of what Meskell (2002)
has recently termed 'negative heritage'. However, they illustrate the manner
in which whole categories of heritage can lie hidden in the landscapes of
everyday life. Whether they truly are hidden or not is beside the point; in
the circumstances described here they are unmentionable and that is what counts.
In many countries of the world quite significant fractions of the history of
the modern era, and the sites associated with this history, remain in the
category of the unmentionable. They are unmentionable precisely because
they are of great significance to at least a fraction of the population, those

who are disempowered. It would be naïve to suppose that governments that are signatory to the 2003 Convention will inventory heritage sites that reflect poorly on their human rights record. All this of course applies mainly to heritage sites of comparatively recent times, but for most people it is these places that evoke the most intense memories and emotions.

Commemoration behind the scenes

Most Balinese now above the age of 45 or 50 are likely to have witnessed at least some of the events of 1965–66, if not the actual killings themselves. Thousands still alive today must have lost children, husbands, lovers, friends and relatives; thousands of others must have actually participated in the executions. Surely the land must still be replete with traces that were visible to these people. It is understandable, according to Adrian Vickers (1989: 172), that 'few Balinese want to relive this time in conversation and most, like survivors of other conflicts, prefer to block it out of their memories'. The question I pose here, though, is whether such blocking would really be sufficient to neutralise the mnemonic potential of a 'traumascape' (Tumarkin 2005). The most eloquent reminders of an event need not be the products or debris, in a direct sense, of that which they signify. Would the gateway through which a lover or child was glimpsed for the last time as he or she was being taken away for execution not be imprinted thereafter, for those left behind, with intimations of loss? We all know how, in cases of deep personal loss, ordinary objects and places can trigger real pain; we know how these objects and places can lie in quiet ambush for us as we move gingerly across the terrain of each new day. So there is the gateway, yes, but also perhaps every laneway and riverbank, a detail here, a detail there, until the familiar local landscape becomes for the survivor a minefield of memory sites.

The way people signify things and landscapes, privately, locally, intimately, animates them in ways that are likely to be invisible to outsiders. At this level, the local meaning of things is intangible in a particular sense. This intangibility, this localised activity taking place 'below the thresholds at which visibility begins', to use Michel de Certeau's (1984: 93) words, can be a form of resistance in the face of larger, national narratives which aim to impose their own ultra-visible truth claims. While not suggesting memory is static or immune to decay, or that it is not changed with every recall, it is nevertheless possible to see how the memory of individuals can preserve an account of events that is subversive to the official version. Not available to surveillance, these private memories constitute a type of 'noise' in the officially imposed silence. In post-1966 Bali, this 'noise' must have been almost deafening for locals and yet quite inaudible to the general Balinese population at a public level or to the generations of tourists who subsequently wandered the beaches and foothills of the island.

There is a sense, then, in which even those who escaped the fate of those in the mass graves were themselves nonetheless buried alive, required as they were to live in a landscape where some of their most intense memories were inadmissible. Erik Mueggler (1998) has described how many victims of the Cultural Revolution in Southwest China subsequently became socially invisible and inaudible, incarcerated as they were within the space of their own memories. His particular use of the word 'encrypted' suggests it can stand for the crypt as a burial site while simultaneously referencing the hidden meaning of an encoded message. In the case of Bali we might usefully think of landscapes encrypted with meaning, populated with traces which it is unwise to draw attention to but which people 'read' privately and perhaps surreptitiously.

All of us carry out this work of signification in the familiar terrain of our everyday lives. My focus has been on traumatic events but our worlds are equally, of course, populated with signs of past pleasures, achievements and satisfactions. If we want to think of the experience of everyday life in terms of heritage, then it is probably true that this heritage is mostly intangible insofar as it consists of places and objects whose significance to us personally will be unreadable archaeologically. Our encrypted landscapes are constructions of our minds. Since heritage practice is unable to work at such a fine-grained level, it follows that most of the heritage that means most to us in the frame of our individual lives will never be the subject of heritage recording or conservation. This observation is not by way of a complaint about heritage practice – who would want to live in a world where all commemoration was public, none private – but by way of an effort to sketch out the parameters of the intangible.

One means by which the fine-grained spatiality of individual lives has become accessible over the last few decades has been through the work of oral history recording. Here, ordinary people who have not been in a position to write or publish their histories have had the opportunity to make them publicly available via audio recordings and written histories based on these recordings. Where attention is given to the spatial dimension, oral history recording can become a means of mapping the intangible. In a recent collaborative oral history recording project carried out with Aboriginal people on the mid-north coast of New South Wales, Australia, an effort was made to map Aboriginal histories of the recent past (that is, post 1820). The aim was to address a lack of recorded heritage places that represented the Aboriginal experience of living in a colonised landscape (Byrne and Nugent 2004). This lack has become increasingly problematic since, for the last several decades, the white settler population of this area has been busily engaged in recording sites representing their own history – village streetscapes, for instance, old farm homesteads, old bridges, banks and courthouses. By filling up the landscape, in a metaphorical sense, with sites of settler heritage the white population, presumably unconsciously, was effacing the

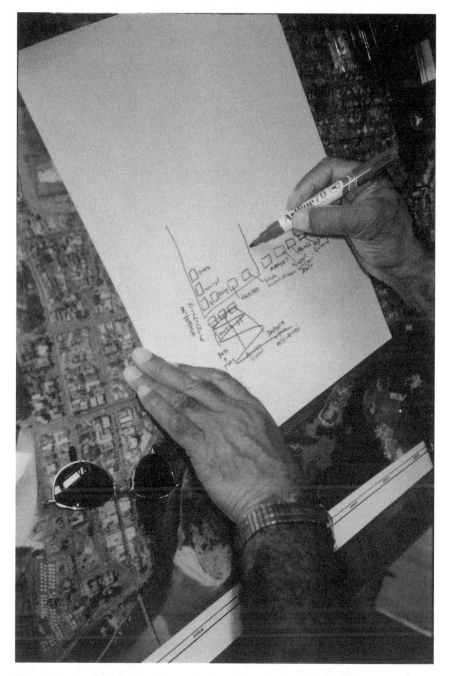

Figure 12.1 An Aboriginal participant in the NSW study draws, from memory, a plan of the location of houses on the Aboriginal reserve at Forster in the 1950s (in the background is an aerial photograph of the town in the 1990s).

historical presence of Aboriginal people whose descendents lacked a comparable technology of history writing or a comparable facility with the discourse of heritage.

The 'intangibility' of Aboriginal people's heritage in the colonised landscape is also a reflection of the tenuousness of their physical footprint in that landscape (Byrne 2003a). As hunter gatherers in the pre-contact landscape, there was always a certain delicacy about their material culture and their modelling of the land: their burials were marked by carved designs on trees, their ceremonial grounds were marked by temporary ground sculptures and raised-earth circles, their artefacts were lightweight and portable and their bark huts were quickly built and easily replaced. They were rapidly dispossessed of their land as the tide of white settler farmers and graziers advanced across their country and, by the mid-nineteenth century, they were living in 'fringe camps' on the edge of settler towns and on tiny Crown reserves. Many of these reserves were later revoked by the government and sold to white farmers (Goodall 1996). The residents of fringe camps were subject to constant pressure by local authorities to move on and the camps themselves were often torn down or bulldozed (Read 1984). On the mid-north coast we stood with our aboriginal interlocutors at the sides of roads gazing into open fields or suburban housing estates while they reminisced about life at these places, a past they could now see no trace of.

Indigenous minorities in settler colonies, in their newly landless state, must fit their lives as best they can into the redrawn map of their former country. Their genius must lie in fitting themselves and their lives into vacant corners and interstices that exist on the settler map, poaching on the space of their colonisers, jumping their fences, walking in the shadows of the settler streetscape (Byrne 2003b). Local Aboriginal people drew for us, on enlarged aerial photographs, the routes they had taken across fields and over fences to reach fishing places along the rivers and on the coast; places they moored their rowboats and places they picnicked (Byrne and Nugent 2004: 73–122). None of the Aboriginal people we interviewed wished for these sites and routes to be conserved on the ground. What they wanted was to record the history of where they had been in this terrain over the last several generations. It was not as if this map had not existed until we came along to record it – it existed in people's minds, transmitted down the generations through the telling of emplaced stories. Now, however, they wanted it to be available (and tangible) to mainstream society; to be accessible, for instance, to white children in the schools of the region.

On the mid-north coast of New South Wales the imprint of Aboriginal post-contact history was, to begin with, physically less substantial than that of European settlers. It was rendered even less tangible by being discursively 'buried' under the weight of proliferating recordings of and commentaries on settler heritage places. I see this as a continuation of the European colonial project in places like Australia: first you settle the land and marginalise the

Figure 12.2 Map showing the coastal town of Forster, NSW, with overlay showing Aboriginal mid-twentieth-century walking tracks, fishing and swimming places, as well as three picnic spots (fire symbol). Wallis Lake is visible on the left showing a jetty where Aboriginal people kept boats for use on the lake.

Indigenous population, then you totalise your historical presence in the landscape by filling it with your recorded traces. Heritage is always a competitive process, it is mired in the politics of tangibility.

Monumentality and its alternatives

Another way of thinking about the relationship of the intangible to the tangible is in relation to monuments. I agree with Tumarkin's (2005: 12) observation that for traumatised people, '[t]he past enters the present as an intruder, not a welcome guest'. But we must acknowledge that many of those who have to live in the present with the legacy of trauma are deeply committed to ensuring that their traumatic past does intrude, that it indeed occupies a permanent place in the landscape of everyday life.

In Central Vietnam, the relatives of the 135 victims of the Ha My massacre, perpetrated by Republic of South Korea troops in February 1968, campaigned to have the victims' remains removed from their mass grave and reburied in a more appropriate place and with appropriate ritual. The new interment site was marked by a monument that was dedicated in 2000 (Kwon 2006: 137–53). The back of the monument was inscribed with a detailed account of what had occurred, an account that related in language of anger and bitterness the shooting of women and children: 'The grievous spirits of the dead were abandoned, having no place to rest, and our fury reached the skin of heaven' (Kwon 2006: 142). Following protests by South Korean diplomats from Saigon, however, the Vietnamese authorities affixed carved marble lotus flowers to the inscription in order to cover it over.

The 'burial' of the Ha My monument inscription beneath a scattering of marble flowers resonates, somewhat, with the way that this part of coastal Central Vietnam is presented to international tourists. The village of Ha My is only some 30 kilometres from the small town of Hoi An which over the last 15 years or so has risen to prominence as a major tourism destination where visitors can witness the architecture and seemingly authentic lifestyle of an old Sino-Vietnamese trading port. Not merely does Hoi An seem to be untouched by war, it seems so remote from Central Vietnam's recent history as to seem to occupy another time and place. No reference can be found there to wartime atrocities in the neighbouring landscape despite the fact that many tourists – those, at least, over the age of about 40 – would remember the My Lai incident through the sensational international press coverage it received when news of it leaked out in November 1969. Hoi An might be compared to the 'touristic utopic landscapes' of the desti-nation resorts described by Ness (2005: 121), except that it is an in situ rather than a fabricated retreat from reality. The same might be said of the utopic landscape of the tourist's Bali where no intimation of the night-mare of 1965 threatens to disturb the fiction of paradise. Essential to the heritage fiction of both places is the visitor's belief that they are experiencing not just authentic place but authentic history. In Bali, as in Hoi An, the present is portrayed as seamlessly connected to an idyllic enduring history of traditional culture.

In the modern era at least, survivors and the bereaved have wished to have physical memorials as a public acknowledgement of suffering and loss, valour and endurance experienced in wartime as well as in natural disasters and other catastrophes. This was true of World Wars I and II where the bodies of dead soldiers were not available for burial at home and where loved ones died in places their relatives and friends at home had never seen and could often scarcely imagine. Jay Winter (1995: 78–116) has argued that World War I monuments were instrumental in allowing many people to express grief which otherwise may have been largely internalised; that people needed to find tangible sites for deaths which otherwise were placeless. But even here the situation was complex. Many of Australia's Australian and New Zealand Army Corps (ANZAC) memorials were actually erected while the Great War was still in progress in an effort to drum up more volunteers in a political situation in which a referendum to allow conscription to be introduced had been twice voted down by an Australian electorate divided as to the war's merits (Inglis 1998: 106–22). Monuments undoubtedly have a constructive role to play in people's efforts to come to terms with the past, indeed of 'mastering' the past (Meskell 2002: 566), but they have also been used for political ends to pack the past away and encourage forgetting (Huyssen 1999).

There are also situations in which the bereaved have pointedly refused to have their loss represented in the form of monuments. The women belonging to the Association of Mothers in Buenos Aires, for instance, steadfastly resist attempts to 'settle' the fate of their children who had disappeared at the hands of the 1976–83 military dictatorship in Argentina, even to the extent of refusing to condone excavation of mass graves and other burial sites by forensic archaeologists (Bosco 2004). They insist their children remain in the category of the disappeared.

A mass grave is, of course, an eminently tangible site in archaeological terms, but we appreciate that it is also a site intended by its creators to be 'intangible' to the extent of being invisible and unknown. It will exist as part of an 'underground', both in the literal sense of being under the ground and in the figurative sense of belonging to that twilight zone in which physical traces of certain events from the 'contemporary past' (Buchli and Lucas 2001) remain hidden. This 'underground' might be taken to stand for the dark side of human nature, representing violence and cruelty; a shadow-land populated by traces of historical events that secrecy, censorship and suppression ensure remain 'intangible' even though they are often under our very noses (Byrne 2007: ix–x). To reiterate one of this chapter's main points, the archaeological record of modern times does not occupy a level playing field. Much of it will remain undocumented and 'unseen' because our eyes and minds are deflected from it.

The fact that the victims of the military regimes in South America in the 1970s and 1980s could be made to simply disappear, underlines the actual tenuousness of human lives: so tangible at one moment and so spectral at another. In 1983 'ghostly silhouettes' began to appear in the streets of Buenos Aires, painted clandestinely by relatives of those who had gone missing at the hands of the military. The silhouettes – outlines of bodies – contained the names of the missing and the dates of their disappearance (Crossland 2002: 123). If the disappearances, the disappeared and those who search for traces of the disappeared, all exist in a kind of twilight zone – the 'underground' I refer to above – then the painted silhouettes of Buenos Aires can be seen as an attempt to connect or anchor this floating zone to the physical surface of the city, an attempt to give physical presence to those who have not just disappeared but become unmentionable. It would be a mistake to think the discourse of heritage, dominated by governments and professionals, now has some kind of monopoly on commemoration-in-place. The latter is a field of social action that still mostly occurs at a local scale, often privately and intimately, without official support or sanction.

With mass graves, it may only be the perpetrators who have knowledge of their precise existence. Unless, that is, one allows that in a poetic sense the ground which surrounds the bodies and harbours them can also be said to know them and remember them. This notion taps into the sacred and mystical association that many cultures have with the soil of their ancestral terrain. When in June 1990 a mass grave was discovered in the desert of Northern Chile, containing the remains of victims of the Pinochet dictatorship who had been held in a nearby detention centre, their relatives printed posters stating that 'the earth spoke to demand justice' (Frazier 1999: 108). Here it is as if the earth itself, rather than a team of investigators, had delivered up the bodies. This resonates with some of the words in the (now hidden) inscription on the Ha My memorial mentioned earlier: 'From now on, the sand dune and the trees that grow on it will remember the history of the tragic killings' (Kwon 2006: 142). This is in reference to a mass grave that was the previous resting place of the massacre victims and is contextualised by the opening lines of the inscription which speak of how the ancestors had lived in harmony with this land for many generations. There is a sense here that they know the soil and the soil knows them. In this construction, the ground is recognised as having agency – it can feel, it can act. One of the outstanding shortcomings of heritage practice at the moment is its failure to acknowledge that for the larger fraction of the world's population old things and places are not inanimate.

A key element in the way the villagers of Central Vietnam engage with their history lies in their relationship with the spirits of the dead. The fact that so many of those who died during the war years endured bad deaths ruptured the ideal in which the spirits of the dead are embraced within the institution of ancestor worship. The war has produced local landscapes populated by restless ghosts who are frequently encountered by the living in apparitions that occur at places the dead had particular attachments to when still alive. Much of Kwon's (2005) ethnographic labour consisted in documenting and understanding the way people try to appease these 'grievous dead' and help them find peace. This provides one tiny window on a whole dimension of everyday life in Southeast Asia that concerns people's relationship with the magical supernatural. One aspect of this relationship, which receives almost no acknowledgement in current heritage practice either by local or international practitioners, is that many or most archaeological sites and ruins are believed to be animated by the presence of ghosts, animist spirits or deities from the realm of popular Buddhism (Byrne in press). Western liberalism, as Povinelli (2002) points out, insists on the need for rational argument or proof for things. The workings of the supernatural in Southeast Asia are simply not available to this kind of argument or proof. To what extent, I wonder, is the promotion of intangible heritage as a field of practice not just liberalism's way of trying to encompass and domesticate realms of experience that lie outside its present field?

The subtlety of the idea that the earth can know and remember the dead and the material delicacy of those ghostly silhouettes in the streets of Buenos Aires both register for me as a kind of counter-heritage. They point to ways of treating the material past without recourse to heritage discourse and they resonate with my uneasiness about heritage practice in general. I believe it can be a force for good, for instance by explaining the nature of the attachment people have to the material past and defending local worlds against effacement by market forces. But in practice it too often displays a profound ignorance of culture theory (an ignorance so evident in most UNESCO Conventions) and is more adept at misrepresenting the local by interpreting it via so-called universal values than at defending it. I wish to quote here some words by Andreas Huyssen (1999: 198), writing about the urge to monumentalism in 1990s Germany:

> The monumental is aesthetically suspect because it is tied to nineteenth-century bad taste, to kitsch, and to mass culture. It is politically suspect because it is seen as representative of nineteenth-century nationalisms and twentieth-century totalitarianisms. It is socially suspect because it is the privileged mode of expression of mass movements and mass politics. It is ethically suspect because in its preference for bigness it indulges in the larger-than-human, in the attempt to overwhelm the individual spectator. It is psychologically suspect because it is tied to narcissistic delusions of grandeur and to imaginary wholeness.

What worries me is that the term 'heritage practice' could too easily be substituted in this passage for the word 'monumental'.

In the present day, the field of cultural heritage is almost entirely concerned with the tangible. Notwithstanding the in-principle acknowledgement by many heritage agencies and practitioners of the importance of intangible heritage, one continues to find that on-ground heritage practice is almost exclusively focused on conserving the physicality of architecture and archaeological sites. And this focus on the tangible all too easily leads to monumentalism. The gravitational pull of the political climate seems always to be towards the global scale (in the form of World Heritage) or the national or state scale (in the form of heritage places that reach thresholds of significance established for national and state/provincial heritage registers). The intangible dimension of this heritage in the form, for instance, of its meaning to ordinary citizens, past and present, in their everyday lives seems mostly to be lost in translation. The drift is towards the larger-than-human scale. I turn now to look the other way, back down along the scale to the intimate and corporeal.

Lost in mass

At the Tuol Sleng Genocide Museum in Phnom Penh where around 17,000 Khmer Rouge and their families, accused of treason, were imprisoned and tortured by their own party between 1975 and 1979 before being executed, individual 'mug shot' photographs are exhibited in an otherwise bare ground floor room of the former high school (Chandler 1999). These photographs, taken by prison photographers for their records, now act to recuperate the individuality of the victims who otherwise are lost in the sheer magnitude of mass death and suffering (Mydans 1997). Tuol Sleng, like the concentration camps in Nazi Europe, was a machine for the mass production of suffering and death. The power of the photographs at the Tuol Sleng museum lies in their ability to unravel the progression that converted individual lives and identities into a barely comprehensible mass. It is as if the museum visitor is propelled in rapid rewind through the space of this progression to land eventually there in that room in front of one frightened face: somebody's parent, somebody's child. Individuality is recuperated in this act and of course the experience for the viewer is almost unbearable. The issue of scale is, I think, central to the whole project of humanising heritage practice. We need to ask ourselves why 17,000 victims are somehow bearable while one frightened face, somehow, is not.

What I have described here is the possibility of experiencing, at second hand and through the medium of a heritage site, the suffering of past individuals, the possibility of bearing witness to their individual lives and deaths, the possibility of making the intangible tangible. And yet one senses that very often our experiences of sites of disaster fail in this respect. The technology available for recapturing and re-presenting past suffering grows ever more sophisticated but the potential this offers for the mass consumption of the past may render the possibility of bearing witness ever more remote. In reflecting upon the mass interest generated by the World Trade Center site in New York, Lynn Meskell (2002: 560) wonders whether it 'will become at best a world commodity fetish or, at worst, a nightmarish theme park'. There is, she observes, 'something inherently disturbing about the incipient musealization of Ground Zero, about the desire to instantly represent it, capture its aura, commodify it, and publicly perform it again and again, simply because we can' (2002: 560). The value in making past suffering 'real' for us in the present lies, one would assume, in persuading us to eschew violence against people in the present. And our capacity for this lies in our simple ability to feel, to emote and empathise. While empathy is surely one of the most basic experiences in the human repertoire, its enactment may be conditional on a certain degree of stillness around us, a space for reflection. Yet it sometimes seems that the news and entertainment media, bombarding our senses with the sights and sounds of devastation and violence, ever ramping up their demands that we feel this or that sensation or gratuitous emotion, aim to prevent us ever having this space.

Yet even in a media-saturated world, archaeology and heritage practice do hold out a promise of being able to facilitate empathetic encounters between people in the present and past lives. Such encounters can probably never be unmediated, tempting though it is to hope for ways to sidestep discourse, ways to hotwire present observers directly to past humanity. The photographs on the wall at Tuol Sleng, like the shoes of Jews killed in a Polish death camp that are now displayed at the Holocaust Memorial Museum in Washington, have gotten there via the discourse of museology. Discourse itself is not the problem; the problem is the way discourse is used and this brings me again to the issue of scale. Will comprehensive inventories of millions of units of intangible heritage bring us any closer to past lives? If we think for a moment of those typological exercises in archaeology that record and analyse thousands of artefacts it is striking that all this effort seems often to take us further from, rather than closer to, any sense of past human presence. The reductive, materialising effect of this work creates landscapes of the past that seem to be inhabited by stone tool traditions and ceramic cultures rather than people.

A key example of mass work in archaeology over the previous few decades has been the recording of hundreds of thousands of archaeological sites in the course of environmental impact assessments which in countries like the USA, Japan, Canada and Australia have become the major employers of professionals in the field. The world's heritage inventories are now bursting with descriptive data on archaeological sites. The moderns, Bruno Latour (1993: 69) observes,

> ... want to keep everything, date everything, because they think they have definitively broken with their past. The more they accumulate revolutions, the more they save; the more they capitalize, the more they put on display in museums. Maniacal destruction is counterbalanced by an equally maniacal conservation. Historians reconstitute the past, detail by detail, all the more carefully inasmuch as it has been swallowed up forever.

The mass recording and inventorying of archaeological sites, in Latour's view of things, can be regarded as symptomatic of our detachment from our ancestors rather than our identification with them. We know them, in a sense, less than we did in pre-Reformation times when their presence was sensed magically and spiritually in old places and objects. Much of the non-Western world still has this identification and communion with past worlds and it is no coincidence that the conservation ethnic, at least in the hypermaterial form in which is it conceived in the West, is pursued much less maniacally there (Byrne in press).

I can appreciate that it may seem offensive to some readers to treat archaeology's 'mass work' in the same breath, as it were, as mass death and mass graves. Nonetheless, the point seems a crucial one to me: archaeology has not been an innocent bystander in modernity's relentless commodification of the past, but archaeology still has a unique potential to counter it by focusing on the individuality of its subjects.

Acts of identification

The contemporary Japanese photographer Miyako Ishiuchi has created a series of photographs that depict personal belongings of her mother, who died in 2000, as well as close-ups of parts of her mother's dead body. She has stated that she wanted the photographs to create a 'contact point' between the present and the past (Itoi 2007). The objects, photographed individually, include used lipsticks, a hairbrush in which strands of hair are entangled in the nylon bristles, and delicate pieces of her mother's undergarments. In the case of the lipstick photographs, the obvious signs of age and usage on the object evoke the past while the viewer's knowledge that the 'wear' on the tip of the lipstick represents its use on Ishiuchi's mother's lips powerfully evokes her mother's individual humanity.

These photographs help illustrate the instrumental continuum between the tangible and the intangible. The lipstick is the tangible part of the equation: its job is to evoke the intangible (in this case, the person of Ishiuchi's dead mother). The lipstick allows us a moment of imaginative connection with the past in which Ishiuchi's mother becomes real as a *person* rather than one of the faceless millions who lived in the past. The lipstick or, more specifically, the photo of the lipstick, does not make that connection by itself; it serves as the contact point or occasion for our own imaginative, empathetic work. In the moment of viewing the image the viewer might picture in his mind an elderly woman in front of a mirror applying lipstick, an image that might morph momentarily into an image of his own mother using lipstick.

The photographs in the *Mother's* series evoke for us not only Ishiuchi's mother. What we are in the presence of here is Ishiuchi's experience of the loss of her mother. Following Marianne Hirsch (2001), there is a key distinction to be made between memory and what she terms 'postmemory'. Writing about the ways in which the Jewish Holocaust is remembered, Hirsch (2001: 9) makes what may seem an obvious point that the experience of actual recollection is available only to the survivors of the Holocaust. For those who come after, including the 'second generation', the Holocaust can only be available to us only via acts of representation, projection and creation. The usefulness of this distinction lies in its drawing our attention to the ways in which these acts facilitate our 'identification with the victim or witness of trauma' (Hirsch 2001: 10). To take the discussion back to Miyako Ishiuchi and her *Mother's* series, Ishiuchi has access both to her recollection of her mother and to her mother's personal effects which serve as contact points to her mother's person. We the viewers only have the personal effects whose 'effect' is amplified by the art of Ishiuchi's photography. One could say that the genius of her photography is that it somehow heightens the tangibility of the objects and their ability to function as a gateway to the intangible (the humanity of Ishiuchi's dead mother).

The archaeological dimension of Ishiuchi's project seems clear. Why is it, though, that we archaeologists seem mostly unable through our 'art' to evoke the individual humanity of the makers, owners and users of the artefacts we handle? How is it that an Aboriginal person in western New South Wales can pick up a stone artefact and sense the spirit of her ancestors simply by rubbing it over her skin (Harrison 2004: 199)? The answer seems to lie in a whole tradition of Western science that has worked to exclude from the act of science the subjectivity of the scientist (Latour 1993). Instead of a 'feeling' archaeology we have the cold hand of an archaeology that cannot make the connection between our lives and past lives.

How different is what I am characterising here as an unfeeling archaeology from antiquarianism, that discourse on the material past in which old objects are an end in themselves rather than a window on past lives? In the eyes of Australia's Aboriginal people the distinction seems hardly to matter. Many Aboriginal people appear to find the spectacle of archaeologists researching their ancestors' remains as offensive as the collection of these remains by the antiquarian 'body hunters' of the nineteenth and early twentieth centuries. Many Aboriginal people also seem as opposed to archaeologists collecting and studying their ancestors' artefacts as they are to the collection and studying of ancestral skeletal remains. There appears to be something especially galling for Indigenous minorities in the spectacle of their colonisers, having taken their land and the lives of so many of their people, now turning to appropriate their ancestors' remains and the stone artefacts that their ancestors left lying on the ground. This is not to say that Aboriginal people would never engage in archaeology – Aboriginal people in some areas work alongside white archaeologists in site assessments and salvage surveys and excavations. The point, here, though is precisely that they are working alongside them. It is no longer a matter of white people interfering with Aboriginal sites in an uncondoned manner.

There is a parallel with natural history in much of the early antiquarian collecting, in the way that Aboriginal graves and stone artefact sites were often treated as if they were naturally occurring phenomena. Aboriginal skeletons were collected much the way that butterflies or rocks were collected. Little or no regard was shown for the feelings of living Aboriginal people who were the descendants or even the immediate kin of the disinterred. As Tom Griffiths (1996) shows in his classic study of antiquarian collecting in Victoria, collectors of Aboriginal stone artefacts naturalised their 'quarry' in the same manner as did the collectors of Aboriginal skeletons (often it was the same people collecting both). In the context of frontier violence, mounted police and posses of white settlers hunted Aboriginal people down and killed or imprisoned them. The artefact collectors to some extent mimicked hunting behaviour:

> ... they talked of 'collecting grounds', 'stamping grounds' and 'beats'. They wrote of their 'hunting' and 'flinting', they boasted of 'pickings', of 'browsing over campsites', of 'bringing back quite a useful bag', of joyfully discovering virgin sites. They moved alertly across the landscape seeking their prey.
>
> (Griffiths 1996: 19)

We white archaeologists can and do lament and disown this history. The problem is that to some degree it owns us. It taints our practice in the eyes of many Aboriginal people. What characterises natural history collecting, antiquarian artefact hunting and grave robbing is a 'disconnect': an absence of an empathetic inter-human relationship between the collector in the present and the person in the past.

While archaeologists now treat Aboriginal artefacts with a certain respect that would not have been evident in the 1950s or 1960s we still, for the most part, do not approach them with feeling. It is difficult to differentiate the tone of most archaeological reports and publications on stone technology from that of, say, geological or botanical writing. There is little or no sense of a common humanity between the writer and the past lives that the artefacts represent. The archaeology of Aboriginal Australia is still primarily focused on the material-tangible, which is to say with objects and the inferences that can be made from them rather than with objects as corporeal extensions of past people.

For Aboriginal people it seems somewhat the opposite. The intangible dominates the tangible. They seem to take for granted that things are not just things. They appear to feel a moral force of responsibility for and a kinship with ancestors whose presence is intimated in surviving things and places. This represents more than just a difference in emphasis on the intangible over the tangible. It represents, I suggest, a radical alternative to conventional Western heritage practice.

Conclusions

The responsibilities that come with adulthood in Indigenous societies appear to include a responsibility to one's ancestors, an ethic that resonates with the efforts of villagers in Central Vietnam to bring peace to the 'grievous dead'. Both are indicative of a more encompassing definition of society or community than is current in the West, one that is inclusive of past generations, even those belonging to the deep past.

It may be worthwhile for those archaeologists with an interest in heritage to reflect on the practice of ancestor worship, the English term for a field of cultural action that remains a dynamic ingredient of society in East and Southeast Asia (for example, Janelli and Janelli 1992; Chambert-Loir and Reid 2002; Faure 2007). I do not mean the various specifics of ancestor worship in these societies but rather the general perspective provided of societies in which people move through daily life with an encompassing sense of relationship to past as well as present generations, one based on the principle that social agency does not end with death and that previous generations have effective presence in the landscape of contemporary everyday life. Clearly this spiritual connectivity is not available to those of us who are non-believers, those of us for instance who are secular modernists. The possibility exists, though, of a cosmopolitan practice of archaeology (Meskell in press) in which archaeologists do their work in a spirit of kinship with global others. If cosmopolitanism can be described as, 'living at home abroad or abroad at home – ways of inhabiting multiple places at once' (Pollock et al. 2002: 11), then a cosmopolitan heritage practice might be one that expands the community of the present to include the community of the past. The 'lateral' connectivity entailed in this cosmopolitanism is not possible, I suggest, without a comparable ability to connect 'vertically' with the community of past others. How, for example, would an archaeologist or heritage practitioner establish a genuine, equitable relationship with a local Thai community as a preliminary to the investigation or conservation of their material past without, by extension, being brought into relationship with the supernatural force that animates their old objects, sites and landscapes (Byrne in press)? Or, again, how can we engage equitably with Aboriginal Australians without being brought into the theatre of their ancestral landscape in which things are not just things?

To conclude on an optimistic note, I predict there will be a growing acceptance in our professions that most people in the world relate to the material past via their emotions, their imaginations, their belief in the supernatural and in the immanence of ancestors. In heritage practice it will come partly via the realisation that conservation solutions that fail to mesh with local beliefs and practices are not solutions at all. It will come, in other words, when authoritarian conservation is rejected as morally unsustainable. We cannot look to UNESCO for leadership here, mired as it appears to be in its own fantasies of universal value. It will come from below rather than above, from people working locally.

In this chapter I have been more concerned with the way that places become intangible than with intangible heritage as defined by the 2003 Convention. Rather than following UNESCO's injunction to go forth to record and conserve intangible heritage (the last thing we need is more of the mass work of archaeologists and heritage professionals) I believe we would be better employed, first, in examining the politics of visibility in the production of heritage and, second, in reconnecting emotionally to the past via the traces we already have recorded.

A good deal of the chapter has been devoted to mass graves and other traces of Cold War violence. The emergence in the last decades of an archaeology of the contemporary past (Buchli and Lucas 2001) provides grounds for optimism. Archaeology, with its increasing interest in the traces of recent events, will not stop state violence but it can give new forensic visibility to deeds that may formerly have escaped notice. Combined with the work of scholars in other fields, such as Kwon (2006) with his remarkable examination of the anthropology of death and grieving in the aftermath of the Vietnam War, there is the potential for a more intimate, finely focused appreciation of how disaster is experienced locally and 'on the ground'. Which is where heritage practice, like archaeology, properly belongs.

Bibliography

Beazley, O.B. (2006) *Drawing a Line Around a Shadow?* Including associative, intangible heritage values on the World Heritage List. PhD thesis, Australian National University.

Bosco, F.J. (2004) 'Human rights politics and scaled performances of memory: conflicts among the *Madres de Plaza de Mayo* in Argentina', *Social and Cultural Geography*, 5(3): 381–402.

Brown, M.F. (2003) *Safeguarding the Intangible*. Available online at: http://www.culturalpolicy. org/commons/comment-print.cfm?ID=12 (Accessed 4 September 2007).

Buchli, V. and Lucas G. (eds) (2001) *Archaeologies of the Contemporary Past*, London: Routledge.

Byrne, D. (1995) 'Buddhist stupa and Thai social practice', *World Archaeology*, 27(2): 266–81.

—— (2003a) 'The ethos of return: erasure and reinstatement of Aboriginal visibility in the Australian historical landscape', *Historical Archaeology*, 37(1): 73–86.

—— (2003b) 'Nervous landscapes: race and space in Australia', *Journal of Social Archaeology*, 3 (2): 169–93.

—— (2007) *Surface Collection: Archaeological Travels in Southeast Asia*, Lanham, MD: AltaMira.

—— (2008) 'Heritage conservation as social action', in G. Fairclough, R. Harrison, J. Jameson and J. Scholfield (eds), *The Heritage Reader*, London: Routledge.

—— (in press) 'Archaeology and the fortress of rationality', in L. Meskell (ed.), *Cosmopolitan Archaeologies*, Durham NC: Duke University Press.

Byrne, D. and Nugent, M. (2004) *Mapping Attachment: A Spatial Approach to Post-contact Heritage*, Sydney: Department of Environmental and Conservation NSW. Available online at: http://www.nationalparks.nsw.gov.au/pdfs/mapping_attachment_part_1.pdf (Accessed 4 September 2007).

Chambert-Loir, H. and Reid A. (2002) *The Potent Dead: Ancestors, Saints and Heroes in Contemporary Indonesia*, Honolulu: University of Hawai'i Press.

Chandler, D. (1999) *Voices from S-21: Terror and History Inside Pol Pot's Secret Prison*, Berkeley: University of California Press.

Cribb, R. (ed.) (1990a) *The Indonesian Killings, 1965–1966*, Melbourne: Centre of Southeast Asian Studies, Monash University.

—— (1990b) 'Editor's introduction', in R. Cribb (ed.), *The Indonesian Killings, 1965–1966*, Melbourne: Centre of Southeast Asian Studies, Monash University.

Crossland, Z. (2002) 'Violent spaces: conflict over the reappearance of Argentina's disappeared', in J. Schofield, W.G. Johnson and C.M. Beck (eds), *Matériel Culture: the Archaeology of Twentieth Century Conflict*, London: Routledge.

de Certeau, M. (1984) *The Practice of Everyday Life*, trans. from the French by S.F. Rendall, Berkeley: University of California Press.

Faure, D. (2007) *Emperor and Ancestor: State and Lineage in South China*, Stanford: Stanford University Press.

Frazier, L.J. (1999) '"Subverted memories": countermourning as political action in Chile', in M. Bal, J. Crewe and L. Sprizer (eds), *Acts of Memory: Cultural Recall in the Present*, Hanover, NH: University Press of New England.

Gonçalves, A. and J. Deacon (2003) *General Report of the Scientific Symposium on 'Place – Memory – Meaning': Preserving Intangible Values in Monuments and Sites*. Available online at: http://www.international.icomos.org/victoriafalls2003/finalreport-rapporteurs.pdf (Accessed 4 September 2007).

Goodall, H. (1996) *Invasion to Embassy: Land in Aboriginal Politics in New South Wales, 1770–1972*, Sydney: Allen and Unwin.

Griffiths, T. (1996) *Hunters and Collectors: The Antiquarian Imagination in Australia*, Cambridge: Cambridge University Press.

Hamilakis, Y. (2002) 'The past as oral history: towards an archaeology of the senses', in Y. Hamilakis, M. Pluciennik and S. Tarlow (eds), *Thinking Through the Body: Archaeologies of Corporeality*, New York: Kluwer Academic.

Harrison, R. (2004) *Shared Landscapes: Archaeologies of Attachment and the Pastoral Industry in New South Wales*, Sydney: Department of Environment and Conservation (NSW) and University of New South Wales Press.

Hirsch, M. (2001) 'Surviving images: holocaust photographs and the work of postmemory', *The Yale Journal of Criticism*, 14(1): 5–37.

Huyssen, A. (1999) 'Monumental seduction', in M. Bal, J. Crewe and L. Sprizer (eds), *Acts of Memory: Cultural Recall in the Present*, Hanover NH: University Press of New England.

Inglis, K.S. (1998) *Sacred Places: War Memorials in the Australian Landscape*, Melbourne: Melbourne University Press.

Itoi, K. (2007) 'Photography: a mother's close up', *Newsweek*, June. Available online at: http://www.msnbc.msn.com/id/8185491/site/newsweek/ (Accessed 5 September 2007).

Janelli, R. and Janelli, D. (1992) *Ancestor Worship and Korean Society*, Stanford: Stanford University Press.

Kwon, H. (2006) *After the Massacre: Commemoration and Consolation in Ha My and My Lai*, Berkeley: University of California Press.

—— (2007) 'Anatomy of US and South Korean massacres in the Vietnamese Year of the Monkey', *Japan Focus*. Available online at: http://japanfocus.org/products/details/2451 (Accessed 21 June 2007).

Latour, B. (1993) *We Have Never Been Modern*, Cambridge, MA: Harvard University Press.

Lewis, N. (1995) *An Empire of the East*, London: Picador.

McKie, R. (1969) *Bali*, Sydney: Angus and Robertson.

Merridale, C. (1996) 'Death and memory in modern Russia', *History Workshop Journal*, 42: 1–18.

Meskell, L. (2002) 'Negative heritage and past mastering in archaeology', *Anthropological Quarterly*, 75(3): 557–74.

—— (ed.) (in press) *Cosmopolitan Archaeologies*, Durham NC: Duke University Press.

Mirsky, J. (1997) 'China: the defining moment,' *The New York Review of Books*, 44(1): 33–6.

Mueggler, E. (1998) 'A carceral regime: violence and social memory in Southwest China', *Cultural Anthropology*, 13(2): 167–92.

Mydans, S. (1997) 'A Cambodian's tale: behind the lens, darkly', *International Herald Tribune*, 27–28 October.

Ness, S.A. (2005) 'Tourism-terrorism: the landscaping of consumption and the darker side of place', *American Anthropologist*, 32(1): 118–40.

Pollock. S., Bhabha, H.K., Breckenridge, C.A. and Chakrabarty, D. (2002) 'Cosmopolitanisms', in C.A. Breckenridge, S. Pollock, H.K. Bhanha and D. Chakrabarty (eds), *Cosmopolitanism*, Durham NC: Duke University Press.

Povinelli, E.A. (2002) *The Cunning of Recognition*, Durham NC: Duke University Press.

Read, P. (1984) '"Breaking up the camps entirely": the dispersal policy in Wiradjuri country 1909–29', *Aboriginal History*, 8(1): 45–55.

Reyolds, H. (1987) *Frontier*, Sydney: Allen and Unwin.

Robinson, G. (1995) *The Dark Side of Paradise: Political Violence in Bali*, Ithaca N.Y.: Cornell University Press.

Smith, L. (2006) *Uses of Heritage*, London: Routledge.

Stoler, A.L. (2002) 'On the uses and abuses of the past in Indonesia', *Asia Survey* 42(4): 642–50.

Taussig, M. (1992) *The Nervous System*, New York: Routledge.

Tumarkin, M. (2005) *Traumascapes*, Melbourne: Melbourne University Press.

UNESCO (2003) *Convention for the Safeguarding of Intangible Cultural Heritage*.

Vickers, A. (1989) *Bali, a Paradise Created*, Ringwood, Victoria: Penguin.

Waterson, R. (1990) *The Living House*, Singapore: Oxford University Press.

Winter, J. (1995) *Sites of Memory, Sites of Mourning: The Great War in European Cultural History*, Cambridge: Cambridge University Press.

Chapter 13

Heritage between economy and politics

An assessment from the perspective of cultural anthropology

Regina Bendix

In the 1990s, a critical cultural historian could exclaim, with considerable frustration, 'Suddenly, cultural heritage is everywhere' (Lowenthal 1996: ix). Since then, scholarship on heritage practices has enjoyed a boom of its own. It is as difficult to categorise the scholarship about it as to comprehend the phenomenon: constitution, use, evaluation, and critique of cultural heritage intertwine in scholarly discourse as much as they do in heritage itself. Thus the 2003 volume *Rethinking Heritage*, edited by Robert Shaman Peckham, assembles contributions from geography, history and art history, landscape planning and philology. This hybrid composition signals that heritage concerns everyone, from the tourism expert to the philosopher of late modernity. Each grouping of practitioners and experts harbours its own conception of heritage; their expectations seldom harmonise with one another. In his introduction, Peckham tries to simplify the range of meanings as follows:

> For most people today 'heritage' carries two related sets of meanings. On the one hand, it is associated with tourism and with sites of historical interest that have been preserved for the nation. Heritage designates those institutions involved in the celebration, management and maintenance of material objects, landscapes, monuments and buildings that reflect the nation's past. On the other hand, it is used to describe a set of shared values and collective memories; it betokens inherited customs and a sense of accumulated communal experiences that are construed as a 'birthright' and are expressed in distinct languages and through other cultural performances.
>
> (Peckham 2003: 1)

The two poles of material and intangible goods entail obligations of preservation, on the one hand, and on the other hand a spectrum of emotions from sentimental affection all the way to aggressively political, collective (mis-)appropriation – which are both consequence and cause of cultural heritage. The consequences are evident in new institutions, expertise and professional profiles; the causes bear witness to seemingly insurmountable problems of group-specific problems and anxieties. The fear of loss, Peckham argues, is what gives rise to instruments of honouring and preserving (Peckham 2003: 4–5). Yet preservation always also entails selection. Not everything is honoured; some aspects must be forgotten, so as to increase the potential for identification of what is selected. Thus, within the potential for identification carried by cultural heritage, conflict also resides: certain marginalised remains of cultural historical memory will have been excluded from the process now being named 'heritagisation'.

Within this jungle of multivalences, the ethnographic approach of cultural anthropology provides a chance to avoid vague and premature appraisals, and focuses instead on the documentation of the processes that foster as well as hinder heritagisation. When doing research in this area, scholars in disciplines such as cultural anthropology[1] often encounter arguments, often outdated, from their own disciplinary history. These have been taken up as tools to legitimise the need for one or another practice to be reclassified as intangible heritage. The very familiarity of these tools or arguments prepares anthropologists to approach heritagisation processes in a reflexive manner. Ethnographic and archival methods in cultural anthropology lead them to understand heritagisation as a cultural practice that has emerged over a long time. Heritagisation itself has tradition. Organisations and institutions have been created to legitimate this practice and to contribute to turning ever more diversified notions of heritage into a self-understood, habitual aspect of culture. Encountering outdated disciplinary knowledge as part and parcel of heritage practices has been – and for some scholars continues to be – an irritant. Alas, the time has come to move beyond ivory-towered outrage at beholding economic and political actors who know how to turn cultural segments into symbolic as well as actual capital. Heritagisation has to be understood as an ingredient of late modern lifeworlds. Understanding knowledge transfers from scholarship – as illogical as they sometimes appear – into this as well as many other cultural practices is a task for a reflexively grounded cultural anthropology.[2]

Over 40 years and more, cultural anthropologists have built a solid scholarly foundation regarding the 'discovery' of economic and political value-added practices of cultural good (Hann 2004: 293; Kasten 2004). The German debate on *Folklorismus*, which began in 1960, continued unabated for several decades (Bausinger 1988; Bendix 1988). Tradition was unmasked as a phenomenon of invention requiring actors and interests (Hobsbawm and Ranger 1983; Johler 2000). The concept of authenticity, so central to nomination processes in the heritage realm, has been thoroughly deconstructed (Bendix 1997; Seidenspinner 2006). Finally, cultural anthropology has acquired a deep awareness of the interdependence of cultural scholarship, nation-building, and the processes of cultivating symbolic cultural capital. Thereby ethnographic work has acquired a reflexivity, disciplinary modesty and diplomacy which will be almost indispensable in taking on heritagisation as a cultural practice – even more so with intangible manifestations, given their naturally more vague contours requiring of actors far more determination in making their case. At the same time, interdisciplinary cooperation remains equally vital for cultural anthropology, for declaring one bit of culture to be heritage opens economic and legal dimensions (Huber 2005: 59 n. 42). Here I present questions and potential lines of inquiry to address these dimensions, based on empirical research with heritage practices in late modern lifeworlds.[3]

Cultural heritage does not exist, it is made. From the warp and weft of habitual practices and everyday experience – the changeable fabric of action and meaning that anthropologists call 'culture' – actors choose privileged excerpts and imbue them with status and value. Motivations and goals may differ, but the effort to ennoble remains the same. Cultural heritage thus represents the opposite of what Michael Herzfeld terms cultural intimacy, those cultural peculiarities that actors seek to hide from outsiders (Herzfeld 2005). The most familiar aspects of cultural workings may be considered problematic or morally compromising, but in their negative aesthetics, unmentioned in any tourism brochures, they nonetheless contribute to everyday life. To understand processes of heritagisation, cultural anthropology pursues two directions of empirical inquiry. The ethnographic gaze will focus first on the actors who generate these processes, exploring their intentions; second, on the specific shape of the value-added mechanism: how the processes are linked to existing forms of everyday life and how new cultural practices are introduced so as to integrate successful cultural-heritage nominations into everyday life. This kind of ethnographic knowledge production is particularly challenging, because there is a demand for such knowledge transfer from institutions like UNESCO to many international NGOs, down to regional and local cultural decision-making institutions. These agencies seek information about the potential 'heritage' itself as much as about the political, legal and economic consequences that heritagisation might have. Ethnographic and cultural historical case studies are particularly pertinent as answers: only such micro approaches, in fact, can properly reveal the local specificity of a global heritage regime.

The shaping of heritage goods

The term *heritage* is both broader and more porous than the older terms used to designate cultural 'inheritance'. In English, the phonemic difference between 'heredity' and 'heritage' steps audibly away from the precise biological notion of succession; it opens up the breadth of all that might potentially be included in cultural heritage, as well as all those who might potentially sun themselves in heritage's rays (Bendix 2000: 37–9). On the global stage of heritage processes, the term broadens further with UNESCO's decision to add Intangible Cultural Heritage to its concern for natural and material heritages.

The spectrum of things with heritage potential in the realm of 'culture' has unfolded over the past three to four centuries on two axes – a social and a temporal one. Initially, value and need for protection was largely bestowed on built monuments of high-cultural or upper-class provenience. The material culture of a nation's dominant ethnic groups could vie for status. Then, testimonies of industrial and working class culture also came to earn the title heritage. While the social axis broadened, the span of passed time that would qualify something to enter the realm of heritage decreased. Even as far back as the periods when the arguments permeating the discourse on cultural heritage were taking shape, this temporal compression is noticeable. The Renaissance and the Enlightenment developed an enthusiasm for classical antiquity; to this, the romantics added the cultural treasures of the Middle Ages. They did not forget classical antiquity, of course, but rather they thickened the stock of cultural patrimony, while awarding a higher value to cultural history. New institutions assisted in making this valuation a self-evident element of social life. Museums as well as preservationist associations on the one hand, innovations in the realm of legal measures on the other, contributed to the slow growth of what Barbara Kirshenblatt-Gimblett (2004) has called 'metacultural operations'. In her view, the honouring, ennobling, preserving and ultimately branding into heritage are processes located on a metalevel, sufficiently removed from self-understood habitus to gaze reflexively upon it, cull segments from it, and bestow special value on them.

Kirshenblatt-Gimblett also notes the temporal thickening in heritage processes. In coining her definition of heritage as 'a new form of cultural production of the present that takes recourse to the past' (Kirshenblatt-Gimblett 1995: 269), and in arguing that time is central to metacultural operations (Kirshenblatt-Gimblett 2004: 59), she points to the key role of the temporal axis.[4] The temporal tensions in cultural heritage matters can manifest in several layers: the non-contemporaneity of the matters and materials under discussion; the presence of things dateable to different pasts in a present- and future-oriented lifeworld; a highly differentiated awareness of history, which has become part and parcel of education and daily life. Juggling such awareness of multiple pasts is in many ways an essential ingredient of being and feeling modern. In our concern to honour cultural pasts, we are reaching for phenomena that are younger and younger. One might even argue that in the case of some cultural innovations, their heritagisation is contemporaneous with their unfolding in daily life.

A case in point is digital cultural heritage. Proponents of this initiative claim, with justification, that the first digital cultural and knowledge achievements are threatened by rapid technological change unless measures are taken to protect and preserve the technologies necessary to access them

(Lohmeier 2006). The success of such initiatives proves that societies today carry a strong sense that heritage preservation is relevant. Without such a nearly habitual commitment, firmly anchored in what is – through UNESCO's efforts – a worldwide mentality, a digital heritage initiative would hardly come to pass. In this case, the educational level and sophistication of digital developers must be kept in mind. Within this interest group, there is naturally also a very high awareness of the cultural ramifications of the digital revolution, coupled with a great deal of discussion, not to say dispute, over to the threat posed by commercial interests in robbing the digital realm of its cultural-commons status (Lessig 1999, 2004; Grassmück 2004).

Thus, one task cultural anthropologists face is research on how the social and temporal axes of heritagisation move ever closer together, choosing present-day cases as well as selected cases from the past. We work and write in a present where the valuing, protection, preservation and competitive evaluation of heritages, on regional to global scales, are natural or obvious; UNESCO's lists of chosen sites and practices dangle before us, an ever-tempting option for actors in the realm of cultural and economic policy-making. From such a present, we might take a look at places and moments in time where there were different, or perhaps no, regimes of comparative cultural (e-)valuation. Personal experience might serve as an example. In the small town in northern Switzerland where I was born, one of the sites considered important was an amphitheatre from Roman times; associated with it was a museum exclusively devoted to the archaeological finds from the Roman settlement. Hence I grew up within a mentality that considered any kind of find from classical antiquity to be worthy of preservation and proper historical contextualisation. Then in my early 30s, I visited a coastal town in southern Turkey, where I was astounded at the ease with which people handled the remnants of antiquity. There was an abundance of them, dating from different eras; the beach seemed positively littered with them. Houses had been constructed out of both new and antique material; the street crews refurbishing the sewage system seemed to be negotiating their way between antique foundations and more recent canal ducts requiring replacement. The sight provided me with a liberating feeling. There was so much potential cultural heritage here that its impact on local mentality was – not nil – but somehow more reasonable than what I had grown up with. In my home town, the Roman finds were one of only a very few touristic resources; people in this Turkish town, by contrast, considered their beach location and climate as their most important economic ticket, not the abundance of antique remains. Turkey certainly features on the UNESCO world heritage lists – with Troy, the old town of Istanbul or the cultural landscape of Pamukkale the most prominent examples – and the country imposes very rigorous conditions on archaeological finds. Yet the richness of its antiquities has created a quite different attitude towards heritage than what I knew from my little

Swiss hometown. There, the Roman finds are rarities and are handled
accordingly, though their quality will probably never suffice for world heritage status. Still, the power of application rhetoric should never be underestimated.

Valence/valuation and the actors bringing it forth

Segments of culture acquire cultural heritage status once particular value is
assigned to them. The predicate 'heritage' is generated from experiential
contexts and knowledges, which in turn take shape in discussions and
application dossiers, employing indicators of valence.[5] How specific actors
approach the task of such upgrading or revaluation is a further process
requiring closer anthropological study. The checklist provided by UNESCO
sets certain parameters, but in a number of points, it remains sufficiently
vague for applicants to insert arguments for their specific locality or cultural
practice. In a number of nations, the process is further aided by the fact that
expert consultants stand ready to assist in carrying an application through
evaluation and selection committees (UNESCO 2003).

Particularly relevant in heritage-making discussions appears to be the
importance accorded to the difference between image and economic value. In
practice, the two types of value overlap or even converge, yet discursively,
much is made of the difference. Thus, cultural heritage is considered to have
high social value and to be endowed with the capacity to foster positive
identification within groups or entire polities. On the global stage, this value
is further heightened. Here, cultural heritage is presented as emanating from
one particular cultural context; actors within this context are claiming cus-
todial care for it in the process of heritagisation. Yet simultaneously, they
assert that all of humanity can share the value of the ennobled piece of culture or cultural practice. Drawing on Werner Sollors' work on the tensions
between descent and consent positions in ethnic politics (Sollors 1986),
Kirshenblatt-Gimblett describes the process as follows: 'World heritage lists
arise from operations that convert selected aspects of localized descent heritage into a translocal consent heritage – the heritage of humanity'
(Kirshenblatt-Gimblett 2006: 170). Achieving and maintaining world heritage status requires economic investments – renovations, protective measures,
and so on – which are discussed only marginally. Discourse labels such costs
as moral responsibilities, naturally important to the custodianship of a world
heritage site or practice. Similarly, selection and award discussions marginalise the potential economic gains that achieving heritage status might bring
about – much as if economic considerations might besmirch or spoil the
purity of heritage. In other contexts, however, such as regional or national
decision-making bodies, the possibility of making economic use of heritage
status, particularly in touristic development, is discussed openly and positively. For example, the central German Tourism Office (*Deutsche Zentrale für*

Tourismus) is a member in the Association of German Heritage Sites and acts within it in a consulting capacity.

The prevalent dichotomisation of image and economic value in public discourse arises from the longstanding modern differentiation between 'genuine' and 'fake' heritage. The fake or inauthentic garnered its bad reputation by lacking uniqueness. The very term *inauthentic* implies a deviation from the originality and hence uniqueness of the genuine.[6] 'Uniqueness' is one of the criteria UNESCO requires for a cultural practice to be welcomed onto the list of world heritages. Quite logically, after something has achieved world heritage status, the danger of losing this very uniqueness preoccupies discussions between responsible actors and their opponents in many local and regional discussions. During the process of heritagisation, actors tend to weave authenticity/inauthenticity arguments into their presentations and documents. Once heritage status has been achieved, however, the intertwining of idealistic and economic components is unavoidable. George Yúdice has convincingly argued that the 'expediency of culture' is ultimately neither harmful nor indictable – rather, it is an unavoidable occurrence, in particular in heterogeneous societies (Yúdice 2003). From the perspective of cultural anthropology, it is interesting to witness the constant attempts to cleanly separate idealistic from economic instrumentalisations of heritage – not least because fields of cultural research collude in this tendency; at various times and purposes they themselves have reintroduced the dichotomy. There is plenty of exploratory as well as reflexive scholarship contemplating the ambiguity of cultural heritage (Csáky and Zeyringer 2000; Csáky and Sommer 2005), but efforts to document specific cases, so as to understand how individuals and communities have turned heritagisation into a cultural practice, are rare. Case-by-case ethnographic documentation is thus very useful to identify specific actors, to follow how they initiate and fight for (or against) particular value additions, and denote how they deploy knowledge transfers from cultural scholarship that is usually outdated. By screening actors' motivations and intentions, one can recognise what types of uses for potential heritage are foreseen or – after a successful nomination – how the results are absorbed and worked with.

The model behind the suggested approach can be seen in Figure 13.1. Culture, and the cultural heritage 'extracted' from it, is lodged in a field of tension generated by the agency and interests of actors in society, politics and economics. From a cultural-anthropological perspective, these three pillars are themselves components of culture at large and, like all of culture, are in a constant, dynamic process of change. In a democratic state, the three pillars cannot be clearly separated. From all three, actors have access to 'culture' and the practices constituting it. From all three, actors may attempt – in divergent ways and with variable levels of urgency – to attribute heightened aesthetic potency to a given segment or excerpt of culture so as to bring forth cultural heritage.

Society

CULTURE

CULTURAL HERITAGE

Politics   Economy

Figure 13.1 A dynamic triangle: three loci of agency producing heritage.

This schematic differentiation of potential loci of agency allows for clearer recognition on two counts:

1. The provenience of a given value-adding initiative will be made visible and put in relation to potential other loci of agency.
2. Through comparing cases from different historical moments, shifts over time in the source of value-adding initiatives will become evident.

At a different historical moment, the pillar 'society' or 'politics' might be replaced by the pillar 'belief' or the 'sacred'. While heritagisation invariably will bring all three areas of activity into contact with one another, different cases will nonetheless show different emphases.

If ennobling a cultural practice up to the status of heritage is a process of canonisation, any such process is also ultimately accompanied by an interest in utilisation. What is interesting to cultural research is the question: what type of use is made of the new value and what kind of criticism of such use is voiced, by whom, and in what specific context? A further important research direction thus concerns the dynamics between social groups – from smallest interest groups to global networks – generated by the needs and practices surrounding cultural heritage.

Interpersonal and societal consequences

Heritage allows close observation of the dynamic between economy and politics, with a focus on 'culture' as an economic good. The process of heritage nomination openly declares this good independent of both spheres; hence, it contributes to intensive discussions between opponents, users and mediators active in the discourses before and after the nomination. However, heritagisation also represents cultural practices that point to other research topics. I look at two examples: mechanisms of social control on the local, regional or even global level, and competition as a regime permeating all spheres of life.

To small-town burghers who are annoyed by urban problems – such as trash in a public park – world heritage status affords a new variable in the game of social control. A voluntary culture caretaker in Goslar, Germany, threatened to call the UNESCO branch office in Bonn to inquire whether excessive trash might not be threatening the town's heritage status (Matt 2006). It is unlikely that these little public nuisances would move UNESCO to put a tangible or intangible heritage onto the red list of threatened world heritage. However, actors on local and regional levels utilise the existence of this international red list to exert social and political control. A case in point is the heated discussion surrounding new architectural projects along the Rhine in Cologne. Had they been built, say their opponents, the urban landscape – into which the cathedral of Cologne is embedded – would have been permanently altered, thus transforming the vista included in the world heritage status of the cathedral. One of the planned buildings had already been erected when the storm broke loose; ultimately, the city decided not to build the rest of the projected structures. Thus was Cologne cathedral, having landed on the red list of endangered heritage sites in 2004, removed from it in 2006 (Kölner Dom 2006). Here as elsewhere, the successful nomination curtailed architectural development: new structures must take into account the image that is to be preserved, or else must be placed elsewhere. Given the importance of innovative architecture in urban development and design, heritage regimes put a major constraint on the system. They may even have some impact on the recruitment of patrons: individuals eager to support innovation or aesthetic transformation in urban spaces are not necessarily equally interested in supporting the stagnation encoded in heritage award policies. All through history, patronage has crucially contributed to the shaping of architectural change. Hence it would be interesting, from an anthropological perspective, to follow up on how the introduction of heritage interests and policies affects patrons as well as urban planners and architects.

More complex still is the situation surrounding the Wartburg, a castle on the UNESCO world heritage list located near Eisenach in Saxony, Germany. The site was famous long before it reached world heritage status in 1999. It was known as an interesting building with architectural traces of different epochs. It was also a pilgrimage site of sorts, as it had served as the refuge in which Martin Luther was hiding from Catholic persecution and where he translated the Bible into German. Election into the UNESCO list, however, put into question other plans in the region. An alternative energy developer had gotten permission in 1993 from the regional council to put up a chain of windmills on a stretch of land near the Wartburg. Construction was to begin in 2005. At that point, defenders of the heritage site voiced objection, arguing that windmills would dramatically alter the landscape around the Wartburg and thus might lead to a loss of its heritage status. They pointed to the economic losses that would be incurred should UNESCO withdraw its seal of approval; they also argued that for many inhabitants, there would be an emotional loss if the landscape around the Wartburg was suddenly altered through the addition of windmills. The investor, as well as local and regional politicians, argued that the region would get increased employment with the windmills and would also make an important contribution to the generation of alternative energy.

At this point, a third set of actors entered the fray. As it turned out, the piece of land in question was or is a habitat for a series of rare bird species, including an endangered type of owl. Environmental activists thus began to argue that windmills might alter the conditions so drastically that this owl would be further threatened. No studies verifying the viability of this claim had been done up to that point, but raising the spectre of the threat was sufficient ground for the Wartburg versus windmill case to enter the courts.[7] Although UNESCO has made no threat to shift the Wartburg onto its red list of endangered sites, the turmoil in Eisenach remains palpable. Signatures have been collected locally in favour of blocking all actions that might threaten the heritage status. The local press also takes sides with the Wartburg custodians; thus here, too, social control makes use of heritage policies. Economic and ecological arguments are available to all contestants in the dispute; hence, the question turns on who can make the biggest moral claim (Sander 2006). For local and regional politicians, heritage thus turns into a tricky arena indeed. It is hard to clearly separate cultural historical, economic, ecological and aesthetic arguments. Twenty years ago, castle, windmills and owls might have cohabited happily: indeed, they could have been placed together on a political platform. If the castle had been elevated to heritage status just as a monument, without making the surrounding forested landscape part of the site, the windmills might have met with less or no resistance. In the meantime, windmills have given rise to momentous arguments, not just about their impact on an ecosystem, but also about their very aesthetics. Thus, in the post-nomination situation, different mechanisms of support and punishment have to be weighed carefully.

UNESCO nominations of humanly built landscapes and of intangible practices pose considerable problems of implementation. It is a great deal easier to set in motion the restoration, maintenance, and protection of, say, a half-timbered façade than to develop a protection policy favourable to an endangered species living in a decaying ruin. The latter requires different measures from the former. The Norwegian town of Rørøs illustrates further facets of such implementation issues. Nominated already in 1980, Rørøs as an old mining town constitutes an example of industrial heritage. Here, too, but differently from Eisenach, the natural surroundings give rise to discussion. When there was still active mining in Rørøs, the surrounding woods had been cut down: timber was required for the mining process. The barren hillsides were part of the surrounding landscape that was nominated, along with the wooden housing structures of the town itself. Alas, Rørøs is now a former mining town; now the regrowth of underbrush and trees is considered problematic by some custodians of Rørøs's heritage status – whereas, of course, environmental activists are relieved to see the recovery of tree growth in the area, judging it a good sign for the health of the ground after long years of industrial work in the area (Bittlinger 2006). Similarly, heritage conservation purists oppose the securing of the town's exclusively wooden houses with fireproofing materials. Heritage regimes and the safety precautions that ought to be available to citizens clearly are at odds.

Intangible heritage also carries new concerns, which evolve into new social practices, though they may be different in timbre. The intangibility of that which has been ennobled requires – logically – mechanisms of making it tangible, so as to fully profit from the new status. This opens the question, however, of who is permitted to do so. Markus Tauschek has begun to document and analyse this development by following the carnival of Binche in Belgium (Tauschek 2007). Unlike a monument or a cultural landscape, an intangible good at first glance appears evanescent. A carnival performance thrives in performance, which in turn is carried by the (mental) competence of those who have traditionalised the practice. Yet naturally, a carnival also lives in photographs, as well as in the material culture of costumes and masks, all of which have been made amply available as highly tangible souvenirs in Binche. The carnival is celebrated not only in Binche but also in neighbouring communities; hence, the people of Binche now struggle to disallow the sale of the likeness of their major masked carnival figure in neighbouring towns. Even the nomination document is an item of material culture, which embodies the valence bestowed upon the tradition. Markus Tauschek has documented the efforts of the principal actors to load this paper document with further potency and turn it into a tangible icon of their intangible possession. As the paper document did not quite capture the enthusiasm for this ascent to world recognition, the town also produced a neon sign announcing the award – certainly not an extension intended by UNESCO, but evidence of the need to somehow rally the local population with recognisable evidence of success.

Heritagisation seeks to ennoble a given intangible practice or a tangible excerpt of culture. Actors faced with 'owning' heritage, or at least being considered the custodians of a site or an intangible practice, will, however, invariably seek to make the new status part of their everyday life, to integrate it into spheres of activity and social interaction. On the 'inside', the nobility thus wears off quite quickly. The symbolic capital inherent in heritage invites social, economic and political contestants to vie for it; heritage becomes another tool or variable in the struggles for power on local and supralocal levels of governance. It is used to add additional contours to a given lifeworld, but also to control other people. Much depends on the ways in which different interest groups take hold of the power potentially inherent in this new toy.

However, the new practice of heritagisation can also open possibilities and have an impact on extant development plans, such as in the realm of urban design, energy, or tourism. One can, therefore, not simply classify this practice as new wine in old bottles, nor is it possible, at this point, simply to reverse the cliché and call it old wine in new bottles. Careful research is necessary to understand the gradations of social control that emerge when a cultural product is transformed into a good of morally and economically enhanced valence. Kirshenblatt-Gimblett (2006) has tried to follow this process for the local-global value exchange in heritage matters. The examples sketched here seek to demonstrate the differentially lodged processes set in motion as cultural heritage gets integrated into everyday lifeworlds and contexts of action.

Heritagisation is, finally, an ideal topic to research the omnipresence of two complementary mechanisms in late modern everyday life: competition and quality control. Competition fosters innovation, production and marketing, and is thus an integral component of modern industrial development. Laws governing patenting rights, for instance, are intended to stimulate producers. If they manage to innovate, they have the opportunity to patent their invention: thus for a limited time, they have sole rights to make a profit from it. The competing variables of quality and price, guide producers and consumers contribute to the dynamic nature of the value scales within a given economy. As the world inches farther and farther into postindustrialism, the interest in broadening the dynamism of economic competition has expanded into work contexts other than (industrial) production. In a service-sector area such as sales or hotel room rental, it is not just the quality of a piece of furniture or the nature of the room that contribute to the price: it is also the quality and nature of service rendered by the sales' clerks and staff. Service behaviour is now part of market competition and has broadened the notion of quality management to include interpersonal behaviours and communicative forms. Arlie Hochschild speaks of the 'managed heart' or emotional labour (Hochschild 1983). Increasingly, everyday life is filled with competitive and evaluative processes, which in turn are coupled with quality control and scales of commendation. While there is today a lot of justified talk about a 'knowledge society' (Nowotny *et al.* 2001) and how knowledge is continuously transferred and instrumentalised in new social contexts, there is equal need to pay attention to 'evaluation society'. Regimes of quality control and evaluation bear witness to the existence of 'audit culture' (Shore 1999; Strathern 2000). The success of such regimes demonstrates how one practice-oriented branch of scholarship, business administration, has permeated social life. Strathern (2000) and Shore (1999) have examined the effects of this in higher education, but its presence in heritagisation is unmistakable. Indeed, these processes are an excellent arena for documenting and fostering a critical understanding of the nature of late modern competitive practices.

In selecting cultural sites or cultural practices as particularly valuable, actors on the heritage stage submit to the rules of competition and their consequences. The selection of cultural heritage is a relatively transparent process; the actors involved in the process are quite visible, thus it is possible to observe the mechanisms they set in motion to make the intangible tangible on the world stage, and to turn what is value-free and obvious into something of special value. This kind of transparency permits a researcher in turn to make visible the components involved in constructing a competitive piece of heritage, and to understand thereby how cultural heritage is canonised. From the vantage point of an 'evaluation society', one could see in proper proportion both small-scale powerplays around world heritage nominations and large-scale moralising and ennobling, as well as their parallel critique. These processes and acts are ultimately just extremes of an economic cultivation, here applied to the fragile resource 'culture'. Although from a cultural anthropological standpoint, the nomination and thus circumscribing of *intangible heritage* and *memory of the world* are close to absurd, they give evidence of a late modern existential order – or help-lessness? – in the face of the capitalist drive to husband all potential resources.

Heritagisation is communicated at a hyper-intensive level – which makes studying it easier for the researcher to use, for instance, the ethnography of communication as a methodological approach. Cases both respectable or simple and explosive are generally talked about in print, online, and in face-to-face settings on and off screen, as well as in growing stacks of memoranda. These media allow the examination of which regimes are being deployed; one can follow the whole spectrum of other issues, far from heritage itself, that are confirmed and achieved – or in some cases foiled or undermined – on the platform of heritage making. In the case of intangible heritage, one may discern issues of inclusion and privileged access, custodianship and benefit of scarce resources – issues, in other words, that are hard to raise on their own. For instance, an annual festivity raised to world heritage level can give rise to discussions of whether non-natives of the town should be permitted to participate in the festivity. The discussion can go both ways, depending on the strength of relevant interest groups. Some may argue that logically, someone born far away could not be part of this local inheritance, while others might argue that world heritage implies an opening up to the world, sharing the knowledge of competent festive, 'intangible' perfor-mance. Likewise, intangible knowledges have always been transported easily, certainly within the immediate environs of a purported place of origin. It is thus not surprising that tradition bearers in towns and villages located near the site of an intangible heritage manifestation seek to showcase festivities of their own that are similar. This in turn can lead to harsh efforts to delimit the freedom of regional competitors to partake of the economic boon of intangible heritage performances, or alternatively, to devise friendly schemes of variable festive dates, so as to allow competitors to profit from migrating seasonal tourists within a single region.

Anthropological attention to heritage matters entails looking at the handling of culture not only as an ideological but also as an economic resource. The role of culture in bolstering identity, thematised since the early nineteenth century, has been carried forward – or, perhaps more to the point, traditionalised – all the way into the UNESCO debates that brought forth the world heritage programmes. Yet, important though the identity factor is, especially emphasised in the moral dimensions of heritage discourses, it is the economic potential of heritage that has grown, long since, to be the primary incitement. The procedures surrounding selection and their competitive nature foster a sense that one is dealing with a finite, or at least a very limited, resource. It is crucial to try to understand the power that resides in this image of a limited reservoir of valuable excerpts of culture, as invoked in the UNESCO Convention of 2003. While many cultural anthropologists have grave reservations about the economic value-adding processes they observe, paying close heed to them is nonetheless essential, not least because economic utilisation will have repercussions on heritage's role in identity discourses.

Privileged access to a particular cultural identity resource has been defended with weapons, not mere words, in both nationalistic and religious contexts. One can postulate, as Yúdice (2003) does somewhat, that a group might also be filled with pride to land on the world heritage list. Such pride might loosen rather than tighten possessive feelings, and allow for a shared ideological ownership, as long as the economic benefits flow primarily to the privileged circle.

The UNESCO Convention is fuelled by the goodwill that was already inherent in the primary tasks UNESCO took on at its founding in 1945: 'Education, Social and Natural Science, Culture and Communication are the means to a far more ambitious goal: to build peace in the minds of man [sic]' (UNESCO 2007). Anthropology's most famous twentieth-century representative, Claude Lévi-Strauss, often a UNESCO consultant, embraced this goal also. When UNESCO celebrated its 60th anniversary in Paris on 16 November 2005, a frail Lévi-Strauss, addressing the assembled crowd, renewed his hope that mutual understanding of cultural difference might contribute to world peace. All the more important is it, then, for cultural anthropologists to study the UNESCO regimes; to follow their impact on local, regional and global actors and their interrelationships; and to uncover new webs of meaning as they arise. One need not be a heritage expert to recognise that peace is not yet forthcoming. Studying deeply the role of the economic utilisation of heritage, and the competitive and evaluative regimes associated with it, is a worthy professional goal.

Acknowledgements

Parts of this paper appeared, in German, as 'Kulturelles Erbe zwischen Wirtschaft und Politik', in Dorothee Hemme, Markus Tauschek and Regina

Bendix (eds), *Prädikat Heritage: Wertschöpfung aus kulturellen Ressourcen*, Münster: LIT, 2007, pp. 337–56. Thanks go to the co-editors of that volume who assist in maintaining a lively discourse on matters of heritage at our institute through their ongoing research, and to Lee Haring for his helpful comments on this paper.

Notes

1 In Europe, cultural anthropology figures under many names, in part shaped by national scholarly histories, in part by efforts to leave behind a compromised label of a field. In Germany, for instance, one jokingly speaks of the 'field of many names' when referring to what was once *Volkskunde*; it is now variously called *Kulturanthropologie*, *Europäische Ethnologie*, *Empirische Kulturwissenschaft*, *Populäre Kulturen*, *Vergleichende Kulturwissenschaft*. In Scandinavia and the Baltics, one finds for the same field the term *Ethnology* (Sweden) or *Cultural History* (Norway) or *Folklore* (Finland, Estonia). In the USA, some cynics speak of their field in the manner of the popstar Prince as 'the field formerly known as folklore' – although a new name thus far does not exist. What is common to this set of names is that scholars are generally more concerned with (predominantly Western) nation-states. Naturally, social anthropology or (extra-European) ethnology is at present equally involved in the research on cultural heritage – uncovering perhaps more heavily colonial ideologies than national or ethnic ones. The present essay draws from literature of both lineages, but for simplicity's sake employs the label cultural anthropology or simply anthropology.

2 Humanities scholars have always had a much harder time than do natural scientists, coming to terms with the fact that their insights do find users and applications in societies. From some of the latter areas of research, polities expect useful results – such as medicine, physics, chemistry or biology. In these areas, knowledge transfer is secured and accepted through agents and processes of professionalisations (cf. Bendix and Welz 2002: 23–6). But the traditional self-image of the humanities is hermeneutically founded, whereby 'culture' is understood as a complex whole that must be understood, but not actively shaped by scholars. An engineer will not feel remorse for designing a new bridge on the basis of new insights from physics. But aside from longstanding areas of scholarly practice, such as the museum, knowledge transfers from the humanities into the public sphere are often hotly debated. Economic actors thus rarely find professionalised brokers of cultural scholarship. Hence processes of adding economic value to tangible and intangible cultural goods have only turned into a hotly debated area in the late twentieth century, even though such processes can arguably be traced back 300 years and more.

3 Some of the case material was compiled in a seminar I taught on 'cultural heritage between economics and politics' at the University of Göttingen in 2006. Thanks are due to the participants who have given permission to cite from their research papers.

4 One might debate, however, whether it really is a 'new' form. As indicated above, the mechanisms of cultural production evident in heritagisation build on a genealogy of practices valorising culture. See Tauschek (2007) and Hemme (2007).

5 In her first theses on heritage, Kirshenblatt-Gimblett spoke of heritage as a 'value added industry' (Kirshenblatt-Gimblett 1995: 370).

6 Lionel Trilling's essay *Sincerity and Authenticity* (1971) is a useful rediscovery for anyone working with heritage, as is Benjamin's (1968) well-known 'Work of Art in the Age of Mechanical Reproduction'. For a consideration of the key place of authenticity discourses in cultural research, see Bendix (1997).

7 At this writing (spring 2008), the case is still pending.

References

Bausinger, H. (1988) 'Da Capo: Folklorismus', in A. Lehmann and A. Kuntz (eds), *Sichtweisen der Volkskunde. Zur Geschichte und Forschungspraxis einer Disziplin*, Berlin: D. Reimer.

Bendix, R. (1988) 'Folklorism, the challenge of a concept', *International Folklore Review*, 6:5–15.

—— (1997) *In Search of Authenticity: The Formation of Folklore Studies*, Madison: University of Wisconsin Press.

—— (2000) 'Heredity, hybridity and heritage from one fin-de-siecle to the next', in J. Pertti (ed.), *Folklore, Heritage Politics and Ethnic Diversity, a Festschrift for Barbro Klein*, Antonen, Botkyrka (Sweden): Multicultural Centre.

Bendix, R. and Welz, G. (2002) *Kulturwissenschaft und Öffentlichkeit*, Frankfurt: Institut für Kulturanthropologie und Europäische Ethnologie.

Benjamin, W. (1968) 'The work of art in the age of mechanical reproduction', in H. Arendt (ed.), trans. H. Zohn, *Illuminations*, New York: Schocken Books.

Bittlinger, L. (2006) 'UNESCO Weltkulturerbe in Norwegen: das Beispiel Roros', Unpublished essay, Institute for Cultural Anthropology/European Ethnology, University of Göttingen.

Csáky, M. and Sommer, M. (eds) (2005) *Kulturerbe Als Soziale Praxis*. Gedächtnis – Erinnerung – Identität, Bd. 6, Innsbruck.

Csáky, M. and Zeyringer, K. (eds) (2000) *Ambivalenz Des Kulturellen Erbes: Vielfachcodierung Des Historischen Gedächtnisses*, Innsbruck: Studien Verlag.

Grassmück, V. (2004) *Freie Software Zwischen Privat-und Gemeineigentum*, Bonn: Bundeszentrale für politische Bildung.

Hann, C. (2004) 'Epilogue: The cartography of copyright cultures versus the proliferation of public properties', in E. Kasten (ed.), *People and the Land: Pathways to Reform in Post-Soviet Siberia*, Berlin: D. Riemer.

Hemme, D. (2007) 'Weltmarke Grimm' – Anmerkungen zum Umgang mit der Ernnung der Grimmschen Kinder – und Hausmärchen zum 'Memory of the World', in D. Hemme, M. Tauschek and R. Bendix (eds), *Prädikat 'Heritage'. Wertschöpfungen Aus Kulturellen Ressourcen*, Münster: Waxmann.

Herzfeld, M. (2005) *Cultural Intimacy: Social Poetics in the Nation-State*, Second Edition, New York: Routledge.

Hobsbawm, E. and Ranger, T. (eds) (1983) *The Invention of Tradition*, Cambridge: Cambridge University Press.

Hochschild, A.R. (1983) *The Managed Heart: Commercialization of Human Feeling*, Berkeley: University of California Press.

Huber, B. (2005) 'Open-source Software und kulturelles Erbe indigener Bevölkerung zwischen Markt und alternativer Rationalität – Von der Anthropologie des Rechtes zu einer Anthropologie als Basis des Rechtes', in M. Seifert and W. Helm (eds), *Recht und Religion Im Alltagsleben: Perspektiven der Kulturforschung*, Passau: Dietmar Klinger.

Johler, R. (2000) *Die Formierung eines Brauches: der Funken-und Holepfannsonntag: Studien aus Vorarlberg, Liechtenstein, Tirol, Südtirol und dem Trentino*, Wien: Selbstverlag des Instituts für Europäische Ethnologie.

Kasten, E. (ed.) (2004) *Properties of Culture – Culture as Property. Pathways to Reform in Post-Soviet Siberia*, Berlin: D. Riemer.

Kirshenblatt-Gimblett, B. (1995) 'Theorizing heritage', *Ethnomusicology*, 39:367–80.

—— (2004) 'Intangible heritage as metacultural production', *Museum*, 56(1–2):52–65.

—— (2006) 'World heritage and cultural economics', in I. Karp, C.A. Kratz, L. Szwaja, T. Ybarra-Frausto, G. Buntinx, B. Kirshenblatt-Gimblett and C. Rassool (eds), *Museum*

Frictions: Public Cultures/Global Transformations, Durham, North Carolina: Duke University Press.

Kölner Dom (2006) *Kölner Dom*. Available online at: http://de.wikipedia.org/wiki/K%C3% B6lner_Dom (Accessed 26 October 2006).

Lessig, L. (1999) *Code and Other Laws of Cyberspace*, New York: Basic Books.

——(2004) *Free Culture: How Big Media Uses Technology and the Law to Lock Down Culture and Control Creativity*, New York: Penguin Press.

Lohmeier, F. (2006) 'Kulturelles Erbe in der Informationsgesellschaft: Aktivitäten zum Schutz von digitalem Kulturerbe und ihre Folgen für den Alltag', unpublished seminar paper. University of Göttingen, Institute for Cultural Anthropology/European Ethnology.

Lowenthal, D. (1996) *Possessed by the Past: The Heritage Crusade and the Spoils of History*, New York: The Free Press.

Matt, K. (2006) 'Ehrenamt Im Bereich Welterbe Am Beispiel der Stadt Goslar', seminar paper. Institute for Cultural Anthropology/European Ethnology, University of Göttingen.

Nowotny, H., Scott, P. and Gibbons, M. (2001) *Rethinking Science: Knowledge and the Public*, Oxford: Blackwell.

Peckham, R.S. (2003) 'Introduction: the politics of heritage and public culture', in R.S. Peckham (ed.), *Rethinking Heritage. Cultures and Politics in Europe*, London: I. B. Tauris.

Sander, S. (2006) 'Weltkulturerbe Wartburg Kontra Windradbau. Über die Unvereinbarkeit von Wirtschaft und Kultur Am Beispiel der Wartburg bei Eisenach', unpublished seminar paper. Institute for Cultural Anthropology/European Ethnology, University of Göttingen.

Seidenspinner, W. (2006) 'Authentizität: Kulturanthropologisch-erinnerungskundliche Annäherungen an ein zentrales Wissenschaftskonzept im Blick auf das Weltkulturerbe', *Volkskunde in Rheinland-Pfalz*, 20:5–39.

Shore, C. (1999) 'Audit cultures and anthropology: neoliberalism in British higher education', *Journal of the Royal Anthropological Institute*, 5:557–76.

Sollors, W. (1986) *Beyond Ethnicity: Consent and Descent in American Culture*, New York: Oxford University Press.

Strathern, M. (2000) *Audit Cultures: Anthropological Studies in Accountability, Ethics, and the Academy*, London: Routledge.

Tauschek, M. 'Plus Oultre' – Welterbe und Kein Ende? Zum Beispiel Binche', in D. Hemme, M. Tauschek and R. Bendix (eds), *Prädikat 'Heritage'. Wertschöpfungen aus kulturellen Ressourcen*, Münster: Waxmann.

Trilling, L. (1971) *Sincerity and Authenticity*, Cambridge, MA: Harvard University Press.

UNESCO (2003) *Third Session of the Intergovernmental Meeting of Experts on the Preliminary Draft Convention for the Safeguarding of the Intangible Cultural Heritage*. Available online at: http://unesdoc.unesco.org/images/0013/001312/131274e.pdf (Accessed 21 March 2008).

—— (2007) *About UNESCO*. Available online at: http://portal.unesco.org/en/ev.php-URL_ID = 3328&URL_DO=DO_TOPIC&URL_SECTION=201.html (Accessed 9 May 2008).

Yüdice, G. (2003) *The Expediency of Culture: Uses of Culture in the Global Era*, Durham: Duke University Press.

Chapter 14

Intangible heritage in the United Kingdom

The dark side of enlightenment?

Frank Hassard

Introduction

The concept of intangible heritage has become the focus of international discussion, which has been augmented by UNESCO and reflects growing concerns about the cultural impact of economic, technological and political forces associated with globalisation. However, its impact on heritage practice in the UK remains limited, due in part to a lack of understanding of the concept and its subsequent lack of formal recognition. It is also due to a prevailing vision of cultural inheritance as residing solely in the *materiality* of the past – tangible heritage; a vision largely fashioned by the scientific/ technical and political-institutional sectors of the West.

This chapter explores the idea of intangible heritage – as developed by UNESCO – and considers how this relates to tangible heritage in the UK. It is argued that these recent developments concerning the 'intangible' in many ways replicate issues that first emerged in the UK in the nineteenth century around the restoration of architecture that led to the founding of the modern Heritage Preservation Movement. This chapter considers how this debate stemmed from contrasting views of the past – one rooted in religion and the other founded on an emerging modern science – in order to reveal the UK's historical trajectory with respect to these two competing paradigmatic domains. It is intended that this will provide greater understanding of this recent recovery of the idea of intangible heritage, and all that this implies in the context of world culture today.

This chapter recommends, finally, that the UK ratify the *UNESCO Convention for the Safeguarding of the Intangible Cultural Heritage* (2003), which in many ways embraces the ideas first expressed in the nineteenth century, but which (despite this) have not been formally recognised in the UK.

Prelude to an era

The question of how far religion has historically shaped the social ordering of knowledge and, by extension, the methodological tools through which cultural inheritance is understood, is an alluring one for anyone considering the relationship between tangible and intangible heritage. It is a question that has tended to be overlooked by a prevailing 'authorised' vision of cultural inheritance which endorses, for the most part, an essentially materialist view of the past in preference to one grounded in 'living' culture – and which might otherwise be embodied today in the concept of intangible heritage (Hassard 2006: 283–5; 2007: 7–8). The European Church Reforms of the 1500s, for example, are important to this discussion because they represent a key turning point in terms of succeeding intellectual developments that shaped European culture. For instance, the period of so-called 'Enlightenment', which can be understood as part of the 'Great Transformation' of modernity – a phrase used to describe the cultural impact of political and economic changes that occurred in Europe from about 1700 to about 1900 (Polanyi [1944] 2002).

The Protestant Reformation set out to reform the Catholic Church of Western Europe. This historic debate is too complex to discuss in detail here but, in its elementary form, disparity centred on the interpretation and re-inscription of the Bible, which had an important impact on how European culture subsequently developed. Essentially, the Roman Catholic view held that the Bible could only be understood through the lens of a tradition of understanding and that its true meaning was not immediately evident to the individual 'lay' reader. The Reformers challenged this view by asserting that 'truth' *was* accessible to the contemporary reader, and that the recovery of the original 'authentic' message as the basis for faith and doctrine could, as a result, be developed *sola scriptura* without reference to tradition (Troeltsch 1912: 62–5; Dawson 1961: 36–43).

The bipolarity between 'continuity' (based on a tradition of understanding) and 'renewal' (augmented by 're-visiting' scripture and omitting tradition) is crucial to understanding the dualistic nature of Western thought and the nature of the society that was to develop in Europe and the West subsequent to these developments. The effect of this transition was widespread and can be understood as reflecting a new hermeneutical consciousness (Gadamer 1975: 146–55) whose emphasis on systematic observation and rational explanation effectively became the basis of modern intellectualism. The Enlightenment, for example, which was directed primarily against the religious tradition of Christianity, propagated free enquiry into the world of ideas and laid the foundations of a new autonomous scientific paradigm that pervaded all aspects of modern society (Shackleton 1969: 259–78; Gadamer 1975: 240–53; Rolston Saul 1992: 38–76).

The search for original meaning became a guiding metaphor in the new era; for example, in the physical sciences Newtonian mechanics searched for *originary* laws, while Darwin searched for *originary* species. The human sciences followed; for example, in politics, economics, history and later the social sciences. Adam Smith's *Wealth of Nations*, first published in 1776, for instance, provided a comprehensive analysis of the fundamental institutions of industrial society and did much to define the new political economy of the time (Seligman 1910: vii–xivi). Smith's advocacy of self-interest in the business world was a landmark in the advancement of scientific economics, commonly known as Capitalism – the satisfaction of material needs, which are artificially stimulated by the same economic powers that find their profit in their stimulation. As one might expect, these developments were supported by greater knowledge of the workings of the natural (material) world enabling greater use of it to serve ever-more political, economic and utilitarian ends.

Francis Bacon (1561–1626), who first recognised the instrumental power of science to transform the worldly conditions of human life (Kitchin 1861: vii–ix), encapsulated the special character of the new scientific age. It was this modern idea of activist science that informed our understanding of technological progress through which humanity would become 'the lords and possessors of nature' (Descartes 1637) and that eventually culminated in industrialisation. This forward-looking spirit was given impetus by the Protestant reaction to clerical tradition – hence capitalistic industrialism was especially successful among the Protestant peoples of Europe (Weber 2003: 95–155).

Culture, conflict and inheritance in the United Kingdom

Through this 'great transformation' the UK emerged as one of the world's most prosperous nations in the nineteenth century. However, at the outset this was not unproblematic as it brought with it humanitarian abuses associated, for instance, with the slave trade, increased use of child labour in extreme working conditions, and hitherto unprecedented environmental pollution. In addition, internal demographic change led to widespread deprivation in the countryside and a dramatic rise in urban poverty contributing to new forms of socio-economic divisions.

It was around this time that an essentially negative critique of modernity became pronounced in certain intellectual circles and which continues to have an important bearing on our understanding of the past. Thomas Carlyle (1795–1881), Augustus Pugin (1812–52), and above all John Ruskin (1819–1900), became important critical voices expressing their concerns for the environment and for the moral and spiritual well-being of humanity, which they believed had been corrupted by a modern secular civilisation dominated by a new metaphysically 'neutral' scientistic order. To them, its materialistic, individualistic characteristics had the effect of liberating humanity's natural impulse to greed. Moreover, its tendency to mechanise human thought and alienate humanity from nature was equally abhorrent to them.

Pugin was an English-born architect, designer and theorist of design. He was an advocate of Gothic architecture, which he believed to be the true

Christian form of architecture and is today perhaps best remembered for his work on churches and the Houses of Parliament, London. In support of his arguments in favour of 'authentic' Gothic, Pugin produced his masterwork, *Contrasts* in 1836 in which he contrasted the glories of medieval architecture and its civilised society with the tired 'pagan' classical constructions that were the product of the degraded, modern, industrial society (Brittain-Catlin 2003). In his second major work, *True Principles of Pointed or Christian Architecture* (1841), Pugin revealed the principles of the medieval builder and the enlightened skill of their artisans. He favoured naturalism in design and the symbolic meaning of every detail of construction and called for a revival of the forgotten crafts (Brittain-Catlin 2003). What we can learn from this is that Pugin essentially worked for a renewed spiritualisation, which he understood as a form of cultural restitution based around the continuity of traditions of practice and related ways of life.

As well as being influenced by the architectural theories of Pugin, as a thinker, Ruskin confessed himself the pupil of Carlyle (see Ruskin [1849] 1909: editor's note). Carlyle was a prominent writer whose work appealed to many Victorians who were grappling with the scientific, technological and political changes that threatened the traditional social order. However, it is above all the figure of John Ruskin who, for much of the second half of the nineteenth century, dominated the English world of art. The combined influence of Pugin and Carlyle is apparent in Ruskin's literary style which was often elevated, subliminal, metaphysical and theological in tone. Like Carlyle, Ruskin criticised the rampant industrialism of his age – described by Carlyle (1829) as the 'Mechanical Age', which had been founded on what he later referred to as the 'dismal science' of economics (Carlyle 1849).

Aside from his personal views on the perceived moral decline of the age, in a lecture in 1884, 'The Storm Cloud of the Nineteenth Century', Ruskin perceptively (and perhaps prophetically) described what he believed to be the environmental costs of mechanical progress that he had observed over 40 years between 1831 and 1871, as follows:

> [I] ... propose to bring to your notice a series of cloud phenomena. ... For the sky is covered with grey cloud – not rain-cloud, but a dry black veil which no ray of sunshine can pierce. ... It looks partly as if it were made of poisonous smoke; very possibly it may be: there are at least two hundred furnace chimneys in a square of two miles on every side of me.
> (1884: 1–30)

Ruskin's concerns for the environment and his critical disposition towards the Mechanical Age represented, for him, the progressive alienation of humanity from nature. Crucially, this informed his understanding of cultural heritage preservation; the traditional arts and crafts were sanctified in the process because they existed in harmony with nature and were not exploitative of it. Again, inspired by the writings of Pugin and Carlyle and by the philosophical transcendentalism and romantic idealism of the period, Ruskin wrote *The Seven Lamps of Architecture* ([1849] 1909) and *The Stones of Venice* ([1851] 2001); two books that were significant in criticising 'restoration' in favour of 'conservation'.

In *The Seven Lamps of Architecture*, for example, Ruskin condemns the 'restorations' of the day in the following terms:

> Neither by the public, nor by those who have the care of public monuments, is the true meaning of the word restoration understood. It means the most total destruction which a building can suffer: a destruction out of which no remnants can be gathered: a destruction accompanied with false description of the thing destroyed. Do not let us deceive ourselves in this important matter; it is impossible, as impossible as to raise the dead, to restore anything that has ever been great or beautiful in architecture. That which I have above insisted upon as the life of the whole, that spirit which is given only by the hand of the workman, never can be recalled. Another spirit may be given by another time, and it is then a new building; but the spirit of the dead workman cannot be summoned up, and commanded to direct other hands, and other thoughts.
>
> ([1849] 1909: 269)

Ruskin did not elucidate the technical aspects of buildings preservation in any detail, mainly because he did not possess the necessary expertise. In typically ideological fashion, he insisted that proper care should prevent the necessity for restoration (Summerson 1966: 27). His thoughts, nonetheless, had a major influence on the heritage preservation movement of the twentieth century (Burman 1995). It is, therefore, imperative to understand just what 'restoration' implied in Ruskin's time. As Summerson has explained:

> What Ruskin mainly understood by restoration was a process very frequently employed in the 1840's and 1850's which consisted in the tooling away at decayed stone to reach a new, firm, and smooth surface. Naturally in this process mouldings [sic] were distorted out of recognition, while all marks of handling and age were lost. And this loss of the visible marks of antiquity [its age-value] was to Ruskin the most dreadful fate which could befall any building.
>
> (1966: 27)

From this, we can understand that restoration then was how we might understand complete reconstruction (or renewal) today and frequently involved complete re-design (see Fawcett 1976 for photographic examples). However, there are two distinct approaches to restoration: one that attempts to take a building (which is valued for its age) back to a perceived earlier or original 'authentic' state, the other which concerns putting back those elements that may have been lost due, for example, to neglect or damage caused by mis-repair. The latter is done with materials/techniques that allow for natural entropic processes to enhance the building's ageing characteristics (and which arguably keep it remaining historically appealing). For the purpose of this discussion, the latter approach can be described as restoration in the *adding to* sense. Crucially, Ruskin was no less critical of restoration in terms of what was frequently *taken away* from their fabric — hence the movement he inspired later became identified with the term 'Anti-Scrape' (Tschudi-Madsen 1976: 63–79).

It would seem, therefore, that Ruskin did not conceive of a building's integrity or its historical authenticity solely in terms of the original fragment (and thus a fixed/static conception), but also in terms of what constituted its symbolic meaning through all times (and thus variable/dynamic). In other words, he recognised that it is the building's being *in* history that is to be understood as constituting its significance. Accordingly, buildings were interpreted as historical documents. For this reason, the post-Ruskinian practice of heritage preservation was concerned with the preservation of 'all times and styles' (Morris 1877), which was based around a philosophy of incremental repair and complementary additions. To that end William Morris, guided by Ruskin, founded the Society for the Protection of Ancient Buildings (SPAB) in 1877, and promoted the cultural significance of traditional arts and crafts practices. Without such expertise, the practice of preservation — in this dynamic incremental sense — was not possible.

The publication of Ruskin's *The Stones of Venice* in 1851 — in particular his essay 'The Nature of Gothic' — was to prove decisive in the practice of heritage preservation. This later became more familiarly known as 'conservation' largely because of a desire to move away from the negative connotations associated with the term 'restoration' that emerged in the latter part of the nineteenth century — and which might be seen as defining the field's own 'pre-scientific' period. In this essay, Ruskin discussed the various elements that composed the inner spirit of Gothic architecture, employing terms such as: 'savageness', 'changefulness', 'naturalism', 'grotesque', 'rigidity' and 'redundance' (Ruskin [1851] 2001: 142). He believed that: 'The charts of the world which have been drawn up by modern science have thrown into a narrow space the expression of a vast amount of knowledge' ([1851] 2001: 143).

There is a sense of loss in Ruskin's words. He appears to be alluding to a 'closure' of thought caused by the growth of modern science, apparently sensing that scientific methodology is reductionist in that it posits a limited consciousness of reality in the act of its enquiry, leading (inevitably) to the loss of certain kinds of what we now term 'tacit knowledge' (Polanyi 1967). Such knowledge, which is frequently culturally and/or geographically located, cannot be codified and can only be transmitted via training or gained through direct personal experience — such as learning a skill — but not in a way that can be easily written down. Tacit knowledge is opposite to the concept of 'explicit knowledge', and for this reason tends to reside outside the methodological limitations of normal scientific protocol, which is essentially, based around the rational explication of observable/measurable phenomena. In such a scheme, that which cannot be explicated in this way tends to be ignored or discredited – hence the metaphysical 'closure' suggested here by Ruskin and the accompanying sense of loss.

In reaction to this, Ruskin identified with what he believed to be the free expression of the Christian spirit in the Gothic artisan:

> Whenever the workman [sic] is utterly enslaved, the parts of the building must of course be absolutely like each other; for the perfection of his execution can only be reached by exercising him in doing only one thing, and giving him nothing else to do. The degree to which the workman is degraded may be thus known at a glance ... if, as in Gothic work, there is perpetual change both in design and execution; the workman must have been altogether set free.
>
> ([1851] 2001: 145–6)

It is apparent then, that Ruskin was criticising the 'alienated' modern worker who he believed had become 'mechanised' in thought and action – leading to a de-spiritualisation and subsequent de-sublimation of their faculties and the loss of their artistic (and tacit) sensibilities. The alienated (or lacerated) consciousness is a concept that was developed by the philosopher, Georg Hegel (1770–1831), who was one of the most influential philosophers in nineteenth-century Europe (Russell 1984: 701–15).

This disinheritance of mind was a process of 'sciencing' or 'naturalisation' in philosophical terms. It may be understood as an outcome of the hermeneutical transition in European thought, which formed the basis of Western materialism, as we know it today. For Ruskin, it was the nature of the material needs of the time and the means used to satisfy them, which in the modern 'political economy', was endorsed by the bureaucratic mechanisms of secular governance. Consequently, the artist or artisan was no longer in a one-to-one relationship with their work; rather they were reduced to a mere mechanical contrivance resulting in disenfranchisement to their work. Ruskin believed that such a worker was not fit to restore the monuments of a bygone age because the unity of the artist and the work of art was lost:

> ... it is again no question of expediency [politico-economic] or feeling whether we shall preserve the buildings of past times or not. We have no right whatever to touch them. They are not ours. They belong partly to those who built them, and partly to all the generations of mankind [sic] who are to follow us.
>
> (Ruskin [1849] 1909: 271)

In fact Ruskin believed that the very worst Gothic architecture was that in which mechanism has taken the place of design (Ruskin [1851] 2001: 169). This understanding led Ruskin to his denunciation of the abstract architectural 'laws' of classical architecture that he saw as analogous to a process of manufacture, rather than profound artistic creativity:

> Exactly so far as architecture works on known rules, and from given models, it is not art, but a manufacture; and it is, of the two procedures, rather less rational (because more easy) to copy capitals or mouldings [sic] from Phidias, and call ourselves architects, than to copy heads and hands from Titian and call ourselves painters.
>
> ([1851] 2001: 148)

Indeed, Ruskin believed, hypothetically, that Titian and Michelangelo would refuse to use modern technology in their artworks because it would separate the artist from the 'flesh and senses of humanity' (O'Hear 1995).

For Ruskin then, the naturalistic qualities of Gothic architecture were represented in the honest use of natural materials – worked with traditional hand processes, while Christian humility was shown in the form and the roughness (or imperfection) of the work (by contrast to Classical 'pride' in exactitude). For him, this was central to its living vitality and noble character (and, therefore, also its historical authenticity, its integrity and its symbolic value). This way of thinking was central to Ruskin's views on restoration (in the repair/maintenance/adding to sense described above) and became enshrined in the philosophy of the nineteenth-century Arts and Crafts Movement which was established shortly after the founding of SPAB. It can, therefore, be argued that both SPAB and the Arts and Crafts Movement were part of the same heritage preservation movement – as conceived by Ruskin and Morris. The 'spirit' of this philosophy embodied respect for the environment (because it was non-industrial and therefore non-exploitative) and the desire to protect historic monuments, while venerating the traditional arts and crafts (but not just in terms of skills, or *process*, but as a way of life) for everything that they had come to symbolise in the modern world. Both cultural *and* environmental sustainability were central to their preservation ethos.

Much of the expertise necessary to maintain the architectural heritage (understood in terms of strictly honest repair) was cultivated through the founding of various training schools and guilds as part of the Arts and Crafts Movement that had been growing since the mid-nineteenth century. Philip Webb and William Lethaby were important figures; Lethaby, for example, founded the Central School of Arts and Crafts, in 1896. In addition to this were the Century Guild of Artists (1882); the Art Workers Guild (1884); the School of Handicraft (1887); the Guild of Handicraft (1888); and the Arts and Crafts Exhibition Society (1888). In fact, one of the first attempts to establish a guild was John Ruskin's own guild of St. George founded in 1871 (Bennett and Pickles n.d.) The Craft Revival was also fuelled by the new ideals of Arts Schools and Colleges in London, Liverpool, Birmingham and Glasgow and their efforts to develop the applied arts. This involved forging links with local industries, the training of local artisans and supporting the development of education in art and craft for the widest possible audiences (Bennett and Pickles n.d.).

With respect to the 'art' of conservation, Lethaby noted that: '... the methods of repair became traditional among the architect members of the Society [SPAB]' (SPAB n.d.). The Lethaby Scholarship was introduced in 1930 in memory of Professor William Lethaby. It aims to cultivate a deep understanding of historical structures and appreciation of the traditional building crafts. The essence of SPAB is practical repair, based on handed-down knowledge and experience which remains true to this day (Venning 2005: 281). In other words, and in true Ruskinian fashion, SPAB philosophy advocates (and sustains) a historiography of *practice* based around the traditional arts and crafts that are considered to have intrinsic value to heritage itself.

This view would appear to be in direct opposition to that expressed by Paul Philippot, an archaeologist and former Director-General of the International Centre for the Study of the Preservation and Restoration of Cultural Property, Rome (ICCROM), who argued that:

> The unique voice of the past is exactly what must be safeguarded by preservation/conservation. The survival of traditional crafts should not mislead one here. What survives of the craftsman's [sic] tradition in the new industrial world [i.e. the Mechanical Age] is its practical skill ... it is no longer a genuine expression either of the past or of the present ... and therefore leads to a faked expression.
>
> (Philippot [1976] 1996: 270)

If this were true, then it would surely mean that much of our built heritage, which has been maintained by traditional skills by the constant renewal of its fabric, would also be fake and the idea of an authentic historical document thrown into question.

Philippot (1996: 268–74) attributes his understanding to the emergence of modern historical consciousness at the end of the eighteenth century which, he claims, brought an end to the traditional link with the past, and that ever since this 'rupture' the past has been considered by Western civilisations as a 'completed development'. This new 'historical distance', he asserts, has produced the conditions necessary for 'a more objective, scientific approach to the past in the form of historical knowledge' (1996: 268). Surely, however, it was the objectifying tendencies of scientific thought that was a determining factor of modern historical consciousness – not the other way around.

Here we have the core of the matter. Such a view is surely contentious – for such traditions are considered by many to be a significant expression of the spiritual, religious and artistic life of the past, which continue to exist in the life of the present. This apparent temporal dilemma has surely arisen because the scientific approach to historiography (and heritage) was based around an essentially positivistic enquiry and the resultant accumulation of factual evidence (or data) about what actually happened *in the past* (Hassard 2007: 8). So conceived, the object – be it a painting, an item of decorative art, a sculpture, an archaeological relic, or a monument – tends to be understood as the product of a single creative instance which is represented chronologically as a series of unrepeatable creative 'events'. However, quite often such tangible heritage has been fashioned – and continues to *be* fashioned – by many hands over an extended period of time. By emphasising the *materiality* of the past (tangible heritage) in this way the scientific approach to the past in the form of historical knowledge failed to notice the historicity of the present embodied in people and the intangible heritage sustained by their activities. In other words, the modern scientific understanding of heritage wishes to accept the inheritance of culture in material form alone, while forgetting the cultural processes by way of which that inheritance has been formed and transmitted.

This dualistic conception of heritage can thus be distinguished as scientific and pre-scientific perspectives – a distinction that is apparent in the original text (still used today) of the Manifesto of SPAB when Morris (1877) used phrases like 'escape the reproach of our learning'; a particular kind of academic learning, and criticised any attempts to 'stay the hand at an arbitrary point'; the basis of scientific conservation as based on an archaeo-museological model, undertaken by those who were 'deaf to the claims of poetry and history in the highest sense of the words'; the supra-sensory metaphysical understanding of cultural inheritance that Morris, Ruskin and their supporters were fully conscious of and which they believed had succumbed to the Mechanical Age. This we may refer to today as intangible heritage. Accordingly, it can be argued that SPAB sought to reconcile the tangible and the intangible heritages, which had become fractured by the progressive tide of modernity and the hermeneutical impasse posed by the emergence of modern historical consciousness.

The problem concerning technology

How then, are we to overcome this dilemma? Surely, a central requirement in preserving the meaning-conferring qualities of any historical document is the processes employed in interventive treatment. Crucially, Ruskin disapproved of any intervention that put the appearance of the building at odds with its structure and substance, which, for him, was unethical – this was the basis of his philosophy of strictly honest repair. For example, Ruskin expressed his view of casting (or machine-work) which replaced the work of hand in the following terms:

> There are two reasons, both weighty, against the substitution of cast or machine work for that of the hand: one, that all cast and machine work is bad, as work; the other, that it is dishonest. ... Its dishonesty, however, which, to my mind, is of the grossest kind, is, I think, a sufficient reason to determine absolute and unconditional rejection of it.
>
> (1865: 240)

In fact, Ruskin abhorred any form of imitation with the intention to deceive; with respect to imitations of marble on wood, he expressed the following:

> There is not a meaner occupation for the human mind than the imitations of the stains and striae of marble on wood. ... the grainer must think of what he is doing; and veritable attention and care, and occasionally considerable skill, are consumed in the doing of a more absolute nothing than I can name in any other department of painful idleness. I know not anything so humiliating as to see a human being, with arms and limbs complete, and apparently a head, and assuredly a soul, yet into the hands of which when you have put a brush and a pallet, it cannot do anything with them but imitate a piece of wood.
>
> (1865: 248)

This demonstrates *unequivocally* that Ruskin respected material substance and techniques used (i.e. process) and not merely the superficial appearance of objects. In studying the hundreds of letters and documents held in the SPAB archives the author has not found a single example of restoration (in the repair/maintenance or *adding to* sense) that was based on superficial appearance alone and did not respect consistency in terms of material substance and process. Every restoration that Morris and Company undertook – from the replacement of stained-glass windows to interior decoration and refurbishment – were all undertaken with traditional materials (always natural) and hand-crafted techniques (for illustrated examples of stained glass by Morris and Co. see Sewter 1974). SPAB philosophy is well represented by the restoration of Kelmscott Manor, the former home of William Morris. With the exception of consolidating water-damaged exterior sills (with synthetic fillers), all of the repair work (which was extensive) was carried out in a 'like-with-like' manner (see Insall 1968).

Ruskin's early influence first became apparent when his criticisms of the restoration work at Tewkesbury Abbey by SPAB were quoted in the *Times*:

> Now there is one thing in the present incomplete state of the work, which had never been intended by Sir Gilbert Scott to remain as it was.

He [Ruskin] alluded to the temporary screen between nave and choir, made of deal, though painted to resemble stone. It was a sham and for that reason and for no other it seemed unworthy of its position in so noble a building as Tewkesbury Abbey.

(Ruskin 1890)

It was a sham because it put the appearance of the building at odds with its underlying structure and substance and precluded any possibility of an 'authentic' interventive treatment process. This Ruskinian ethic is the antithesis of the kind of so-called 'neutral' restoration carried out today in the name of scientific conservation based purely on the superficial appearance of tangible heritage – as, for example, informed by Cesare Brandi's influential *Theory of Restoration* ([1963] 2005: 51) and embodied in the archaeological concept of *anastylosis*.

In spite of this, the literature that has built up in recent times within the discipline of 'scientific' conservation has claimed to foster a Ruskinian conception of heritage preservation ('conservation'). It has done so as the profession seeks (through its ethical strictures) to distance itself from its craft-based 'restoration' origins – a phenomenon that has recently been described by Larsen (1999) as 'a paradigm shift from craft to science'. The European Confederation of Conservator-Restorers' Organisations (ECCO), for example, defines the conservation professional in the following terms:

The Conservator-Restorer is neither an artist nor a craftsperson. Whereas the artist or craftsperson is engaged in creating new objects or in maintaining or repairing objects in a functional sense, the Conservator-Restorer is engaged in the preservation of cultural property.

(ECCO 1993: 12)

This definition was taken from an earlier one provided by the International Council of Museums (ICOM) in 1984. A similar understanding of the role of the 'scientific' conservator was also expressed by Brandi's colleague Giulo Argan (cited in Brandi [1963] 2005: 172–4) and is arguably indicative of Brandi's influence on the Heritage Movement of the post-World War II period. It is worth highlighting once more then, that Brandi's approach to restoration is based on a limited understanding of authenticity as residing solely in the superficial appearance of objects (as the above definition underlines).

The overly simplistic understanding of what it means to 'conserve' and to 'restore' implied here relates to Ruskin's public criticisms of his contemporary, the French architect Eugene Emmanuel Viollet-le-Duc's approach to the restoration of architecture. This historical argument is a complex one, and present understanding within the field of conservation (which is largely limited to art-historical studies) does not sufficiently take account of the fact that the issues between Ruskin and Viollet-le-Duc did not only relate to the extent of, or the stylistic qualities of, the interventions as typically implied. In fact, as this chapter has argued, Ruskin and his supporters were *no less* concerned with the kinds of processes used.

In this regard, Viollet-le-Duc was an advocate of the use of the newly available materials of industrial production. These materials (and therefore techniques) he believed would extend the life of the building because they were superior to those used in the past. To Viollet-le-Duc, it was illogical to repair or reconstruct a building with traditional materials when more refined and better materials and methods were available: 'There is another overriding condition that must always be kept in mind in restoration work. It is this: both the methods and the materials of construction employed by the restorer must always be of superior quality' (Viollet-le-Duc [1868] 1990: 214).

However, for Ruskin and his supporters the historical record of the building was destroyed by such 'improvements'. Buildings, Ruskin believed, had to be recognised (and maintained) with reference to their own specific history and with due regard to architectural propriety in relation to this. It was largely for this reason that Ruskin believed new architectural construction should be produced only from materials that would weather with the passage of time. Otherwise, the building would eventually become symbolically depleted – negating the meaning-conferring qualities of the historical document; Demel (1997) provides an illustrated account of this argument. What we can understand from this is that Viollet-le-Duc's work represented a clear indication of the difference between the pre-industrial, historically transcendent craft-based perspective – which sustains intangible heritage – and that of the so-called Mechanical Age, which Ruskin reviled because it did not. The argument clearly centred on the role of technology (and materials) in restoration practice (the term used here generically).

Viollet-le-Duc's preference for modern materials/techniques has been explained by Bressani (1989) as the outcome of his views of history and his (questionable) understanding of progress. In 'Notes on Viollet-le-Duc's Philosophy of History: Dialectics and Technology', Bressani draws on Classical mythology (namely Doxius and Epergos) to explain the dialectical forces of tradition and renewal which represent the fundamental duality of the world. Viollet-le-Duc is entirely on the side of modern technological culture (or the Mechanical Age), which he sees as humanity's emancipation from nature through scientific/technological inventiveness – understood as progress. Epergos is the active principle of renovation – and thus represents scientific knowledge; while Doxius is the passive imagination – representing the past, or tradition. Epergos is the active imagination, representing the will to transform, improve and/or control. For Viollet-le-Duc the source of all Western progress is the Greek intellect (i.e., scientific knowledge). Thus, Doxius and Epergos also symbolise the opposition of science to tradition – a paradox that can also be understood as reflecting dialectical forces between pre- and post-Enlightenment philosophical positions.

Thus, according to Viollet-le-Duc, the sciences: '... are not the result of the labours of our predecessors [they] ... make us, in fact, capable of forgetting all that was done before us' (Viollet-le-Duc cited in Bressani 1989: 348). In other words, for Viollet-le-Duc history comes to an 'end' with science – a view which is consistent with the view expressed by Philippot (1996) with respect to modern 'scientific' historicism and its privileged sense of rupture and discontinuity, noted above. In this scheme, the scientific construction of the heritage field leads to a dead end – its presiding scientific methodology would appear to have resulted in a kind of 'time wall'. This is why, within this paradigm, the physical object is suspended (frozen) in time and why ethical principles such as 'reversibility' (reversible treatments) have come into existence – which is often used to legitimise the use of modern 'non-like' materials/techniques in restoration in preference to 'like-for-like' means – which would sustain traditions of practice. However, in fact, no act of treatment intervention can be undone by merely removing its material outcome because the act itself is necessarily part of history. To imply that it can is an illusion caused by modern historicism and the subsequent 'time wall' it would appear to have resulted in.

This dilemma is also apparent in the ideas of Viollet-le-Duc, who, although wanting to forget the past, relies on his understanding of history for his conception of progress. Paradoxically, he saw progress in scientific methodology, deriving from antiquity in the Greek intellect – which is necessarily backward looking. What tends to give the impression of progress is modern technology, the proliferation of which became synonymous with science in the eighteenth century – as an outcome of the world-changing spirit of the Enlightenment. However, the methodology itself is ancient and by no means progressive. It is for this reason that, with respect to the practice of restoration, the scientific/technological revolution of the heritage field in the post-World War II period – the so-called 'paradigm shift' – is entirely Viollet-le-Ducian in character. Moreover, its public denunciation of the traditional arts and crafts is by no means Ruskinian. This understanding has become inverted by prevailing discourse within the scientific/technical and political-institutional sectors throughout much of the Western world.

Here we come to the heart of the matter concerning technology: surely the Ruskin/Morris philosophy sought to arrest the sense of rupture with the past brought about by modern historicism – by supporting the traditional arts and crafts and the idea of a historical document (sustained by a process of incremental repair). This was their understanding of historical authenticity. The idea that heritage preservation should be based solely on the superficial appearance of a tangible record and not also on the substances and processes employed in its preservation is not entirely consistent with the Ruskin/Morris philosophy. This philosophy understood heritage in terms of process too, and was based on memory and meaning, and a living mediation of the past and the present – and surely *not* forgetfulness. It was metaphysically productive, traditional and artistic in character *not* scientistically reductive and technologically progressive in its orientation. In short, it sought synergy between the tangible and intangible inheritance of humanity.

This understanding is remarkably consistent with UNESCO's contemporary interpretation of intangible heritage in terms of the cultural value it attributes to 'traditional craftsmanship' as expressed in the *UNESCO Convention for the Safeguarding of the Intangible Cultural Heritage* (2003). This Convention should be understood in relation to the *Nara Document on Authenticity* (1994) which was adopted by the *UNESCO Operational Guidelines for the Implementation of the World Heritage Convention* in 2005; Section II.E Point 82 states the following:

> Depending on the type of cultural heritage, and its cultural context, properties may be understood to meet the conditions of authenticity if their cultural values (as recognized in the nomination criteria proposed) are truthfully and credibly expressed through a variety of attributes including: form and design; materials and substance; use and function; traditions, techniques and management systems; location and setting; language and other forms of intangible heritage; spirit and feeling; [and]: other internal and external factors.

What we can understand from this is that post-Nara the practice of restoration/repair/maintenance and any action that *adds to* the historical document became bound to the concept of authenticity and is today understood in relation to intangible heritage. This more comprehensive understanding of cultural inheritance will necessitate significant changes to heritage preservation practice throughout the international heritage community.

Conclusion

The concept of intangible heritage – as conceived by UNESCO – is today central to the debate around cultural diversity in the context of world culture. It represents a re-orientation in thinking about the relationship of culture and its inheritance brought about largely because of concerns relating to the cultural impact of globalisation, and is essentially opposed to an established vision of heritage residing solely in the *materiality* of the past. However, key international documents of recent years reveal that there has been a general movement towards a reconciliation of the tangible and intangible domains brought about by a new understanding of the concept of authenticity. By moving from a view grounded in materials and form to one grounded in *process*, the practice of restoration can now be understood, generically, as: *the methodological moment when the intangible 'adheres' itself to the tangible and becomes the historical document of the future*. Traditions of practice, understood as a manifestation of intangible heritage, are central to this realisation. This correlation between authenticity, restoration and traditions of practice is based upon the understanding that both the tangible and intangible domains are co-related and inter-dependent when it comes to their preservation and safeguarding, respectively.

This synthesis of the tangible and intangible heritages can thus be understood as indicative of a wider epistemological (and hermeneutical) shift in understanding heritage and its relationship to the present. This chapter has argued that this has the effect of overcoming the impasses of modern historicism that has dominated Western culture since the period of so-called European Enlightenment. It has attempted to show how this impasse has its origins in the European Church Reforms of the preceding centuries, which strengthened the division between humanity and nature polarising our understanding of the world into subjective/objective realities. It was the latter 'objectivating paradigm' that gave shape to a new scientific episte-mology that emerged at the forefront of the succeeding period of Enlightenment which, in turn, shaped our understanding of heritage as based solely on a tangible record. The 'subjective' paradigm existed beyond its methodological limitations – and hence the historicity of civilisation itself was overlooked leading to a fracture between the tangible and intangible heritages that contemporary theory seeks to redress.

The chapter has also argued that the cultural impact of this historic tran-sition lay at the heart of concerns that emerged in the UK in the nineteenth century. These concerned the practice of restoration (in the generic sense) and the subsequent Preservation Movement's veneration of traditional arts and crafts practices – which were understood to be the cultural expression of a 'pre-scientific' era. It revealed how this was an essentially 'anthropocentric' vision of heritage that was informed by (and informed) a critical ideology of modernity which emerged as a reaction to what was perceived to be the metaphysically reductive, environmentally destructive and apodictic char-acter of the Mechanical Age – which, to them, represented the 'dark' side of Enlightenment. The nineteenth-century Heritage Movement anticipated recent developments in global heritage theory in that it also aimed to syn-thesise the tangible and intangible domains – and the past with the pre-sent – through an elevated concept of what constitutes an authentic historical document.

This observation makes more comprehensible the idea of the intangible as it relates to Western culture by revealing clear similarities between the nineteenth century and present-day concerns relating to world heritage and the (now) global problem of sustaining cultural divergence. Finally, with its unique historical trajectory, the UK must surely now embrace the idea of the intangible by ratifying the *UNESCO Convention for the Safeguarding of the Intangible Cultural Heritage* (2003) and formally move the heritage sector into a new era and towards a synthesis of the 'tangible' and 'intangible' inheri-tance of humanity in line with contemporary theory.

Acknowledgements

I should like to thank Dr Reg Winfield, Buckinghamshire New University, UK for his assistance in drafting this chapter.

Bibliography

Bennett, D. and Pickles, D. (n.d.) 'Head Hand & Heart: "The Arts and Crafts Movement in Great Britain 1850–1915"'. Available online at: http://www.artscrafts.org.uk/branches/handicrafts.html (Accessed 15 May 2005).

Brandi, C. ([1963] 2005) *Theory of Restoration*, Florence: Nardini Editore.

Bressani, M. (1989) 'Notes on Viollet-le-Duc's philosophy of history: Dialectics and technology', in E. MacDougall (ed.), *Journal of the Society of Architectural Historians* XLVIII, Chicago: Society of Architectural Historians.

Brittain-Catlin, T. (2003) *Contrasts or a Parallel between the Noble Edifices of the Middle Ages, and Corresponding Buildings of the Present Day: Shewing the Present Decay of Taste* (A. Pugin 1836) and *True Principles of Pointed or Christian Architecture* (A. Pugin 1841), combined facsimile edition, Reading: Spire Books.

Burman, P. (1995) 'A question of ethics', in *The Conservation and Repair of Ecclesiastical Buildings*, London: Cathedral Communications. Available online at: http://www.building-conservation.com/articles/ethics/ethics.htm (Accessed 18 April 2005).

Carlyle, T. (1829) 'Sign of the times', first published in *The Edinburgh Review*; reprinted (1858) in *The Collected Works of Thomas Carlyle*, Vol. 3. London: Chapman and Hall. Available online at: http://www.victorianweb.org/authors/carlyle/signs1.html (Accessed 15 May 2006).

—— (1849) 'Occasional discourse on the Negro question', *Fraser's Magazine*, 40(December): 670–9; reprinted in H. Traill (ed.) (1898) *Collected Works of Thomas Carlyle*, Vol. 11, London: Chapman and Hall.

Dawson, C. (1961) *The Crisis of Western Education*, New York: Sheed and Ward.

Demel, S. (1997) *Architectural Additions*, unpublished MA thesis, Columbia University. Available online at: http://www.demel.net/th-ch1.html (Accessed 3 December 2005).

Descartes. R. (1637) *Discourse on the Method of Rightly Conducting One's Reason and of Seeking Truth*; text prepared by I. and G. Newby (1993), University of Illinois, Project Gutenberg. Available online at: http://www.gutenberg.org/etext/59 (Accessed 14 March 2007).

European Confederation of Conservator-Restorers' Organizations (ECCO) (1993) 'Professional guidelines I: The role of the conservator-restorer', *ECCO Official Papers*, Brussels: ECCO.

Fawcett, J. (ed.) (1976) *The Future of the Past: Attitudes to Conservation 1174–1974*, London: Thames and Hudson.

Gadamer, H. (1975) *Truth and Method*, London: Sheed and Ward.

Hassard, F. (2006) Heritage, *Hermeneutics and Hegemony: A Study of Ideological Division in the Field of Conservation-Restoration*, unpublished PhD thesis, Brunel University.

—— (2007) 'Understanding the past in a contemporary context; towards a new methodology', in G. Lasker, H. Schinzel and Karel Boullart (eds), *Art and Science Vol. 5*. Proceedings of the 19th International Conference on Systems Research, Informatics and Cybernetics, Tecumseh: International Institute for Advanced Studies.

Insall, D. (1968) 'Kelmscott Manor, the home of William Morris and its Repair for the Society of Antiquaries London'. Available online at: http://www.international.icomos.org/monumentum/ (Accessed 30 September 2003).

International Council of Museums (ICOM) (1984) 'The conservator-restorer: A definition of the profession', *ICOM – Code of Ethics*. Available online at: http://www.encore-edu.org/encore/documents/ICOM1984.html (Accessed 18 April 2004).

Kitchin, G. (ed.) (1861) *The Advancement of Learning*, London: Dent.

Larsen, R. (1999) 'Comments to FULCO – a framework of competence for conservator-restorers in Europe', *ENCoRE Newsletter*. Available online at: http://www.kulturnet.dk/homes/ks/encore/ (Accessed 7 February 2005).

Morris, W. (1877) 'The manifesto for the Society for the Protection of Ancient Buildings (SPAB)'. Available online at: http://www.spab.org.uk/html/what-is-spab/the-manifesto/ (Accessed 15 May 2005).

O'Hear, A. (1995) 'Art and technology: an old tension', in R. Fellows (ed.), *Philosophy and Technology*, Cambridge: Cambridge University Press.

Philippot, P. ([1976] 1996) 'Historic preservation: philosophy, criteria, guidelines I', in N.S. Price, M.K. Talley (Jr.) and A.M. Vaccaro (eds), *Historical and Philosophical Issues in the Conservation of Cultural Heritage*, Los Angeles: The J. Paul Getty Trust.

Polanyi, K. ([1944] [1957] 2002) *The Great Transformation: The Political and Economic Origins of Our Time*, Boston: Beacon Press by arrangement with Rinehart & Company, Inc.

Polanyi, M. (1967) *The Tacit Dimension*, New York: Archer Books.

Rolston Saul, J. (1992) *Voltaire's Bastards*, New York: The Free Press.

Ruskin, J. (1865) *Selections from the Writings of John Ruskin*, London: Smith Elder and Co.

—— (1884) 'The storm-cloud of the nineteenth century: Two lectures delivered at the London Institution February 4th and 11th, 1884', in *The Complete Works of John Ruskin*, vol. XXIV; text prepared by J. Sutherland and S. Flanagan (2006), Project Gutenberg. Available online at: http://www.gutenberg.org/files/20204/20204.txt (Accessed 10 January 2007).

—— (1890) 'The restoration of Tewkesbury Abbey', letter to *The Times*, 6th September 1890 – available at the SPAB archives.

—— ([1849] 1909) *The Seven Lamps of Architecture*, London: Cassell.

—— ([1851] 2001), *The Stones of Venice*, edited and abridged by J. Links, London: Pallas Editions.

Russell, B. ([1946] 1984) *A History of Western Philosophy*, London: Counterpoint.

Seligman, E. (1910) 'Introduction to Smith, A. (1776) An inquiry into the nature and the causes of the wealth of nations', in E. Rhys (ed.), London: Dent.

Sewter, A. (ed.) (1974) *The Stained Glass of William Morris and His Circle: Text and Illustrations*, New Haven: Yale University Press.

Shackleton, R. (1969) 'Free enquiry and the world of ideas', in A. Cobban (ed.), *The Eighteenth Century*, London: Thames and Hudson.

Society for the Protection of Ancient Buildings (SPAB) (n.d.). Available online at: http://www.spab.org.uk/html/ (Accessed 15 June 2007).

Summerson, J. (1966) 'Ruskin, Morris, and the "Anti-Scrape" philosophy', in *Historic Preservation Today: Essays Presented to the Seminar on Preservation and Restoration*, Williamsburg, Virginia: University Press of Virginia.

Troeltsch, E. (1912) *Protestantism and Progress: A Historical Study of the Relation of Protestantism to the Modern World*, Boston: Beacon Press.

Tschudi-Madsen, S. (1976) *Restoration and Anti-Restoration: A Study in English Restoration Philosophy*, Oslo: Universitetsforlaget.

UNESCO (2003) *Convention for the Safeguarding of the Intangible Cultural Heritage*.

—— (2005) *Operational Guidelines for the Implementation of the World Heritage Convention*. Available at: http://whc.unesco.org/archive/opguide05-en.pdf (Accessed 15 March 2006).

UNESCO, ICCROM and ICOMOS (1994) *Nara Document on Authenticity*, Nara, Japan.

Venning, P. (2005) 'The continuing work of the SPAB', in C. Miele (ed.), *From William Morris: Building Conservation and the Arts and Crafts Cult of Authenticity, 1877–1939*, New Haven: Yale University Press.

Viollet-le-Duc, E. ([1868] 1990) *The Foundations of Architecture: Selections from the Dictionnaire Raisonne*; reprint trans. D. Whitehead, New York: Brazillier.

Weber, M. ([1905] 2003) *The Protestant Ethic and the Spirit of Capitalism*, New York: Dover.

Chapter 15

'The envy of the world?'

Intangible heritage in England

Laurajane Smith and Emma Waterton

Introduction

On Friday 20 January 2006, Romania became the 30th country to ratify UNESCO's *Convention for the Safeguarding of the Intangible Cultural Heritage*, thereby allowing the Convention to enter into force after a 30-month gestation period (Smeets 2006: 1). Heralded as ' ... a major step forward in the international efforts to protect the world's cultural heritage', the Convention sits alongside UNESCO's 1972 *Convention Concerning the Protection of the World Cultural and Natural Heritage* (Matsuura 2004: 1; chapters this volume). What this means is that there are now *three* overarching categories of heritage operating at the international level: 'tangible', 'natural' and 'intangible'. However, while the latter Convention remains a prominent international instrument, it is notable that England has yet to ratify or accept it – and it does not look likely that they will any time soon. Thus, while England prides itself on being '... the envy of the world' (English Heritage 2003: 1; Thurley 2004: 19) in terms of its management of 'tangible' and 'natural' heritage, it seems rather less concerned with the category of 'intangible'. From this, we might assume that for England at least, 'intangible heritage' is something set apart, assumed to deal with non-Western or non-European culture, and something that is ethnically, culturally, politically and socially distinct from the types of heritage associated with the categories of 'tangible' and 'natural'.

Quite the opposite, however, the aim of this chapter is to argue that heritage *is* intangible (see also Byrne this volume). Moreover, we argue that the palpable discomfort with which intangibility has been greeted in England reflects a wider failure to recognise the cultural legitimacy of the concept. Drawing on an analysis of discourse, this chapter will illustrate the ways in which a particular Western discourse, which Smith (2006) has labelled the *authorised heritage discourse* (henceforth AHD), has worked to impede not only the possibility of the UK signing up to the 2003 Convention, but also formally recognising the relevance of intangibility within Britain, and England in particular. Moreover, this discomfort with intangible heritage, which is illustrated with reference to interview data collected between 2004 and 2006, has implications for the way the concept of heritage is used in England, and the social and political work it does. The interviews used in this chapter were conducted with English Heritage and Department for Culture Media and Sport (DCMS) staff, in which they were asked specifically about the relevance of the 2003 Convention. These interviews are also supplemented with reflective commentary from practitioners associated with the World Heritage Centre and the Intangible Cultural Heritage Section of UNESCO, Paris, and others involved in the drafting of the 2003 Convention.

The authorised heritage discourse

As Alpha Oumar Konare (cited in Munjeri 2004: 12) remarked in the Preamble to UNESCO's First Proclamation of Masterpieces of the Oral and Intangible Heritage of Humanity, '... the protection of intangible heritage is a long struggle'. Indeed, the issue of intangibility remains an uncomfortable one for many Western countries. At the outset of this chapter, we suggested that this discomfort could in large part be understood through an analysis of 'discourse', but what does discourse mean? As an analytical category, 'discourse' is understood to do a number of things: (a) it contributes to the way people act, interact and organise their interactions; (b) it figures in the way the world is represented, helping to construct, unify, and maintain specific social relations; and (c) it constitutes and defines the social identities and subject positions from which we speak (Fairclough 1992, 2003; Marston 2004: 36; Waterton *et al.* 2006). 'Discourse' is thus given a significant amount of muscle; not only as a linguistic concept, but also as a concept that has significant social effects (Fairclough 2003: 3). Indeed, the ways in which we write, talk and think about heritage issues *matter*. They matter because they influence and reflect not only the ways in which we act, but also how we identify and manage heritage in practice. Subsequently, it is possible to argue that the traditional understanding of heritage – as a tangible and built corpus consisting of sites, monuments and buildings – is not simply a commonsense reflection of reality, but is one discourse out of many that has come to dominate.

Smith (2006) has labelled this discourse the AHD, which is a way of seeing heritage that developed over a considerable period of time, and owes many of its characteristics to an evocative mixing of Enlightenment and Romanticist philosophies. A sense of permanence and continuity permeates this discourse, which brings with it a need for the protection of 'authentic' fabric from damage and/or destruction for the ultimate benefit of future generations (Glendinning 2003: 362; Edensor 2005: 11; Karlström 2005: 345). The idea of inheritance, whereby current generations are conceived of as 'stewards' or 'caretakers' of the past, is important, as it works to specifically disengage certain social actors in the present (that is, non-experts) from an active use of heritage. Likewise, the privileging of aesthetic value and authenticity, generally associated with William Morris and John Ruskin and their desire for the 'historicity of buildings', undermines the experiences and understandings emergent from non-expertise (Nassar 2003: 469; Waterton 2007: 34; Hassard this volume). A significant underpinning of the English conservation ethic is the idea of inherent value. This conceptualisation underwrites much of the legal and policy processes that define the way heritage is conserved and managed in the UK (see Emerick 2003; Smith 2006; Waterton 2007). The authenticity of heritage is deemed to lie in the degree to which it may be perceived to be in its 'original' state and underwrites the philosophy of 'conserve as found' championed by Ruskin ([1849] 1899). This sense of the 'authentic' nature of heritage means that material culture is understood to not only symbolise, but actually 'embody', heritage cultural values. The physical fabric, which in the ideal should not be altered lest the authenticity of place suffers, becomes the central concern of heritage management and conservation. Quite simply, this is because the values through which we interpret heritage have become confused with the object itself.

The AHD also constructs an authorised mentality, which is deployed to understand and deal with social problems centred on claims to identity and memory. As such, it is in a position to continually legitimise and de-legitimise a range of cultural and social values. To this end, heritage agencies such as English Heritage and the National Trust become part of the process of maintaining certain historical identities and narratives. A range of alternative constructions of heritage are subsequently subdued and disarmed, inevitably rendered invisible both in a policy sense and in practice. While the AHD developed some time ago, recent research by Waterton (2007, 2009) into the analysis of a range of contemporary policy documents reveals its continued reoccurrence and naturalisation. Here, the AHD, and the cultural practices designed to manage that sense of 'heritage', have assumed a 'taken-for-granted' quality, remaining unquestioned in English public policy. For us, this makes apparent the social and ideological effects of discourse, revealing the seemingly innocuous form of power that underpins the management process. It also fleshes out the argument that a particular construction of 'heritage' has been – and continues to be – bolstered and protected by the very language we use, and is buried within the internal consistencies of public policy and practice.

The intangibility of heritage

In contrast to the assumption of heritage central to the AHD, this chapter starts from the premise that all heritage is intangible. Like Kirshenblatt-Gimblett (2004: 57), we suggest that the creation of a dichotomy between different 'types' of heritage is exclusive in its own way. As such, we argue that heritage cannot be defined by its materiality or non-materiality, but rather by what is done with it. Thus, whether we are dealing with historic houses, industrial sites and archaeological ruins, or traditional dance and the retelling of oral histories and storylines, we are dealing with the same thing: and what we are dealing with – what heritage *is* – is the performance and negotiation of identity, values and a sense of place.

The idea of the intangibility of all heritage lies in four interlinked observations expanded upon below. First, it lies in the realisation that at its core, 'heritage' is simply a shifting range of intangible cultural values that are used to give meaning to places and events. As Dawson Munjeri (2004: 13) observes 'the tangible can only be understood and interpreted through the intangible'. Second, it lies in the social and cultural 'affect' of heritage and the intangible, but no less 'real' or material, social and political consequences that heritage has in validating individual and collective senses of place, identity and collective memories. Third, it lies in the way heritage is constructed in, and through, discourse, and subsequent ways in which dominant heritage discourses regulate and govern not only what is defined as heritage and its use, but the social and political consequence that it has. This consequence is linked to the way heritage may be understood to be incorporated within the processes of remembering and forgetting. An interlinked relationship exists between heritage and memory and so, fourth, the intangibility of heritage reflects its relationship with memory.

The idea of heritage developed here is itself also based on the observation that it is not inherently valuable. Heritage values are not innate to heritage objects or places, or indeed to the 'intangible' expressions as defined under the 2003 Convention. As Smith (2006) has argued elsewhere, the subject of management is the values and meanings that are symbolised or represented at, and by, these places. Objects, places or events of 'heritage' are given heritage values *through* the performances of selecting and placing them on 'heritage' lists or registers. These values are then reinforced through the performances of management and conservation, interpretation and visitation. The cultural values, meanings and narratives engendered by these performances are then diffused out into everyday social contexts to underwrite individual and collective cultural, national and/or sub-national community identities (Abercrombie and Longhurst 1998). In this way, heritage undertakes cultural 'work' in defining and authorising the values and identities of social groups or other collectives. However, this work is often obscured by the Western authorised heritage discourse's preoccupation with monumentality and the materiality of heritage places. Thus, the heritage gaze is directed away from the *affect* of heritage onto the cultural 'object' or 'intangible event' itself. This 'affect' may be regulated and governed within the context of certain discourses, or, as Thrift (2004) notes, designed into spaces and places.

One of the key consequences of the heritage performance is the way in which it is used to legitimise and authorise identity. That heritage and identity are linked is a well-established concern in the literature on heritage, but to assume that that is 'all' heritage does misunderstand the extent of the heritage 'affect'. The values that inform any sense of identity are also used to construct ways of understanding and making the present meaningful and comprehensible. Heritage is not 'simply' about identity; it is also about creating and maintaining a sense of *place*; and this sense of place is not only about a physical or geographical sense of belonging, but is also concerned with placing ourselves within social space. That is, heritage is a process through which individuals and collectives negotiate their social position and 'place' within particular societies. At an international level, nation-states use heritage to negotiate their sense of 'place' in relation to each other. The World Heritage List, for instance, which is often gently critiqued through the analogy of a beauty pageant, is a process whereby states, sometimes quite cynically, attempt to assert their status in 'world' history and cultural achievement. Indeed, as one commentator noted:

> It is an ethical concept ... the focus on Western Europe has nothing, in principle, to do with the World Heritage committee itself. It has to do with those state parties which have beyond 30 [world heritage] sites – Spain, Italy, the UK, Germany and France, for example – and they don't stop nominating ... they don't stop nominating ... because it is a prestige issue.
>
> (Interview 7, World Heritage Centre, 10 January 2005)

Heritage thus becomes a cultural tool that nations, societies, communities and individuals use to facilitate self, identity and belonging. Moreover, it becomes a cultural and social framework for dealing with the present. It is also a highly emotive process, with very real emotional power. This power works to reinforce the social and cultural values given to heritage and helps to legitimise the sense of place, belonging and identities that those values engender.

One of the ways these processes are put into operation is through the performances of commemoration and remembering, which are themselves often emotionally charged. Heritage places or events are not simply a collective *aide-mémoire,* but are an active component of a cultural toolkit for remembering and forgetting. As James Wertsch (2002) argues, remembering (and by inference forgetting) is not a passive process, but one that is actively engaged in. Nor is memory an objective or neutral construct. Rather, our collective and individual memories are continually interpreted and reinterpreted through our experiences in the present, and are actively engaged with to help us not only understand the present, but negotiate collective and individual desires and aspirations (Wertsch 2002). Heritage is about remembering (and forgetting) and, like remembering, heritage is a process in which the past and the present intertwine to negotiate and understand the present. More importantly, traditional Western discourses of heritage that stress its materiality work to make intangible memories more 'tangible' by linking them to places, objects and spaces. By linking memory and remembering to the tangible, processes of remembering become more open to state regulation and control – they can be preserved, conserved, lost or destroyed and, above all, collected onto lists and registers (Figlio 2003: 152).

The Western authorised heritage discourses that define or emphasise the materiality of heritage work to render the intangible tangible. Through their association with material objects and places, ephemeral memories and intangible expressions of identities, senses of place and social values are all made tangible. They are also thus made tractable and open to regulation and control. In a very real sense, this is what heritage is about and what it does – it is part of the processes of social and cultural regulation. This process of regulation can occur at state/national level, through public policy and statutes, and through NGOs concerned with the management and conservation/preservation of heritage resources. International Conventions are, of course, another way in which social and cultural debates are regulated – the 2003 Convention included. Even though these are self-perceived as acts of management and administration, such processes are simultaneously engaged in a performance concerned with the regulation and creation of consensus history, national identity, collective memories, and social and cultural values.

Importantly, the public is not a passive audience to these performances. They, too, become active in a range of ways, although most obviously through the visiting of heritage sites or museums. Although self-defined as activities of leisure or tourism, these activities are also performances in which the visitor – and indeed site manager and museum curator – engages in the active construction of cultural and social meanings and messages. Indeed, as much of the cultural tourism literature acknowledges, visiting heritage sites is an experience and is valued as such by visitors (Prentice et al. 1998; McIntosh and Prentice 1999; Prentice 2001; Poria et al. 2003). Visitors are not passive receptors of the interpreter's messages, nor are they necessarily interested in being 'educated' about the value and history of heritage, as various visitor studies have demonstrated (Moscardo 1996; Prentice et al. 1998; McIntosh and Prentice 1999). Rather, visitors are quite active in the way that they use sites and exhibitions to reminisce and construct a sense of place and identity (see for instance, Urry 1996; Dicks 2000; Bagnall 2003; Poria et al. 2003; Smith 2006, among others).

It is also vital to note that these performances can occur both within and outside the AHD. While the AHD may often operate at state levels to regulate heritage performances, such performances will – and do – occur, not only outside the AHD, but also in opposition to it. As Tunbridge and Ashworth (1996) identify, heritage is dissonant (see also Tunbridge 1998;

Graham *et al.* 2000). What may be 'comfortable' and 'worthy' as heritage to someone will *always* be 'uncomfortable' and problematic to another. Indeed, any heritage item, place or event inevitably exists within a complex and interacting web of conflicting and multiple meanings and values. This contested nature of heritage is well documented and should need no elaboration. Nonetheless, there is a significant hesitancy in the heritage literature – as with the idea of intangibility – to actively incorporate the idea of dissonance into definitions of heritage. Instead, there is an active desire to separate an idea of dissonant heritage from an idea of heritage as something inherently 'good' and 'great'. As with the tendency to separate the 'tangible' from 'intangible', this simply operates as an attempt to keep difficult and problematic notions of heritage from complicating visions of a comfortable and comforting heritage. Much of the debate about how to 'manage' or safeguard intangible heritage has centred on issues of how to deal not only with its mutable quality, but, more importantly, how to deal with the cultural and identity politics that are often identified as an essential aspect of intangible heritage. What is interesting here is the degree to which this dissonance is seen as a *particular* problematic of intangible heritage – as if, in some way, tangible heritage does not also engage with such issues (see for instance, Nas 2002; Kurin 2004). However, dissonance, like intangibility, is also core to understanding the nature of heritage and the work that it does. This is because heritage is *about* the regulation and negotiation of the multiplicity of meaning of the past, and it is about the arbitration and mediation of the cultural and social politics of identity, belonging and exclusion.

Intangibility in England

Recently, heritage policy – both nationally and internationally – has been characterised by an attempt to fuse an explicitly *material* perspective with a distinctly *social* one. In England, this can be observed through recent initiatives within the heritage sector that are geared towards 'public value' and 'social inclusion'. Collectively, these policies are built around the assumptions of the AHD. As such, the more rounded theorisation of heritage recently offered within the heritage literature is absented, nor do they fully incorporate the range of meanings, values and experiences we engage with when we think, feel and speak about the past in the present. This inability to recognise accounts of heritage that extend beyond those offered by the AHD is underpinned by the same discursive predisposition that prevents management practices in England from recognising the legitimacy and *relevance* of intangible heritage. The naturalisation of a particular 'way of seeing' has worked to sustain and shape the parameters of social debates regarding heritage issues. Ideas pertaining to national importance, objective and immutable value, aesthetics, and authenticity have acted as reference points for developing policy, becoming key markers by which to orientate an approach to the management and interpretation of heritage (Jenkins 1996: 127). Moreover, these reference points have been uncritically accepted as common sense.

This line of argument can be illustrated with reference to a number of policy debates in England, in which discourses of social inclusion and intangibility have been reshaped and regulated by the AHD. In the late 1990s, issues of intangibility, social inclusion and cultural diversity, for example, began to gain political importance internationally (see chapters Part 1, this volume), and it should come as no surprise that these issues became visible within the English policy sphere. Our contention, however, is that this timeframe simultaneously saw a tightening of the AHD. As such, any broadened definitions of heritage initially put forward from this time onwards were closed down or obscured, and the emphasis on materiality and physicality made more prominent. For example, at the start of the Governmental Review of Policies Relating to the Historic Environment undertaken in 1999–2001, it was proposed that heritage be defined as:

> ... all the physical and intangible remains of the past that people can see, understand, feel or remember in the present world ...
>
> (English Heritage 2000a: 1)

At the end of this review period, the above definition had been significantly modified, such that what eventually emerged was a far more muted – and qualified – nod to intangibility:

> The historic environment is all the physical evidence for past human activity, and its associations, that people can see, understand and feel in the present world.
>
> (English Heritage 2000b: 5)

This was underpinned by the assertion that:

> [the review] must be about tangible not intangible culture.
>
> (English Heritage 2000c: 3)

> The other Working Groups have moved away from the idea of 'heritage' to the wider idea of the historic environment, which encompasses all of the physical remains of the past.
>
> (English Heritage 2000e: 5)

Through the review process, the concept of 'intangible' was removed and replaced by 'physical' evidence or remains. This carries the assumption that associations, feelings and understandings are intimately tied up with 'physical evidence', and will not occur in isolation from physicality. Such an assumption is based on the belief that, ultimately, heritage is tangible, although, as the additive clause 'and its associations' points out, there are intangible elements to this tangibility. Regardless of this additive, however, the point remains that this definition of heritage holds at its core 'materiality', around which these other activities (seeing, understanding, feeling, and associating) revolve. The core of 'physical and intangible', as set up in the first statement, is reconfigured to include only the physical, with intangibles pushed out so that they become understood only in the sense of elaborative relationships.

This is not a minor semantic quibble. Rather, it is a telling instance of the AHD in operation. The dominance given to the 'tangible' and 'material', along with the discomfort associated with ideas of 'the intangible', makes a potent textual appearance; and it is an appearance that has since remained across more recent reviews of heritage protection in England, culminating in the 2007 White Paper and the Draft Heritage Protection Bill (2008) scheduled for debate in the House of Commons in the 2008/9 session. This discomfort was illustrated by exchanges that took place in a number of interviews:

INTERVIEWEE: The UK has not said that it will ratify that convention [the *Convention for the Safeguarding of Intangible Cultural Heritage*, 2003] and I think it will be quite a long time before it does.
INTERVIEWER: What are the reasons for that?
INTERVIEWEE: It is just difficult to see how you could apply a convention of that sort in the UK context ... it is not relevant ... it just does not fit with the UK approach ... I think it would be very difficult to bring in a convention that says we are actually going to list this sort of stuff and protect it. What are the obvious examples you come up with? Morris Dancing? As intangible heritage and so on? The UK has no intangible heritage.
(Interview 1, English Heritage, 4 July 2005)

In this extract, the interviewee takes up an explicit and conscious stance with regards to intangibility in the UK, which, for our purposes, usefully sets out an overtly negative position: intangibility is marked out as 'irrelevant', 'difficult' and incomprehensible. In the last statement of this extract, the interviewee offers what discourse analysts refer to as a 'truth modality', in which the possibility of intangibility is categorically shut down with the offering of an authoritative judgement that vigorously denies the existence of intangible heritage in the UK. Importantly, there is no ambiguity to this claim. In another interview with staff from English Heritage, the following qualification was offered:

And in fact, broadly speaking, you could say that some people's definition of cultural heritage also encompasses museums and possibly intangible heritage as well. Probably in terms of what we do the historic environment is actually a safer term ... yes, it is correctional.
(Interview 2, English Heritage, 4 July 2005)

This interviewee was far more cautious in their assessment of intangibility, a point observable not only in the hedged claim that 'some people's definition ... also encompasses ... possibly intangible heritage', but by the use of the modal verb 'could' and adverb 'probably'. While this reveals a less stringent commitment to the absence of intangibility in the UK, it also suggests that the failure to embrace the concept rests less with its applicability and more with the difficulty this concept poses within the dominant management process. Coining the term 'historic environment', which is emphatically *material*, allows the management process to deliberately and consciously limit itself to the arbitration and regulation of meaning and values tied up with tangible and material objects. This qualification that the 'historic environment' is safer, and therefore a *correctional* term used to prevent the incorporation of ideas of intangibility, is thus particularly telling, revealing as much to do with the discomfort of dealing with difficult heritage as it does about the supposed irrelevance of intangibility for the UK. The following extract offers a reflection on this discomfort:

INTERVIEWEE: It is what [the Inspector of Ancient Monuments] and I are battling against all the time, saying 'No, we are not archaeologists, we are cultural heritage managers, and we deal with as much above ground as we do below ground, and most of the time we are actually dealing with intangible heritage ...

INTERVIEWER: So who in English Heritage is dealing with the intangible heritage you just mentioned?

INTERVIEWEE: No one, nobody deals with intangibles.

(Interview 3, English Heritage, 10 November 2004)

In this extract, the interviewee begins to undo the categorical work undertaken by Interviewee 1. Through a series of elaborative statements, the interviewee presents a situation within which intangible heritage exists – and not just peripherally, but 'most of the time' – and yet it is something that remains unacknowledged. It is at this point that the work of discourse becomes more apparent, such that the ways in which heritage professionals operating within the AHD talk about heritage, along with how they *act* and what they *do*, effectively obfuscate or ignore the possibility of its existence. It is not so much the case that it simply *doesn't* exist in the UK, but that it causes a conceptual problem. Thus, when we argue that this is a problem of discourse, we are not suggesting that language use, in itself, prevents its existence. What we are arguing is that if it cannot be conceived, and recognised, within the structural, social and discursive relationships of the management process *it simply cannot be managed*.

The impression of discomfort or cultural irrelevance was also noted by a range of practitioners observing England's attempts to engage with notions of intangibility:

INTERVIEWER: ... it was just a sense that they [the British] didn't know what people were talking about [in terms of intangible cultural heritage]?

INTERVIEWEE: Yeah, I mean it was the making of much-ado-about nothing for them ... all this intangible cultural heritage. It was like 'who is this, what is this about, for what, for who? Do you want us to go out and collect, like stories from Gypsies or something? Who? Where? ... At that time is was just, it was like ... what is this? It was unfathomable to be talking about something like this, there was, kind of, no sense of relevance. Here you have what was looked at in many countries as giving pride to the unrepresented as a matter of course, which for many people are the major cultures in those countries. Whereas I think for the folks in the UK, this was marginal, not very important stuff, for people who don't, aren't and can't encapsulate the identity of *our* cultural heritage.

(Interview 6, Smithsonian Institution, April 2006)

INTERVIEWEE: We have intangible heritage and Indigenous heritage existing all over the world. It is the way they [England] see their own heritage which is the problem, because they don't consider rituals and traditions, for example with the mining industry in the UK, as being both tangible and intangible heritage – then it is a problem in their own view.

(Interview 4, UNESCO, World Heritage Centre, Paris, 10 January 2006)

INTERVIEWEE: Intangibles are relevant to every country – the intangibles ARE heritage ... that is what heritage is. We have trouble communicating this idea to Western countries who want to see things in a different way. We have trouble with England, who resist very strongly this way of thinking. They are stuck in their own mindset.

(Interview 5, UNESCO, The Intangible Heritage Section, Paris, 12 January 2006)

In all three extracts above, the problems encountered within the UK in terms of the idea of intangibility are not tied up with the existence or relevance of intangible heritage per se, but with the ability of the management process in the UK to comprehend it. Each extract is thus principally constructed around two existential assumptions: 1) that heritage is, inevitably, about intangibles; and 2) that the UK, specifically, has difficulty reconciling that notion with the dominant understanding of heritage. The idea that heritage is 'good', 'safe' and 'tangible' has been so successfully absorbed into the UK management process that any attempts to deviate away from, or disrupt, this cultural norm are met with incomprehensibility. It is the outcome of a dominant discourse process that is so staunch in its defence of a particular stance that it cannot, and will not, allow new conceptual or theoretical insights to permeate its core beliefs.

Conclusion

The advent of the *Convention for the Safeguarding of the Intangible Cultural Heritage* formally recognised the 'intangible' as a third category of heritage within the international policy arena. In contrast to recent assertions that it is 'the envy of the world' in terms of its possession and management of tangible and natural heritage, the UK greeted this category of heritage with uncharacteristic silence. In this chapter, we sought to examine this silence, and have suggested that it is a consequence of a wider failure to comprehend the relevance of 'intangibility' within the UK context. We have argued that this is a problem of discourse and have specifically related it to the enactment and naturalisation of a dominant heritage discourse, the AHD, which explicitly privileges the materiality of heritage. As such, references to qualities of heritage that stand outside the AHD are met with varying degrees of indifference, discomfort and incomprehensibility, a point that we have documented through the analysis of both policy and interview material. Thus, while the 2003 Convention clearly identifies intangibility as a significant issue, this chapter has reflected upon the causes of its muted reception within England.

Essentially, we have argued that the AHD is particularly striking within the UK heritage context, where it holds a significant position of hegemony within the public policy and management process. Here, it acts as a potent influence, not only in terms of the way heritage is constructed, defined and understood, but how the overarching management process organises its interactions, maintains its social relations and creates an authoritative position from which to 'speak' about heritage issues. Operating from within the confines of the AHD, the management process is unable to accommodate the realities of intangible heritage, nor, indeed, acknowledge that it is a concept that operates at the core of what heritage *is* and the work we do whenever we engage with it. If heritage is intangible – if all heritage is really represented by the values and cultural meanings that we give not only to tangible sites and places, but also to intangible events, performances and so forth – then ultimately what we preserve in the conservation and management processes are cultural and social values and narratives. For us, heritage is something that is done at sites and places, or at or in intangible events and performances – the moment of heritage is a moment when cultural, social and political values and meanings are recognised, scrutinised, accepted, reworked or otherwise negotiated. In failing to acknowledge the legitimacy of intangible heritage within the UK context, the management process in that country inevitably becomes a process that simply engages cultural stasis and status.

Bibliography

Abercrombie, N. and Longhurst, B. (1998) *Audiences: A Sociological Theory of Performance and Imagination*, London: Sage.

Bagnall, G. (2003) 'Performance and performativity at heritage sites', *Museum and Society*, 1 (2):87–103.

Dicks, B. (2000) *Heritage, Place and Community*, Cardiff: University of Wales Press.

Edensor, T. (2005) *Industrial Ruins: Space, Aesthetics and Materiality*, Oxford: Berg Publishers.

Emerick, K. (2003) *From Frozen Monuments to Fluid Landscapes. The Conservation and Preservation of Ancient Monuments from 1882 to the Present*, unpublished PhD thesis, Department of Archaeology, York: University of York.

English Heritage (2000a) *Working Group 1*: Final Draft of the Discussion Papers – Annex. Unpublished document, London: English Heritage.

—— (2000b) *Viewpoint: Understanding*, London: English Heritage.

—— (2000c) 'Working Group 3: Minutes of the Third Meeting, Wednesday 21 June 2000, Kensington Palace'. Unpublished document, London: English Heritage.

—— (2000d) 'Working Group 4: Minutes of the Third Meeting, Friday 16 June 2000, Savile Row'. Unpublished document, London: English Heritage.

—— (2000e) *Viewpoint: Enriching*, London: English Heritage.

—— (2003) *DCMS Consultation Paper: Protecting the Historic Environment – Making the System Work Better – The English Heritage Response*, London: English Heritage.

Fairclough, N. (1992) *Discourse and Social Change*, Cambridge: Polity Press.

—— (2003) *Analysing Discourse: Textual Analysis for Social Research*, London: Routledge.

Figlio, K. (2003) 'Getting to the beginning: identification and concrete thinking in historical consciousness', in S. Radstone and K. Hodgkin (eds), *Regimes of Memory*, 152–66. London: Routledge.

Glendinning, M. (2003) 'The conservation movement: a cult of the modern age', *Transactions of the Royal Historical Society*, 13:359–76.

Graham, B., Ashworth G. and Tunbridge, J. (2000) *A Geography of Heritage: Power, Culture and Economy*, London: Arnold.

Jenkins, R. (1996) *Social Identity*, London: Routledge.

Karlström, A. (2005) 'Spiritual materiality: heritage preservation in a Buddhist world?', *Journal of Social Archaeology*, 5(3):338–55.

Kirshenblatt-Gimblett, B. (2004) 'Intangible heritage as metacultural production', *Museum International*, 56(1–2):52–63.

Kurin, R. (2004) 'Safeguarding intangible cultural heritage in the 2003 UNESCO Convention: a critical appraisal', *Museum International*, 56(1–2):66–76.

Mcintosh, A. and Prentice, R. (1999) 'Affirming authenticity: consuming cultural heritage', *Annals of Tourism Research*, 26(3):589–612.

Marston, G. (2004) *Social Policy and Discourse Analysis: Policy Change in Public Housing*, Hants: Ashgate Publishing Limited.

Matsuura, K. (2004) 'Preface: views and visions of the intangible', *Museum International*, 221/222:4–5.

Moscardo, G. (1996) Mindful visitors: heritage and tourism , *Annals of Tourism Research*, 23 (2):376–97.

Munjeri, D. (2003) 'Intangible heritage in Africa: could it be a case of 'much-ado-about nothing'?' Paper presented at the ICOMOS 14th General Assembly and Scientific Symposium, Victoria Falls, Zimbabwe. Available online at: http://www.international. icomos.org/victoriafalls2003/munjeri_eng.htm (Accessed 22nd February 2008).

—— (2004) Tangible and intangible heritage: from difference to convergence , *Museum International,* 56(1–2):12–20.

Nas, P. (2002) 'Masterpieces of Oral and Intangible Culture: reflections on the UNESCO world heritage list', *Current Anthropology,* 43(1):139–48.

Nassar, N. (2003) 'Planning for urban heritage places: reconciling conservation, tourism, and sustainable development', *Journal of Planning Literature,* 17(4):467–79.

Poria, Y., Butler, R. and Airey, D. (2003) 'The core of heritage tourism', *Annals of Tourism Research,* 30(1):238–54.

Prentice, R. (1998) 'Recollections of museum visits: a case study of remembered cultural attraction visiting on the Isle of Man', *Museum Management and Curatorship,* 17(1):41–64.

—— (2001) 'Experiential cultural tourism: museums and the marketing of the new romanticism of evoked authenticity', *Museum Management and Curatorship,* 19(1):5–26.

Prentice, R., Witt, S. and Hamer, C. (1998) 'Tourism as experience: the case of heritage parks', *Annals of Tourism Research,* 25(1):1–24.

Ruskin, J. ([1849] 1899) *Seven Lamps of Architecture,* London: George Allen.

Smeets, R. (2006) 'The intangible heritage convention: it's official! Ratified by 30 States in record time, the ICH Convention enters into force on 20 April 2006', *The Intangible Heritage Messenger,* 1:1.

Smith, L. (2006) *Uses of Heritage,* London: Routledge.

Thrift, N. (2004) 'Intensities of feeling: towards a spatial politics of affect', *Geografiska Annaler,* 86(B):57–78.

Thurley, S. (2004) 'The heritage protection review', *The Institute of Field Archaeologists Yearbook and Directory,* 2004:19–21.

Tunbridge, J.E. (1998) 'The question of heritage in European cultural conflict', in B. Graham (ed.), *Modern Europe: Place, Culture, Identity,* London: Arnold.

Tunbridge, J. and Ashworth, G. (1996) *Dissonant Heritage: The Management of the Past as a Resource in Conflict,* Chichester: Wiley.

Urry, J. (1996) 'How societies remember the past', in S. Macdonald and G. Fyfe (eds), *Theorising Museums,* Oxford: Blackwells.

Waterton, E. (2007) *Rhetoric and 'Reality': Politics, Policy and the Discourses of Heritage in England,* Unpublished PhD thesis, University of York.

—— (2009, in press) 'Sights of sites: Picturing heritage, power and exclusion', *Journal of Heritage Tourism.*

Waterton, E., Smith, L. and Campbell, G. (2006) 'The utility of discourse analysis to heritage studies: The Burra Charter and social inclusion', *International Journal of Heritage Studies,* 12 (4):339–55.

Wertsch, J.V. (2002) *Voices of Collective Remembering,* Cambridge: Cambridge University Press.

Index

Related titles from Routledge

New Heritage
New Media and Cultural Heritage
Edited by Yehuda Kalay, Thomas Kvan and Janice Affleck

The use of new media in the service of cultural heritage is a fast growing field, known variously as virtual or digital heritage. *New Heritage*, under this denomination, broadens the definition of the field to address the complexity of cultural heritage such as the related social, political and economic issues. This book is a collection of 20 key essays, of authors from 11 countries, representing a wide range of professions including architecture, philosophy, history, cultural heritage management, new media, museology and computer science, which examine the application of new media to cultural heritage from a different points of view. Issues surrounding heritage interpretation to the public and the attempts to capture the essence of both tangible (buildings, monuments) and intangible (customs, rituals) cultural heritage are investigated in a series of case studies.

Current discourses arising subsequent to the marriage of new media and cultural heritage are explored, such as the ongoing debate regarding the status of the original and the copy. Challenges addressed in creating cultural heritage virtual environments, such as engagement and evaluation, are presented, and lessons learned from case studies of digital applications in both formal and informal learning environments as well as theoretical and technical frameworks are discussed along with the related methodological limitations. This book is essential reading for those people wishing to understand the key debates in 'new heritage' and appraise the growing innovations applied to cultural heritage.

ISBN10: 0-415-77355-5 (hbk)
ISBN10: 0-415-77356-3 (pbk)

ISBN13: 978-0-415-77355-3 (hbk)
ISBN13: 978-0-415-77356-0 (pbk)

Available at all good bookshops
For ordering and further information please visit:
www.routledge.com

Difficult Heritage
Negotiating the Nazi Past in Nuremberg and Beyond
Sharon Macdonald

How does a city or a nation deal with a legacy of perpetrating atrocity? How are contemporary identities negotiated and shaped in the face of concrete reminders of a past that most wish they did not have?

Difficult Heritage focuses on the case of Nuremberg – a city whose name is indelibly linked with Nazism – to explore these questions and their implications. Using an original in-depth research, using archival, interview and ethnographic sources, it provides not only fascinating new material and perspectives, but also more general original theorizing of the relationship between heritage, identity and material culture.

The book looks at how Nuremberg has dealt with its Nazi past post-1945. It focuses especially, but not exclusively, on the city's architectural heritage, in particular, the former Nazi party rally grounds, on which the Nuremburg rallies were staged. The book draws on original sources, such as city council debates and interviews, to chart a lively picture of debate, action and inaction in relation to this site and significant others, in Nuremberg and elsewhere. In doing so, *Difficult Heritage* seeks to highlight changes over time in the ways in which the Nazi past has been dealt with in Germany, and the underlying cultural assumptions, motivations and sources of friction involved.

Whilst referencing wider debates and giving examples of what was happening elsewhere in Germany and beyond, *Difficult Heritage* provides a rich in-depth account of this most fascinating of cases. It also engages in comparative reflection on developments underway elsewhere in order to contextualize what was happening in Nuremberg and to show similarities to and differences from the ways in which other 'difficult heritages' have been dealt with elsewhere. By doing so, the author offers an informed perspective on ways of dealing with difficult heritage, today and in the future, discussing innovative museological, educational and artistic practice.

ISBN13: 978-0-415-41991-8 (hbk)
ISBN13: 978-0-415-41992-5 (pbk)